COMPETITIVE STRATEGY

Techniques for Analyzing Industries and Competitors

Michael E. Porter

Free Press
New York   London   Toronto   Sydney

*f*P

FREE PRESS
A Division of Simon & Schuster, Inc.
1230 Avenue of the Americas
New York, NY 10020

First Free Press Export Edition 2004

FREE PRESS and colophon are trademarks
of Simon & Schuster, Inc.

For information regarding special discounts for bulk purchases,
please contact Simon & Schuster Special Sales at 1-800-456-6798
or business@simonandschuster.com

Manufactured in the United States of America

20 19 18 17 16 15 14 13 12 11

Library of Congress Cataloging-in-Publication Data

Porter, Michael E.
    Competitive strategy: techniques for analyzing industries and competitors:
with a new introduction/ Michael E. Porter.
        p. cm.
    Originally published: New York : Free Press, c1980.
    Includes bibliographical references and index.
    1.Competition. 2. Industrial management. I. Title.
HD41.P67   1998
658—dc21   98—9580
                            CIP

ISBN: 0-7432-6088-0

fP

Books by Michael E. Porter

The Competitive Advantage of Nations (1990)

Competitive Advantage: Creating and Sustaining Superior Performance (1985)

Cases in Competitive Strategy (1982)

Competition in the Open Economy (with R.E. Caves and A.M. Spence) (1980)

Interbrand Choice, Strategy and Bilateral Market Power (1976)

Contents

Introduction   ix

Preface   xvii

Introduction, 1980   xxi

PART I   *General Analytical Techniques*

CHAPTER 1   THE STRUCTURAL ANALYSIS OF INDUSTRIES   3

Structural Determinants of the
    Intensity of Competition   5
Structural Analysis and
    Competitive Strategy   29
Structural Analysis and
    Industry Definition   32

CHAPTER 2   GENERIC COMPETITIVE STRATEGIES   34

Three Generic Strategies   35
Stuck in the Middle   41
Risks of the Generic Strategies   44

CHAPTER 3   A FRAMEWORK FOR COMPETITOR ANALYSIS   47

The Components of Competitor
    Analysis   49
Putting the Four Components
    Together—The Competitor
    Response Profile   67
Competitor Analysis and
    Industry Forecasting   71
The Need for a Competitor
    Intelligence System   71

CHAPTER 4   MARKET SIGNALS   75

Types of Market Signals   76
The Use of History in Identifying
    Signals   86
Can Attention to Market Signals
    Be a Distraction?   87

CHAPTER 5   COMPETITIVE MOVES   88

Industry Instability: The Likelihood
    of Competitive Warfare   89
Competitive Moves   91
Commitment   100
Focal Points   105
A Note on Information and Secrecy   106

CHAPTER 6   STRATEGY TOWARD BUYERS AND SUPPLIERS   108

Buyer Selection   108
Purchasing Strategy   122

CHAPTER 7   STRUCTURAL ANALYSIS WITHIN INDUSTRIES   126

Dimensions of Competitive Strategy   127
Strategic Groups   129
Strategic Groups and a Firm's
    Profitability   142
Implications for Formulation
    of Strategy   149
The Strategic Group Map as an
    Analytical Tool   152

CHAPTER 8   INDUSTRY EVOLUTION   156

Basic Concepts in Industry
    Evolution   157
Evolutionary Processes   163
Key Relationships in Industry
    Evolution   184

PART II   *Generic Industry Environments*

CHAPTER 9   COMPETITIVE STRATEGY IN FRAGMENTED
             INDUSTRIES   191

What Makes an Industry
    Fragmented?   196

Overcoming Fragmentation   200
Coping with Fragmentation   206
Potential Strategic Traps   210
Formulating Strategy   213

CHAPTER 10   COMPETITIVE STRATEGY IN EMERGING
                          INDUSTRIES   215

The Structural Environment   216
Problems Constraining Industry
     Development   221
Early and Late Markets   225
Strategic Choices   229
Techniques for Forecasting   234
Which Emerging Industries to
     Enter   235

CHAPTER 11   THE TRANSITION TO INDUSTRY MATURITY   237

Industry Change during Transition   238
Some Strategic Implications of
     Transition   241
Strategic Pitfalls in Transition   247
Organizational Implications of
     Maturity   249
Industry Transition and the General
     Manager   252

CHAPTER 12   COMPETITIVE STRATEGY IN DECLINING
                          INDUSTRIES   254

Structural Determinants of
     Competition in Decline   255
Strategic Alternatives in Decline   267
Choosing a Strategy for Decline   271
Pitfalls in Decline   273
Preparing for Decline   274

CHAPTER 13   COMPETITION IN GLOBAL INDUSTRIES   275

Sources and Impediments to Global
     Competition   277
Evolution to Global Industries   287
Competition in Global Industries   291
Strategic Alternatives in Global
     Industries   294

Trends Affecting Global
Competition   295

PART III   *Strategic Decisions*

CHAPTER 14   THE STRATEGIC ANALYSIS OF VERTICAL
             INTEGRATION   300

Strategic Benefits and Costs of
    Vertical Integration   302
Particular Strategic Issues in
    Forward Integration   315
Particular Strategic Issues in
    Backward Integration   317
Long-Term Contracts and the
    Economics of Information   318
Illusions in Vertical Integration
    Decisions   322

CHAPTER 15   CAPACITY EXPANSION   324

Elements of the Capacity Expansion
    Decision   325
Causes of Overbuilding Capacity   328
Preemptive Strategies   335

CHAPTER 16   ENTRY INTO NEW BUSINESSES   339

Entry through Internal Development   340
Entry through Acquisition   350
Sequenced Entry   356

APPENDIX A   PORTFOLIO TECHNIQUES IN
             COMPETITOR ANALYSIS   361
APPENDIX B   HOW TO CONDUCT AN INDUSTRY ANALYSIS   368

Bibliography   383
Index   389
About the Author   397

Introduction

When *Competitive Strategy* was first published eighteen years ago, I hoped that it would have an impact. There were reasons to hope, because the book rested on a body of research that had stood the test of peer review, and the draft chapters had survived the scrutiny of my MBA and executive students.

The reception of the book and the role it has played in launching a new field, however, exceeded my most optimistic expectations. Most business school students around the world are exposed to the ideas in the book, invariably in core courses on policy or strategy, but often in specialized elective courses on competitive strategy and also in fields such as economics, marketing, technology management, and information systems. Practitioners in both large and small companies have internalized the ideas, as I learn from numerous thoughtful letters, personal conversations, and now E-mails. Most strategic consultants use the ideas in the book, and entire firms have emerged to assist companies in employing them. Budding financial analysts must read the book prior to certification.

Competitive strategy, and its core disciplines of industry analysis, competitor analysis, and strategic positioning, are now an accepted part of management practice. That a large number of thoughtful practitioners have embraced the book as a powerful tool has fulfilled a career-long desire to influence what happens in the real world.

Competitive strategy has also become an academic field in its own right. Now rich with its own competing ideas, this field is prominent among management researchers. It has also become a thriving area of inquiry among economists. The extent and vitality of the body of literature that traces in some way from the book, whether pro or con, is enormously gratifying. The number of outstanding scholars who are working in this field—some of whom I have had the privilege of teaching, mentoring, and writing with— has fulfilled my central aspiration of influencing the path of knowledge.

The re-issue of *Competitive Strategy* has led me to ponder the reasons for the book's impact. They are clearer to me now with the passage of time. Competition has always been central to the agenda of companies, but it certainly did not hurt that the book came at a time when companies all over the world were struggling to cope with growing competition. Indeed, competition has become one of the enduring themes of our time. The rising intensity of competition has continued until this day, and spread to more and more countries. Translations of the book in mainland China (1997) or into Czech, Slovak, Hungarian, Polish, or Ukrainian would have been unthinkable in 1980.

The book filled a void in management thinking. After several decades of development, the role of general managers versus specialists was becoming better defined. Strategic planning had become widely accepted as the important task of charting a long-term direction for an enterprise. Early thinkers in the field such as Kenneth Andrews and C. Roland Christensen had raised some important questions in developing a strategy, as I note in *Competitive Strategy*'s original introduction. Yet there were no systematic, rigorous tools for answering these questions—assessing a company's industry, understanding competitors, and choosing a competitive position. Some newly founded strategy consulting firms had moved to fill this void, but the ideas they put forward, such as the experience curve, rested on a single presumed basis of competition and a single type of strategy.

Competitive Strategy offered a rich framework for understanding the underlying forces of competition in industries, captured in the "five forces." The framework reveals the important differences among industries, how industries evolve, and helps companies find a unique position. *Competitive Strategy* provided tools for capturing the richness and heterogeneity of industries and companies while providing a disciplined structure for examining them. The book also brought structure to the concept of competitive advantage through defining it in terms of cost and differentiation, and linking it directly to profitability. Managers looking for concrete ways to tackle strategic planning's difficult questions quickly embraced the book, which rang true to practitioners.

The book also signaled a new direction and provided an impetus for economic thinking. The economic theory of competition at the time was highly stylized. Economists focused mainly on industries; companies were presumed equal or differing primarily in size or in unexplained differences in efficiency. The prevailing view of industry structure encompassed seller concentration and a few sources of barriers to entry. Managers were all but absent in economic models, with virtually no latitude to affect competitive outcomes. Economists were concerned mainly with the societal and public policy consequences of alternative industry structures and patterns of competition. The aim was to push "excess" profits down. Few economists had ever even considered the question of what the nature of competition implied for company behavior, or how to push profits up. Moreover, economists also lacked the tools to model competition among small numbers of firms whose behavior affected each other. *Competitive Strategy* identified a range of phenomena that economists, armed with new game-theoretic techniques, have begun to explore mathematically for the first time.

My training and assignments—first an MBA, then an economics PhD, then the unique Harvard Business School challenge of using the case method to teach practitioners—revealed the gap between actual competition and the stylized models. They also created a sense of urgency to develop tools that would inform actual choices in real markets. With rich industry and company knowledge from many case studies, I was able to offer a more sophisticated view of industry competition and bring some structure to the question of how a firm could outperform its rivals. Industry structure involved five forces, not two. Competitive positions could be thought of in terms of cost, differentiation, and scope. In my theory, managers had important latitude to influence industry structure and to position the company relative to others.

Market signaling, switching costs, barriers to exit, cost versus differentiation, and broad versus focused strategies were just some of the new concepts explored in the book that proved to be fertile avenues for research, including the use of game theory. My approach helped open up new territory for economists to explore, and offered economists in business schools a way of moving beyond the teaching of standard economic concepts and models. *Competitive Strategy* has not only been widely used in teaching but has motivated and served as a starting point in other efforts to bring economic thinking to bear on practice.[1]

What has changed since the book was published? In some ways, everything has changed. New technologies, new management tools, new growth industries, and new government policies have appeared and reappeared. But in another sense, nothing has changed. The book provides an underlying framework for examining competition that transcends industries, particular technologies, or management approaches. It applies to high-tech, low-tech, and service industries. The advent of the Internet can alter barriers to entry, reshape buyer power, or drive new patterns of substitution, for example, yet the underlying forces of industry competition stay the same. Industry changes make the ideas in the book even more important, because of the need to rethink industry structure and boundaries. While 1990s companies may look very different than 1980s companies or 1970s companies, superior profitability within an industry still rests on relative cost and differentiation. One may believe that faster cycle time or total quality hold the key to competing, but the acid test comes in how these practices affect industry rivalry, a company's relative cost position, or its ability to differentiate itself and command a price premium.

The ideas in the book have endured for the very reason that they addressed the underlying fundamentals of competition in a way that is independent of the specifics of the ways companies go about competing. A number of other books on competition have come and gone because they were really about special cases, or were grounded not in the principles of competitive strategy but in particular competitive practices. That is not to say that *Competitive Strategy* is the last word on the subject. Quite the contrary, and there is much im-

[1] Notable examples include S. Oster, *Modern Competitive Analysis*, Second Edition, Oxford University Press, 1994; A. Dixit and B. Nalebuff, *Thinking Strategically: The Competitive Edge in Business, Politics, and Everyday Life*, W. W. Norton & Company, New York, 1991; and D. Besanko, D. Dranove; and M. Shanley, *The Economics of Strategy*, Northwestern University, 1996.

portant thinking that has advanced knowledge, and more will follow. *Competitive Strategy* remains, however, an enduring foundation and grounding point for thinking about industry competition and positioning within industries to which other ideas can be added and integrated.

What would I modify or change? This is a challenging question for any author to answer objectively. *Competitive Strategy* could clearly be enriched in the form of new examples, in both old and new industries. The concepts are just as powerful in services as in products, and more service examples could be added. The frameworks have been applied in virtually all significant countries, and an internationalization of the examples would be very much in order. While the industries, companies, and countries change, however, the power of the concepts is enduring.

On the level of ideas, I can honestly say that there is nothing yet that I am persuaded to retract. This does not mean that we have not pushed learning further. Various parts of the framework have been tested, challenged, deepened, and importantly extended by others, mostly academics. It is a source of pride, and some discomfort, that *Competitive Strategy* has so often been a foil for other authors. It is impossible here to do justice to this literature, which offers much new insight. The supplier side has been fleshed out, for example, as has our understanding of the theoretical underpinnings of barriers to entry. Also, while firms inevitably have a bargaining relationship with suppliers and buyers, firms can enhance total value to be divided by working cooperatively with buyers, suppliers, and producers of complementary products. This was developed in my later book *Competitive Advantage*, and in subsequent literature.[2] Finally, empirical work has verified many of *Competitive Strategy*'s propositions.

Competitive Strategy has certainly stirred its share of controversy. Some of it involves misunderstandings, and suggests areas where the presentation could be clearer. For example, some have criticized the book for implying a static framework in a world that is rapidly changing. Nothing static was ever intended. Each part of the framework—industry analysis, competitor analysis, competitive positioning—stresses conditions that are subject to change. Indeed, the frameworks reveal the *dimensions* of change that will be the most significant. Much of the book is about how to understand and deal

---

[2] The most important single contribution is A. Brandenburger and B. Nalebuff, *Co-opetition*, Currency/Doubleday, New York, 1996.

with change: e.g., industry evolution (Chapter 8); emerging industries (Chapter 10); dealing with industry maturity (Chapter 11); declining industries (Chapter 12); and globalization (Chapter 13). Companies can never stop learning about their industry, their rivals, or ways to improve or modify their competitive position.

Another misunderstanding revolves around the need to choose between low cost and differentiation. My position is that being the *lowest* cost producer and being truly differentiated and commanding a price premium are rarely compatible. Successful strategies require choice or they can be easily imitated. Becoming "stuck in the middle"—the phrase I introduced—is a recipe for disaster. Sometimes companies such as Microsoft get so far ahead that they seem to avoid the need for strategic choices, but this becomes their ultimate vulnerability.

This never meant companies could ignore cost in the pursuit of differentiation, or ignore differentiation in the pursuit of lowest cost. Nor should companies forgo improvements in one dimension that involve no sacrifice in the other. Finally, a lowest-cost or differentiated position, whether broad or focused, involves constant improvement. A strategic position is a path, not a fixed location. I have recently introduced the distinction between operational effectiveness and strategic position that helps to clarify some of this confusion.[3]

Other controversies raised by the book, however, reflect real differences of opinion. A school of thought has emerged which argues that industries are not important to strategy, because industry structure and boundaries are said to change so rapidly or because profitability is seen as dominated by individual firm position. I have always argued that *both* industry and position are important, and that ignoring either one exposes a firm to peril. Industry differences in average profitability are large and enduring. Recent statistical evidence confirms the importance of industry in explaining both firm profitability and stock market performance, and finds that industry differences are remarkably stable even in the 1990s.[4] It also suggests that industry attributes are important in explaining the dispersion of

---

[3] M. E. Porter, "What is Strategy?," *Harvard Business Review,* November-December 1996.

[4] In assessing the statistical evidence, it is important also to note that the relative contribution of industry in explaining profitability is biased downward by overly broad SIC code industry definitions, overly broad line of business definitions in financial reporting, and the fact that partitioning of variance techniques artificially diminishes the measured contribution of industry. See A. McGahan and M.E. Porter, "What Do We Know About Variance in Accounting Profitability?," Harvard Business School manuscript, August 1997.

profitability within industries.[5] It is hard to concoct a logic in which the nature of the arena in which firms compete would not be important to performance outcomes.

Industry structure, embodied in the five competitive forces, provides a way to think about how value is created and divided among existing and potential industry participants. It highlights the fact that competition is more than just rivalry with existing competitors. While there can be ambiguity about where to draw industry boundaries, one of the five forces always captures the essential issues in the division of value. Some have argued for the addition of a sixth force, most often government or technology. I remain convinced that the roles of government or technology cannot be understood in isolation, but through the five forces.

Another school of thought asserts that factor market (input) conditions take primacy over industry competition in determining company performance. Again, there is no empirical evidence to weigh against the considerable evidence about the role of industry, and supplier conditions are part of industry structure. While resources, capabilities, or other attributes related to input markets have a place in understanding the dynamics of competition, attempting to disconnect them from industry competition and the unique positions that firms occupy vis-à-vis rivals is fraught with danger. The value of resources and capabilities is inextricably bound with strategy. No matter how much we learn about what goes on inside firms, then, understanding industries and competitors will continue to be essential to guide what firms should aim to do.

Finally, in recent years there have been some who argue that firms should not choose competitive positions at all but concentrate on, variously, staying flexible, incorporating new ideas, or building up critical resources or core competencies that are portrayed as independent of competitive position.

I respectfully disagree. Staying flexible in strategic terms renders competitive advantage almost unobtainable. Jumping from

---

[5] See also A. McGahan and M.E. Porter, "How Much Does Industry Matter, Really?," *Strategic Management Journal,* July 1997, pp. 15–30; A. McGahan and M.E. Porter, "The Persistence of Shocks to Profitability," Harvard Business School working paper, January 1997; A. McGahan and M.E. Porter, "The Emergence and Sustainability of Abnormal Profits," Harvard Business School working paper, May 1997; A. McGahan, "The Influence of Competitive Positioning on Corporate Performance," Harvard Business School working paper, May 1997; and J.W. Rivkin, "Reconcilable Differences: The Relationship Between Industry Conditions and Firm Effects," unpublished working paper, Harvard Business School, 1997.

strategy to strategy makes it impossible to be good at implementing any of them. Continuous incorporation of new ideas is important to maintaining operational effectiveness. But this is surely not at all inconsistent with having a consistent strategic position.

Concentrating only on resources/competencies and ignoring competitive position runs the risk of becoming inward looking. Resources or competencies are most valuable for a particular position or way of competing, not in and of themselves. While the resource/competency perspective can be useful, it does not diminish the crucial need in a particular business to understand industry structure and competitive position. Again, the need to connect competitive ends (a company's position in the marketplace) and means (what elements allow it to attain that position) is not just crucial but essential.

Competitive Strategy was written at a different time, and spawned not only extensions but competing perspectives. Yet in a curious way, appreciation of the importance of strategy is growing today. Preoccupation with issues internal to companies over the last decade had limits that are becoming apparent, and there is a renewed awareness of the importance of strategy. With greater perspective and less youthful enthusiasm, I hope we can now see, more clearly than ever, the place of competitive strategy in the broader palette of management, and develop a renewed appreciation for an integrated view of competition.

Michael E. Porter
Brookline, Massachusetts
January 1998

Preface

This book, which marks an important place in an intellectual journey that I have been on for much of my professional life, grows out of my research and teaching in industrial organization economics and in competitive strategy. Competitive strategy is an area of primary concern to managers, depending critically on a subtle understanding of industries and competitors. Yet the strategy field has offered few analytical techniques for gaining this understanding, and those that have emerged lack breadth and comprehensiveness. Conversely, since economists have long studied industry structure, but mostly from a public policy perspective, economic research has not addressed itself to the concerns of business managers.

As one teaching and writing in both business strategy and industrial economics, my work at the Harvard Business School over the past decade has sought to help bridge this gap. The genesis of this book was in my research on industrial economics, which began with my doctoral dissertation and has continued since. The book became a fact as I prepared material to use in the Business Policy course at the school in 1975 and as I developed a course called Industry and Competitive Analysis and taught it to MBA and executive students over the last several years. I not only drew on statistically based scholarly research in the traditional sense but also on studies of hundreds of industries that have been the result of preparation of teaching materials, my own research, supervision of dozens of industry studies by teams of MBA students, and my work with U.S. and international companies.

This book is written for practitioners who need to develop strategy for a particular business and for scholars trying to understand competition better. It is also directed at others who want to understand their industry and competitors. Competitive analysis is important not only in the formulation of business strategy but also in corporate finance, marketing, security analysis, and many other areas of business. I hope that the book will offer valuable insight to practitioners in many different functions and at many organizational levels.

It is also hoped that the book will contribute to the development of sound public policy toward competition. *Competitive Strategy* examines the way in which a firm can compete more effectively to strengthen its market position. Any such strategy must occur in the context of rules of the game for socially desirable competitive behavior, established by ethical standards and through public policy. The rules of the game cannot achieve their intended effect unless they anticipate correctly how businesses respond strategically to competitive threats and opportunities.

I have had considerable help and support in making this book a reality. The Harvard Business School lent a unique setting in which to do this research, and Deans Lawrence Fouraker and John McArthur have provided useful comments, institutional support, and, most importantly, encouragement right from the beginning. The Division of Research at the School extended much of the financial support for the study, in addition to support from the General Electric Foundation. Richard Rosenbloom, as Director of the Division of Research, has been not only a patient investor but also a valued source of commentary and advice.

The study would not have been possible without the efforts of a highly talented and dedicated group of research associates who have worked with me over the last five years in conducting industry research and preparing case material. Jessie Bourneuf, Steven J. Roth, Margaret Lawrence, and Neal Bhadkamkar—all MBA's from Harvard—have each spent at least one year working with me full time on the study.

I have also benefited very much from research by a number of my doctoral students in the area of competitive strategy. Kathryn Harrigan's work on declining industries was a major contribution to Chapter 12. Work by Joseph D'Cruz, Nitin Mehta, Peter Patch, and

George Yip has also enriched my appreciation of important topics covered in the book.

My colleagues at Harvard and associates in outside firms have played a central role in developing the book. Research that I co-authored with Richard Caves, a valued friend and colleague, made an important intellectual contribution to the book; he has also commented perceptively on the entire manuscript. Members of the Business Policy faculty at Harvard, particularly Malcolm Salter and Joseph Bower, helped me to sharpen my thinking and offered valued support. Catherine Hayden, Vice President of Strategic Planning Associates, Inc. has been a continued source of ideas, besides commenting on the entire manuscript. Joint research and innumerable discussions with Michael Spence increased my understanding of strategy. Richard Meyer has taught my course in Industry and Competitive Analysis with me, and stimulated my thinking in many areas. Mark Fuller was of assistance through his work with me on case development and industry studies. Thomas Hout, Eileen Rudden, and Eric Vogt—all of the Boston Consulting Group—contributed to Chapter 13. Others who have offered encouragement and useful comments on the manuscript in its various stages include Professors John Lintner, C. Roland Christensen, Kenneth Andrews, Robert Buzzell, and Norman Berg; as well as John Nils Hanson (Gould Corporation), John Forbus (McKinsey and Company), and my editor Robert Wallace.

I also owe a great debt to Emily Feudo and particularly Sheila Barry, both of whom managed the production of the manuscript and added to my peace of mind and productivity as I worked on this study. Finally, I would like to thank my students in Industry and Competitive Analysis, Business Policy, and Field Studies in Industry Analysis courses for their patience in serving as the guinea pigs while trying out the concepts in this book, but more importantly for their enthusiasm in working with the ideas and helping me clarify my thinking in innumerable ways.

Introduction, 1980

Every firm competing in an industry has a competitive strategy, whether explicit or implicit. This strategy may have been developed explicitly through a planning process or it may have evolved implicitly through the activities of the various functional departments of the firm. Left to its own devices, each functional department will inevitably pursue approaches dictated by its professional orientation and the incentives of those in charge. However, the sum of these departmental approaches rarely equals the best strategy.

The emphasis being placed on strategic planning today in firms in the United States and abroad reflects the proposition that there are significant benefits to gain through an *explicit* process of formulating strategy, to insure that at least the policies (if not the actions) of functional departments are coordinated and directed at some common set of goals. Increased attention to formal strategic planning has highlighted questions that have long been of concern to managers: What is driving competition in my industry or in industries I am thinking of entering? What actions are competitors likely to take, and what is the best way to respond? How will my industry evolve? How can the firm be best positioned to compete in the long run?

Yet most of the emphasis in formal strategic planning processes has been on asking these questions in an organized and disciplined way rather than on answering them. Those techniques that have been advanced for answering the questions, often by consulting firms, either address the diversified company rather than the industry perspective or consider only one aspect of industry structure, like the behavior of costs, that cannot hope to capture the richness and complexity of industry competition.

This book presents a comprehensive framework of analytical techniques to help a firm analyze its industry as a whole and predict the industry's future evolution, to understand its competitors and its own position, and to translate this analysis into a competitive strategy for a particular business. The book is organized into three parts. Part I presents a general framework for analyzing the structure of an industry and its competitors. The underpinning of this framework is the analysis of the five competitive forces acting on an industry and their strategic implications. Part I builds on this framework to present techniques for the analysis of competitors, buyers, and suppliers; techniques for reading market signals; game theoretic concepts for making and responding to competitive moves; an approach to mapping strategic groups in an industry and explaining differences in their performance; and a framework for predicting industry evolution.

Part II shows how the analytical framework described in Part I can be used to develop competitive strategy in particular important types of industry environments. These differing environments reflect fundamental differences in industry concentration, state of maturity, and exposure to international competition. These differing environments are crucial in determining the strategic context in which a business competes, the strategic alternatives available, and the common strategic errors. Part II examines fragmented industries, emerging industries, the transition to industry maturity, declining industries, and global industries.

Part III of the book completes the analytical framework by systematically examining the important types of strategic decisions that confront firms in competing in a single industry: vertical integration, major capacity expansion, and entry into new businesses. (Divestment is considered in detail in Chapter 12 in Part II.) The analysis of each strategic decision draws on application of the general analytical tools of Part I as well as on other economic theory and on administrative considerations in managing and motivating an organization. Part III is designed not only to help a company make these key decisions but also to give it insight into how its competitors, customers, suppliers, and potential entrants might make them.

To analyze competitive strategy for a particular business, the reader can draw on the book in a number of ways. First, the general analytical tools of Part I can be utilized. Second, the chapter or chapters from Part II that bear on the key dimensions of the firm's industry can be used to provide some more specific guidance for strategy formulation in the business's particular environment. Finally, if the business is considering a particular decision, the reader can refer to the appropriate chapter in Part III. Even if a particular decision is not imminent, Part III will usually be helpful in reviewing decisions that have already been made and in examining the past and present decisions of competitors.

Whereas the reader can dip into a particular chapter, a great deal is gained by having a working understanding of the entire framework as a starting point for attacking a particular strategic problem. The parts of the book are meant to enrich and reinforce each other. Sections seemingly not important to the firm's own position may well be crucial in looking at competitors, and the broad industry circumstances or the strategic decision currently on the table may change. Reading the full book may appear formidable, but the effort will be rewarded in terms of the speed and clarity with which a strategic situation can then be assessed and a competitive strategy developed.

It will soon be apparent from reading the book that a comprehensive analysis of an industry and its competitors requires a great deal of data, some of it subtle and difficult to obtain. The book aims to provide the reader with a framework for deciding what data is particularly crucial, and how it can be analyzed. Reflecting the practical problems of doing such an analysis, however, Appendix B provides an organized approach to actually conducting an industry study, including sources of field and published data as well as guidance in field interviewing.

This book is written for *practitioners*, that is, managers seeking to improve the performance of their businesses, advisors to managers, teachers of management, security analysts or other observers trying to understand and forecast business success or failure, or government officials seeking to understand competition in order to formulate public policy. The book is drawn from my research in industrial economics and business strategy and my teaching experience in the MBA and executive programs at the Harvard Business School. It draws upon detailed studies of hundreds of industries with all varieties of structures and at widely differing states of maturity. The book is not written from the viewpoint of the scholar or in the style of my more academically oriented work, but it is hoped that scholars will nevertheless be interested in the conceptual approach, the extensions to the theory of industrial organization, and the many case examples.

Review: The Classic Approach to Formulation of Strategy

Essentially, developing a competitive strategy is developing a broad formula for how a business is going to compete, what its goals should be, and what policies will be needed to carry out those goals. To serve as a common starting point for the reader before plunging into the analytical framework of this book, this section will review a classic approach to strategy formulation[1] that has become a standard in the field. Figures I-1 and I-2 illustrate this approach.

Figure I-1 illustrates that competitive strategy is a combination of the *ends* (goals) for which the firm is striving and the *means* (policies) by which it is seeking to get there. Different firms have different words for some of the concepts illustrated. For example, some firms use terms like "mission" or "objective" instead of "goals," and some firms use "tactics" instead of "operating" or "functional policies." Yet the essential notion of strategy is captured in the distinction between ends and means.

Figure I-1, which can be called the "Wheel of Competitive Strategy," is a device for articulating the key aspects of a firm's competitive strategy on a single page. In the hub of the wheel are the

---

[1]This section draws heavily on work by Andrews, Christensen, and others in the Policy group at the Harvard Business School. For a more complete articulation of the concept of strategy see Andrews (1971); and more recently Christensen, Andrews, and Bower (1977). These classic accounts also discuss the reasons why explicit strategy is important in a company, as well as the relationship between strategy formulation and the broader role and functions of general management. Planning strategy is far from the only thing that general management does or should do.

GOALS

Definition of how the business is going to compete

Objectives for profitability growth, market share, social responsiveness, etc.

Product Line

Target Markets

Marketing

Sales

Distribution

Manufacturing

Labor

Purchasing

Research and Development

Finance and Control

FIGURE I-1.   The Wheel of Competitive Strategy

firm's goals, which are its broad definition of how it wants to compete and its specific economic and noneconomic objectives. The spokes of the wheel are the key operating policies with which the firm is seeking to achieve these goals. Under each heading on the wheel a succinct statement of the key operating policies in that functional area should be derived from the company's activities. Depending on the nature of the business, management can be more or less specific in articulating these key operating policies; once they are specified, the concept of strategy can be used to guide the overall behavior of the firm. Like a wheel, the spokes (policies) must radiate from and reflect the hub (goals), and the spokes must be connected with each other or the wheel will not roll.

Figure I-2 illustrates that at the broadest level formulating competitive strategy involves the consideration of four key factors that

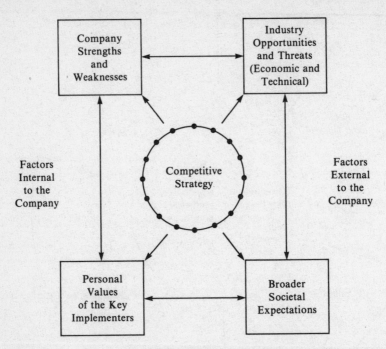

FIGURE I-2.   Context in Which Competitive Strategy Is Formulated

determine the limits of what a company can successfully accomplish. The company's strengths and weaknesses are its profile of assets and skills relative to competitors, including financial resources, technological posture, brand identification, and so on. The personal values of an organization are the motivations and needs of the key executives and other personnel who must implement the chosen strategy. Strengths and weaknesses combined with values determine the internal (to the company) limits to the competitive strategy a company can successfully adopt.

The external limits are determined by its industry and broader environment. Industry opportunities and threats define the competitive environment, with its attendant risks and potential rewards. Societal expectations reflect the impact on the company of such things as government policy, social concerns, evolving mores, and many others. These four factors must be considered before a business can develop a realistic and implementable set of goals and policies.

The appropriateness of a competitive strategy can be determined by testing the proposed goals and policies for consistency, as shown in Figure I-3.

FIGURE I-3 Tests of Consistency[a]

Internal Consistency

> Are the goals mutually achievable?
>
> Do the key operating policies address the goals?
>
> Do the key operating policies reinforce each other?

Environmental Fit

> Do the goals and policies exploit industry opportunities?
>
> Do the goals and policies deal with industry threats (including the risk of competitive response) to the degree possible with available resources?
>
> Does the timing of the goals and policies reflect the ability of the environment to absorb the actions?
>
> Are the goals and policies responsive to broader societal concerns?

Resource Fit

> Do the goals and policies match the resources available to the company relative to competitors?
>
> Does the timing of the goals and policies reflect the organization's ability to change?

Communication and Implementation

> Are the goals well understood by the key implementers?
>
> Is there enough congruence between the goals and policies and the values of the key implementers to insure commitment?
>
> Is there sufficient managerial capability to allow for effective implementation?

[a]These questions are a modified version of those developed in Andrews (1971).

These broad considerations in an effective competitive strategy can be translated into a generalized approach to the formulation of strategy. The outline of questions in Figure I-4 gives such an approach to developing the optimal competitive strategy.

FIGURE I-4 Process for Formulating a Competitive Strategy

A. What is the Business Doing Now?

>   1. Identification
>   What is the implicit or explicit current strategy?
>
>   2. Implied Assumptions*
>   What assumptions about the company's relative position, strengths and weaknesses, competitors, and industry trends must be made for the current strategy to make sense?

*Given the premise that managers honestly try to optimize the performance of their businesses, the current strategy being followed by a business must reflect assumptions management is making about its industry and the business's relative position in the industry. Understanding and

B.   What is Happening in the Environment?

   1. Industry Analysis

      What are the key factors for competitive success and the important in-
dustry opportunities and threats?

   2. Competitor Analysis

      What are the capabilities and limitations of existing and potential com-
petitors, and their probable future moves?

   3. Societal Analysis

      What important governmental, social, and political factors will present
opportunities or threats?

   4. Strengths and Weaknesses

      Given an analysis of industry and competitors, what are the company's
strengths and weaknesses *relative to present and future competitors*?

C.   What Should the Business be Doing?

   1. Tests of Assumptions and Strategy

      How do the assumptions embodied in the current strategy compare with
the analysis in B above? How does the strategy meet the tests in Figure I-3?

   2. Strategic Alternatives

      What are the feasible strategic alternatives given the analysis above? (Is
the current strategy one of these?)

   3. Strategic Choice

      Which alternative best relates the company's situation to external oppor-
tunities and threats?

Although the process shown in Figure I-4 may be intuitively
clear, answering these questions involves a great deal of penetrating
analysis. It is answering these questions that is the purpose of this
book.

---

addressing these implied assumptions can be crucial to giving strategic advice. Usually a great
deal of convincing data and support must be mustered to change these assumptions, and this is
where much if not most attention needs to be focused. The sheer logic of the strategic choice is
not enough; it will not be convincing if it ignores management's assumptions.

COMPETITIVE STRATEGY

I
General Analytical Techniques

Part I lays the analytical foundation for the development of competitive strategy, built on the analysis of industry structure and competitors. Chapter 1 introduces the concept of structural analysis as a framework for understanding the five fundamental forces of competition in an industry. This framework is the starting point from which much of the subsequent discussion in the book begins. The structural analysis framework is used in Chapter 2 to identify at the broadest level the three generic competitive strategies that can be viable in the long run.

Chapters 3, 4, and 5 deal with the other key part of the formulation of competitive strategy: competitor analysis. In Chapter 3 a framework for analyzing competitors is presented. which aids in diagnosing probable moves by competitors and their ability to react. Chapter 3 gives detailed questions that can help the analyst to assess a particular competitor. Chapter 4 shows how company behavior gives off a variety of types of market signals that can be used to enrich competitor analysis and as a basis for taking strategic actions. Chapter 5 sets forth a primer for making, influencing, and reacting to competitive moves. Chapter 6

1

elaborates on the concept of structural analysis for developing strategies toward buyers and suppliers.

The final two chapters of Part I bring industry and competitor analysis together. Chapter 7 shows how to analyze the nature of competition *within* an industry, employing the concept of strategic groups and the principle of mobility barriers that are deterrents to shifts in strategic position. Chapter 8 concludes the discussion of general analytical techniques by examining ways of predicting the process of industry evolution and some of the implications of that evolution for competitive strategy.

1
The Structural Analysis
of Industries

The essence of formulating competitive strategy is relating a company to its environment. Although the relevant environment is very broad, encompassing social as well as economic forces, the key aspect of the firm's environment is the industry or industries in which it competes. Industry structure has a strong influence in determining the competitive rules of the game as well as the strategies potentially available to the firm. Forces outside the industry are significant primarily in a relative sense; since outside forces usually affect all firms in the industry, the key is found in the differing abilities of firms to deal with them.

The intensity of competition in an industry is neither a matter of coincidence nor bad luck. Rather, competition in an industry is rooted in its underlying economic structure and goes well beyond the behavior of current competitors. The state of competition in an industry depends on five basic competitive forces, which are shown in Figure 1-1. The collective strength of these forces determines the ultimate profit potential in the industry, where profit potential is measured in terms of long run return on invested capital. Not all industries have the same potential. They differ fundamentally in their ultimate profit potential as the collective strength of the forces dif-

3

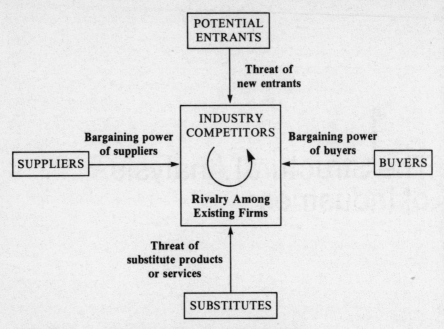

FIGURE 1-1.   Forces Driving Industry Competition

fers; the forces range from intense in industries like tires, paper, and steel—where no firm earns spectacular returns—to relatively mild in industries like oil-field equipment and services, cosmetics, and toiletries—where high returns are quite common.

This chapter will be concerned with identifying the key *structural* features of industries that determine the strength of the competitive forces and hence industry profitability. The goal of competitive strategy for a business unit in an industry is to find a position in the industry where the company can best defend itself against these competitive forces or can influence them in its favor. Since the collective strength of the forces may well be painfully apparent to all competitors, the key for developing strategy is to delve below the surface and analyze the sources of each. Knowledge of these underlying sources of competitive pressure highlights the critical strengths and weaknesses of the company, animates its positioning in its industry, clarifies the areas where strategic changes may yield the greatest payoff, and highlights the areas where industry trends promise to hold the greatest significance as either opportunities or threats. Understanding these sources will also prove to be useful in considering areas for diversification, though the primary focus here is on strategy in individual industries. Structural analysis is the fundamental underpinning for formulating competitive strategy and a key building block for most of the concepts in this book.

To avoid needless repetition, the term "product" rather than "product or service" will be used to refer to the output of an industry, even though the principles of structural analysis developed here apply equally to product and service businesses. Structural analysis also applies to diagnosing industry competition in any country or in an international market, though some of the institutional circumstances may differ.[1]

Structural Determinants of the Intensity of Competition

Let us adopt the working definition of an industry as the group of firms producing products that are close substitutes for each other. In practice there is often a great deal of controversy over the appropriate definition, centering around how close substitutability needs to be in terms of product, process, or geographic market boundaries. Because we will be in a better position to treat these issues once the basic concept of structural analysis has been introduced, we will assume initially that industry boundaries have already been drawn.

Competition in an industry continually works to drive down the rate of return on invested capital toward the competitive floor rate of return, or the return that would be earned by the economist's "perfectly competitive" industry. This competitive floor, or "free market" return, is approximated by the yield on long-term government securities adjusted upward by the risk of capital loss. Investors will not tolerate returns below this rate in the long run because of their alternative of investing in other industries, and firms habitually earning less than this return will eventually go out of business. The presence of rates of return higher than the adjusted free market return serves to stimulate the inflow of capital into an industry either through new entry or through additional investment by existing competitors. The strength of the competitive forces in an industry deter-

---

[1]Chapter 13 discusses some of the particular implications of competing in global industries.

mines the degree to which this inflow of investment occurs and drives the return to the free market level, and thus the ability of firms to sustain above-average returns.

The five competitive forces—entry, threat of substitution, bargaining power of buyers, bargaining power of suppliers, and rivalry among current competitors—reflect the fact that competition in an industry goes well beyond the established players. Customers, suppliers, substitutes, and potential entrants are all "competitors" to firms in the industry and may be more or less prominent depending on the particular circumstances. Competition in this broader sense might be termed *extended rivalry*.

All five competitive forces jointly determine the intensity of industry competition and profitability, and the strongest force or forces are governing and become crucial from the point of view of strategy formulation. For example, even a company with a very strong market position in an industry where potential entrants are no threat will earn low returns if it faces a superior, lower-cost substitute. Even with no substitutes and blocked entry, intense rivalry among existing competitors will limit potential returns. The extreme case of competitive intensity is the economist's perfectly competitive industry, where entry is free, existing firms have no bargaining power against suppliers and customers, and rivalry is unbridled because the numerous firms and products are all alike.

Different forces take on prominence, of course, in shaping competition in each industry. In the ocean-going tanker industry the key force is probably the buyers (the major oil companies), whereas in tires it is powerful original equipment (OEM) buyers coupled with tough competitors. In the steel industry the key forces are foreign competitors and substitute materials.

The underlying structure of an industry, reflected in the strength of the forces, should be distinguished from the many short-run factors that can affect competition and profitability in a transient way. For example, fluctuations in economic conditions over the business cycle influence the short-run profitability of nearly all firms in many industries, as can material shortages, strikes, spurts in demand, and the like. Although such factors may have tactical significance, the focus of the analysis of industry structure, or "structural analysis," is on identifying the basic, underlying characteristics of an industry rooted in its economics and technology that shape the arena in which competitive strategy must be set. Firms will each have unique strengths and weaknesses in dealing with industry structure, and industry structure can and does shift gradually over time. Yet understanding industry structure must be the starting point for strategic analysis.

A number of important economic and technical characteristics of an industry are critical to the strength of each competitive force. These will be discussed in turn.

THREAT OF ENTRY

New entrants to an industry bring new capacity, the desire to gain market share, and often substantial resources. Prices can be bid down or incumbents' costs inflated as a result, reducing profitability. Companies diversifying through acquisition into the industry from other markets often use their resources to cause a shake-up, as Philip Morris did with Miller beer. Thus acquisition into an industry with intent to build market position should probably be viewed as entry even though no entirely new entity is created.

The threat of entry into an industry depends on the *barriers to entry* that are present, coupled with the *reaction* from existing competitors that the entrant can expect. If barriers are high and/or the newcomer can expect sharp retaliation from entrenched competitors, the threat of entry is low.

BARRIERS TO ENTRY

There are six major sources of barriers to entry:

Economies of Scale.　Economies of scale refer to declines in unit costs of a product (or operation or function that goes into producing a product) as the absolute volume *per period* increases. Economies of scale deter entry by forcing the entrant to come in at large scale and risk strong reaction from existing firms or come in at a small scale and accept a cost disadvantage, both undesirable options. Scale economies can be present in nearly every function of a business, including manufacturing, purchasing, research and development, marketing, service network, sales force utilization, and distribution. For example, scale economies in production, research, marketing, and service are probably the key barriers to entry in the mainframe computer industry, as Xerox and General Electric sadly discovered.

Scale economies may relate to an entire functional area, as in the case of a sales force, or they may stem from particular operations or activities that are part of a functional area. For example, in the manufacture of television sets, economies of scale are large in color tube production, and they are less significant in cabinetmaking and set assembly. It is important to examine each component of costs separately for its particular relationship between unit cost and scale.

Units of multibusiness firms may be able to reap economies similar to those of scale if they are able to *share operations or functions* subject to economies of scale with other businesses in the company. For example, the multibusiness company may manufacture small electric motors, which are then used in producing industrial fans, hairdryers, and cooling systems for electronic equipment. If economies of scale in motor manufacturing extend beyond the number of motors needed in any one market, the multibusiness firm diversified in this way will reap economies in motor manufacturing that exceed those available if it only manufactured motors for use in, say, hairdryers. Thus related diversification around common operations or functions can remove volume constraints imposed by the size of a given industry.[2] The prospective entrant is forced to be diversified or face a cost disadvantage. Potentially shareable activities or functions subject to economies of scale can include sales forces, distribution systems, purchasing, and so on.

The benefits of sharing are particularly potent if there are *joint costs*. Joint costs occur when a firm producing product *A* (or an operation or function that is part of producing *A*) must inherently have the capacity to produce product *B*. An example is air passenger services and air cargo, where because of technological constraints only so much space in the aircraft can be filled with passengers, leaving available cargo space and payload capacity. Many of the costs must be borne to put the plane into the air and there is capacity for freight regardless of the quantity of passengers the plane is carrying. Thus the firm that competes in both passenger and freight may have a substantial advantage over the firm competing in only one market.

---

[2]For this entry barrier to be significant it is crucial that the shared operation or function be subject to economies of scale which extend beyond the size of any one market. If this is not the case, cost savings of sharing can be illusory. A company may see its costs decline as overhead is spread, but this depends solely on the presence of *excess capacity* in the operation or function. These economies are short-run economies, and once capacity is fully utilized and expanded the true cost of the shared operation will become apparent.

This same sort of effect occurs in businesses that involve manufacturing processes involving by-products. The entrant who cannot capture the highest available incremental revenue from the by-products can face a disadvantage if incumbent firms do.

A common situation of joint costs occurs when business units can share *intangible* assets such as brand names and know-how. The cost of creating an intangible asset need only be borne once; the asset may then be freely applied to other business, subject only to any costs of adapting or modifying it. Thus situations in which intangible assets are shared can lead to substantial economies.

A type of economies of scale entry barrier occurs when there are economies to vertical integration, that is, operating in successive stages of production or distribution. Here the entrant must enter integrated or face a cost disadvantage, as well as possible foreclosure of inputs or markets for its product *if* most established competitors are integrated. Foreclosure in such situations stems from the fact that most customers purchase from in-house units, or most suppliers "sell" their inputs in-house. The independent firm faces a difficult time in getting comparable prices and may become "squeezed" if integrated competitors offer different terms to it than to their captive units. The requirement to enter integrated may heighten the risks of retaliation and also elevate other entry barriers discussed below.

Product Differentiation.   Product differentiation means that established firms have brand identification and customer loyalties, which stem from past advertising, customer service, product differences, or simply being first into the industry. Differentiation creates a barrier to entry by forcing entrants to spend heavily to overcome existing customer loyalties. This effort usually involves start-up losses and often takes an extended period of time. Such investments in building a brand name are particularly risky since they have no salvage value if entry fails.

Product differentiation is perhaps the most important entry barrier in baby care products, over-the-counter drugs, cosmetics, investment banking, and public accounting. In the brewing industry, product differentiation is coupled with economies of scale in production, marketing, and distribution to create high barriers.

Capital Requirements.   The need to invest large financial resources in order to compete creates a barrier to entry, pratically if the capital is required for risky or unrecoverable up-front advertising or research and development (R&D). Capital may be necessary not only for production facilities but also for things like customer credit, inventories, or covering start-up losses. Xerox created a major capital barrier to entry in copiers, for example, when it chose to rent copiers rather than sell them outright which greatly increased the need for working capital. Whereas today's major corporations have the financial resources to enter almost any industry, the huge capital requirements in fields like computers and mineral extraction limit the pool of likely entrants. Even if capital is available on the capital markets, entry represents a risky use of that capital which should be reflected in risk premiums charged the prospective entrant; these constitute advantages for going firms.[3]

Switching Costs.   A barrier to entry is created by the presence of *switching costs*, that is, one-time costs facing the buyer of switching from one supplier's product to another's. Switching costs may include employee retraining costs, cost of new ancillary equipment, cost and time in testing or qualifying a new source, need for technical help as a result of reliance on seller engineering aid, product redesign, or even psychic costs of severing a relationship.[4] If these switching costs are high, then new entrants must offer a major improvement in cost or performance in order for the buyer to switch from an incumbent. For example, in intravenous (IV) solutions and kits for use in hospitals, procedures for attaching solutions to patients differ among competitive products and the hardware for hanging the IV bottles are not compatible. Here switching encounters great resistance from nurses responsible for administering the treatment and requires new investments in hardware.

Access to Distribution Channels.   A barrier to entry can be created by the new entrant's need to secure distribution for its product. To the extent that logical distribution channels for the product have already been served by established firms, the new firm must persuade the channels to accept its product through price breaks, cooperative advertising allowances, and the like, which reduce profits. The manufacturer of a new food product, for example, must per-

[3]In some industries suppliers are willing to help finance entry in order to increase their own sales (oil tankers, logging equipment). This obviously lowers effective capital barriers to entry.

[4]Switching costs may also be present for the seller. Switching costs and some of their implications will be discussed more fully in Chapter 6.

suade the retailer to give it space on the fiercely competitive super-market shelf via promises of promotions, intense selling efforts to the retailer, or some other means.

The more limited the wholesale or retail channels for a product are and the more existing competitors have these tied up, obviously the tougher entry into the industry will be. Existing competitors may have ties with channels based on long relationships, high-quality service, or even exclusive relationships in which the channel is solely identified with a particular manufacturer. Sometimes this barrier to entry is so high that to surmount it a new firm must create an entirely new distribution channel, as Timex did in the watch industry.

Cost Disadvantages Independent of Scale. Established firms may have cost advantages not replicable by potential entrants no matter what their size and attained economies of scale. The most critical advantages are factors such as the following:

- Proprietary product technology: product know-how or design characteristics that are kept proprietary through patents or secrecy.
- Favorable access to raw materials: established firms may have locked up the most favorable sources and/or tied up foreseeable needs early at prices reflecting a lower demand for them than currently exists. For example, Frasch sulphur firms like Texas Gulf Sulphur gained control of some very favorable large salt dome sulphur deposits many years ago, before mineral rightholders were aware of their value as a result of the Frasch mining technology. Discoverers of sulphur deposits were often disappointed oil companies who were exploring for oil and not prone to value them highly.
- Favorable locations: established firms may have cornered favorable locations before market forces bid up prices to capture their full value.
- Government subsidies: preferential government subsidies may give established firms lasting advantages in some businesses.
- Learning or experience curve: in some businesses, there is an observed tendency for unit costs to decline as the firm gains more cumulative experience in producing a product. Costs decline because workers improve their methods and become more efficient (the classic learning curve), layout improves,

specialized equipment and processes are developed, better performance is coaxed from equipment, product design changes make manufacturing easier, techniques for measurement and control of operations improve, and so on. Experience is just a name for certain kinds of technological change and may apply not only to production but also to distribution, logistics, and other functions. As is the case with scale economies, cost declines with experience relate not to the entire firm but arise from the individual operations or functions that make up the firm. Experience can lower costs in marketing, distribution, and other areas as well as in production or operations within production, and each component of costs must be examined for the effects of experience.

Cost declines with experience seem to be the most significant in businesses involving a high labor content performing intricate tasks and/or complex assembly operations (aircraft manufacture, shipbuilding). They are nearly always the most significant in the early and growth phase of a product's development, and later reach diminishing proportional improvements. Often economies of scale are cited among the reasons that costs decline with experience. Economies of scale are dependent on volume per period, and *not* on cumulative volume, and are very different analytically from experience, although the two often occur together and can be hard to separate. The dangers of lumping scale and experience together will be discussed further.

If costs decline with experience in an industry, and *if the experience can be kept proprietary by established firms*, then this effect leads to an entry barrier. Newly started firms, with no experience, will have inherently higher costs than established firms and must bear heavy start-up losses from below- or near-cost pricing in order to gain the experience to achieve cost parity with established firms (if they ever can). Established firms, particularly the market share leader who is accumulating experience the fastest, will have higher cash flow because of their lower costs to invest in new equipment and techniques. However, it is important to recognize that pursuing experience curve cost declines (and scale economies) may require substantial up-front capital investment for equipment and startup losses. If costs continue to decline with volume even as cumulative volume gets very large, new entrants may never catch up. A number of firms, notably Texas Instruments, Black and Decker, Emerson Electric, and others have built successful strategies based on the experience curve through aggressive investments to build cumulative volume early in the development of industries, often by pricing in anticipation of future cost declines.

The decline in cost from experience can be augmented if there are diversified firms in the industry who *share* operations or functions subject to such a decline with other units in the company, or where there are related activities in the company from which incomplete though useful experience can be obtained. When an activity like the fabrication of raw material is shared by several business units, experience obviously accumulates faster than it would if the activity were used solely to meet the needs in one industry. Or when the corporate entity has related activities within the firm, sister units can receive the benefits of their experience at little or no cost since much experience is an intangible asset. This sort of shared learning accentuates the entry barrier provided by the experience curve, provided the other conditions for its significance are met.

Experience is such a widely used concept in strategy formulation that its strategic implications will be discussed further.

Government Policy.   The last major source of entry barriers is government policy. Government can limit or even foreclose entry into industries with such controls as licensing requirements and limits on access to raw materials (like coal lands or mountains on which to build ski areas). Regulated industries like trucking, railroads, liquor retailing, and freight forwarding are obvious examples. More subtle government restrictions on entry can stem from controls such as air and water pollution standards and product safety and efficacy regulations. For example, pollution control requirements can increase the capital needed for entry and the required technological sophistication and even the optimal scale of facilities. Standards for product testing, common in industries like food and other health-related products, can impose substantial lead times, which not only raise the capital cost of entry but also give established firms ample notice of impending entry and sometimes full knowledge of the new competitor's product with which to formulate retaliatory strategies. Government policy in such areas certainly has direct social benefits, but it often has secondary consequences for entry which are unrecognized.

EXPECTED RETALIATION

The potential entrant's expectations about the reaction of existing competitors also will influence the threat of entry. If existing competitors are expected to respond forcefully to make the entrant's stay in the industry an unpleasant one, then entry may well be deterred. Conditions that signal the strong likelihood of retaliation to entry and hence deter it are the following:

- a history of vigorous retaliation to entrants;
- established firms with substantial resources to fight back, including excess cash and unused borrowing capacity, adequate excess productive capacity to meet all likely future needs, or great leverage with distribution channels or customers;
- established firms with great commitment to the industry and highly illiquid assets employed in it;
- slow industry growth, which limits the ability of the industry to absorb a new firm without depressing the sales and financial performance of established firms.

THE ENTRY DETERRING PRICE

The condition of entry in an industry can be summarized in an important hypothetical concept called the *entry deterring price*: the prevailing structure of prices (and related terms such as product quality and service) which just balances the potential rewards from entry (forecast by the potential entrant) with the expected costs of overcoming structural entry barriers and risking retaliation. If the current price level is higher than the entry deterring price, entrants will forecast above-average profits from entry, and entry will occur. Of course the entry deterring price depends on entrants' expectations of the future and not just current conditions.

The threat of entry into an industry can be eliminated if incumbent firms choose or are forced by competition to price below this hypothetical entry deterring price. If they price above it, gains in terms of profitability may be short-lived because they will be dissipated by the cost of fighting or coexisting with new entrants.

PROPERTIES OF ENTRY BARRIERS

There are several additional properties of entry barriers that are crucial from a strategic standpoint. First, entry barriers can and do change as the conditions previously described change. The expiration of Polaroid's basic patents on instant photography, for instance, greatly reduced its absolute cost entry barrier built by proprietary technology. It is not surprising that Kodak plunged into the market. Product differentiation in the magazine printing industry has all but disappeared, reducing barriers. Conversely, in the auto industry, economies of scale increased with post-World War II automation and vertical integration, virtually stopping successful new entry.

Second, although entry barriers sometimes change for reasons largely outside the firm's control, the firm's strategic decisions also can have a major impact. For example, the actions of many U. S. wine producers in the 1960s to step up introductions of new products, raise advertising levels, and undertake national distribution surely increased entry barriers by raising economies of scale in the industry and making access to distribution channels more difficult. Similarly, decisions by members of the recreational vehicle industry to vertically integrate into parts manufacture in order to lower costs have greatly increased the economies of scale there and raised the capital cost barriers.

Finally, some firms may possess resources or skills which allow them to overcome entry barrier into an industry more cheaply than most other firms. For example, Gillette, with well-developed distribution channels for razors and blades, faced lower costs of entry into disposable lighters than did many other firms. The ability to share costs also provides opportunities for low-cost entry. (In Chapter 16 we will explore the implications of factors like these for entry strategy in some detail).

EXPERIENCE AND SCALE AS ENTRY BARRIERS

Although they often coincide, economies of scale and experience have very different properties as entry barriers. The presence of economies of scale *always* leads to a cost advantage for the large-scale firm (or firm that can share activities) over small-scale firms, presupposing that the former have the most efficient facilities, distribution systems, service organizations, or other functional activities for their size.[5] This cost advantage can be matched only by attaining comparable scale or appropriate diversification to allow cost sharing. The large-scale or diversified firm can spread the fixed costs of operating these efficient facilities over a large number of units,

[5]And presupposing that the large-scale firm does not nullify its advantage through product line proliferation.

whereas the smaller firm, even if it has technologically efficient facilities, will not fully utilize them.

Some limits to economies of scale as an entry barrier, from the strategic standpoint of incumbents, are as follows:

- Large-scale and hence lower costs may involve trade-offs with other potentially valuable barriers to entry such as product differentiation (scale may work against product image or responsive service, for example) or the ability to develop proprietary technology rapidly.
- Technological change may penalize the large-scale firm if facilities designed to reap scale economies are also more specialized and less flexible in adapting to new technologies.
- Commitment to achieving scale economies by using existing technology may cloud the perception of new technological possibilities or of other new ways of competing that are less dependent on scale.

Experience is a more ethereal entry barrier than scale, because the mere presence of an experience curve does not insure an entry barrier. Another crucial prerequisite is that the experience be proprietary, and not available to competitors and potential entrants through (1) copying, (2) hiring a competitor's employees, or (3) purchasing the latest machinery from equipment suppliers or purchasing know-how from consultants or other firms. Frequently, experience cannot be kept proprietary; even when it can, experience may accumulate more rapidly for the second and third firms in the market than it did for the pioneer because followers can observe some aspects of the pioneer's operations. Where experience cannot be kept proprietary, new entrants may actually have an advantage if they can buy the latest equipment or adapt to new methods unencumbered by having operated the old way in the past.

Other limits to the experience curve as an entry barrier are as follows:

- The barrier can be nullified by product or process innovations leading to a substantially new technology and thereby creating an entirely new experience curve.[6] New entrants can leapfrog the industry leaders and alight on the new experience curve, to which the leaders may be poorly positioned to jump.

[6]For an example of this development drawn from the history of the automobile industry, see Abernathy and Wayne (1974), p. 109.

- Pursuit of low cost through experience may involve trade-offs with other valuable barriers, such as product differentiation through image or technological progressiveness. For example, Hewlett-Packard has erected substantial barriers based on technological progressiveness in industries in which other firms are following strategies based on experience and scale, like calculators and minicomputers.
- If more than one strong company is building its strategy on the experience curve, the consequences for one or more of them can be nearly fatal. By the time only one rival is left pursuing such a strategy, industry growth may have stopped and the prospects of capturing the experience curve benefits long since evaporated.
- Aggressive pursuit of cost declines through experience may draw attention away from market developments in other areas or may cloud perception of new technologies that nullify past experience.

INTENSITY OF RIVALRY AMONG EXISTING COMPETITORS

Rivalry among existing competitors takes the familiar form of jockeying for position—using tactics like price competition, advertising battles, product introductions, and increased customer service or warranties. Rivalry occurs because one or more competitors either feels the pressure or sees the opportunity to improve position. In most industries, competitive moves by one firm have noticeable effects on its competitors and thus may incite retaliation or efforts to counter the move; that is, firms are *mutually dependent*. This pattern of action and reaction may or may not leave the initiating firm and the industry as a whole better off. If moves and countermoves escalate, then all firms in the industry may suffer and be worse off than before.

Some forms of competition, notably price competition, are highly unstable and quite likely to leave the entire industry worse off from the standpoint of profitability. Price cuts are quickly and easily matched by rivals, and once matched they lower revenues for all firms unless industry price elasticity of demand is high enough. Advertising battles, on the other hand, may well expand demand or enhance the level of product differentiation in the industry for the benefit of all firms.

Rivalry in some industries is characterized by such phrases as "warlike," "bitter," or "cutthroat," whereas in other industries it is termed "polite" or "gentlemanly." Intense rivalry is the result of a number of interacting structural factors.

Numerous or Equally Balanced Competitors. When firms are numerous, the likelihood of mavericks is great and some firms may habitually believe they can make moves without being noticed. Even where there are relatively few firms, if they are relatively balanced in terms of size and perceived resources, it creates instability because they may be prone to fight each other and have the resources for sustained and vigorous retaliation. When the industry is highly concentrated or dominated by one or a few firms, on the other hand, then there is little mistaking relative strength, and the leader or leaders can impose discipline as well as play a coordinative role in the industry through devices like price leadership.

In many industries foreign competitors, either exporting into the industry or participating directly through foreign investment, play an important role in industry competition. Foreign competitors, although having some differences that will be noted later, should be treated just like national competitors for purposes of structural analysis.

Slow Industry Growth. Slow industry growth turns competition into a market share game for firms seeking expansion. Market share competition is a great deal more volatile than is the situation in which rapid industry growth insures that firms can improve results just by keeping up with the industry, and where all their financial and managerial resources may be consumed by expanding with the industry.

High Fixed or Storage Costs. High fixed costs create strong pressures for all firms to fill capacity which often lead to rapidly escalating price cutting when excess capacity is present. Many basic materials like paper and aluminum suffer from this problem, for example. The significant characteristic of costs is fixed costs relative to value added, and not fixed costs as a proportion of total costs. Firms purchasing a high proportion of costs in outside inputs (low value added) may feel enormous pressures to fill capacity to break even, despite the fact that the absolute proportion of fixed costs is low.

A situation related to high fixed costs is one in which the product, once produced, is very difficult or costly to store. Here firms will also be vulnerable to temptations to shade prices in order to insure sales. This sort of pressure keeps profits low in industries like lobster fishing and the manufacture of certain hazardous chemicals and some service businesses.

Lack of Differentiation or Switching Costs. Where the product or service is perceived as a commodity or near commodity, choice by the buyer is largely based on price and service, and pressures for intense price and service competition result. These forms of competition are particularly volatile, as has been discussed. Product differentiation, on the other hand, creates layers of insulation against competitive warfare because buyers have preferences and loyalites to particular sellers. Switching costs, described earlier, have the same effect.

Capacity Augmented in Large Increments. Where economies of scale dictate that capacity must be added in large increments, capacity additions can be chronically disruptive to the industry supply/demand balance, particularly where there is a risk of bunching capacity additions. The industry may face recurring periods of overcapacity and price cutting, like those that afflict the manufacture of chlorine, vinyl chloride, and ammonium fertilizer. The conditions leading to chronic overcapacity are discussed in Chapter 15.

Diverse Competitors. Competitors diverse in strategies, origins, personalities, and relationships to their parent companies have differing goals and differing strategies for how to compete and may continually run head on into each other in the process. They may have a hard time reading each other's intentions accurately and agreeing on a set of "rules of the game" for the industry. Strategic choices right for one competitor will be wrong for others.

Foreign competitors often add a great deal of diversity to industries because of their differing circumstances and often differing goals. Owner-operators of small manufacturing or service firms may as well, because they may be satisfied with a subnormal rate of return on their invested capital to maintain the independence of self-ownership, whereas such returns are unacceptable and may appear irrational to a large publicly held competitor. In such an industry, the posture of the small firms may limit the profitability of the larger concern. Similarly, firms viewing a market as an outlet for excess capacity (e.g., in the case of dumping) will adopt policies contrary to those of firms viewing the market as a primary one. Finally, differences in the relationship of competing business units to their corporate parents is an important source of diversity in an industry as well. For example, a business unit that is part of a vertical chain of businesses in its corporate organization may well adopt different and perhaps contradictory goals than a free-standing firm competing in the same industry. Or a business unit that is a "cash cow" in its parent company's portfolio of businesses will behave differently than one that is being developed for long-run growth in view of a lack of other opportunities in the parent. (Some techniques for identifying diversity in competitors will be developed in Chapter 3.)

High Strategic Stakes. Rivalry in an industry becomes even more volatile if a number of firms have high stakes in achieving success there. For example, a diversified firm may place great importance on achieving success in a particular industry in order to further its overall corporate strategy. Or a foreign firm like Bosch, Sony, or Philips may perceive a strong need to establish a solid position in the U. S. market in order to build global prestige or technological credibility. In such situations, the goals of these firms may not only be diverse but even more destabilizing because they are expansionary and involve potential willingness to sacrifice profitability. (Some techniques for assessing strategic stakes will be developed in Chapter 3.)

High Exit Barriers. Exit barriers are economic, strategic, and emotional factors that keep companies competing in businesses even though they may be earning low or even negative returns on investment. The major sources[7] of exit barriers are the following:

- Specialized assets: assets highly specialized to the particular business or location have low liquidation values or high costs of transfer or conversion.
- Fixed costs of exit: these include labor agreements, resettlement costs, maintaining capabilities for spare parts, and so on.
- Strategic interrelationships: interrelationships between the business unit and others in the company in terms of image, marketing ability, access to financial markets, shared facilities, and so on. They cause the firm to attach high strategic importance to being in the business.

[7]For a fuller treatment see Chapter 12, which also illustrates how diagnosing exit barriers is crucial in developing strategies for declining industries.

- Emotional barriers: management's unwillingness to make economically justified exit decisions is caused by identification with the particular business, loyalty to employees, fear for one's own career, pride, and other reasons.
- Government and social restrictions: these involve government denial or discouragement of exit out of concern for job loss and regional economic effects; they are particularly common outside the United States.

When exit barriers are high, excess capacity does not leave the industry, and companies that lose the competitive battle do not give up. Rather, they grimly hang on and, because of their weakness, have to resort to extreme tactics. The profitability of the entire industry can be persistently low as a result.

SHIFTING RIVALRY

The factors that determine the intensity of competitive rivalry can and do change. A very common example is the change in industry growth brought about by industry maturity. As an industry matures its growth rate declines, resulting in intensified rivalry, declining profits, and (often) a shake-out. In the booming recreational vehicle industry of the early 1970s nearly every producer did well, but slow growth since then has eliminated the high returns, except for the strongest competitors, not to mention forcing many of the weaker companies out. The same story has been played out in industry after industry: snowmobiles, aerosol packaging, and sports equipment are just a few examples.

Another common change in rivalry occurs when an acquisition introduces a very different personality to an industry, as has been the case with Philip Morris' acquisition of Miller Beer and Procter and Gamble's acquisition of Charmin Paper Company. Also, technological innovation can boost the level of fixed costs in the production process and raise the volatility of rivalry, as it did in the shift from batch to continuous-line photofinishing in the 1960s.

Although a company must live with many of the factors that determine the intensity of industry rivalry—because they are built into industry economics—it may have some latitude in improving matters through strategic shifts. For example, it may try to raise buyers' switching costs by providing engineering assistance to customers to design its product into their operations or to make them dependent for technical advice. Or the firm can try to raise product differentiation through new kinds of services, marketing innovations, or product changes. Focusing selling efforts on the fastest growing segments of the industry or on market areas with the lowest fixed costs can reduce the impact of industry rivalry. Also, if it is feasible a company can try to avoid confronting competitors with high exit barriers and can thus sidestep involvement in bitter price cutting, or it can lower its own exit barriers. (Competitive moves will be explored in detail in Chapter 5.)

EXIT BARRIERS AND ENTRY BARRIERS

Although exit barriers and entry barriers are conceptually different, their joint level is an important aspect of the analysis of an industry. Often exit and entry barriers are related. Substantial economies of scale in production, for example, are usually associated with specialized assets, as is the presence of proprietary technology.

Taking the simplified case in which exit and entry barriers can be either high or low:

Exit Barriers

		Low	High
Entry Barriers	Low	Low, stable returns	Low, risky returns
	High	High, stable returns	High, risky returns

FIGURE 1-2. Barriers and Profitability

The best case from the viewpoint of industry profits is one in which entry barriers are high but exit barriers are low. Here entry will be deterred, and unsuccessful competitors will leave the industry. When both entry and exit barriers are high, profit potential is high but is usually accompanied by more risk. Although entry is deterred, unsuccessful firms will stay and fight in the industry.

The case of low entry and exit barriers is merely unexciting, but the worst case is one in which entry barriers are low and exit barriers are high. Here entry is easy and will be attracted by upturns in economic conditions or other temporary windfalls. However, capacity will not leave the industry when results deteriorate. As a result capacity stacks up in the industry and profitability is usually chronically poor. An industry might be in this unfortunate position, for example, if suppliers or lenders will readily finance entry, but once in, the firm faces substantial fixed financing costs.

PRESSURE FROM SUBSTITUTE PRODUCTS

All firms in an industry are competing, in a broad sense, with industries producing substitute products. Substitutes limit the potential returns of an industry by placing a ceiling on the prices firms in the industry can profitably charge.[8] The more attractive the price-performance alternative offered by substitutes, the firmer the lid on industry profits.

Sugar producers confronted with the large-scale commercialization of high fructose corn syrup, a sugar substitute, are learning this lesson today, as have the producers of acetylene and rayon who faced extreme competition from alternative, lower-cost materials for many of their respective applications. Substitutes not only limit profits in normal times, but they also reduce the bonanza an industry can reap in boom times. In 1978 the producers of fiberglass insulation enjoyed unprecedented demand as a result of high energy costs and severe winter weather. But the industry's ability to raise prices was tempered by the plethora of insulation substitutes, including cellulose, rock wool, and styrofoam. These substitutes are bound to become an ever stronger limit on profitability once the current round of plant additions has boosted capacity enough to meet demand (and then some).

Identifying substitute products is a matter of searching for other products that can perform the same *function* as the product of the industry. Sometimes doing so can be a subtle task, and one which leads the analyst into businesses seemingly far removed from the industry. Securities brokers, for example, are being increasingly confronted with such substitutes as real estate, insurance, money market funds, and other ways for the individual to invest capital, accentuated in importance by the poor performance of the equity markets.

Position vis-à-vis substitute products may well be a matter of *collective* industry actions. For example, although advertising by one firm may not be enough to bolster the industry's position against

[8]The impact of substitutes can be summarized as the industry's overall elasticity of demand.

a substitute, heavy and sustained advertising by all industry participants may well improve the industry's collective position. Similar
arguments apply to collective response in areas like product quality
improvement, marketing efforts, providing greater product availability, and so on.

Substitute products that deserve the most attention are those
that (1) are subject to trends improving their price-performance
tradeoff with the industry's product, or (2) are produced by industries earning high profits. In the latter case, substitutes often come
rapidly into play if some development increases competition in their
industries and causes price reduction or performance improvement.
Analysis of such trends can be important in deciding whether to try
to head off a substitute strategically or to plan strategy with it as
inevitably a key force. In the security guard industry, for example,
electronic alarm systems represent a potent substitute. Moreover,
they can only become more important since labor-intensive guard
services face inevitable cost escalation, whereas electronic systems
are highly likely to improve in performance and decline in costs.
Here, the appropriate response of security guard firms is probably to
offer packages of guards and electronic systems, based on a redefinition of the security guard as a skilled operator, rather than to try to
outcompete electronic systems across the board.

BARGAINING POWER OF BUYERS

Buyers compete with the industry by forcing down prices, bargaining for higher quality or more services, and playing competitors
against each other—all at the expense of industry profitability. The
power of each of the industry's important buyer groups depends on
a number of characteristics of its market situation and on the relative importance of its purchases from the industry compared with
its overall business. A buyer group is powerful if the following circumstances hold true:

*It is concentrated or purchases large volumes relative to seller
sales.* If a large portion of sales is purchased by a given buyer this
raises the importance of the buyer's business in results. Large-
volume buyers are particularly potent forces if heavy fixed costs
characterize the industry—as they do in corn refining and bulk
chemicals, for example—and raise the stakes to keep capacity filled.

The products it purchases from the industry represent a significant fraction of the buyer's costs or purchases. Here buyers are prone to expend the resources necessary to shop for a favorable price and purchase selectively. When the product sold by the industry in question is a small fraction of buyers' costs, buyers are usually much less price sensitive.

The products it purchases from the industry are standard or undifferentiated. Buyers, sure that they can always find alternative suppliers, may play one company against another, as they do in aluminum extrusion.

It faces few switching costs. Switching costs, defined earlier, lock the buyer to particular sellers. Conversely, the buyer's power is enhanced if the seller faces switching costs.

It earns low profits. Low profits create great incentives to lower purchasing costs. Suppliers to Chrysler, for example, are complaining that they are being pressured for superior terms. Highly profitable buyers, however, are generally less price sensitive (that is, of course, if the item does not represent a large fraction of their costs) and may take a longer run view toward preserving the health of their suppliers.

Buyers pose a credible threat of backward integration. If buyers either are partially integrated or pose a credible threat of backward integration, they are in a position to demand bargaining concessions.[9] The major automobile producers, General Motors and Ford, are well known for using the threat of self-manufacture as a bargaining lever. They engage in the practice of *tapered integration*, that is, producing some of their needs for a given component in-house and purchasing the rest from outside suppliers. Not only is their threat of further integration particularly credible, but also partial manufacture in-house gives them a detailed knowledge of costs which is a great aid in negotiation. Buyer power can be partially neutralized when firms in the industry offer a threat of forward integration into the buyers' industry.

The industry's product is unimportant to the quality of the buyers' products or services. When the quality of the buyers' products is very much affected by the industry's product, buyers are generally less price sensitive. Industries in which this situation exists in-

[9]If buyers' motivations to integrate are based more on safety of supply or other non-price factors this may imply that firms in the industry must offer great price concessions to forestall integration.

clude oil-field equipment, where a malfunction can lead to large losses (witness the enormous cost of the recent failure of a blowout preventor in a Mexican offshore oil well), and enclosures for electronic medical and test instruments, where the quality of the enclosure can greatly influence the user's impression about the quality of the equipment inside.

The buyer has full information. Where the buyer has full information about demand, actual market prices, and even supplier costs, this usually yields the buyer greater bargaining leverage than when information is poor. With full information, the buyer is in a greater position to insure that it receives the most favorable prices offered to others and can counter suppliers' claims that their viability is threatened.

Most of these sources of buyer power can be attributed to consumers as well as to industrial and commercial buyers; only a modification of the frame of reference is necessary. For example, consumers tend to be more price sensitive if they are purchasing products that are undifferentiated, expensive relative to their incomes, or of a sort where quality is not particularly important to them.

The buyer power of wholesalers and retailers is determined by the same rules, with one important addition. Retailers can gain significant bargaining power over manufacturers when they can *influence consumers' purchasing decisions*, as they do in audio components, jewelry, appliances, sporting goods, and other products. Wholesalers can gain bargaining power, similarly, if they can influence the purchase decisions of the retailers or other firms to which they sell.

ALTERING BUYER POWER

As the factors described above change with time or as a result of a company's strategic decisions, naturally the power of buyers rises or falls. In the ready-to-wear clothing industry, for example, as the buyers (department stores and clothing stores) have become more concentrated and control has passed to large chains, the industry has come under increasing pressure and has suffered falling margins. The industry has been unable to differentiate its product or engender switching costs that lock in its buyers enough to neutralize these trends, and the influx of imports has not helped.

A company's choice of buyer groups to sell to should be viewed as a crucial strategic decision. A company can improve its strategic posture by finding buyers who possess the least power to influence it adversely—in other words, *buyer selection*. Rarely do all the buyer groups a company sells to enjoy equal power. Even if a company sells to a single industry, segments usually exist within that industry which exercise less power (and that are therefore less price sensitive) than others. For example, the replacement market for most products is less price sensitive than the OEM market. (I will explore buyer selection as a strategy more fully in Chapter 6.)

BARGAINING POWER OF SUPPLIERS

Suppliers can exert bargaining power over participants in an industry by threatening to raise prices or reduce the quality of purchased goods and services. Powerful suppliers can thereby squeeze profitability out of an industry unable to recover cost increases in its own prices. By raising their prices, for example, chemical companies have contributed to the erosion of profitability of contract aerosol packagers because the packagers, facing intense competition from self-manufacture by their buyers, accordingly have limited freedom to raise their prices.

The conditions making suppliers powerful tend to mirror those making buyers powerful. A supplier group is powerful if the following apply:

It is dominated by a few companies and is more concentrated than the industry it sells to. Suppliers selling to more fragmented buyers will usually be able to exert considerable influence in prices, quality, and terms.

It is not obliged to contend with other substitute products for sale to the industry. The power of even large, powerful suppliers can be checked if they compete with substitutes. For example, suppliers producing alternative sweeteners compete sharply for many applications even though individual firms are large relative to individual buyers.

The industry is not an important customer of the supplier group. When suppliers sell to a number of industries and a particular industry does not represent a significant fraction of sales, suppliers are much more prone to exert power. If the industry is an important customer, suppliers' fortunes will be closely tied to the industry and they will want to protect it through reasonable pricing and assistance in activities like R&D and lobbying.

The suppliers' product is an important input to the buyer's business. Such an input is important to the success of the buyer's manufacturing process or product quality. This raises the supplier power. This is particularly true where the input is not storable, thus enabling the buyer to build up stocks of inventory.

The supplier group's products are differentiated or it has built up switching costs. Differentiation or switching costs facing the buyers cut off their options to play one supplier against another. If the supplier faces switching costs the effect is the reverse.

The supplier group poses a credible threat of forward integration. This provides a check against the industry's ability to improve the terms on which it purchases.

We usually think of suppliers as other firms, but *labor* must be recognized as a supplier as well, and one that exerts great power in many industries. There is substantial empirical evidence that scarce, highly skilled employees and/or tightly unionized labor can bargain away a significant fraction of potential profits in an industry. The principles in determining the potential power of labor as a supplier are similar to those just discussed. The key additions in assessing the power of labor are its *degree of organization*, and whether the supply of scarce varieties of labor can *expand*. Where the labor force is tightly organized or the supply of scarce labor is constrained from growing, the power of labor can be high.

The conditions determining suppliers' power are not only subject to change but also often out of the firm's control. However, as with buyers' power the firm can sometimes improve its situation through strategy. It can enhance its threat of backward integration, seek to eliminate switching costs, and the like. (Chapter 6 will explore some implications of suppliers' power for purchasing strategy more fully.)

GOVERNMENT AS A FORCE IN INDUSTRY COMPETITION

Government has been discussed primarily in terms of its possible impact on entry barriers, but in the 1970s and 1980s government at all levels must be recognized as potentially influencing many if not all aspects of industry structure both directly and indirectly. In many industries, government *is* a buyer or supplier and can influence industry competition by the policies it adopts. For example, government plays a crucial role as a buyer of defense-related products and as a supplier of timber through the Forest Service's control of vast timber reserves in the western United States. Many times government's role as a supplier or buyer is determined more by political factors than by economic circumstances, and this is probably a fact of life. Government regulations can also set limits on the behavior of firms as suppliers or buyers.

Government can also affect the position of an industry with substitutes through regulations, subsidies, or other means. The U. S. government is strongly promoting solar heating, for example, using tax incentives and research grants. Government decontrol of natural gas is quickly eliminating acetylene as a chemical feedstock. Safety and pollution standards affect relative cost and quality of substitutes. Government can also affect rivalry among competitors by influencing industry growth, the cost structure through regulations, and so on.

Thus no structural analysis is complete without a diagnosis of how present and future government policy, at all levels, will affect structural conditions. For purposes of strategic analysis it is usually more illuminating to consider how government affects competition *through* the five competitive forces than to consider it as a force in and of itself. However, strategy may well involve treating government as an actor to be influenced.

Structural Analysis and Competitive Strategy

Once the forces affecting competition in an industry and their underlying causes have been diagnosed, the firm is in a position to identify its strengths and weaknesses relative to the industry. From a strategic standpoint, the crucial strengths and weaknesses are the firm's posture vis-à-vis the underlying causes of each competitive force. Where does the firm stand against substitutes? Against the sources of entry barriers? In coping with rivalry from established competitors?

An effective competitive strategy takes offensive or defensive action in order to create a *defendable* position against the five competitive forces. Broadly, this involves a number of possible approaches:

- positioning the firm so that its capabilities provide the best defense against the existing array of competitive forces;
- influencing the balance of forces through strategic moves, thereby improving the firm's relative position; or

- anticipating shifts in the factors underlying the forces and responding to them, thereby exploiting change by choosing a strategy appropriate to the new competitive balance before rivals recognize it.

POSITIONING

The first approach takes the structure of the industry as given and matches the company's strengths and weaknesses to it. Strategy can be viewed as building defenses against the competitive forces or as finding positions in the industry where the forces are weakest.

Knowledge of the company's capabilities and of the causes of the competitive forces will highlight the areas where the company should confront competition and where avoid it. If the company is a low-cost producer, for example, it may choose to sell to powerful buyers while it takes care to sell them only products not vulnerable to competition from substitutes.

INFLUENCING THE BALANCE

A company can devise a strategy that takes the offensive. This posture is designed to do more than merely cope with the forces themselves; it is meant to alter their causes.

Innovations in marketing can raise brand identification or otherwise differentiate the product. Capital investments in large-scale facilities or vertical integration affect entry barriers. The balance of forces is partly a result of external factors and partly within a company's control. Structural analysis can be used to identify the key factors driving competition in the particular industry and thus the places where strategic action to influence the balance will yield the greatest payoff.

EXPLOITING CHANGE

Industry evolution is important strategically because evolution, of course, brings with it changes in the structural sources of competition. In the familiar product life-cycle pattern of industry development, for example, growth rates change, advertising is said to decline as the business becomes more mature, and the companies tend to integrate vertically.

These trends are not so important in themselves; what is critical is whether they affect the structural sources of competition. Consider vertical integration. In the maturing minicomputer industry, extensive vertical integration is taking place, both in manufacturing and in software development. This very significant trend is greatly raising economies of scale as well as the amount of capital necessary to compete in the industry. This in turn is raising barriers to entry and may drive some smaller competitors out of the industry once growth levels off.

Obviously, the trends holding the highest priority from a strategic standpoint are those that affect the most important sources of competition in the industry and those that bring new structural factors to the forefront. In contract aerosol packaging, for example, the trend toward less product differentiation is now dominant. This trend has increased buyers' powers, lowered the barriers to entry, and intensified rivalry.

Structural analysis can be used to predict the eventual profitability of an industry. In long-range planning the task is to examine each competitive force, forecast the magnitude of each underlying cause, and then construct a composite picture of the probable profit potential of the industry.

The outcome of such an exercise may differ a great deal from the existing industry structure. Today, for example, the solar heating business is populated by dozens and perhaps hundreds of companies, none with a major market position. Entry is easy, and competitors are battling to establish solar heating as a superior substitute for conventional heating methods.

The potential of solar heating will depend largely on the shape of the future barriers to entry, the improvement of the industry's position relative to substitutes, the ultimate intensity of competition, and the power captured by buyers and suppliers. These characteristics will, in turn, be influenced by such factors as the likelihood of establishment of brand identities, whether significant economies of scale or experience curves in equipment manufacture will be created by technological change, what will be the ultimate capital costs to enter, and the eventual extent of fixed costs in production facilities. (The process of industry structural evolution and the forces driving it will be explored in detail in Chapter 8.)

DIVERSIFICATION STRATEGY

The framework for analyzing industry competition can be used in setting diversification strategy. It provides a guide for answering the extremely difficult question inherent in diversification decisions:

"What is the potential of this business?" The framework may allow a company to spot an industry with a good future before this good future is reflected in the prices of acquisition candidates.

The framework can also help identify particularly valuable types of relatedness in diversification. For example, relatedness that allows the firm to overcome key entry barriers through shared functions or pre-existing relationships with distribution channels can be a fruitful basis for diversification. All these issues will be explored in more detail in Chapter 16.

Structural Analysis and Industry Definition

A great deal of attention has been directed at defining the relevant industry as a crucial step in competitive strategy formulation. Numerous writers have also stressed the need to look beyond product to function in defining a business, beyond national boundaries to potential international competition, and beyond the ranks of one's competitors today to those that may become competitors tomorrow. As a result of these urgings, the proper definition of a company's industry or industries has become an endlessly debated subject. An important motive in this debate is the fear of overlooking latent sources of competition that may someday threaten the industry.

Structural analysis, by focusing broadly on competition well beyond existing rivals, should reduce the need for debates on where to draw industry boundaries. Any definition of an industry is essentially a choice of where to draw the line between established competitors and substitute products, between existing firms and potential entrants, and between existing firms and suppliers and buyers. Drawing these lines is inherently a matter of degree that has little to do with the choice of strategy.

If these broad sources of competition are recognized, however, and their relative impact assessed, then where the lines are actually drawn becomes more or less irrelevant to strategy formulation. Latent sources of competition will not be overlooked, nor will key dimensions of competition.

Definition of an industry is *not* the same as definition of where the firm wants to compete (defining *its* business), however. Just because the industry is defined broadly, for example, does not mean that the firm can or should compete broadly; and there may be strong benefits to competing in a group of related industries, as has been discussed. Decoupling industry definition and that of the businesses the firm wants to be in will go far in eliminating needless confusion in drawing industry boundaries.

USE OF STRUCTURAL ANALYSIS

This chapter has identified a large number of factors that can potentially have an impact on industry competition.[10] Not all of them will be important in any one industry. Rather the framework can be used to identify rapidly what are the crucial structural features determining the nature of competition in a particular industry. This is where the bulk of the analytical and strategic attention should be focused.

2
Generic Competitive Strategies

Chapter 1 described competitive strategy as taking offensive or defensive actions to create a defendable position in an industry, to cope successfully with the five competitive forces and thereby yield a superior return on investment for the firm. Firms have discovered many different approaches to this end, and the best strategy for a given firm is ultimately a unique construction reflecting its particular circumstances. However, at the broadest level we can identify three internally consistent generic strategies (which can be used singly or in combination) for creating such a defendable position in the long run and outperforming competitors in an industry. This chapter describes the generic strategies and explores some of the requirements and risks of each. Its purpose is to develop some introductory concepts that can be built upon in subsequent analysis. Succeeding chapters of this book will have much more to say about how to translate these broad generic strategies into more specific strategies in particular kinds of industry situations.

Three Generic Strategies

In coping with the five competitive forces, there are three potentially successful generic strategic approaches to outperforming other firms in an industry:

1. overall cost leadership
2 differentiation
3. focus.

Sometimes the firm can successfully pursue more than one approach as its primary target, though this is rarely possible as will be discussed further. Effectively implementing any of these generic strategies usually requires total commitment and supporting organizational arrangements that are diluted if there is more than one primary target. The generic strategies are approaches to outperforming competitors in the industry; in some industries structure will mean that all firms can earn high returns, whereas in others, success with one of the generic strategies may be necessary just to obtain acceptable returns in an absolute sense.

OVERALL COST LEADERSHIP

The first strategy, an increasingly common one in the 1970s because of popularization of the experience curve concept, is to achieve overall cost leadership in an industry through a set of functional policies aimed at this basic objective. Cost leadership requires aggressive construction of efficient-scale facilities, vigorous pursuit of cost reductions from experience, tight cost and overhead control, avoidance of marginal customer accounts, and cost minimization in areas like R&D, service, sales force, advertising, and so on. A great deal of managerial attention to cost control is necessary to achieve these aims. Low cost relative to competitors becomes the theme running through the entire strategy, though quality, service, and other areas cannot be ignored.

Having a low-cost position yields the firm above-average returns in its industry despite the presence of strong competitive forces. Its cost position gives the firm a defense against rivalry from competitors, because its lower costs mean that it can still earn returns after its competitors have competed away their profits through rivalry. A low-cost position defends the firm against powerful buyers because buyers can exert power only to drive down prices to the level of the next most efficient competitor. Low cost provides a defense against powerful suppliers by providing more flexibility to cope with input cost increases. The factors that lead to a low-cost position usually also provide substantial entry barriers in terms of scale economies or cost advantages. Finally, a low-cost position usually places the firm in a favorable position vis-à-vis substitutes relative to its competitors in the industry. Thus a low-cost position protects the firm against all five competitive forces because bargaining can only continue to erode profits until those of the next most efficient competitor are eliminated, and because the less efficient competitors will suffer first in the face of competitive pressures.

Achieving a low overall cost position often requires a high relative market share or other advantages, such as favorable access to raw materials. It may well require designing products for ease in manufacturing, maintaining a wide line of related products to spread costs, and serving all major customer groups in order to build volume. In turn, implementing the low-cost strategy may require heavy up-front capital investment in state-of-the art equipment, aggressive pricing, and start-up losses to build market share. High market share may in turn allow economies in purchasing which lower costs even further. Once achieved, the low-cost position provides high margins which can be reinvested in new equipment and modern facilities in order to maintain cost leadership. Such reinvestment may well be a prerequisite to sustaining a low-cost position.

The cost leadership strategy seems to be the cornerstone of Briggs and Stratton's success in small horsepower gasoline engines, where it holds a 50 percent worldwide share, and Lincoln Electric's success in arc welding equipment and supplies. Other firms known for successful application of cost leadership strategies to a number of businesses are Emerson Electric, Texas Instruments, Black and Decker, and Du Pont.

A cost leadership strategy can sometimes revolutionize an industry in which the historical bases of competition have been otherwise and competitors are ill-prepared either perceptually or economically to take the steps necessary for cost minimization. Harnischfeger is in the midst of a daring attempt to revolutionize the rough-terrain crane industry in 1979. Starting from a 15 percent market share,

Harnischfeger redesigned its cranes for easy manufacture and service using modularized components, configuration changes, and reduced material content. It then established subassembly areas and a conveyorized assembly line, a notable departure from industry norms. It ordered parts in large volumes to save costs. All this allowed the company to offer an acceptable quality product and drop prices by 15 percent. Harnischfeger's market share has grown rapidly to 25 percent and is continuing to grow. Says Willis Fisher, general manager of Harnischfeger's Hydraulic Equipment Division:

> We didn't set out to develop a machine significantly better than anyone else but we did want to develop one that was truly simple to manufacture and was priced, intentionally, as a low cost machine.[1]

Competitors are grumbling that Harnischfeger has "bought" market share with lower margins, a charge that the company denies.

DIFFERENTIATION

The second generic strategy is one of differentiating the product or service offering of the firm, creating something that is perceived *industrywide* as being unique. Approaches to differentiating can take many forms: design or brand image (Fieldcrest in top of the line towels and linens; Mercedes in automobiles), technology (Hyster in lift trucks; MacIntosh in stereo components; Coleman in camping equipment), features (Jenn-Air in electric ranges); customer service (Crown Cork and Seal in metal cans), dealer network (Caterpillar Tractor in construction equipment), or other dimensions. Ideally, the firm differentiates itself along several dimensions. Caterpillar Tractor, for example, is known not only for its dealer network and excellent spare parts availability but also for its extremely high-quality durable products, all of which are crucial in heavy equipment where downtime is very expensive. It should be stressed that the differentiation strategy does not allow the firm to ignore costs, but rather they are not the primary strategic target.

Differentiation, if achieved, is a viable strategy for earning above-average returns in an industry because it creates a defensible position for coping with the five competitive forces, albeit in a dif-

[1] "Harnischfeger's Dramatic Pickup in Cranes," *Business Week*, August 13, 1979.

ferent way than cost leadership. Differentiation provides insulation against competitive rivalry because of brand loyalty by customers and resulting lower sensitivity to price. It also increases margins, which avoids the need for a low-cost position. The resulting customer loyalty and the need for a competitor to overcome uniqueness provide entry barriers. Differentiation yields higher margins with which to deal with supplier power, and it clearly mitigates buyer power, since buyers lack comparable alternatives and are thereby less price sensitive. Finally, the firm that has differentiated itself to achieve customer loyalty should be better positioned vis-à-vis substitutes than its competitors.

Achieving differentiation may sometimes preclude gaining a high market share. It often requires a perception of exclusivity, which is incompatible with high market share. More commonly, however, achieving differentiation will imply a trade-off with cost position if the activities required in creating it are inherently costly, such as extensive research, product design, high quality materials, or intensive customer support. Whereas customers industrywide acknowledge the superiority of the firm, not all customers will be willing or able to pay the required higher prices (though most are in industries like earthmoving equipment where despite high prices Caterpillar has a dominant market share). In other businesses, differentiation may not be incompatible with relatively low costs and comparable prices to those of competitors.

FOCUS

The final generic strategy is focusing on a particular buyer group, segment of the product line, or geographic market; as with differentiation, focus may take many forms. Although the low cost and differentiation strategies are aimed at achieving their objectives industrywide, the entire focus strategy is built around serving a particular target very well, and each functional policy is developed with this in mind. The strategy rests on the premise that the firm is thus able to serve its narrow strategic target more effectively or efficiently than competitors who are competing more broadly. As a result, the firm achieves either differentiation from better meeting the needs of the particular target, or lower costs in serving this target, or both. Even though the focus strategy does not achieve low cost or differentiation from the perspective of the market as a whole, it does achieve one or both of these positions vis-à-vis its narrow market target. The difference among the three generic strategies are illustrated in figure 2-1.

The firm achieving focus may also potentially earn above-average returns for its industry. Its focus means that the firm either has a low cost position with its strategic target, high differentiation, or both. As we have discussed in the context of cost leadership and differentiation, these positions provide defenses against each competitive force. Focus may also be used to select targets least vulnerable to substitutes or where competitors are the weakest.

For example, Illinois Tool Works has focused on specialty markets for fasteners where it can design products for particular buyer needs and create switching costs. Although many buyers are uninterested in these services, some are. Fort Howard Paper focuses on a narrow range of industrial-grade papers, avoiding consumer products vulnerable to advertising battles and rapid introductions of new products. Porter Paint focuses on the professional painter rather than the do-it-yourself market, building its strategy around serving the professional through free paint-matching services, rapid delivery of as little as a gallon of needed paint to the worksite, and free coffee rooms designed to provide a home for professional painters at factory stores. An example of a focus strategy that achieves a low-cost

FIGURE 2-1. Three Generic Strategies

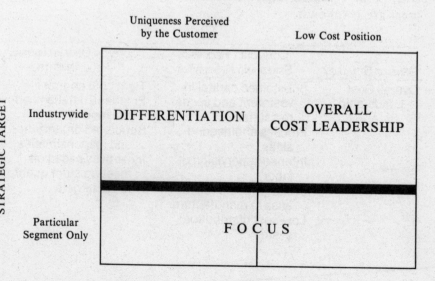

STRATEGIC ADVANTAGE

	Uniqueness Perceived by the Customer	Low Cost Position
Industrywide	DIFFERENTIATION	OVERALL COST LEADERSHIP
Particular Segment Only	FOCUS	

STRATEGIC TARGET

position in serving its particular target is seen in Martin-Brower, the third largest food distributor in the United States. Martin-Brower has reduced its customer list to just eight leading fast-food chains. Its entire strategy is based on meeting the specialized needs of the customers, stocking only their narrow product lines, order taking procedures geared to their purchasing cycles, locating warehouses based on their locations, and intensely controlling and computerizing record keeping. Although Martin-Brower is not the low-cost distributor in serving the market as a whole, it is in serving its particular segment. Martin-Brower has been rewarded with rapid growth and above-average profitability.

The focus strategy always implies some limitations on the overall market share achievable. Focus necessarily involves a trade-off between profitability and sales volume. Like the differentiate strategy, it may or may not involve a trade-off with overall cost position.

OTHER REQUIREMENTS OF THE GENERIC STRATEGIES

The three generic strategies differ in dimensions other than the functional differences noted above. Implementing them successfully requires different resources and skills. The generic strategies also imply differing organizational arrangements, control procedures, and inventive systems. As a result, sustained commitment to one of the strategies as the primary target is usually necessary to achieve success. Some common implications of the generic strategies in these areas are as follows:

GENERIC STRATEGY	COMMONLY REQUIRED SKILLS AND RESOURCES	COMMON ORGANIZATIONAL REQUIREMENTS
Overall Cost Leadership	Substained capital investment and access to capital	Tight cost control
	Process engineering skills	Frequent, detailed control reports
	Intense supervision of labor	Structured organization and responsibilities
	Products designed for ease in manufacture	Incentives based on meeting strict quantitative targets
	Low-cost distribution system	

GENERIC STRATEGY	COMMONLY REQUIRED SKILLS AND RESOURCES	COMMON ORGANIZATIONAL REQUIREMENTS
Differentiation	Strong marketing abilities Product engineering Creative flair Strong capability in basic research Corporate reputation for quality or technological leadership Long tradition in the industry or unique combination of skills drawn from other businesses Strong cooperation from channels	Strong coordination among functions in R&D, product development, and marketing Subjective measurement and incentives instead of quantitative measures Amenities to attract highly skilled labor, scientists, or creative people
Focus	Combination of the above policies directed at the particular strategic target	Combination of the above policies directed at the particular strategic target

The generic strategies may also require different styles of leadership and can translate into very different corporate cultures and atmospheres. Different sorts of people will be attracted.

Stuck in the Middle

The three generic strategies are alternative, viable approaches to dealing with the competitive forces. The converse of the previous discussion is that the firm failing to develop its strategy in at least one of the three directions—a firm that is "stuck in the middle"—is in an extremely poor strategic situation. This firm lacks the market share, capital investment, and resolve to play the low-cost game, the industrywide differentiation necessary to obviate the need for a low-cost position, or the focus to create differentiation or a low-cost position in a more limited sphere.

The firm stuck in the middle is almost guaranteed low profitability. It either loses the high-volume customers who demand low prices or must bid away its profits to get this business away from low-cost firms. Yet it also loses high-margin businesses—the cream—to the firms who are focused on high-margin targets or have achieved differentiation overall. The firm stuck in the middle also probably suffers from a blurred corporate culture and a conflicting set of organizational arrangements and motivation system.

Clark Equipment may well be stuck in the middle in the lift truck industry in which it has the leading overall U.S. and worldwide market share. Two Japanese producers, Toyota and Komatsu, have adopted strategies of serving only the high-volume segments, mini-mized production costs, and rock-bottom prices, also taking advantage of lower Japanese steel prices, which more than offset transportation costs. Clark's greater worldwide share (18 percent; 33 percent in the United States) does not give it clear cost leadership given its very wide product line and lack of low-cost orientation. Yet with its wide line and lack of full emphasis to technology Clark has been unable to achieve the technological reputation and product differentiation of Hyster, which has focused on larger lift trucks and spent aggressively on R&D. As a result, Clark's returns appear to be significantly lower than Hyster's, and Clark has been losing ground.[2]

The firm stuck in the middle must make a fundamental strategic decision. Either it must take the steps necessary to achieve cost leadership or at least cost parity, which usually involve aggressive investments to modernize and perhaps the necessity to buy market share, or it must orient itself to a particular target (focus) or achieve some uniqueness (differentiation). The latter two options may well involve shrinking in market share and even in absolute sales. The choice among these options is necessarily based on the firm's capabilities and limitations. Successfully executing each generic strategy involves different resources, strengths, organizational arrangements, and managerial style, as has been discussed. Rarely is a firm suited for all three.

Once stuck in the middle, it usually takes time and sustained effort to extricate the firm from this unenviable position. Yet there seems to be a tendency for firms in difficulty to flip back and forth over time among the generic strategies. Given the potential inconsistencies involved in pursuing these three strategies, such an approach is almost always doomed to failure.

These concepts suggest a number of possible relationships between market share and profitability. In some industries, the prob-

[2]See Wertheim (1977).

lem of getting caught in the middle may mean that the smaller (focused or differentiated) firms and the largest (cost leadership) firms are the most profitable, and the medium-sized firms are the least profitable. This implies a U-shaped relationship between profitability and market share, as shown in Figure 2-2. The relationship in Figure 2-2 appears to hold in the U.S. fractional horsepower electric motor business. There GE and Emerson have large market shares and strong cost positions, GE also having a strong technological reputation. Both are believed to earn high returns in motors. Baldor and Gould (Century) have adopted focused strategies, Baldor oriented toward the distributor channel and Gould toward particular customer segments. The profitability of both is also believed to be good. Franklin is in an intermediate position, with neither low cost nor focus. Its performance in motors is believed to follow accordingly. Such a U-shaped relationship probably also roughly holds in the automobile industry when viewed on a global basis, with firms like GM (low cost) and Mercedes (differentiate) the profit leaders. Chrysler, British Leyland, and Fiat lack cost position, differentiation, or focus—they are stuck in the middle.

However, the U-shaped relationship in Figure 2-2 does not hold in every industry. In some industries, there are no opportunities for focus or differentiation—it's solely a cost game—and this is true in a number of bulk commodities. In other industries, cost is relatively unimportant because of buyer and product characteristics. In these kinds of industries there is often an inverse relationship between market share and profitability. In still other industries, competition is so intense that the only way to achieve an above-average return is

FIGURE 2-2

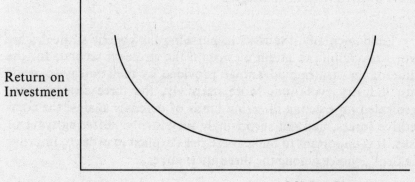

Return on Investment

Market Share

through focus or differentiation—which seems to be true in the U.S. steel industry. Finally, low overall cost position may not be incompatible with differentiation or focus, or low cost may be achievable without high share. For an example of the complex combinations that can result, Hyster is number two in lift trucks but is more profitable than several of the smaller producers in the industry (Allis-Chalmers, Eaton) who do not have the share to achieve either low costs or enough product differentiation to offset their cost position.

There is *no single relationship* between profitability and market share, unless one conveniently defines the market so that focused or differentiated firms are assigned high market shares in some narrowly defined industries and the industry definitions of cost leadership firms are allowed to stay broad (they must because cost leaders often do not have the largest share in every submarket). Even shifting industry definition cannot explain the high returns of firms who have achieved differentiation industrywide and hold market shares below that of the industry leader.

Most importantly, however, shifting the way the industry is defined from firm to firm begs the question of deciding which of the three generic strategies is appropriate for the firm. This choice rests on picking the strategy best suited to the firm's strengths and one least replicable by competitors. The principles of structural analysis should illuminate the choice, as well as allow the analyst to explain or predict the relationship between share and profitability in any particular industry. I will discuss this issue further in Chapter 7, where structural analysis is extended to consider the differing positions of firms within a particular industry.

Risks of the Generic Strategies

Fundamentally, the risks in pursuing the generic strategies are two: first, failing to attain or sustain the strategy; second, for the value of the strategic advantage provided by the strategy to erode with industry evolution. More narrowly, the three strategies are predicated on erecting differing kinds of defenses against the competitive forces, and not surprisingly they involve differing types of risks. It is important to make these risks explicit in order to improve the firm's choice among the three alternatives.

RISKS OF OVERALL COST LEADERSHIP

Cost leadership imposes severe burdens on the firm to keep up its position, which means reinvesting in modern equipment, ruthlessly scrapping obsolete assets, avoiding product line proliferation and being alert for technological improvements. Cost declines with cumulative volume are by no means automatic, nor is reaping all available economies of scale achievable without significant attention.

Cost leadership is vulnerable to the same risks, identified in Chapter 1, of relying on scale or experience as entry barriers. Some of these risks are

- technological change that nullifies past investments or learning;
- low-cost learning by industry newcomers or followers, through imitation or through their ability to invest in state-of-the-art facilities;
- inability to see required product or marketing change because of the attention placed on cost;
- inflation in costs that narrow the firm's ability to maintain enough of a price differential to offset competitors' brand images or other approaches to differentiation.

The classic example of the risks of cost leadership is the Ford Motor Company of the 1920s. Ford had achieved unchallenged cost leadership through limitation of models and varieties, aggressive backward integration, highly automated facilities, and aggressive pursuit of lower costs through learning. Learning was facilitated by the lack of model changes. Yet as incomes rose and many buyers had already purchased a car and were considering their second, the market began to place more of a premium on styling, model changes, comfort, and closed rather than open cars. Customers were willing to pay a price premium to get such features. General Motors stood ready to capitalize on this development with a full line of models. Ford faced enormous costs of strategic readjustment given the rigidities created by heavy investments in cost minimization of an obsolete model.

Another example of the risks of cost leadership as a sole focus is provided by Sharp in consumer electronics. Sharp, which has long followed a cost leadership strategy, has been forced to begin an aggressive campaign to develop brand recognition. Its ability to sufficiently undercut Sony's and Panasonic's prices was eroded by cost increases and U.S. antidumping legislation, and its strategic position was deteriorating through sole concentration on cost leadership.

RISKS OF DIFFERENTIATION

Differentiation also involves a series of risks:

- the cost differential between low-cost competitors and the differentiated firm becomes too great for differentiation to hold brand loyalty. Buyers thus sacrifice some of the features, services, or image possessed by the differentiated firm for large cost savings;
- buyers' need for the differentiating factor falls. This can occur as buyers become more sophisticated;
- imitation narrows perceived differentiation, a common occurrence as industries mature.

The first risk is so important as to be worthy of further comment. A firm may achieve differentiation, yet this differentiation will usually sustain only so much of a price differential. Thus if a differentiated firm gets too far behind in cost due to technological change or simply inattention, the low cost firm may be in a position to make major inroads. For example, Kawasaki and other Japanese motorcycle producers have been able to successfully attack differentiated producers such as Harley-Davidson and Triumph in large motorcycles by offering major cost savings to buyers.

RISKS OF FOCUS

Focus involves yet another set of risks:

- the cost differential between broad-range competitors and the focused firm widens to eliminate the cost advantages of serving a narrow target or to offset the differentiation achieved by focus;
- the differences in desired products or services between the strategic target and the market as a whole narrows;
- competitors find submarkets *within* the strategic target and outfocus the focuser.

3
A Framework for
Competitor Analysis

Competitive strategy involves positioning a business to maximize the value of the capabilities that distinguish it from its competitors. It follows that a central aspect of strategy formulation is perceptive competitor analysis. The objective of a competitor analysis is to develop a profile of the nature and success of the likely strategy changes each competitor might make, each competitor's probable response to the range of feasible strategic moves other firms could initiate, and each competitor's probable reaction to the array of industry changes and broader environmental shifts that might occur. Sophisticated competitor analysis is needed to answer such questions as "Who should we pick a fight with in the industry, and with what sequence of moves?" "What is the meaning of that competitor's strategic move and how seriously should we take it?" and "What areas should we avoid because the competitor's response will be emotional or desperate?"

Despite the clear need for sophisticated competitor analysis in strategy formulation, such analysis is sometimes not done explicitly or comprehensively in practice. Dangerous assumptions can creep into managerial thinking about competitors: "Competitors cannot be systematically analyzed," "We know all about our competitors because we compete with them every day." Neither assumption is generally true. A further difficulty is that in-depth competitor analysis requires a great deal of data, much of which is not easy to find without considerable hard work. Many companies do not collect information about competitors in a systematic fashion, but act on the basis of informal impressions, conjectures, and intuition gained through the tidbits of information about competitors every manager continually receives. Yet the lack of good information makes it very hard to do sophisticated competitor analysis.

There are four diagnostic components to a competitor analysis (see Figure 3-1): future *goals*, current *strategy*, *assumptions*, and *capabilities*.[1] Understanding these four components will allow an informed prediction of the competitor's response profile, as articulated in the key questions posed in Figure 3-1. Most companies develop at least an intuitive sense for their competitors' current strategies and their strengths and weaknesses (shown on the right side of Figure 3-1). Much less attention is usually directed at the left side, or understanding what is really driving the behavior of a competitor—its future goals and the assumptions it holds about its own situation and the nature of its industry. These driving factors are much harder to observe than is actual competitor behavior, yet they often determine how a competitor will behave in the future.

This chapter will present a basic framework for competitor analysis, which will be extended or enriched in subsequent chapters. Each component of competitor analysis in Figure 3-1 will be treated in subsequent sections by developing a set of questions that can be asked about competitors, with somewhat more stress placed on diagnosing competitor goals and assumptions. In these more subtle areas, it will be important to go beyond mere categorization to suggest some techniques and clues for identifying what a particular competitor's goals and assumptions actually are. Having discussed each component of competitor analysis, we will then examine how the components can be put together to answer the questions posed in Figure 3-1. Finally, some concepts for collecting and analyzing competitor data will be briefly discussed, in view of the importance of the data-gathering task in competitor analysis.

Although the framework and questions presented here are stated in terms of competitors, the same ideas can also be turned

[1]Although we usually treat future goals as part of strategy, it will be analytically useful to separate goals and current strategy in competitor analysis.

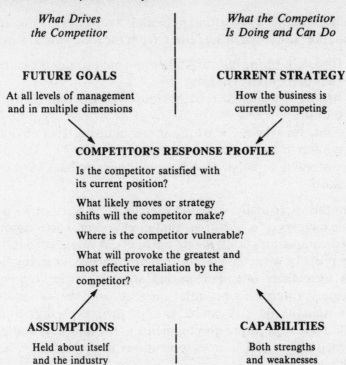

*What Drives
the Competitor*

*What the Competitor
Is Doing and Can Do*

FUTURE GOALS

At all levels of management
and in multiple dimensions

CURRENT STRATEGY

How the business is
currently competing

COMPETITOR'S RESPONSE PROFILE

Is the competitor satisfied with
its current position?

What likely moves or strategy
shifts will the competitor make?

Where is the competitor vulnerable?

What will provoke the greatest and
most effective retaliation by the
competitor?

ASSUMPTIONS

Held about itself
and the industry

CAPABILITIES

Both strengths
and weaknesses

FIGURE 3-1   The Components of a Competitor Analysis

around to provide a framework for self-analysis. The same concepts
provide a company with a framework for probing its own position in
its environment. And beyond this, going through such an exercise
can help a company understand what conclusions *its competitors are
likely to draw about it*. This is part of sophisticated competitor analysis because these conclusions shape a competitor's assumptions and
hence behavior, and are crucial to making competitive moves (see
Chapter 5).

The Components of Competitor Analysis

Before discussing each component of competitor analysis, it is
important to define which competitors should be examined. Clearly
all significant *existing competitors* must be analyzed. However, it
also may be important to analyze the *potential competitors* that may

come on the scene. Forecasting potential competitors is not an easy task, but they can often be identified from the following groups:

- firms not in the industry but who could overcome entry barriers particularly cheaply;
- firms for whom there is obvious synergy from being in the industry;
- firms for whom competing in the industry is an obvious extension of the corporate strategy;
- customers or suppliers who may integrate backward or forward.

Another potentially valuable exercise is to attempt to predict probable *mergers or acquisitions* that might occur, either among established competitors or involving outsiders. A merger can instantaneously propel a weak competitor into prominence, or strengthen an already formidable one. Forecasting acquiring firms follows the same logic as forecasting potential entrants. Forecasting acquisition targets within the industry can be based on their ownership situation, ability to cope with future developments in the industry, and potential attractiveness as a base of operations in the industry, among other things.

FUTURE GOALS

The diagnosis of competitors' goals (and how they will measure themselves against these goals), the first component of competitor analysis, is important for a variety of reasons. A knowledge of goals will allow predictions about whether or not each competitor is satisfied with its present position and financial results, and thereby, how likely that competitor is to change strategy and the vigor with which it will react to outside events (for instance, the business cycle) or to moves by other firms. For example, a firm placing a high value on stable sales growth may react very differently to a business downturn or a market share increase by another company than a firm most interested in maintaining its rate of return on investment.

Knowing a competitor's goals will also aid in predicting its reactions to strategic changes. Some strategic changes will threaten a competitor more than others, given its goals and any pressures it may face from a corporate parent. This degree of threat will affect the probability of retaliation. Finally, a diagnosis of a competitor's goals helps interpret the seriousness of initiatives the competitor takes. A strategic move by a competitor which addresses one of its central goals or seeks to restore performance against a key target is not a casual matter. Similarly, a diagnosis of its goals will help determine whether a corporate parent will seriously support an initiative taken by one of its business units or whether it will back that business unit's retaliation against moves of competitors.

Although one most often thinks of financial goals, a comprehensive diagnosis of a competitor's goals will usually include many more qualitative factors, such as its targets in terms of market leadership, technological position, social performance, and the like. Diagnosis of goals should also be at multiple management levels. There are corporate-wide goals, business unit goals, and even goals that can be deduced for individual functional areas and key managers. The goals of higher levels play a part in, but do not fully determine, the goals lower down.

The following diagnostic questions help to determine a competitor's present and future goals. We begin by considering the business unit or division, which in some cases will comprise the competitor's entire corporate entity. Then we examine the impact of the corporate parent on the future goals of the business unit in the diversified company.

BUSINESS UNIT GOALS

1. What are the stated and unstated *financial goals* of the competitor? How does the competitor make the trade-offs inherent in goal setting, such as the trade-off between long-run and short-run performance? Between profits and growth in revenue? Between growth and ability to pay regular dividends?

2. What is the competitor's *attitude toward risks*? If financial objectives essentially consist of profitability, market position (share), rate of growth, and desired level of risk, how does the competitor appear to balance these factors?

3. Does the competitor have economic or noneconomic organizational *values or beliefs*, either widely shared or held by senior management, which importantly affect its goals? Does it want to be the market leader (Texas Instruments)? The industry statesman (Coca-Cola)? The maverick? The technological leader? Does it have a tradition or history of following a particular strategy or functional policy that has been institutionalized into a goal? Strongly held views about product design or quality? Locational preferences?

4. What is the *organizational structure* of the competitor (functional structure, presence or absence of product managers, separate R&D laboratory, etc.)? How does the structure allocate responsibility and power for such key decisions as resource allocation, pricing, and product changes? The competitor's organizational structure provides some indication about the relative status of the various functional areas and the coordination and emphasis that are deemed strategically important. For example, if the sales department is headed by a senior vice-president who reports directly to the president, it is an indication that sales is more influential than manufacturing if manufacturing is headed by a director who reports to the senior vice-president for administration. Where responsibility for decisions is assigned will give clues about the perspective top management wants to bring to bear on them.

5. What *control and incentive* systems are in place? How are executives compensated? How is the sales force compensated? Do managers hold stock? Is there a deferred compensation system in place? What measures of performance are tracked regularly? How often? All these things, though sometimes difficult to discern, yield important clues about what the competitor believes is important and how its managers will respond to events in view of their rewards.

6. What *accounting system* and conventions are in place? How does the competitor value inventory? Allocate costs? Account for inflation? These sorts of accounting policy issues can strongly influence the competitor's perceptions of its performance, what its costs are, the way it sets prices, and so on.

7. What kinds of *managers* comprise the leadership of the competitor, particularly the Chief Executive Officer (CEO)? What are their backgrounds and experience?[2] What kinds of younger managers seem to be getting rewarded, and what is their apparent emphasis? Are there any patterns in the places from which outsiders are hired into the company as an indication of a direction the company might be taking? Bic Pen, for example, had an explicit policy of hiring from outside the industry because it believed it needed to take an unconventional strategy. Are retirements imminent?

8. How much apparent *unanimity* is there among management about future direction? Are their management factions favoring different goals? If so, this may lead to sudden shifts in strategy as power shifts. Unanimity, conversely, may lead to great staying power and even stubbornness in the face of adversity.

[2]Some potentially illuminating questions about managers' backgrounds and experience are discussed below.

9. What is the composition of the *board*? Does it have enough outsiders to exercise effective outside review? What kinds of outsiders are on the board, and what are their backgrounds and company affiliations? How do they manage in their own firms, or what interests do they represent (banks? lawyers?)? The composition of the board can provide clues about the company's orientation, posture toward risk, and even preferred strategic approaches.

10. What *contractual commitments* may limit alternatives? Are there any debt covenants that will limit what goals can be? Restrictions due to licensing or joint venture agreements?

11. Are there any *regulatory, antitrust, or other governmental or social constraints* on the behavior of the firm that will affect such things as its reaction to moves of a smaller competitor or the probability that it will try to gain a larger market share? Has the competitor had any antitrust problems in the past? For what reasons? Has it entered into any consent decrees? Such restraints or even just a history may sensitize a firm so that it foregoes reacting to strategic events unless some essential element if its business is threatened. The firm attempting to capture a small share of a market from an industry leader can enjoy some protection as a result of such constraints, for example.

THE CORPORATE PARENT AND BUSINESS UNIT GOALS

If the competitor is a unit of a larger company, its corporate parent is likely to impose constraints or requirements on the business unit that will be crucial to predicting its behavior. The following questions need to be asked in addition to those just discussed:

1. What are the current *results* (sales growth, rate of return, etc.) *of the parent company*? As a first approximation, this gives an indication of the parent's targets that may be translated into market share objectives, pricing decisions, pressure for new products, and so on, for its business unit. A business unit performing worse than the parent as a whole is usually feeling the pressure. A business unit of a parent with a long string of unbroken financial improvement will be unlikely to take an action that can jeopardize the record.

2. What are the *overall goals of the parent*? In view of these, what are the parent's probable needs from its business unit?

3. What *strategic importance* does the parent attach to the particular business unit in terms of its overall corporate strategy? Does the corporation view this business as a "base business" or one on the periphery of its operation? Where does the business fit into the parent's portfolio? Is this business seen as a growth area and one of the

keys to the future of the corporation, or is it considered mature or stable and a source of cash? The strategic importance of the business unit will have a major influence on the goals it is expected to meet, and assessing strategic importance is discussed further below.

4. Why did the parent *get into this business* (because of excess capacity, need for vertical integration, to exploit distribution channels, for marketing strength)? This factor will give some further indication of the way in which the parent views the contribution of the business and the probable pressure it will place on the unit's strategic posture and behavior.

5. What is the *economic relationship* between the business and others in the parent company's portfolio (vertical integration, complementary to other businesses, shared R&D)? What does this relationship imply for special requirements the corporation may place on the unit relative to the way it would behave as a free-standing company? Shared facilities, for example, may mean that the unit is under pressure to cover overhead or absorb excess capacity generated by its sister units. Or if the unit is complementary to another division in the parent, the parent may choose to take the profits elsewhere. Interrelationships with other units in the company may also imply cross-subsidies in one direction or another.

6. What are the corporate-wide *values or beliefs* of top management? Do they seek technological leadership in all their businesses? Do they desire level production and the avoidance of layoffs to carry out a corporate policy against unions?[3] These sorts of corporate-wide values and beliefs will usually have an effect on the business unit.

7. Is there a *generic strategy* that the parent has applied in a number of businesses and may attempt in this one? For example, Bic Pen has employed a strategy of low-price, standardized, disposable products produced at very high volumes with heavy advertising to compete in the areas of writing instruments, cigarette lighters, pantyhose, and now razors. Haynes Corporation is in the process of applying the L'eggs strategy in pantyhose to such diverse businesses as cosmetics, men's underwear, and socks.

8. Given the *performance and needs of other units* in the corporation and the overall strategy, what sorts of sales targets, hurdles for return on investment, and constraints on capital might be placed

---

[3] A policy against layoffs, for example, would imply the building of big inventories in downturns, and possibly the willingness to give up market share in upturns. Such policies are in place at a number of major U. S. corporations.

on the competitor unit? Will it be able to compete successfully against other units in its corporate organization for corporate capital given its performance vis-à-vis these other units and the corporation's goals for it? Is the business unit either actually or potentially big enough to command the attention and support of the parent company, or will it be left on its own and assigned low priority in terms of managerial attention? What are the investment capital requirements of the other units of the company? Given any clues available about the priorities its parent company places on the various units and the amount of funds available after dividends, how much will be left for the unit?

9. What are the parent company's *diversification plans*? Is the parent planning to diversify into other areas that will consume capital or which provide an indication of the long-run emphasis that will be placed on the unit? Is the parent moving in directions that will bolster the unit through opportunities for synergy? Reynolds recently purchased Del Monte, for example, which should give a shot in the arm to Reynold's consumer food businesses because of Del Monte's distribution system.

10. What clues does the *organizational structure* of the competitor's corporate parent provide about the relative status, position, and goals of the unit in the eyes of the corporate parent? Does the unit report directly to the chief executive or an influential group vice-president, or is it a small part of a larger organizational entity? Has a "comer" in the organization been placed in charge or a manager on his way out? The organizational relationships will also give clues about actual or probable strategy. For example, if a cluster of electrical product divisions are grouped under an electrical products general manager, a coordinated strategy among them is more likely than if they are independent divisions, particularly if an influential executive has been made group general manager. It is important to note that clues derived from reporting relationships must be combined with other indications before confidence in them can be complete since organizational relationships can be merely cosmetic.

11. How is divisional management *controlled and compensated* in the overall corporate scheme? What is the frequency of reviews? The size of bonus relative to salary? What is the bonus based on? Is there stock ownership? These questions have clear implications for divisional goals and behavior.

12. What kinds of *executives* seem to be rewarded by the corporate parent, as an indication of the types of strategic behavior rein-

forced by corporate senior management and thereby of divisional management's goals? How rapidly do managers typically move in and out of the unit to other units in the parent company? The answer may provide some evidence about their time horizons and the manner in which they balance risky strategies versus safer ones.

13. Where does the corporate parent *recruit from*? Has current management been promoted from within—which may mean that past strategy will be continued—or from outside the division or even outside the company? What functional area did the current general manager come from (an indication of the strategic emphasis top management may want to bring to bear)?

14. *Does the corporation as a whole have any antitrust, regulatory, or social sensitivities* which may spill over to affect the business unit?

15. Does its corporate parent or particular top managers in the organization have an *emotional attachment* to the unit? Is the unit one of the early businesses of the company? Are any past chief executives of the unit now in top corporate jobs? Did current top management make the decision to acquire or to develop the unit? Were any programs or moves of the unit begun under the leadership of such a manager? These sorts of relationships may signal that disproportionate attention and support will be given to the unit. They may also indicate exit barriers.[4]

PORTFOLIO ANALYSIS AND COMPETITOR'S GOALS

When a competitor is part of a diversified company, analysis of its parent company's collection of businesses can be a potentially revealing exercise in answering some of the questions just posed. The full range of techniques available for analyzing a business portfolio can be used to answer questions about the needs the competitor unit is fulfilling in the eyes of the parent company.[5] The most revealing technique for portfolio analysis of the competitor is the one the competitor uses itself.

- What criteria are used to classify businesses at the competitor's parent if a classification scheme is in use? How is each business classified?

---

[4] Exit barriers are discussed in Chapters 1 and 12.
[5] Appendix A briefly describes some of the approaches commonly used by companies today to classify their portfolio.

- Which businesses are being counted on to be cash cows?
- Which businesses are candidates for harvest or divestment given their position in the portfolio?
- Which businesses are the habitual sources of stability to off-set fluctuations elsewhere in the portfolio?
- Which businesses represent defensive moves to protect other major businesses?
- Which businesses are the most promising areas the parent company has in which to invest resources and build market position?
- Which businesses have a lot of "leverage" in the portfolio? These businesses are ones where performance changes will have a significant impact on the performance of the parent overall in terms of stability, earnings, cash flow, sales growth, or costs. Such businesses will be protected vigorously.

Portfolio analysis of the parent will provide clues to what the objectives of the business unit will be; how hard it will fight to maintain its position and performance along dimensions such as return on investment, share, cash flow, and so on; and how likely it is to attempt to change its strategic position.

Competitors' Goals and Strategic Positioning

One approach in formulating strategy is to look for positions in the market where a firm can meet its objectives without threatening its competitors. When competitors' goals are well understood, there may be a place where everyone is relatively happy. Of course such positions do not always exist, particularly when one takes into account that new entrants may be tempted into an industry where existing firms are all doing well. In most cases the firm has to force competitors to compromise their goals in order for the firm to meet its objectives. To do so it needs to find a strategy it can defend against existing competitors and new entrants through some distinctive advantages.

Analysis of competitors' goals is crucial, because it helps the firm avoid strategic moves that will touch off bitter warfare by threatening competitors' ability to achieve key goals. For example, portfolio analysis can separate cash cows and harvest businesses from those the parent is trying to build. It is often quite possible to gain position against a cash cow if this does not threaten its cash flow to the parent, but it is potentially explosive to try to gain against a business the competitor's parent is attempting to build (or one to which it has emotional attachments). Similarly, a business that is counted on to achieve stable sales may fight aggressively to do so even at the expense of profits, whereas it will react much less to a move designed to boost a competitor's profits though leaving market shares the same. These are just some examples of how analysis of goals can begin to answer the questions about competitors' behavior posed in Figure 3-1.

ASSUMPTIONS

The second crucial component in competitor analysis is identifying each competitor's assumptions. These fall into two major categories:

- The competitor's assumptions about *itself*
- The competitor's assumptions about *the industry and the other companies in it*

Every firm operates on a set of assumptions about its own situation. For example, it may see itself as a socially conscious firm, as the industry leader, as the low-cost producer, as having the best sales force, and so on. These assumptions about its own situation will guide the way the firm behaves and the way it reacts to events. If it sees itself as the low-cost producer, for example, it may try to discipline a price cutter with price cuts of its own.

A competitor's assumptions about its own situation may or may not be accurate. Where they are not, this provides an intriguing strategic lever. If a competitor believes it has the greatest customer loyalty in the market and it does not, for example, a provocative price cut may be a good way to gain position. The competitor might well refuse to match the price cut believing that it will have little impact on its share, only to find that it loses significant market position before it recognizes the error in its assumption.

Just as each competitor holds assumptions about itself, every firm also operates on assumptions about its industry and competitors. These also may or may not be correct. For example, Gerber Products had steadfastly believed that births would increase ever since the 1950s, even though the birth rate has been declining steadily and the actual upturn in births may just have occurred in 1979. There are also many examples of firms that greatly over- or underestimated their competitors' staying power, resources, or skills.

Examining assumptions of all types can identify biases or *blind spots* that may creep into the way managers perceive their environment. The blind spots are areas where a competitor will either not see the significance of events (such as a strategic move) at all, will perceive them incorrectly, or will perceive them only very slowly. Rooting out these blind spots will help the firm identify moves with a lower probability of immediate retaliation and identify moves where retaliation, once it comes, is not effective.

The following questions are directed toward identifying competitors' assumptions and also areas where they are likely *not* to be completely dispassionate or realistic:

1. What does the competitor appear to *believe about its relative position*—in cost, product quality, technological sophistication, and other key aspects of its business—based on its public statements, claims of management and sales force, and other indications? What does it see as its strengths and weaknesses? Are these accurate?

2. Does the competitor have strong *historical or emotional identification* with particular products or with particular functional policies, such as an approach to product design, desire for product quality, manufacturing location, selling approach, distribution arrangements, and so on, which will be strongly held to?

3. Are there *cultural, regional, or national differences* that will affect the way in which competitors perceive and assign significance to events? To take one of many examples, West German companies are sometimes very oriented toward production and product quality, at the expense of unit costs and marketing.

4. Are there *organizational values or canons* which have been strongly institutionalized and will affect the way events are viewed? Are there some policies that the company's founder believed in strongly that may still linger?

5. What does the competitor appear to believe about *future demand* for the product and about the *significance of industry trends*? Will it be hesitant to add capacity because of unfounded uncertainties about demand, or likely to overbuild for the opposite reason? Is it prone to misestimate the importance of particular trends? Does it believe the industry is concentrating, for example, when it may not be? These are all wedges around which strategies can be built.

6. What does the competitor appear to believe about the goals and capabilities of its *competitors*? Will it over- or underestimate any of them?

7. Does the competitor seem to believe in industry *"conventional wisdom"* or historic rules of thumb and common industry approaches that do not reflect new market conditions?[6] Examples of conventional wisdom are such notions as "Everyone must have a full line," "Customers trade up," "One must control sources of raw material in this business," "Decentralized plants are the most efficient manufacturing system," "One needs a large number of dealers," and so on. Identifying situations where conventional wisdom is inappropriate or can be changed yields advantages in terms of the timeliness and effectiveness of a competitor's retaliation.

8. A competitor's assumptions may well be subtly influenced by, as well as reflected in, its *current strategy*. It may see new industry events through filters defined by its past and present circumstances, and this may not lead to objectivity.

THE SIGNIFICANCE OF PERCEIVING BLIND SPOTS OR CONVENTIONAL WISDOM

The recent resurgence of Miller Breweries provides an example of the benefits that accrue to the perception of blind spots. Miller, acquired by Philip Morris and not bound by conventional wisdom like many family-owned breweries, has introduced Lite Beer, a 7-ounce bottle, and a domestically brewed Lowenbrau Beer at a 25 percent price premium over Michelob (the leading domestic premium beer). According to reports, most breweries laughed at Miller's moves, but many have now grudgingly followed as Miller made major gains in market share.[7]

Another situation in which the recognition of outdated conventional wisdom has been credited with yielding great rewards is in the turnaround of Paramount Pictures. Two new senior executives with backgrounds in network television management have violated many industry norms in the movie industry—preselling of films, releasing films simultaneously in large numbers of theaters, and so on—and registered major gains in market share.[8]

---

[6]These are particularly likely to exist in industries composed of competitors with a long tradition in the industry.

[7]For a brief account, see *Business Week*, November 8, 1976.

[8]For a brief description, see *Business Week*, November 27, 1978.

HISTORY AS AN INDICATOR OF GOALS AND ASSUMPTIONS

One of the often powerful indicators of a competitor's goals and assumptions with respect to a business is its history in the business. The following questions suggest some ways to examine these areas:

1. What is the competitor's current financial performance and market share, *compared to* that of the relatively recent past? This can be a good first indication of future goals, particularly if results of the "rememberable" past were somewhat better and provide a tangible and annoyingly visible indicator of the competitor's potential. The competitor will almost always be striving to regain the performance of the recent past.

2. What has been the competitor's *history in the marketplace* over time? Where has it failed or been beaten, and thus perhaps not likely to tread again? The memory of past failures, and the impediments to further moves in those areas they bring, can be very lasting and given disproportionate weight. This is particularly true in generally successful organizations. For example, some argue that a past failure with discount stores delayed Federated Department Stores' reentry into this area of retailing for seven years.

3. In what areas has the competitor *starred or succeeded* as a company? In new product introductions? Innovative marketing techniques? Others? In such areas the competitor may feel confident to initiate a move again or to do battle in the event of a provocation.

4. How has the competitor *reacted* to particular strategic moves or industry events in the past? Rationally? Emotionally? Slowly? Quickly? What approaches have been employed? To what sorts of events has the competitor reacted poorly, and why?

MANAGERIAL BACKGROUNDS AND ADVISORY RELATIONSHIPS

Another key indicator of a competitor's goals, assumptions, and probable future moves is where its leadership has come from and what the managers' track records and personal successes and failures have been.

1. The *functional background* of top management is one key measure of its orientation and perception of the business and appropriate goals. Leaders with financial backgrounds can often em-

phasize different strategic directions, based on what they feel comfortable with, than leaders with backgrounds in marketing or production. Current examples could be Edwin Land's penchant for radical innovation as a solution to strategic problems at Polaroid, and McGee's strategy of retrenchment to energy-related activities at Gulf Oil.

2. A second clue to the top managers' assumptions, goals, and probable future moves is the *types of strategies* that have worked or not worked for them personally in their careers. For example, if cutting costs was a successful remedy for a problem facing the CEO in the past, it may be adopted the next time a remedy is needed.

3. Another dimension of the top managers' backgrounds that can be important is the *other businesses* they have worked in and what rules of the game and strategic approaches have been characteristic of those businesses. For example, Marc Roijtman applied a strategy of salesmanship, implemented successfully in industrial equipment, to the farm equipment business when he assumed the presidency of J. I. Case in the mid-1960s. R. J. Reynolds has recently brought in new leadership from consumer packaged food and toiletries companies that has introduced many of the product management and other practices characteristic of those businesses. And the recently retired top management of Household Finance Corporation (HFC) came from the retail industry. Rather than bolster HFC's strong position in consumer credit and capitalize on the consumer credit boom, the company spent its resources diversifying into retailing. A new CEO, promoted from the consumer finance division, has reversed this direction. This tendency to reuse concepts that have worked in the past applies to senior executives coming from law firms, consulting firms, and from other companies in the industry. All can bring to the competitor a perspective and tool kit of remedies to some extent reflecting their past.

4. Top managers can be greatly influenced by *major events* they have lived through, such as a sharp recession, traumatic energy shortage, major loss due to currency fluctuations, and so on. Such events sometimes broadly affect the perspective of the manager in a wide range of areas and can influence strategic choices accordingly.

5. Indications of top managers' perspectives can also be gained from their *writing and speaking*, their *technical background* or patent history where applicable, *other firms* they come into frequent contact with (such as through boards of directors they sit on), their outside activities, and a range of other clues limited only by the imagination.

6. Management consulting firms, advertising agencies, investment banks, and other *advisors* used by the competitor can be important clues. What other companies use these advisors and what have they done? What conceptual approaches and techniques are the advisors known for? The identity of a competitor's advisors and a thorough diagnosis of them can provide an indication of future strategic changes.

CURRENT STRATEGY

The third component of competitor analysis is developing statements of the current strategy of each competitor. A competitor's strategy is most usefully thought of as its key operating policies in each functional area of the business and how it seeks to interrelate the functions. This strategy may be either explicit or implicit—one always exists in one form or the other. The principles of strategy identification have been discussed in the Introduction.

CAPABILITIES

A realistic appraisal of each competitor's capabilities is the final diagnostic step in competitor analysis. Its goals, assumptions, and current strategy will influence the *likelihood, timing, nature*, and *intensity* of a competitor's reactions. Its strengths and weaknesses will determine its *ability* to initiate or react to strategic moves and to deal with environmental or industry events that occur.

Since the notion of a competitor's strengths and weaknesses is relatively clear, I will not dwell on it here. Broadly, strengths and weaknesses can be assessed by examining a competitor's position with respect to the five key competitive forces discussed in Chapter 1, an analysis I will pursue in Chapter 7. Taking a narrower perspective, Figure 3-2 gives a summary framework for looking at a competitor's strengths and weaknesses in each key area of the business.[9] A list such as this can be made more useful by asking some additional, synthesizing questions.

[9]For other sources of areas to look at in assessing capabilities, see Robert Buchele, "How to Evaluate a Firm," *California Management Review*, Fall 1962, pp. 5–16; "Checklist for Competitive and Competence Profiles," in H. I. Ansoff, *Corporate Strategy* (New York: McGraw-Hill, 1965), pp. 98–99; Chapter 2 in W. H. Newman and J. P. Logan, *Strategy, Policy and Central Management*, 6th ed. (Cincinnati: South-Western Publishing, 1971); Chapter 5 in W. E. Rothschild, *Putting It All Together* (New York: AMACOM, 1979).

FIGURE 3-2   Areas of Competitor Strengths and Weaknesses

Products

> Standing of products, from the user's point of view, in each market segment
> Breadth and depth of the product line

Dealer/Distribution

> Channel coverage and quality
> Strength of channel relationships
> Ability to service the channels

Marketing and Selling

> Skills in each aspect of the marketing mix
> Skills in market research and new product development
> Training and skills of the sales force

Operations

> Manufacturing cost position—economies of scale, learning curve, newness of equipment, etc.
> Technological sophistication of facilities and equipment
> Flexibility of facilities and equipment
> Proprietary know-how and unique patent or cost advantages
> Skills in capacity addition, quality control, tooling, etc.
> Location, including labor and transportation cost
> Labor force climate; unionization situation
> Access to and cost of raw materials
> Degree of vertical integration

Research and Engineering

> Patents and copyrights
> In-house capability in the research and development process (product research, process research, basic research, development, imitation, etc.)
> R&D staff skills in terms of creativity, simplicity, quality, reliability, etc.
> Access to outside sources of research and engineering (e.g., suppliers, customers, contractors)

Overall Costs

> Overall relative costs
> Shared costs or activities with other business units
> Where the competitor is generating the scale or other factors that are key to its cost position

Financial Strength

> Cash flow
> Short- and long-term borrowing capacity (relative debt/equity ratio)

FIGURE 3-2   Continued

New equity capacity over the foreseeable future

Financial management ability, including negotiation, raising capital, credit, inventories, and accounts receivable

Organization

Unity of values and clarity of purpose in the organization

Organizational fatigue based on recent requirements placed on it

Consistency of organizational arrangements with strategy

General Managerial Ability

Leadership qualities of CEO; ability of CEO to motivate

Ability to coordinate particular functions or groups of functions (e.g., manufacturing with research coordination)

Age, training, and functional orientation of management

Depth of management

Flexibility and adaptability of management

Corporate Portfolio

Ability of corporation to support planned changes in all business units in terms of financial and other resources

Ability of corporation to supplement or reinforce business unit strengths

Other

Special treatment by or access to government bodies

Personnel turnover

CORE CAPABILITIES

- What are the competitor's capabilities in each of the functional areas? What is it best at? Worst at?
- How does the competitor measure up to the tests of the consistency of its strategy (presented in the Introduction)?
- Are there any probable changes in those capabilities as the competitor matures? Will they increase or diminish over time?

ABILITY TO GROW

- Will the competitor's capabilities increase or diminish if it grows? In which areas?
- What is the competitor's capacity for growth in terms of people, skills and plant capacity?

- what is the competitor's *sustainable growth* in financial terms? Given a Du Pont analysis, can it grow with the industry?[10] Can it increase market share? How sensitive is sustainable growth to raising outside capital? To achieving good short-term financial results?

QUICK RESPONSE CAPABILITY

- what is the competitor's capacity to respond quickly to moves by others, or to mount an immediate offensive? This will be determined by factors such as the following:
  - uncommitted cash reserves
  - reserve borrowing power
  - excess plant capacity
  - unintroduced but on-the-shelf new products

ABILITY TO ADAPT TO CHANGE

- What are the competitor's fixed versus variable costs? Its cost of unused capacity? These will influence its probable responses to change.
- What is the competitor's ability to adapt and respond to changed conditions in each functional area? For example, can the competitor adapt to
  - competing on cost?
  - managing more complex product lines?
  - adding new products?
  - competing on service?
  - escalation in marketing activity?
- Can the competitor respond to possible exogenous events such as
  - a sustained high rate of inflation?
  - technological changes which make obsolete existing plant?
  - a recession?
  - increases in wage rates?
  - the most probable forms of government regulation that will affect this business?
- Does the competitor have *exit barriers* which will tend to keep it from scaling down or divesting its operations in the business?

[10] Sustainable growth $= \left(\frac{\text{asset}}{\text{turnover}} \right) \times \left(\begin{array}{c} \text{after tax} \\ \text{return} \\ \text{on sales} \end{array} \right) \times \left(\frac{\text{assets}}{\text{debt}} \right) \times \left(\frac{\text{debt}}{\text{equity}} \right) \times \left(\begin{array}{c} \text{fraction of} \\ \text{earnings} \\ \text{retained} \end{array} \right)$

- Does the competitor share manufacturing facilities, a sales force, or other facilities or personnel with other units of its corporate parent? These may provide constraints to adaptation and/or may impede cost control.

STAYING POWER

- what is the ability of the competitor to sustain a protracted battle, which may put pressure on earnings or cash flow? This will be a function of considerations such as the following:
  - ○ cash reserves
  - ○ unanimity among management
  - ○ long time horizon in its financial goals
  - ○ lack of stock market pressure

Putting the Four Components Together—The Competitor Response Profile

Given an analysis of a competitor's future goals, assumptions, current strategies, and capabilities, we can begin to ask the critical questions that will lead to a profile of how a competitor is likely to respond.

OFFENSIVE MOVES

The first step is to predict the strategic changes the competitor might initiate.

1. *Satisfaction with current position.* Comparing the competitor's (and its parent company's) goals with its current position, is the competitor likely to attempt to initiate strategic change?

2. *Probable moves.* Based on the competitor's goals, assumptions, and capabilities relative to its existing position, what are the most probable strategic changes the competitor will make? These will reflect the competitor's views about the future, what it believes its strengths to be, which of its rivals it thinks are vulnerable, how it likes to compete, the biases brought to the business by top management, and other considerations suggested by the preceding analysis.

3. *Strength and seriousness of moves.* The analysis of a competitor's goals and capabilities can be used to assess the expected

strength of these probable moves. It is also important to assess what the competitor may *gain* from the move. For example, a move that will allow the competitor to share costs with another division, thereby dramatically changing its relative cost position, may be a lot more significant than a move that leads to an incremental gain in marketing effectiveness. An analysis of the probable gain from the move coupled with knowledge of the competitor's goals will give an indication of how serious the competitor will be in pursuing the move in the face of resistance.

DEFENSIVE CAPABILITY

The next step in building a response profile is to construct a list of the range of feasible strategic moves a firm in the industry might make and a list of the possible industry and environmental changes that might occur. These can be assessed against the following criteria to determine the competitor's defensive capability, with inputs coming from the analysis in previous sections.

1. *Vulnerability*. To what strategic moves and governmental, macroeconomic or industry events would the competitor be most vulnerable? What events have asymmetrical profit consequences, that is, affect a competitor's profits more or less than they affect the initiating firm's? What moves would require so much capital to retaliate against or follow that the competitor cannot risk them?

2. *Provocation*. What moves or events are such that they will provoke a retaliation from competitors even though retaliation may be costly and lead to marginal financial performance? That is, what moves threaten a competitor's goals or position so much that it will be forced to retaliate, like it or not? Most competitors will have *hot buttons*, or areas of the business where a threat will lead to a disproportionate response. Hot buttons reflect strongly held goals, emotional commitments, and the like. Where possible, they are to be avoided.

3. *Effectiveness of retaliation*. To what moves or events is the competitor impeded from reacting to quickly and/or effectively given its goals, strategy, existing capabilities, and assumptions? What courses of action might be taken in which the competitor would not be effective if it tries to match or emulate them?

Figure 3-3 presents a simple schematic diagram for analyzing a competitor's defensive capabilities. The left-hand column lists first

FIGURE 3-3 A Scheme for Assessing a Competitor's Defensive Capability

Events	Vulnerability of the Competitor to the Event	Degree to which the Event will Provoke Retaliation by the Competitor	Effectiveness of the Competitor's Retaliation to the Event
Feasible Strategic Moves by our Firm			
List all alternatives such as:			
Fill out the line			
Increase product quality and service			
Reduce price and compete on costs			
Feasible Environmental Changes			
List all changes such as:			
Major increase in raw material costs			
Downturn in sales			
Increase in cost con-sciousness of buyers			

the feasible strategic moves some firm might make and then the environmental and industry changes that could possibly occur (including probable moves by competitors). These events can then be subjected to the questions listed across the top. The resulting matrix should help pick the most effective strategy, given the reality that competitors will respond, and can facilitate rapid response to industry and environmental events that will expose a competitor's weaknesses. (Concepts for making competitive moves are discussed in detail in Chapter 5.)

PICKING THE BATTLEGROUND

Assuming that competitors will retaliate to moves a firm initiates, its strategic agenda is selecting the *best battleground* for fighting it out with its competitors. This battleground is the market segment or dimensions of strategy in which competitors are ill-prepared, least enthusiastic, or most uncomfortable about competing. The best battleground may be competition based on costs, centered at the high or low end of the product line, or other areas.

The ideal is to find a strategy that competitors are frozen from reacting to given their present circumstances. The legacy of their past and current strategy may make some moves very costly for competitors to follow, while posing much less difficulty and expense for the initiating firm. For example, when Folger's Coffee invaded Maxwell House strongholds in the east with price cutting, the cost of matching these cuts were enormous for Maxwell House because of its large market share.

Another key strategic concept deriving from competitor analysis is creating a situation of *mixed motives* or conflicting goals for competitors. This strategy involves finding moves for which retaliation, though effective, would hurt the competitor's broader position. For example, as IBM responds to the threat of the minicomputer with its own minicomputer, it may hasten the decline in growth of its large computers and accelerate the changeover to minicomputers. Placing competitors in a situation of conflicting goals can be a very effective strategic approach for attacking established firms that have been successful in their markets. Small firms and newly entered firms often have very little legacy in the existing strategies in the industry and can reap great rewards from finding strategies that penalize competitors for their stake in these existing strategies.

Realistically, competitors will not often be completely frozen or even torn by mixed motives. In this case, the questions posed above should help to identify those strategic moves that will put the initiating firm in the best position to fight the competitive battle when it comes. This means taking advantage of an understanding of competitor goals and assumptions to avoid effective retaliation whenever possible and picking the battlefield where the firm's distinctive ability represents the most formidable artillery.

Competitor Analysis and Industry Forecasting

An analysis of each significant existing and potential competitor can be used as an important input to forecasting future industry conditions. The knowledge of each competitor's probable moves and capacity to respond to change can be summed up, and competitors can be seen as interacting with each other on a simulated basis to answer questions such as the following:

- What are the implications of the interaction of the probable competitors' moves that have been identified?
- Are firms' strategies converging and likely to clash?
- Do firms have sustainable growth rates that match the industry's forecasted growth rate, or will a gap be created that will invite entry?
- Will probable moves combine to hold implications for industry structure?

The Need for a Competitor Intelligence System

Answering these questions about competitors creates enormous needs for data. Intelligence data on competitors can come from many sources: reports filed publicly, speeches by a competitor's management to security analysts, the business press, the sales force, a firm's customers or suppliers that are common to competitors, inspection of a competitor's products, estimates by the firm's engineering staff, knowledge gleaned from managers or other personnel who have left the competitor's employment, and so on. Souces of data are described in more detail in Appendix B. It is unlikely that data to support a full competitor analysis could be compiled in one massive effort. The data to make the subtle judgments implied by these questions usually come in trickles rather than rivers and must be put together over a period of time to yield a comprehensive picture of the competitor's situation.

Compiling the data for a sophisticated competitor analysis probably requires more than just hard work. To be effective, there is the need for an organized mechanism—some sort of competitor intelligence *system*—to insure that the process is efficient. The elements of a competitor intelligence system can vary according to the particular firm's needs, based on its industry, its staff capability, and its managements' interests and talents. Figure 3-4 diagrams the functions that must be performed in developing the data for sophisticated competitor analysis and gives some options for how each function might be performed. In some companies all these functions can be performed effectively by one person, but this seems to be the exception rather than the rule. There are numerous sources for field data and published data, and many individuals in a company can usually contribute. Furthermore, compiling, cataloging, digesting, and communicating these data in an effective fashion are usually beyond the capabilities of one person.

One observes a variety of alternative ways firms organize to perform these functions in practice. They range from a competitor analysis group that is part of the planning department and performs all the functions (perhaps drawing on others in the organization for collecting field data); to a competitor intelligence coordinator who performs the compiling, cataloging, and communication functions; to a system in which the strategist does it all informally. All too often, however, no one is made responsible for the competitor analysis at all. There seems to be no single correct way to collect competitor data, but it is clear that someone must take an active interest or much useful information will be lost. Top management can do a lot to stimulate the effort by requiring sophisticated profiles of competitors as part of the planning process. As a minimum, some manager with the responsibility to serve as the focal point for competitor intelligence gathering seems to be necessary.

Each of the functions can also be performed in a number of different ways, as noted in Figure 3-4. The options shown cover a range of degrees of sophistication and completeness. A small firm may not

FIGURE 3-4   Functions of a Competitor Intelligence System

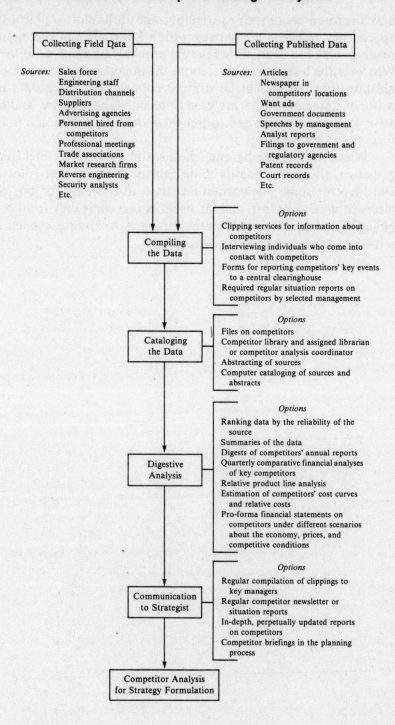

Collecting Field Data

Sources: Sales force
Engineering staff
Distribution channels
Suppliers
Advertising agencies
Personnel hired from
competitors
Professional meetings
Trade associations
Market research firms
Reverse engineering
Security analysts
Etc.

Collecting Published Data

Sources: Articles
Newspaper in
competitors' locations
Want ads
Government documents
Speeches by management
Analyst reports
Filings to government and
regulatory agencies
Patent records
Court records
Etc.

Compiling the Data

Options

Clipping services for information about
competitors
Interviewing individuals who come into
contact with competitors
Forms for reporting competitors' key events
to a central clearinghouse
Required regular situation reports on
competitors by selected management

Cataloging the Data

Options

Files on competitors
Competitor library and assigned librarian
or competitor analysis coordinator
Abstracting of sources
Computer cataloging of sources and
abstracts

Digestive Analysis

Options

Ranking data by the reliability of the
source
Summaries of the data
Digests of competitors' annual reports
Quarterly comparative financial analyses
of key competitors
Relative product line analysis
Estimation of competitors' cost curves
and relative costs
Pro-forma financial statements on
competitors under different scenarios
about the economy, prices, and
competitive conditions

Communication to Strategist

Options

Regular compilation of clippings to
key managers
Regular competitor newsletter or
situation reports
In-depth, perpetually updated reports
on competitors
Competitor briefings in the planning
process

Competitor Analysis for Strategy Formulation

have the resources or staff to attempt some of the more sophisticated approaches, whereas a company with a large stake in successfully reading some key competitors should probably be doing all of them. Whatever the level of sophistication, the importance of the communication function cannot be stressed enough. Gathering data is a waste of time unless they are used in formulating strategy, and creative ways must be devised to put these data in concise and usable form to top management.

Whatever the mechanism chosen for competitor intelligence gathering, there are benefits to be gained from one that is formal and involves some documentation. It is all too easy for bits and pieces of data to be lost, and the benefits that come only from combining these bits and pieces thereby foregone. Analyzing competitors is too important to handle haphazardly.

4
Market Signals

A market signal is any action by a competitor that provides a direct or indirect indication of its intentions, motives, goals, or internal situation. The behavior of competitors provides signals in a myriad of ways. Some signals are bluffs, some are warnings, and some are earnest commitments to a course of action.[1] Market signals are indirect means of communicating in the marketplace, and most if not all of a competitor's behavior can carry information that can aid in competitor analysis and strategy formulation.

Recognizing and accurately reading market signals, then, is of major significance for developing competitive strategy, and reading signals from behavior is an essential supplement to competitor analysis (Chapter 3). Knowledge of signaling is also important for effective competitive moves, to be discussed in Chapter 5. A prerequisite to interpreting signals accurately is to develop a baseline competitor analysis: an understanding of competitors' future goals, assumptions about the market and themselves, current strategies, and capabilities. Reading market signals, a second-order form of competitor analysis, rests on subtle judgments about competitors based on the

[1]There is substantial evidence to be found in the experimental literature on oligopolies, as well as in casual observation of competitive behavior, that market signaling occurs. For an interesting experimental study that verifies the importance of signaling, see Fouraker and Siegel (1960).

comparison of known aspects of their situations with their behavior. As we will see, the many subtleties in interpreting signals will require ongoing comparisons between behavior and the sort of competitor analysis in Chapter 3.

Types of Market Signals

Market signals can have two fundamentally different functions: they can be truthful indications of a competitor's motives, intentions, or goals or they can be bluffs. Bluffs are signals designed to mislead other firms into taking or not taking an action to benefit the signaler. Discerning the difference between a bluff and a true signal can often involve subtle judgments.

Market signals take a variety of forms, depending on the particular competitor behavior involved and the medium employed. In discussing different forms of signals, it will be important to indicate how they may be used as bluffs, and how a bluff and a true signal might be distinguished.

The important forms of market signals are as follows:

PRIOR ANNOUNCEMENTS OF MOVES

The form, character, and timing of prior announcements can be potent signals. A prior announcement is a formal communication made by a competitor that it either *will* or *will not* take some action, such as building a plant, changing price, and so on. An announcement does not necessarily insure that an action will be taken; announcements can be made that are not carried out in practice, either because nothing was done or a later announcement nullified the action. This property of announcements adds to their signaling value, as will be discussed.

In general, prior announcements can serve a number of signaling functions that are not mutually exclusive. First, they can be attempts to stake out a commitment to take an action for the purposes of *preempting* other competitors. If a competitor announces a major new capacity addition which is sufficient to meet all expected industry growth, for example, it may be trying to dissuade other firms from adding capacity, which would lead to industry overcapacity.

Or as has been typical of IBM, a competitor may announce a new product well before it is ready for the marketplace, seeking to get buyers to wait for its new product rather than buy a competitor's product in the interim.[2] Berkey, for example, has charged in its anti-trust suit against Kodak that Eastman Kodak disclosed new camera products far in advance of production to discourage sales of competing products.

Second, announcements can be *threats* of actions to be taken if a competitor follows through with a planned move. If firm *A* learns of competitor *B*'s intentions to lower its price on selected items in the product line (or competitor *B* announces such intentions), for example, then firm *A* might announce the intention to lower its price significantly below *B*'s. This may deter *B* from going through with the price change, because *B* now knows that *A* is unhappy with the lower price and is willing to start a price war.

Third, announcements can be *tests of competitor sentiments*, taking advantage of the fact that they need not necessarily be carried out. Firm *A* might announce a new warranty program to see how others in the industry will react. If they react predictably, then *A* will follow through with the change as planned. If competitors send signals of displeasure or announce somewhat different warranty programs than *A* has proposed, then *A* might either withdraw the planned move or announce a revised warranty program to match that of its competitors.

This sequence of actions suggests a fourth role of announcements related to their role as threats. Announcements can be a means of *communicating pleasure or displeasure* with competitive developments in the industry.[3] Announcing a move that falls in line with a competitor's move might indicate pleasure, whereas announcing a punishing move or a substantially different approach to the same end can indicate displeasure.

A fifth and common function of announcements is to serve as conciliatory steps aimed at *minimizing the provocation* of a forth-

---

[2] See Brock (1975).

[3] Competitors can also comment on their pleasure or displeasure *directly* through interviews, speeches to security analysts, and so on. But announcing that they will do something, in response to a firm's move, is usually a more binding commitment to their position than mere statements of pleasure or displeasure. This is because reneging on an announcement carries a greater cost in credibility than taking an action inconsistent with what was said in an interview or speech. Sometimes interviews and speeches are used to signal displeasure to cause another firm to change its mind, and if this tactic is not successful an announcement is made that the firm will follow the move.

coming strategic adjustment. The announcement seeks to avoid having a strategic adjustment touch off a round of unwelcomed retaliation and warfare. For example, firm *A* might decide that price levels need to be adjusted downward in the industry. Announcing this move well ahead of time, and justifying it in terms of specific changes in costs, can avoid having firm *B* read the price change as an aggressive bid for market share and retaliating vigorously. This role of announcements is particularly common when a necessary strategic adjustment is not meant to be aggressive. However, announcements like these can also be designed to lull competitors into a sense of security in order to facilitate the implementation of an aggressive move. This is one of many instances when a signal can be a double-edged sword.

A sixth function of announcements is to *avoid costly simultaneous moves* in areas like capacity additions, where bunching of new plant additions would lead to overcapacity. Firms might announce expansion plans well in advance, facilitating the scheduling of capacity additions by competitors in a sequence that will minimize overcapacity.[4]

A final function of announcements can be *communication with the financial community*, for purposes of boosting stock price or improving the reputation of the company. This common practice means that firms often have a public relations motive in presenting their situation in the best possible light. Announcements of this character can cause trouble by sending inappropriate signals to competitors.

Announcements can also sometimes serve the purpose of coalescing *internal support* for a move. Committing the firm to do something publicly can be a way of cutting off internal debate about its desirability. Announcements of financial goals not infrequently serve this function of rallying support.

It should be clear from the above discussion that an entire competitive battle can be waged through announcements before a single dollar of resources is expended. A fairly recent sequence of announcements among producers of computer memories provides an illustration of this occurrence. Texas Instruments announced a price for random access memories to be available two years hence. One week later, Bowmar announced a lower price. Three weeks later, Motorola announced an even lower price. Finally, two weeks after

---

[4]Such a process not infrequently breaks down. See Chapter 15, "Capacity Expansion."

this, Texas Instruments announced a price of half of Motorola's, and the other firms decided not to produce the product. Thus, before any major investments were actually made, Texas Instruments had won the battle.[5] Similarly, trading announcements back and forth can settle the size of a price change or form of a new dealer rebate program without the need to disrupt the market and risk a battle by actually introducing one scheme and then having to change or withdraw it later.

Discerning whether a prior announcement is an attempt at preemption or is a conciliatory move is obviously a crucial distinction to make correctly. A place to start in making such a distinction is with an analysis of the lasting benefits that might accrue to the competitor from preemption.[6] If there are such lasting benefits, a preemptive motive must be taken as a strong possibility. If there are few benefits from preemption, on the other hand, or if the competitor acting in its narrow self-interest could have done better through a surprise move, then conciliation may be indicated. An announcement that discloses an action much less damaging to others than it might have been, given the competitor's capabilities, may usually be viewed as conciliatory. Another clue to motives is the timing of the announcement relative to when the action is set to occur. Announcements far in advance of a move tend to be conciliatory, other things being equal, though it is difficult to generalize completely.

It should be clearly noted that announcements can be *bluffs*, because they need not always be carried out. As described, an announcement can be a way to communicate a firm's commitment to carrying out a threat for purposes of causing a competitor to either back down from or tone down a move or to not initiate it in the first place. For example, a firm can announce a large plant designed to maintain its share of industry capacity in the face of other capacity announcements it seeks to have cancelled, where the effect of its plant will be to create major overcapacity in the industry. If a bluff for these purposes fails, there may be little incentive for the bluffer to carry out the threat. However, whether or not a threat or other commitment is carried out has critical implications for the credibility of future commitments and future announcements. In extreme cases

[5]For such an outcome to occur Texas Instruments must have also credibly demonstrated its commitment, from other actions, that it *would* actually sell memories at the low prices. Without this, entry by competitors would not have been deterred. (See Chapter 5.)

[6]Chapter 15 discusses the conditions supporting a preemptive strategy.

an announcement can be a bluff designed to trick competitors into expending resources in gearing up to defend against a nonexistent threat.

Prior announcements by competitors can and do occur in a variety of media: official press releases, speeches by management to securities analysts, interviews with the press, and other forms. The medium chosen for the announcement is one clue to its underlying motives. The more formal the announcement, the more the announcing firm wants to be sure that the message will be heard, and the broader the audience it probably seeks to reach. The medium for the announcement also affects who will see it. An announcement in a specialized trade journal is likely to be noticed only by competitors or other industry participants. This may carry a different connotation from an announcement made to a broad audience of security analysis or to the national business press. A prior announcement to a broad audience may be a way of establishing a "public" commitment to do something that is perceived by competitors as being hard to back down from, with the consequent deterrent value.[7]

ANNOUNCEMENTS OF RESULTS OR ACTIONS AFTER THE FACT

Firms often announce (verify) plant additions, sales figures, and other results or actions after they have occurred. Such announcements may carry signals, particularly to the degree that they disclose data that are hard to get otherwise and/or are surprising for the announcing firm to make public. The after-the-fact announcement has the function of insuring that other firms know and take note of the data disclosed—which can influence their behavior.

Like any announcement, an ex post announcement can be wrong or more likely misleading, although this does not seem to be common. Many such announcements refer to data like market shares that are not audited nor are subject to full SEC screening procedures and liability. Firms sometimes announce misleading data if they believe such data can be preemptive or can communicate commitment. An example of this tactic is announcing sales figures that include the sales of some related products outside the narrow product category in the total, that is, inflating apparent market share. Another tactic

---

[7]See Chapter 5 for a discussion of the significance of commitment and deterrence in competitive situations.

is to quote final capacity for a new plant, even though reaching that capacity will take a second addition, while representing the final capacity implicitly as initial capacity.[8] If the firm can learn about or deduce such misleading practices, they will carry important signals about the competitor's objectives and true competitive strengths.

PUBLIC DISCUSSIONS OF THE INDUSTRY BY COMPETITORS

It is not uncommon for competitors to comment on industry conditions, including forecasts of demand and prices, forecasts of future capacity, the significance of external changes such as material cost increases, and so on. Such commentary is laden with signals because it may expose the commenting firm's assumptions about the industry on which it is presumably building its own strategy. As such, this discussion can be a conscious or unconscious attempt to get other firms to operate under the same assumptions and thereby minimize the chances of mistaken motives and warfare. Such commentary can also contain implicit pleas for price discipline: "Price competition is still very harsh. The industry is doing a lousy job of passing along increased costs to the consumer."[9] "The problem in this industry is that some firms do not recognize that these current prices will be detrimental to our ability to grow and produce a quality product in the long run."[10] Or discussions of the industry may contain implicit pleas that other firms add capacity in an orderly fashion, not engage in excessive advertising competition, not break ranks in dealing with large customers, or any number of other things, as well as implicit promises to cooperate if others act "properly."

Of course, the firm making the comments may be seeking to interpret industry conditions in such a way as to improve its own position. It may prefer that prices fall, for example, and may therefore describe industry conditions so that its competitors' prices appear too high, even though competitors might truly be better off holding their price levels. This possibility implies that firms reading the sig-

[8]This action is to be clearly distinguished from announcing existing capacity accurately and also simultaneously announcing plans for future expansion.

[9]President of Sherwin-Williams Coating Group, commenting on the paint industry in "A Thin Coating of Profit for Paint Makers," *Business Week*, August 14, 1977.

[10]Executive of a leading commodities producer in a speech to security analysts.

nals in their competitor's commentary must verify industry conditions themselves and search for areas in which a competitor's position might be improved by its interpretation of the facts, thereby compromising its intentions.

In addition to commentary on the industry generally, competitors sometimes comment on their rival's moves directly: "The recent extension of credit to dealers was inappropriate for X and Y reasons." Such commentary can signal an indication of pleasure or displeasure with a move, but like any other public announcement, there are alternative interpretations of its purposes. It may be self-serving by slanting the interpretation of the desirability of the competitor's move so that its own position is improved.

Sometimes firms praise competitors by name or the industry generally. This has occurred, for example, in hospital management. Such praise is usually a conciliatory gesture aimed at reducing tensions or ending undesirable practices. It is most common in industries in which all firms are affected by the industry's collective image with the customer group or financial community.

COMPETITORS' DISCUSSIONS AND EXPLANATIONS OF THEIR OWN MOVES

Competitors often discuss their own moves in public or in forums where the discussion is likely to reach other firms. A common example of the latter is to discuss a move with major customers or distributors, in which case the discussion will almost surely be circulated around the industry.

A firm's explanation or discussion of its own move can serve, consciously or unconsciously, at least three purposes. First, it may be an attempt to get other firms to see the logic of a move and hence follow it or to communicate that the move is not to be taken as a provocation. Second, explanations or discussions of moves can be preemptive gestures. Firms introducing a new product or entering a new market sometimes fill the press with stories about how costly and difficult the move was to make. This may deter other firms from trying. Finally, such discussions of moves may be an attempt to communicate commitment. The competitor can stress the large amount of resources expended and its long-run commitment to a new area to try to convince rivals that it is there to stay and to not attempt to displace it.

COMPETITORS' TACTICS RELATIVE TO WHAT THEY COULD HAVE DONE

Relative to what a competitor could have feasibly chosen to do, the prices and advertising levels actually chosen, the size of capacity additions, specific product characteristics adopted, and so on, all carry important signals about motives. To the degree that its choices of strategic variables was the worst it could have taken with respect to damaging other firms, this is a strong aggressive signal. If it could have hurt competitors more with strategies other than the one chosen, which were within its set of feasible alternatives (e.g., a price higher than the competitor's cost might justify), this potentially signals conciliation. A competitor behaving in a way inconsistent with its narrowly defined self-interest may implicitly be signaling conciliation as well.

MANNER IN WHICH STRATEGIC CHANGES ARE INITIALLY IMPLEMENTED

A competitor's new product can be initially introduced in a peripheral market, or it can immediately be aggressively sold to the key customers of its rivals. A price change may be made initially on products that represent the heart of a competitor's product line, or the price changes can be first put into effect in product or market segments where the competitor does not have a great interest. A move can be made at the normal time of the year for adjustments of its type, or it can be made at an unusual time. These are just examples of how the manner in which almost any strategic change is implemented can help differentiate between a competitor's desire to inflict a penalty and its desire to make a move in the best interests of the industry as a whole. As usual where such motives are involved, however, there is the risk of bluffs.

DIVERGENCE FROM PAST GOALS

If a competitor has historically produced products exclusively at the high end of the product spectrum, its introduction of a significantly inferior product is an indication of a potential major realignment in goals or assumptions. Such a divergence from past goals in any other area of strategy carries a similar message. These divergences should probably lead to a period of intense attention to signaling and competitor analysis.

DIVERGENCE FROM INDUSTRY PRECEDENT

A move that diverges from industry norms is usually an aggressive signal. Examples include discounting products that have never been discounted in the industry and plant construction in an entirely new geographic area or new country.

THE CROSS-PARRY

When one firm initiates a move in one area and a competitor responds in a different area with one that affects the initiating firm, the situation can be called a *cross-parry*. This situation occurs not infrequently when firms compete in different geographic areas or have multiple product lines that do not completely overlap. For example, an East-Coast-based firm entering the western market may see a western firm in turn entering the eastern market. A situation not far from this occurred in the roasted coffee industry. Maxwell House has long been strong in the East, whereas Folger's strength is in the West. Folger's, acquired by Procter and Gamble, moved to increase its penetration in the eastern markets through some aggressive marketing. Maxwell countered, in part, by cutting prices and raising marketing expenditures in some of Folger's key western markets. Another example may be occurring in the machinery sector. Deere entered the earthmoving industry in the late 1950s with a strategy similar to Caterpillar's. Deere has recently pushed even harder to penetrate some of Caterpillar's key markets. Rumors are now rampant that Caterpillar is planning to enter the farm equipment industry, where Deere is strong.[11]

The cross-parry response represents a choice by the defending firm *not* to counter the initial move directly but to counter it indirectly. By responding indirectly, the defending firm may well be trying not to trigger a set of destructive moves and countermoves in the encroached-upon market but yet clearly to signal displeasure and raise the threat of serious retaliation later.

[11] A rumor, as well as an actual move, can serve as a cross-parry.

If the cross-parry is directed toward one of the original initiator's "bread and butter" markets, it may be interpreted as a serious warning. If it is directed toward a minor market, it may signal a warning of things to come but also the hope of not triggering any unsettling or hasty counterresponse by the original initiator. A response in a minor market may also signal that the defender will raise the ante with a more threatening cross-parry later if the initiator does not back off.

The cross-parry can be a particularly effective way to discipline a competitor if there is a great divergence of market shares. For example, if the cross-parry involves a price cut, the cost of meeting this price cut for the firm with the bigger share may be a lot greater than for the firm sending the signal. This fact can increase the pressure placed on the original instigator to back off.

An implication of all this analysis is that maintaining a small position in such cross-markets can be a useful potential deterrent.

THE FIGHTING BRAND

A form of signal related to the cross-parry is the *fighting brand*. A firm threatened or potentially threatened by another can introduce a brand that has the effect—whether this is the only motivation for the brand or not—of punishing or threatening to punish the source of the threat. For example, Coca-Cola introduced a new brand called Mr. Pibb in the mid-1970s which tasted very much like Dr. Pepper, a brand that was gaining market share. Maxwell House introduced a coffee brand called Horizon, which had similar characteristics and package design to Folger's, in some markets where Folger's was seeking to gain position. Fighting brands can be meant as warnings or deterrents or as shock troops to absorb the brunt of a competitive attack. They are also often introduced with little push or support *before* any serious attack occurs, thereby serving as a warning. Fighting brands can also be used as offensive weapons as part of a larger campaign.

PRIVATE ANTITRUST SUITS

If a firm files a private antitrust suit challenging a competitor, it can be taken as a signal of displeasure or in some cases as harassment or a delaying tactic. Private suits can thus be viewed a lot like cross-parries. Since a private suit can be dropped at any time by the initiating firm, it is potentially a mild signal of displeasure relative to, for example, a competitive price cut. The suit may be saying, "You have pushed too far this time and had better back off," without taking the risks that would accompany a direct confrontation in the marketplace. For the weaker firm suing the stronger firm, the suit may be a way of sensitizing the stronger firm so that it will not undertake any aggressive actions while the suit is outstanding. If the stronger firms feels itself under legal scrutiny, its power may be effectively neutralized.

For large firms suing smaller firms, private antitrust suits can be thinly veiled devices to inflict penalties. Suits force the weaker firm to bear extremely high legal costs over a long period of time and also divert its attention from competing in the market. Or, following the argument above, a suit can be a low-risk way of telling the weaker firm that it is attempting to bite off too much of the market. The oustanding suit can be left effectively dormant through legal maneuvering and selectively activated (inflicting costs on the weaker firm) if the weaker firm shows signs of misreading the signal.

The Use of History in Identifying Signals

Studying the historical relationship between a firm's announcements and its moves, or between other varieties of potential signals and the subsequent outcomes, can greatly improve one's ability to read signals accurately. Searching for signs a competitor may have inadvertently given before making changes in the past can also help to uncover new types of unconscious signals unique to that competitor. Do certain activities by the sales force always precede a product change? Do product introductions always occur after a national sales meeting? Do price changes in the existing line always precede the introduction of a new product? Does the competitor always announce capacity addition when its level of capacity utilization reaches a certain figure?

Of course, in interpreting such signals there is always the possibility of divergence from past behavior; ideally a full competitor analysis will uncover economic and organizational reasons why such a divergence might occur ahead of time.

Can Attention to Market Signals Be a Distraction?

Given the subtlety of interpreting market signals, one can take the view that too much attention to them can be a counterproductive distraction. Rather than getting all tangled up second-guessing competitors' words and actions, holds this view, companies should focus their time and energy on competing.

Although situations might be imagined in which top management become so preoccupied with signals that the important tasks of managing the business and building a strong strategic position were neglected, this hardly justifies abandoning this potentially valuable source of information. Strategy formulation inherently contains some explicit or implicit assumptions about competitors and their motives. Market signals can add greatly to the firm's stock of knowledge about competitors, and therefore improve the quality of these assumptions. Ignoring them is like ignoring competitors altogether.

5
Competitive Moves

In most industries a central characteristic of competition is that firms are mutually dependent: firms feel the effects of each others' moves and are prone to react to them. In this situation, which economists call an oligopoly, the outcome of a competitive move by one firm depends at least to some extent on the reactions of its rivals.[1] "Bad" or "irrational" reactions by competitors (even weaker competitors) can often make "good" strategic moves unsuccessful. Thus success can be assured only if the competitors choose to or are influenced to respond in a non-destructive way.

In an oligopoly the firm often faces a dilemma. It can pursue the interests (profitability) of the industry as a whole (or of some subgroup of firms), and thereby not incite competitive reaction, or it can behave in its own narrow self-interest at the risk of touching off retaliation and escalating industry competition to a battle. The dilemma arises because choosing strategies or responses that avoid the risk of warfare and make the industry as a whole better off (strategies that can be called *cooperative*) may mean that the firm gives up potential profits and market share.

The situation is analogous to the classis Prisoners' Dilemma in game theory, one version of which goes as follows. Two prisoners sit

[1] An oligopoly falls in between a monopoly, where there is only one firm, and the perfectly competitive industry, where there are so many firms and entry is so easy that firms do not really affect each other but respond to overall market conditions.

in jail, each with the choice of squealing on each other or maintaining silence. If neither prisoner squeals, both go free. If they both squeal, both get hanged. If one prisoner talks and the other does not, however, the squealer not only gets off scot-free but also collects a bounty for his trouble. Both prisoners taken together are better off if they can avoid squealing at all. But acting in his own self-interest, each prisoner has an even greater incentive to squeal provided the other does not have the same idea. Translating this problem into the setting of oligopoly, if firms are cooperative they all can make a reasonable profit. However, if one firm makes a self-interested strategic move to which others do not retaliate effectively, it can earn even higher profits. If its competitors retaliate vigorously against the move, though, everybody can be worse off than if they were all cooperative.

This chapter presents some principles for making competitive moves in such a setting. It considers both offensive moves to improve position and defensive moves to deter competitors from taking undesirable actions. First, this chapter draws on Chapter 1 to explore the general likelihood of competitive outbreaks in an industry, which sets the context in which any offensive or defensive move must be made. Next, some important considerations in making various kinds of competitive moves are examined, including nonthreatening or cooperative moves, threatening moves, and moves designed for deterrence. This discussion will illustrate the crucial role of established *commitment* in making moves, and approaches to doing so will be examined in detail. Finally, some approaches that firms take to promote industry cooperation will be discussed briefly.

In addition to drawing on Chapter 1, this chapter will necessarily draw on the basic principles of competitor analysis described in Chapter 3 and the discussion of market signals in Chapter 4. Competitor analysis is obviously a prerequisite to considering any offensive or defensive move, and market signals are tools both for understanding competitors and for use in actually implementing competitive moves.

Industry Instability: The Likelihood of Competitive Warfare

The first question for the firm in considering offensive or defensive moves is the general degree of instability in the industry or the industry-wide conditions that may mean a move will touch off widespread warfare. Some industries require much softer treading than others. The underlying *structure* of an industry, discussed in Chapter 1, determines the intensity of competitive rivalry and the general ease or difficulty that cooperative or warfare-avoiding outcomes can be found. The greater the number of competitors, the more equal their relative power, the more standardized their products, the higher their fixed costs and other conditions that tempt them to try to fill capacity, and the slower the industry's growth, the greater is the likelihood that there will be repeated efforts by firms to pursue their own self-interest. They will take actions like shading prices (squealing), where almost sure retaliation will touch off recurring bouts of retaliation that keep profits low. Similarly, the more diverse or asymmetrical are competitors' goals and perspectives, the greater their strategic stakes in the particular business and the less segmented the market, the harder it will be to properly interpret each others' moves and sustain a cooperative outcome. Broadly speaking, both offensive and defensive moves are more risky if these conditions favor intense rivalry.

Some other conditions in an industry can make outbreaks of rivalry more or less likely. A history of competing or *continuity of interaction* among the parties can promote stability since it facilitates the building of trust (the belief that competitors are not out to bankrupt each other), and leads to more accurate forecasts of how competitors will react. Conversely, lack of continuity will raise the chances of competitive outbreaks. Continuity of interaction not only depends on a stable group of competitors but also is aided by a stable group of general managers of these competitors.

Multiple bargaining areas, or situations in which firms are interacting in more than one competitive arena, can also facilitate a stable outcome in an industry. For example, if two firms compete in both the U.S. and European markets, one firm's gain in the U.S. market might be offset by the other firm's gains in Europe, gains which neither firm would tolerate individually. Multiple markets provide a way in which one firm can reward another for not attacking it,[2] or conversely, provide a way of disciplining a renegade. *Interconnections* through joint ventures or joint participations can also promote stability in an industry through fostering a cooperative orientation and exposing the players to fairly complete information about each other. Full information is usually stabilizing because it

[2]Or "side payments" in the jargon of game theory.

mpetitors' performance is impaired little if at all measured y *their own criteria*.

example of a move combining a number of these character- was Timex's entry into the watch industry in the early 1950s.[3] x's entry strategy was to produce a very low-price watch (with-jeweled bearings), which was so inexpensive that it did not pay to ve it repaired. This watch was sold through drugstores and other nconventional watch outlets instead of through jewelry stores. he Swiss dominated the world watch industry at the time with high-quality, high-priced watches sold through jewelry stores and marketed as precision instruments. The Swiss industry was growing briskly in the early 1950s. The Timex watch was so different from the Swiss watch that the Swiss did not seem to perceive it as competition at all. It did not threaten their image of quality, nor did it threaten their position with jewelers or as the leading producers of high-quality, high-priced watches. The Timex watch probably created primary demand initially, rather than taking sales from the Swiss. Furthermore, the Swiss were growing, and Timex was no threat to their performance at all initially. As a result, Timex was able to gain a secure foothold in the lower end of the market without even attracting the attention of the Swiss.

Executing moves so as to improve everyone's position requires that competitors *understand* that the move is not threatening. Such moves can be a common and recurring adaptation necessary because of changed industry conditions. Yet all three categories of non-threatening moves involve some risk that the move may be misinterpreted as aggression.

Firms can use a wide variety of mechanisms to avoid misinterpretation in such situations, though none is foolproof. Active market signaling (Chapter 4) through announcements, public commentary about the change, and the like is one option in indicating benign intentions. For example, an elaborate discussion in the press of cost increases that justify making a price change may help communicate intentions. The firm making such a move also can discipline competitors who fail to follow, such as through selective advertising campaigns or selling efforts directed at those competitors' customers. Another approach to easing risks of misinterpretation is

[3]For background, see *Note on the Watch Industries in Switzerland, Japan and the United States*, Intercollegiate Case Clearinghouse 9-373-090; and *Timex (A)*, Intercollegiate Case Clearinghouse 6-373-080.

helps firms avoid mistaken reactions and keeps them from attempting ill-advised strategic initiatives.

Industry structure influences the position of the competitors, the pressures on them to make aggressive moves, and the degree to which their interests are likely to conflict. Structure thus sets the basic parameters within which competitive moves are made. However, structure does not fully determine what will take place in a market. Rivalry also depends on the particular situations of individual competitors. Another step in assessing industry instability and the general context for making moves is *competitor analysis*. Using the techniques described in Chapter 3, it is necessary to examine the probable moves each competitor will make, the threat provided by moves made by its rivals, and the ability of each competitor to defend itself effectively against such moves. This analysis is a prerequisite to developing strategies for deterrence or in deciding where and how to make offensive moves. Here it will be assumed that such analysis has already been done.

The final part of assessing industry instability is determining the nature of the information flow among firms in the market, including the extent of their shared knowledge of industry conditions, and ability to communicate intentions effectively through signaling. This flow of information will be a central focus of this chapter.

Competitive Moves

Because in an oligopoly a firm is partly dependent on the behavior of its rivals, selecting the right competitive move involves finding one whose outcome is quickly determined (no protracted or serious battle takes place) and also skewed as much as possible toward the firm's own interests. That is, the goal for the firm is to avoid destabilizing and costly warfare, which spells poor results for all participants, but yet still outperform other firms.

One broad approach is to use superior resources and capabilities to *force* an outcome skewed toward the interests of the firm, overcoming and outlasting retaliation—we might call this the *brute force approach*. This sort of approach is possible only if the firm possesses clear superiorities, and it is stable only as long as the firm maintains these superiorities and as long as competitors do not misread them and incorrectly attempt to change their positions.

Some companies seem to view competitive moves as entirely a game of brute force: sheer resources are massed to attack a rival. A firm's strengths and weaknesses (Chapter 3) certainly help define the opportunities and threats it faces. However, even sheer resources are often not enough to insure the right outcome if competitors will be tough (or worse, desperate or seemingly irrational) in their responses or if competitors are pursuing greatly different objectives. Moreover, possession of clear strengths is not always realistically available to every firm seeking to improve its strategic position. Finally, even with clear strengths, a war of attrition is costly to the victor and vanquished alike and is best avoided.

Competitive moves are also a game of finesse. The game can be structured and moves selected and executed in such a way as to maximize their outcome no matter what resources are available to the firm. Ideally, a battle of retaliation never begins at all. Making competitive moves in oligopoly is best thought of as a combination of whatever brute force the firm can muster, applied with finesse.

COOPERATIVE OR NONTHREATENING MOVES

Moves that do not threaten competitors' goals are a place to begin in searching for ways to improve position. Based on a thorough analysis of competitors' goals and assumptions, using the framework in Chapter 3, there may be moves the firm can make to increase its profits (or even its share) that do not reduce the performance of its significant competitors or threaten their goals unduly. Three categories of such moves can be usefully distinguished:

- moves that improve the firm's position and *improve* competitors' positions *even if* they do not match them;
- moves that improve the firm's position and *improve* competitors' positions *only if* a significant number match them;
- moves that improve the firm's position because competitors *will not* match them.

The first case involves the least risk if such moves can be identified. One possibility is that the firm may be engaged in practices that not only diminish its performance but also spill over to diminish the performance of competitors, such as an inappropriate advertising campaign or poor pricing structure out of line with the industry. The existence of such possibilities is a reflection of weak past strategy.

The second case is more commo[n]
moves that would improve ever[y]
lowed. For example, if every f[irm]
years to one year, all the firms'
would increase, provided that aggr[e]
sensitive to warranty terms. Another
that calls for a price adjustment. The p[rice]
that all firms may not follow, because the
their positions absolutely, is not optimal for
firm with the highest product reliability will lo[se]
vantage if the warranty period is reduced. Compe[titors]
follow because one or more firms see the chance to i[mprove rel]
ative position by not following, assuming that others d[o].

In selecting a move of this second type, the key step[s]
sessing the impact of the move on each and every major [competi]
tor, and (2) assessing the pressures on each competitor to for[go the]
benefits of cooperating for the possible benefits of breaking r[anks].
This assessment is a problem in competitor analysis. When mak[ing]
moves whose success is contingent on competitors following, the ris[k]
is that competitors will not follow. This risk is not great if the chosen
move can be cheaply rescinded or if shifts in relative company position are either slow to occur or easy to redress. However, such a move can be very risky if the relative positions potentially gained by firms that choose not to participate are significant and hard to win back.

Identifying the third category of nonthreatening moves—moves that competitors will not follow—depends on a careful understanding of the opportunities provided by competitors' particular goals and assumptions. It involves finding moves to which competitors will not respond because they do not perceive a need to do so. For example, a competitor may attach little significance to the Latin American market, focusing instead on Canada as an export opportunity. Inroads into Latin America at the expense of local companies may not matter at all to this competitor.

Moves will be perceived as nonthreatening if:

- competitors do not even notice, because the adjustments are largely internal for the firm making them;
- competitors will not be concerned about them because of their self-perceptions or assumptions about the industry and how to compete in it;

reliance on a traditional industry leader. In some industries, one firm historically takes the leadership role in adjusting to new conditions; other firms wait for it to move first and then follow. Another mechanism is to associate prices or other decision variables to some readily visible index, such as the consumer price index, to facilitate adjustments. Focal points, to be discussed below, are a coordinating mechanism that can also be employed.

THREATENING MOVES

Many moves that would significantly improve a firm's position do threaten competitors, since this is the essence of oligopoly. Thus a key to the success of such moves is predicting and influencing retaliation. If retaliation is rapid and effective, then such a move may leave the mover no better off or even worse off. If retaliation is very bitter, the initiator can actually come out a lot worse off than it started.

In considering threatening moves, the key questions are as follows:

1. How *likely* is retaliation?
2. How *soon* will retaliation come?
3. How *effective* will retaliation potentially be?
4. How *tough* will retaliation be, where toughness refers to the willingness of the competitor to retaliate strongly even at its own expense?
5. Can retaliation be *influenced*?

Because the framework for competitor analysis in Chapter 3 addresses a number of these questions, we will concentrate our attention here on predicting lags in retaliation to offensive moves. Many of these considerations can be turned around to help develop defensive strategy. Influencing retaliation will also be discussed in the section on commitment later in this chapter.

LAGS IN RETALIATION

Other things being equal, the firm will want to make the move that gives it the most time before its competitors can effectively retaliate. In a defensive context, the firm will want competitors to believe that it will retaliate quickly and effectively to their moves. Lags in retaliation stem from four basic sources:

- perceptual lags;
- lags in mounting a retaliatory strategy;
- inability to pinpoint retaliation, which raises its short-run cost;
- lags caused by conflicting goals or mixed motives.

The first source, *perceptual lags*, involves delay in competitors perceiving or noticing the initial strategic move, either because the move was kept secret or introduced quietly away from competitors' centers of attention (e.g., with small customers or foreign customers). Sometimes, by being secretive or keeping a low profile, a firm can make a move or build a new capability before competitors can effectively retaliate. Also, competitors may not immediately perceive a move as significant because of their goals, perceptions of the marketplace, and so on. The example of the introduction of the Timex watch serves here as well. Long after Timex began to cut into the sales of the Swiss and American producers, the Timex watch was seen by them as an inferior junk product not requiring retaliation.

Perceptual lags depend partly on the mechanisms firms have in place for monitoring competitive behavior, and these lags can be influenced. When competitors are dependent on outside statistical sources like trade associations to provide the base data against which they compute market share, then they may not be able to notice moves until such data are published. Perceptual lags may sometimes be lengthened by *diversionary tactics*, such as introducing a product or making some other move in an area away from that in which the key initiative is to take place. From a defensive point of view perceptual lags may be shortened by having a competitor monitoring system in place which continually assembles data from the field salesforce, distributors, and so on. With careful monitoring, competitors can actually learn about moves ahead of time because the competitor must make advance commitments for advertising space, equipment delivery, and the like. If systems for competitor monitoring are known to competitors, all the better for deterrence.

Lags in mounting a retaliatory campaign vary with the type of initial move. Retaliation to a price cut can be immediate, but it may take years for a defensive research effort to match a product change or for modern capacity to be put on stream to match a competitor's new plant. A new automobile model requires three years from planning to introduction, for example. A large, modern blast furnace for producing pig iron or an integrated papermaking plant requires three to five years to build.

These lags in retaliation can also be influenced by a firm's actions. A firm can pick offensive moves against which competitors face a slow process of mounting effective retaliation, given natural lead times coupled with internal weaknessses. From a defensive standpoint, retaliation time can be shortened by building up retaliatory resources even though they may never be used. For example, new product offerings may be developed but held in reserve, machinery can be ordered at the risk of modest cancellation payments, and so on.

Lags caused by the *inability to pinpoint retaliation* are analogous to the problem of having to disassemble an entire television set to replace one faulty transistor. Particularly for larger firms reacting to moves by smaller ones, retaliatory moves may have to be generalized to all customers rather than restricted to the customers or market segments that are being contested. For example, to match a price cut by a small competitor, a large firm may have to give a price discount to all its customers, at enormous expense. If a firm can find moves that are much less costly for it to make than they are for its competitors to respond to, it can produce lags in retaliation and sometimes even deter retaliation altogether.

Lags in retaliation caused by *conflicting goals or mixed motives* are a final important situation which has wide applicability in the study of competitive interaction. This is the situation, introduced in Chapter 3, in which one firm makes a move that threatens some of a competitor's business, but if the competitor retaliates quickly and vigorously, it hurts itself elsewhere in its business. This effect potentially creates a lag in retaliation (and a reduction in its effectiveness) or even prevents retaliation altogether. Part of the lag may be in the extra time needed to thrash out internal conflicts.

Finding a situation that catches the key competitor or competitors with conflicting goals is at the heart of many company success stories. The slow Swiss reaction to the Timex watch provides an example. Timex sold its watches through drugstores, rather than through the traditional jewelry store outlets for watches, and emphasized very low cost, the need for no repair, and the fact that a watch was not a status item but a functional part of the wardrobe. The strong sales of the Timex watch eventually threatened the financial and growth goals of the Swiss, but it also raised an important dilemma for them were they to retaliate against it directly. The Swiss had a big stake in the jewelry store as a channel and a large investment in the Swiss image of the watch as a piece of fine precision jewelry. Aggressive retaliation against Timex would have helped legitimize the Timex concept, threatened the needed cooperation of jewelers in selling Swiss watches, and blurred the Swiss product image. Thus the Swiss retaliation to Timex never really came.

There are many other examples of this principle at work. Volkswagen's and American Motor's early strategies of producing a stripped-down basic transportation vehicle with few style changes created a similar dilemma for the Big Three auto producers. They had a strategy built on trade-up and frequent model changes. Bic's recent introduction of the disposable razor has put Gillette in a difficult position: if it reacts it may cut into the sales of another product in its broad line of razors, a dilemma Bic does not face.[4] Finally, IBM has been reluctant to jump into minicomputers because the move will jeopardize its sales of larger mainframe computers.

Finding strategic moves that will benefit from a lag in retaliation, or making moves so as to maximize the lag, are key principles of competitive interaction. However, seeking to delay retaliation cannot be made a principle of strategy without qualification. A slow but tough retaliation may leave the initiating firm worse off than a quick but less effective one. Thus to the extent that there is a trade-off between the lag in retaliation and the effectiveness and toughness of that retaliation, the firm will have to balance the two in selecting a move.

DEFENSIVE MOVES

Thus far we have been talking about offensive moves, but the need to deter or defend against moves by competitors can be equally important. The problem of defense, of course, is the opposite of the problem of offense. Good defense is creating a situation in which competitors, after doing the analysis described above or actually attempting a move, will conclude that the move is unwise. As with offensive moves, defense can be achieved by forcing competitors to back down after a battle. However, the most effective defense is to *prevent the battle altogether*.

[4]For a description of Bic's move, see "Gillette: After the Diversification That Failed," *Business Week,* February 28, 1977.

To prevent a move, it is necessary that competitors expect retaliation with a high degree of certainty and believe that the retaliation will be effective. Some approaches to achieving this effect have been discussed and others will be introduced as part of the generalized concept of creating *commitment*, discussed below.

Even if a move cannot be prevented, however, there are some other approaches to defense,

DISCIPLINE AS A FORM OF DEFENSE

If a competitor makes a move and the firm immediately and surely retailiates against it, this disciplining action can lead the aggressor to expect that retaliation will always occur. The more the disciplining firm is able to aim its retaliation specifically at the initiator, and the more it can communicate that its target is the initiator rather than any other firm, the more effective such discipline is likely to be. For example, a fighting brand which is a copy of a particular competitor's product is more effective discipline than a more generalized new product.[5] Conversely, if the retaliation must be generalized (e.g., a price cut that applies to all customers and not just those shared with the initiating price cutter), the more expensive and less effective the discipline is likely to be. Also, when the response to a move must be generalized rather than focused on the firm initiating the battle, retaliation runs a greater risk of starting a chain reaction of moves and countermoves—which makes discipline more risky.

DENYING A BASE

Once a competitor's move has occurred, the denial of an adequate base for the competitor to meet its goals, coupled with the expectation that this state of affairs will continue, can cause the competitor to withdraw. New entrants, for example, usually have some targets for growth, market share, and ROI, and some time horizon for achieving them. If a new entrant is denied its targets and becomes convinced that it will be a long time before they are met, then it may withdraw or deescalate. Tactics for denying a base include strong price competition, heavy expenditures on research, and so on. Attacking new products in the test-market phase can be an effective way to foretell a firm's future willingness to fight and can be less expensive than waiting for the introduction to actually occur. Another

[5]For examples of fighting brands, see Chapter 4.

tactic is using special deals to load customers up with inventory, thereby removing the market for the product and raising the short-run cost of entry. It can be worth paying a substantial short-run price to deny a base if a firm's market position is threatened. Essential to such a strategy, however, is a good hypothesis about what a competitor's performance targets and time horizon are.

An example of such a situation may be Gillette's withdrawal from digital watches. Although claiming it had won significant market shares in test markets, Gillette bowed out, citing the substantial investments required to develop technology and margins lower than those available in other areas of its business. Texas Instruments' strategy of aggressive pricing and rapid technological development in digital watches probably had a substantial impact on this decision.

Commitment

Perhaps the single most important concept in planning and executing offensive or defensive competitive moves is the concept of commitment. Commitment can guarantee the likelihood, speed, and vigor of retaliation to offensive moves and can be the cornerstone of defensive strategy. Commitments influence the way competitors perceive their positions and those of rivals. Establishing commitment is essentially a form of communicating the firm's resources and intentions unequivocally.[6] Competitors face uncertainty about a firm's intentions and the extent of its resources. Communicating commitment reduces the uncertainty and causes the players to calculate their rational strategies from new assumptions, which avoids warfare. For example, if a firm can commit itself unequivocally to vigorously repulsing a given move, its competitors may take this reaction as a certainty rather than a probability in formulating their own strategies. They are thus less likely to act in the first place. The trick in competitive interactions is to stake out commitments in such a way as to maximize the firm's own market position.

[6] It should be stressed that the term *communication* is not used in the literal sense. Nevertheless, some modes of signaling and establishing commitments are under review by the U.S. antitrust authorities because of the concern that they may be effective in leading to tacit collusion in industries. Although this interpretation is novel and unproven, managers must be aware of its existence.

There are three major types of commitment in the competitive setting, each designed to achieve deterrence of a different type:

- commitment that the firm is unequivocally sticking with a move it is making;
- commitment that the firm will retaliate and continue to retaliate if a competitor makes certain moves;
- commitment that the firm will take no action or forgo an action.

If the firm can convince its rivals that it is commited to a strategic move it is making or plans to make, it increases the chances that rivals will resign themselves to the new position and not expend the resources to retaliate or try to cause the firm to back down. Thus commitment can *deter retaliation*. The more entrenched and stubborn the firm appears in its intentions to carry out a move, the more likely this outcome is. If competitors perceive a grim and committed competitor, they may be convinced that if they retaliate the competitor will countermove to keep its new position, and so on in a downward spiral.

The second form of commitment is analogous, but it relates to a firm's reaction to possible initiatives by competitors. If the firm can convince its rivals that it will retaliate strongly and with certainty to their moves, they may conclude that it is not worth making the move at all. This role of commitment is to *deter threatening moves* in the first place. The more competitors perceive the prospect of dogged, bitter retaliation to the point of severely hurting everyone's profits, the less likely they are of initiating the chain of events in the first place. This is analogous to the situation in which the robber says, "stick 'em up, I want your money," and the deranged-looking victim says "If you take it, I will explode this bomb and kill us both!"

The third form of commitment, that of not taking a damaging action, might be termed *creating trust*. This form of commitment can be important in deescalating competitive battles. For example, if the firm can convince its rivals that it will follow a price increase rather than attempt to undercut it, it may help stop a price war.

The persuasiveness of a commitment is related to the degree to which it appears *binding and irreversible*. The value of a commitment is as a deterrent, and deterrent value increases with the certainty with which the competitor sees the commitment being honored. The irony is that if the deterrent fails, the firm may be sorry it has made the commitment (the victim doesn't really want to blow himself up). The firm faces the difficult trade-off of reneging on its commitment, reducing its credibility in subsequent situations, or paying the price of fulfilling the commitment.

Both the fact of a commitment and its timing are crucial. The firm that can commit itself *first* may be in the position to make other firms take its behavior as given in their maximizing calculations about what to do, thereby skewing the outcome in its favor. This can be especially effective when firms basically are seeking a stable outcome but disagree on its precise form. When two firms are locked in a vigorous battle for position and have widely divergent interests, early commitment may be less helpful.[7]

COMMUNICATING COMMITMENT

Communicating commitment, either to pursue a move or to retaliate against a competitor's action, can be done through a variety of mechanisms and with a variety of signaling devices. The building blocks of a credible commitment are the following:

- assets, resources, and other mechanisms to carry out the commitment quickly;
- a clear intention to carry out the commitment, including a history of adherance to past commitments;
- inability to back down or perceived moral resolve not to back down;
- ability to detect compliance to the terms to which the commitment refers.

The necessity of having the *mechanisms* to carry out a commitment in order to communicate its seriousness is obvious. If a firm appears unbeatable, a battle is unlikely to occur. Particularly visible assets for carrying out commitments are excess cash reserves, excess production capacity,[8] a large corps of salespersons, extensive research facilities, small positions in a competitor's other businesses which can be used in retaliation, and fighting brands. Less visible assets are such things as on-the-shelf but unintroduced new products

[7]For experimental evidence that supports this conclusion, see Deutsch (1960).

[8]For a discussion of the related point that excess capacity can provide a deterrent to entry, see Spence (1977).

which are set to go directly against a competitor's key market. *Discipline mechanisms* is a term applied to such assets or resources, which are intended to punish a competitor if it makes a move undesirable from the point of view of the firm. Many of the assets listed above can be effective discipline mechanisms.

The building of such assets to carry out a commitment can play an important role in establishing commitment. Mere possession of the assets is not enough, however. Competitors must know about their presence for them to have deterrent value. Insuring that competitors are aware of the assets to carry out commitments sometimes involves public announcements, discussions with customers that will spread around the industry, and cooperation with the business press to the point of producing articles noting the existence of such assets. Highly visible resources are particularly valuable as deterrents since they minimize the risk of being misread or ignored by competitors.

The clear intention to carry out a commitment must similarly be communicated for a commitment to be credible. One way to do so is through a pattern of consistent behavior. The past is usually used by competitors as an indication of how reliable and tough a firm is likely to be in its reactions, and a well-orchestrated series of past reaction (which may be on less important or even trivial matters) can be a persuasive signal of future intentions. The clear intention to carry out a commitment is also enhanced by noticeable actions that reduce the lag in retaliating, like defensive R&D programs already underway which are known to competitors. Announcements or leaks of the intention to carry out a commitment are also communicating devices, although they do not usually communicate with the seriousness of past behavior.

Extremely effective in communicating commitment are known factors that make it *difficult and costly if not impossible for the firm to back down*. For example, a publicized long-term contract with a supplier or customer is an indication of a long-run stake in trying to enter and stay in a market. So is buying a plant rather than leasing it, or entering a market as a fully integrated producer rather than just an assembler. Commitment to retaliate to a competitor's moves can be made irreversible by written or verbal agreements with retailers or customers to meet price cuts, guarantees of an equivalent quality product, cooperative advertising support to meet a competitor's action, and so on. Declaring commitments to the industry or financial community in public statements, publicizing targets for market share, and a variety of other devices can let competitors know that a firm will be embarrassed publicly if it has to back down. This knowledge will tend to deter them from trying to force it to do so.

Pursuing this line of thinking, the more the competitor thinks the firm is bordering on being irrational in pursuing its commitment, the more wary it will be in taking that firm on. Irrationality is communicated in competitive situations by such things as past actions, lawsuits, and public statements. Behavior that tells competitors the firm is serious can occur in all parts of a business. What is said to suppliers, to customers, to distribution channels, and in public can communicate more or less seriousness about being in the business or about sticking to a commitment for the long haul.

It is important to note that great resources are not always necessary for commitment to be communicated. The firm with a large market share or broad product line, for example, will usually have conflicting goals in retaliating to some moves, as previously discussed. The small firm, however, may have much to gain and little to lose by initiating a move or by retaliating to others' moves. A price cut the firm initiates may have an enormous impact on the large competitor, given that competitor's higher volume, for example. Although the smaller firm has fewer resources to carry out its threats, it can also partially compensate through toughness or irrationality.

Finally, the *ability of a firm to detect compliance* is central to the effectiveness of its commitment to retaliate. If a competitor believes it can "cheat" and go undetected, it may be tempted to do so. But if the firm can *demonstrate* its ability to know immediately of any price shading, quality adjustments, or forthcoming new products, for example, its commitment to retaliate becomes more credible. *Known* systems of monitoring sales, talking to customers, and for interviewing distributors are examples of ways to communicate a high probability of detection. It should be noted that buyers may have the incentive to report secret price cuts even if they do not actually occur in order to encourage discounting. This can undermine the stability of a market where information is poor or suppliers cannot verify buyer claims.

An evolving competitive battle involving Baxter Travenol Laboratories in intravenous solutions, blood containers, and related disposable health care products is an interesting example of some of these ideas about commitment.[9] Baxter ($800 million), in a strong market position, faces a challenge from the McGaw division of American Hospital Supply Corporation ($1.5 billion), developer of

---

[9] For a description, see "A Miracle of Sorts," *Forbes*, November 15, 1977.

a new container for intravenous solutions. Although the Food and Drug Administration had not given its approval to the new competitive product as of November 1977, Baxter reportedly had already begun to take action to communicate its commitment to resist the entry. Hospital purchasing agents were reporting increased price competition. Baxter was reported to be offering large discounts on many lines and was going especially hard after McGaw accounts. Baxter also had been spending heavily on research and had engaged in reportedly vicious price cutting when another competitor entered the market in the early 1970s. Baxter's toughness and resolve in meeting this recent competitive challenge has apparently been well communicated.

TRUST AS A COMMITMENT

Our discussion has focused on communicating commitment to stick with a move or to retaliate, but in some situations firms find it desirable to make commitments to *not* make a damaging move or to end aggression. Although this course may seem easy, competitors are usually wary of a firm's conciliatory gesture, especially if they have been stung by that firm in the past. They may also be wary if letting down their guard gives the initiating firm a chance of getting a jump on them that is hard to recoup. How, then, do firms actually go about communicating conciliation or building trust?

Once again the range of possibilities observed in practice is large, and the principles already described in communicating commitment apply. A persuasive way to communicate trustworthiness is for the firm to *demonstrably* take some diminution in its performance that accrues to the benefit of competitors. For example, there is substantial evidence that General Electric yielded market share in cyclical downturns in the turbine generator business to avoid severe price deterioration and took the share back in cyclical upturns.[10]

Focal Points

A problem leading to instability in oligopoly is in coordinating the expectations of competitors about what the eventual market outcome will be. To the extent that competitors have divergent expecta-

[10]Sultan (1974), vol. 1.

tions, jockeying will continue to occur and the prospect of outbreaks of warfare is likely. Thomas Schelling's work on game theory[11] suggests that an important part of reaching an outcome in such a setting is the discovery of a *focal point*, or some prominent resting place on which the competitive process can converge its expectations. The power of focal points resides in the need and desire of competitors to mutually achieve some stable outcome to avoid difficult and unsettling moves and countermoves. Focal points can take the form of logical price points, percentage markup pricing rules, round-number divisions of market shares, informal sharings of the market on some geographic or customer basis, and so on. The theory of focal points is that competitive adjustments will finally settle on such a point, which then serves as a natural sticking place.

The concept of focal points raises three implications for competitive rivalry. First, firms should seek to identify a desirable focal point as early as possible. The faster the focal point can be reached, the less the costs of jockeying around searching for it are likely to be. Second, industry prices or other decision variables may be simplified so that a focal point can be identified. This may involve, for example, establishing standard grades or products to replace a complex array of items in the line. Third, it is in the firm's interest to try to set up the game to make the focal point that is best for it seem to emerge. This may mean introducing a terminology in the industry that leads to a desirable focal point, such as talking in terms of prices per square foot rather than in terms of absolute prices. It can also take the form of structuring the *sequence* of strategic moves in such a way as to make a satisfactory focal point (from the firm's prospective) appear to emerge naturally.

A Note on Information and Secrecy

In part because of the proliferation of the business press and increased requirements for public filings, companies are disclosing more and more about themselves. Although some of this is legally required, much of what is written in annual reports, stated in interviews or speeches, or comes out via other means is not statutorily required. Disclosure may stem more from concern with the stock mar-

[11]Schelling (1960).

ket, managers' pride, inability to control statements by employees, or simply from lack of attention.

As should be clear from the discussion in this chapter, information is crucial to both offensive and defensive competitive moves. Sometimes selective release of information can serve very useful purposes, in market signaling, communicating commitment, and the like; but often information about plans or intentions can make it a great deal easier for competitors to formulate strategy. For example. if an impending new product is disclosed in detail, competitors will be able to focus their resources in preparing a response. Contrast this situation with the one in which disclosure of the new product's nature is very vague; competitors are then obliged to prepare a range of defensive strategies, depending on what shape the new product actually takes.

Selective disclosure of information about itself is a crucial resource the firm has in making competitive moves. The disclosure of any information should only be made as an integral part of competitive strategy.

6
Strategy Toward Buyers and Suppliers

This chapter develops some of the implications of structural analysis for buyer selection, or the choice of target customers or customer groups. It also explores some implications of structural analysis for purchasing strategy. Policies toward both buyers and toward suppliers are often looked at too narrowly, with the primary focus on operating problems. Yet through attention to broad issues of strategy toward buyers and suppliers, the firm may be able to improve its competitive position and reduce its vulnerability to their exercise of power.

Buyer Selection

Most industries sell their products or services not to a single buyer but to a range of different buyers. The bargaining power of this group of buyers, viewed in aggregate terms, is one of the key competitive forces determining the potential profitability of an industry. Chapter 1 has examined some of the structural conditions that make an industry's buyer group as a whole more or less powerful.

Yet it is rare that the buyer group facing an industry is homogeneous from a structural standpoint. Many producer-goods industries, for example, sell products to firms in a wide variety of businesses that use the product in differing ways. These firms can differ widely in their volumes of purchases, the importance of the product as an input to their production processes, and so on. Buyers of consumer goods can also vary a great deal in the quantity of a product they purchase, in income, in education, and along many other dimensions.

An industry's buyers can also differ in their purchasing needs. Different buyers may require differing levels of customer service, desired product quality or durability, needed information in sales presentations, and so on. These differing purchasing needs are one reason why buyers have different structural bargaining power.

Buyers differ not only in their structural position but also in their growth potential, and hence in the probable growth of their volume of purchases. Selling an electronic component to a firm like Digital Equipment in the rapidly growing minicomputer industry offers greater prospects for growth than selling the same component to a black and white television manufacturer.

Finally, for a variety of reasons the costs of servicing individual buyers differ. In electronic component distribution, for example, servicing buyers who order components in small quantities is a great deal more costly (as a percentage of sales) than serving higher-volume purchasers because the costs of servicing an order are largely fixed with respect to quantity shipped. The primary costs are paperwork, processing, and handling, which are not greatly affected by the number of components involved.

As a result of this heterogeneity, *buyer selection*—the choice of target buyers—becomes an important strategic variable. Broadly speaking, the firm should sell to the most favorable buyers possible, to the extent it has any choice. Buyer selection can strongly affect the growth rate of the firm and can minimize the disruptive power of buyers. Buyer selection with attention to structural considerations is an especially important strategic variable in mature industries and in those where barriers caused by product differentiation or technological innovation are hard to sustain.

Some concepts for buyer selection will be developed below. After identifying the characteristics of favorable, or "good," buyers, some strategic implications of buyer selection will be discussed. One such key implication is that a firm can not only find good buyers but also can *create* them.

A FRAMEWORK FOR BUYER SELECTION AND STRATEGY

There are four broad criteria, drawn from the previous discussion, that determine the quality of buyers from a strategic standpoint:

- Purchasing needs versus company capabilities

- Growth potential

- Structural position $\Big\langle$ intrinsic bargaining power
  propensity to exercise this bargaining power in demanding low prices

- Cost of servicing

Buyers' different purchasing needs carry strategic implications if a firm has differing capabilities for serving these needs relative to competitors. The firm will improve its competitive advantage, other things being equal, if it targets its efforts toward buyers whose particular needs it is in the best relative position to serve. The significance of the growth potential of buyers for strategy formulation is self-evident. The higher the growth potential of a buyer, the more probably its demands for the firm's product will be increasing over time.

Buyers' structural position is usefully divided into two parts for purposes of strategic analysis. Intrinsic bargaining power is the leverage the buyers can potentially exert over sellers, given their clout and the alternative sources of supply available. This leverage *may or may not* be exercised, however, because buyers also differ in their propensity to exercise their bargaining power to force down a seller's margins. Some buyers, even though they may purchase large quantities, are not particularly price sensitive. Or they are willing to trade price against other product attributes in a way that preserves the margins of the sellers. Both intrinsic bargaining power and the propensity to exercise it are crucial strategically, because unexercised power is a threat that can be unleashed by industry evolution. Buyers who have not been price sensitive can rapidly become so as their industries mature, for example, or as some substitute product begins to put pressure on their own margins.

The final key buyer characteristic from a strategic standpoint is the costs to the firm of servicing particular buyers. If these costs are high, then buyers that are "good buyers" based on other criteria may lose their attraction, because the costs more than offset any higher margins or lower risks in serving them.

These four criteria do *not* necessarily all move in the same direction. The buyers with the greatest growth potential can also be the most powerful and/or the most ruthless in exercising their power, though not necessarily. Or the buyers with little bargaining power and low price sensitivity may be so costly to service that the benefits of higher realized prices may be outweighed. Finally, the buyers the firm is best suited to serve may fail all the other tests. Thus the ultimate choice of the best target buyers is often a weighing and balancing process among these factors, measured against the firm's goals.

To assess where a particular buyer falls with respect to the four criteria is a matter of applying the concepts of structural and competitor analysis to their situations. Some of these factors will now be discussed.

PURCHASING NEEDS RELATIVE TO A FIRM'S CAPABILITIES

The need to match buyers' particular purchasing needs with the relative capabilities of the firm is self-evident. Such a match will allow the firm to achieve the highest level of product differentiation vis-à-vis its buyers compared to competitors. It should also minimize the cost of serving these buyers relative to competitors. For example, if the firm has strong engineering and product development skills it will achieve the greatest relative advantage in serving the buyers who place greatest stress on custom varieties. Or if the firm enjoys an efficient logistical system relative to its competitors, this advantage will be maximized by serving the buyers for whom cost is crucial or for whom the logistics of reaching them are most complex.

Diagnosing the purchasing needs of particular buyers is a matter of identifying all the factors that enter into each buyer's purchase decision and the factors involved in executing the purchase transaction (shipping, delivery, order processing). These can then be ranked for individual buyers or buyer groups within the total buyer population. Identifying the firm's own relative capabilities can draw on the tools of competitor analysis presented in Chapter 3.

BUYER'S GROWTH POTENTIAL

The growth potential of a buyer in an industrial business is determined by three straightforward conditions:

- the growth rate of its industry;
- the growth rate of its primary market segment(s);
- its change in market share in the industry and in key segments.

The growth rate of the buyer's industry will depend on a variety of factors, such as the position of the industry vis-à-vis substitute products, the growth of the buyer group to which it sells, and so on. The broad factors determining long-run industry growth are described in Chapter 8, "Industry Evolution."

Some market segments within an industry will usually be growing faster than others. Thus the buyer's growth potential also depends in part on what segments it is primarily serving or those it could and will potentially serve. Assessing the growth potential of particular segments requires basically the same analysis as assessing the growth potential of the industry, although at a lower level of aggregation.

The market share of a buyer in its industry and in particular market segments is the third element in growth analysis. Both the buyer's current share and the likelihood that this share will move up or down is a function of the buyer's competitive situation. Assessing this state requires a competitor analysis as well as a diagnosis of present and future industry structure, as is outlined in other chapters.

All three of these elements jointly determine the growth potential of the buyer. If a particular buyer is in a strong position to gain share, for example, it may offer possibilities for substantial growth even in a mature or declining industry.

The growth potential of a household buyer is determined by an analogous set of factors:

- demographics;
- quantity of purchases.

The first factor, demographics, determines the future size of a particular consumer segment. The number of well-educated consumers over twenty-five will be increasing rapidly, for example. Any stratum of income, education, marital status, age, and so on can be similarly analyzed by using demographic techniques.

The quantity of the product or service the particular consumer segment will purchase is the other key determinant of its growth prospects. This will be determined by such factors as the existence of substitutes, social trends which shift underlying needs, and so forth. As with demand for industrial goods, the underlying factors determining long-run demand for consumer goods will be discussed in Chapter 8.

INTRINSIC BARGAINING POWER OF BUYERS

The factors that determine the intrinsic bargaining power of particular buyers or buyer segments are similar to those described in Chapter 1, which determine the power of the industry's buyer group as a whole, although they will need to be extended somewhat. Here I will present the criteria that identify buyers *without* much intrinsic bargaining power, relative to others, because these will be good buyers for purposes of buyer selection:

They purchase small quantities relative to the sales of sellers. Small-volume buyers will have less leverage to demand price concessions, freight absorption, and other special considerations. The volume of purchases of a particular buyer will be most significant in giving it bargaining leverage when the seller has high fixed costs.

They lack qualified alternative sources. If the particular buyers' needs are such that there are few alternative products that will meet them satisfactorily, their bargaining leverage is limited. For example, if the buyer needs an unusually high-precision part because of the design of the final product, there may be few sellers that can supply it. A good buyer, using this criterion, is one who has a need for features of the particular seller's product or service that are unique. Qualified alternative sources can also be limited by needs for extensive testing or field trials to insure seller compliance with needed specifications, such as is common in telecommunications equipment.

They face high shopping, transactions, or negotiating costs. Buyers who face particular difficulties in securing alternative quotes, negotiating, or conducting transactions generally have less intrinsic power. The cost to them of finding a new brand or new supplier is great, and they are forced to stick with their existing ones. For example, buyers located in isolated geographic areas may have such difficulties.

They lack a credible threat of backward integration. Buyers who are in a poor position to backward integrate lose an important bargaining lever. The buyers of a product usually differ greatly in this ability. For example, of the numerous purchases of sulfuric acid, only the large users, who are fertilizer manufacturers or oil companies, are really in this position. The other buyers of sulfuric acid have less bargaining leverage. The factors that determine the feasibility of backward integration by a particular buyer are discussed in Chapter 14, "The Strategic Analysis of Vertical Integration."

They face high fixed costs of switching suppliers. Some buyers will face particularly high switching costs because of their situations. For example, they may have tied the specifications of their product to that of a particular supplier or made heavy investments in learning how to use a particular supplier's equipment.

The major sources of switching costs are as follows:

- costs of modifying products to match a new supplier's product;
- costs of testing or certifying a new supplier's product to insure substitutability;
- investments in retraining employees;
- investments required in new ancillary equipment that is necessary to use a new supplier's products (tools, test equipment, etc.);
- cost of establishing new logistical arrangements;
- psychic costs of severing a relationship.

Any of these can be higher for particular buyers than for others.

Switching costs may also afflict the seller, who may have to bear fixed costs of changing buyers. Switching costs facing sellers yield bargaining power to buyers.

PRICE SENSITIVITY OF BUYERS

Individual buyers can also differ greatly in their propensity to exercise whatever bargaining power they have in bargaining down seller margins. Buyers who are not price sensitive at all, or who are willing to trade price for performance characteristics of the product, are usually good buyers. Once again the conditions determining the price sensitivity of individual buyers are similar to those determining the price sensitivity of the buyer group as a whole, presented in Chapter 1, with a number of extensions.

Buyers who are *not* sensitive to price tend to fall into one or more of the following categories:

The cost of the product is a small part of the cost of the buyer's product cost and/or purchasing budget. If the product is a relatively low-cost item, the perceived benefits of price shopping and bargaining tend to be low. Note that the relevant cost is the total cost of the product per period, not the unit cost. Unit costs may be low, but the number of units purchased may make the item very important. The efforts of the consumer or purchasing agent, whichever is applicable, will tend to be directed toward the higher-cost items. For industrial buyers, this often means that senior, specialist purchasing agents and company executives buy high-cost items, and more junior, generalist purchasing agents handle all the low-cost items as a group. For consumer buyers, a low-cost item does not justify the high costs of shopping and product comparison. As a result, convenience may be a major motive in purchase, and purchase will be based on less "objective" criteria.

The penalty for product failure is high relative to its cost. If a product that fails or does not meet expectations causes the particular buyer to pay a substantial penalty, then the buyer will tend not to be price sensitive. The buyer will be much more concerned about quality, willing to pay a premium for it, and will tend to stick with products that have proven themselves in the past. A good example of this product characteristic is found in the electrical products industry. Here electrical controls sold to buyers for use in production machines may encounter lower price sensitivity than controls sold to buyers using them for more mundane applications. Failure of the controls for a piece of expensive production equipment can idle it as well as a number of workers, if not an entire production line. Products sold to buyers who will use them in interrelated systems may also imply particularly high failure costs, because failure of the product may bring the whole system down.

Effectiveness of the product (or service) can yield major savings or improvement in performance. Turning the previous condition around, if the product or service can save the buyer time and money if it performs well or can improve the performance of the buyer's product, then the buyer will tend to be insensitive to price. For example, an investment banker's or consultant's services can produce major savings through accurate pricing of stock issues, valuation of acquisition candidates or approaches to solving company problems. Buyers with particularly difficult pricing decisions, or with high stakes in solving problems, will tend to be willing to pay a premium for the very best advice. Another example is provided by the "logging" of oil fields. Companies like Schlumberger use sophisticated electronic techniques to detect the probable presence of oil in rock formations. Accurate readings can yield major savings in drilling costs, and oil drilling companies happily pay high fees for this service, particularly the companies that face very difficult and costly wells because of great depth or offshore location. Related to savings like these are savings to the buyer from timely delivery, rapid product servicing in the event of breakdowns, and many others. Some buyers are willing to pay premiums to companies that can perform well in areas such as these. Products that can yield the buyer improvements in performance include such things as prescription drugs and electronic equipment.

The buyer competes with a high-quality strategy to which the purchased product is perceived to contribute. Those buyers competing with a high-quality strategy are often quite sensitive about the inputs they purchase. If they perceive that the input enhances the performance of their product or if the brand of the input carries prestige value which will reinforce their high-quality strategy, they will tend to be insensitive to the price of inputs. For these reasons manufacturers of costly machinery often will pay a premium for electric motors or generators made by the prestige supplier.

The buyer seeks a custom designed or differentiated variety. If the buyer wants a specially designed product, then this desire is often (though not always) accompanied by the willingness to pay a premium price for it. This situation can lock the buyer into a particular supplier or suppliers, and it may be willing to pay a premium to keep those suppliers happy. Such buyers may also believe that such extra effort deserves compensation. A good example of a company built on such a strategy is Illinois Tool Works, who goes to elaborate lengths to custom design its fasteners to specific customer's needs. This policy has led to high margins and great customer loyalty.

A buyer with high intrinsic bargaining power, however, may demand unique or custom products but not be willing to pay extra for them. Serving these buyers puts the seller in the worst of situations, because it elevates costs without elevating margins.

The buyer is very profitable and/or can readily pass on the cost of inputs. Highly profitable buyers tend to be less price sensitive than those in marginal financial condition, unless the purchased product is a major cost item. Some of this attitude may be based on the fact that the highly profitable buyers fall into one of the categories listed above, and part may be attributable to a higher propensity to assure the seller a fair return. Although it could be argued that highly profitable buyers are that way because they are good bargainers, in practice it seems that the priorities of such buyers are placed less on aggressive bargaining over price and more in other areas.

The buyer is poorly informed about the product and/or does not purchase from well-defined specifications. Buyers who are poorly informed about the cost of an input, demand conditions, or criteria on which alternative brands should be evaluated tend to be less price sensitive than very well-informed buyers. If buyers are very well informed about the state of demand and suppliers' costs, on the other hand, they can be ruthless price bargainers. This is the case with many large purchasers of commodities. Poorly informed buyers, however, tend to be swayed by subjective factors and to be less certain about squeezing suppliers' margins. However, the buyer must not be so poorly informed as to not recognize that competing products differ.

The motivation of the actual decision maker is not narrowly defined as the cost of inputs. The price sensitivity of the buyer depends in part on the motivation of the actual purchaser or decision maker in the buyer's organization, which can vary a great deal from buyer to buyer. For example, purchasing agents are often rewarded for cost savings, which makes them very narrowly price oriented, whereas plant managers may have a longer-run outlook based on plant productivity.[1] Depending on the size of the company and many other factors, a purchasing agent, plant manager, or even senior executive may be the actual decision maker. In consumer goods, different members of the family may be the decision maker for different products. Different consumers can have different motivation systems. The more the decision maker's motivation is not narrowly defined as minimizing the cost of inputs, the less price sensitive the buyer is likely to be.

---

[1]For a discussion of this point see Corey (1976).

The factors promoting price insensitivity can work jointly. For example, most buyers of Letraset, a high-speed transfer process for lettering artwork and drawings, are architects and commercial artists. For them the cost of the lettering is small compared to the cost of their time, and attractive lettering reflects strongly on the overall impression left by design work they have done. Architects and artists are most concerned with instant availability of a large selection of different lettering styles. As a result, buyers of Letraset tend to be extremely price insensitive and have allowed Letraset to earn very high margins.

The factors discussed above also mean that *large buyers are not necessarily the most price sensitive*. For example, large buyers of construction machinery use their equipment heavily and generally purchase a wide line of machines, preferring to deal with one supplier. A single supplier allows them to take advantage of parts interchangeability and interacting with a single service organization. They are willing to pay a premium for a reliable line of machines, so that they can be kept intensively utilized, and for products whose service costs are low. Small contractors, on the other hand, only purchase a few types of construction machinery and often use them less intensively. They are much more sensitive about purchase price since the cost of equipment is a major cost item to them.

COSTS OF SERVING BUYERS

The costs of serving different buyers of a product can vary greatly, usually for one of the following reasons:

- order size;
- selling direct versus through distributors;
- required lead time;
- steadiness of order flow for purposes of planning and logistics;
- shipping cost;
- selling cost;
- need for customization or modification;

Many of the costs of serving buyers can be hidden, and some are quite subtle. They can be obscured by overhead allocation. Usually to ascertain the cost of serving different types of buyers a firm must do a special study, because data in sufficient detail are rarely a part of normal operating statements.

BUYER SELECTION AND STRATEGY

The notion that buyers differ along the four dimensions previously discussed means that the choice of buyers can be a critical strategic variable. Not all firms have the luxury of selecting their buyers, and not all industries have buyers that differ significantly along these dimensions. In many cases, however, the option of buyer selection is present.

The basic strategic principle in buyer selection is to *seek out and attempt to sell to the most favorable buyers* available based on the criteria outlined above. As was noted earlier, the four criteria may yield conflicting implications for the attractiveness of a particular buyer. The buyer with the most growth potential may also have the most power and be the most price sensitive, for example. Thus the choice of the best buyer must balance all four criteria against the capabilities of the firm relative to its competitors.

Different firms will be in differing positions to select buyers. A firm with high product differentiation may be able to sell to good buyers that are unavailable to many of its competitors, for example. The intrinsic power of buyers may also vary for different firms. A very large firm or one with unique product variety may be less affected by the size of the buyer than a smaller firm, to cite just one possibility. Finally, firms have differing capabilities with respect to serving particular buyers' needs. Thus the *most favorable buyers to sell to will depend on the position of the individual firm* in some respects.

There are a number of other strategic implications of buyer selection:

The firm with a low-cost position can sell to powerful, price-sensitive buyers and still be successful. If a firm is the low-cost producer, no matter how powerful or price sensitive the buyer the firm will be able to earn above-average margins for its industry, because the seller can meet the prices of its competitors and still earn better returns than they do. But there is an element of circularity in this statement in some businesses. The seller may sometimes have to sell to "lousy" buyers if it is to achieve a cost advantage because it needs the volume.

The firm without a cost advantage or differentiation must be selective about its buyers if it desires an above-average return. Without a cost advantage, the firm must focus its efforts on buyers who are less price sensitive if it is to outperform the industry average. This requirement may mean that such a firm must deliberately give up sales volume in order to maintain such a focus. Without a cost advantage, building volume for its own sake is self-defeating because it exposes the firm to less and less favorable buyers. This principle reinforces the notion of generic strategies described in Chapter 2. If the firm cannot achieve cost leadership, it must be careful not to become stuck in the middle by selling to powerful buyers.

Good buyers can be created (or the quality of buyers improved) through strategy. Some of the characteristics of buyers that make them favorable can be influenced by the firm. For example, one important strategy is to *build up switching costs*—by persuading the customer to design the firm's product into his product, by developing custom varieties, by assistance in training of customer personnel to use the firm's product, and so on. Furthermore, clever selling can *shift the decision maker* for the product from an individual who is price sensitive to one who is less price sensitive. The product or service can be improved to yield potential savings to particular types of buyers; and many other actions can be taken to improve the quality of the buyer from the firm's point of view, by affecting the characteristics of good buyers previously identified.

This analysis suggests that one way in which the formulation of strategy can be viewed is to create favorable buyers. It is obviously better, as a matter of strategy, to create good buyers that are locked into the particular firm rather than to create ones that will be good buyers for any competitor.

The basis of buyers' choice can be broadened. An approach to creating good buyers which is so important as to warrant separate discussion is broadening the basis of buyers' choice. Ideally, the basis can be shifted away from purchase price and in directions where the firm has some distinctive abilities or where switching costs can be created.

There are two fundamental ways to broaden buyers' choice. The first is to *increase the value added* the firm provides to the buyer,[2] which involves such tactics as

- providing responsive customer service;
- providing engineering assistance;
- providing credit or rapid delivery;
- creating new features of the product.

[2]Theodore Levitt would term this selling the buyer an "augmented" product; see Levitt (1969).

The notion here is simple. Increasing value added broadens the attributes on which choice is potentially based. It may allow the transformation of a product which is a commodity itself to one that can be differentiated.

A distinct but related way to broaden the basis of buyers' choice is to redefine the way the buyer *thinks* about the product's function, even if the product and service offering itself is the same. Here the buyer is shown that the cost or value of the product to him is not only the initial purchase price but involves such additional factors as[3]

- resale value;
- maintenance cost and downtime over the product's life;
- fuel cost;
- revenue generating capacity;
- cost of installation or attachment.

If the buyer can be convinced that such factors as these enter into the actual total cost or value of the product, then the firm has the potential opportunity of demonstrating that its product has superior performance along these dimensions and thereby justifies a price premium and buyer loyalty. Of course, the firm must be able to deliver on its promises of superiority, and its claims must be to some extent distinctive vis-à-vis its competitors or the potential higher margins will soon be eroded. Widening the basis of buyers' choice requires a combination of effective marketing on this basis and product development that supports the story convincingly. General Electric has practiced this strategy very successfully for decades in the large turbine generator industry.

High-cost buyers can be eliminated. A commonly used strategy to boost return on investment is to eliminate the high-cost buyers from the customer base. This tactic can often be quite effective since there is a common tendency to proliferate marginal customers, particularly in the growth phase of an industry's development. Eliminating high cost buyers is also often fruitful since the costs of serving individual buyers are rarely studied. However, it is crucial to recognize that there are other aspects to the desirability of buyers than merely their costs of servicing. High-cost buyers can be very price insensitive, for example, and amenable to price increases that more

[3]This notion has been carefully developed by McKinsey and Company in the notion of the "economic value to the customer." See Forbus and Mehta (1979).

than cover the cost of serving them once the true cost of serving them has been ascertained. Or high-cost buyers may offer significant contributions to a firm's growth which can be essential in reaping economies of scale or necessary for other strategic purposes. Thus a decision to eliminate high-cost customers should involve a study of all four elements of buyer attractiveness.

The quality of buyers can change over time. Many of the factors determining a buyer's quality can change. As an industry matures, for example, buyers tend to become more price sensitive in many businesses because their own margins are squeezed and they are more expert purchasers. From a strategic standpoint, then, it is important not to base a strategy on selling to buyers whose quality will erode. Conversely, early recognition of a buyer group that is likely to become particularly favorable represents a major strategic opportunity. Penetrating such buyers early may be easy if they have low switching costs and few other competitors are interested. Once in the door, switching costs can be elevated through strategy.

Switching costs should be considered in making strategic moves. In view of the potential importance of switching costs, the impact of all strategic moves on switching costs should be considered. For example, the presence of switching costs means that it is often much cheaper for a customer to upgrade or augment an already purchased product then replace it altogether with another brand. This consideration may allow the firm with units already in place to earn very high margins on upgrading, as long as upgrading is priced properly in relation to the cost of competitors' new units.

Purchasing Strategy

The analysis of suppliers' power in Chapter 1 coupled with a reverse application of the principles of buyer selection can help a firm in formulating purchasing strategy. Although there are many aspects of purchasing strategy, procedures, and organization that go well beyond the scope of this book, some issues can be usefully examined by using the industry structure framework. Key issues in purchasing strategy from a structural standpoint are as follows:

- stability and competitiveness of the supplier pool;
- optimal degree of vertical integration;

- allocation of purchases among qualified suppliers;
- creation of maximum leverage with chosen suppliers.

The first issue is the stability and competitiveness of suppliers. From a strategic point of view, it is desirable to purchase from suppliers who will maintain or improve their competitive position in terms of their products and services. This factor insures that the firm will purchase inputs of adequate or superior quality/cost to insure its own competitiveness. Similarly, selecting suppliers who will continue to be able to meet the firm's needs will minimize the costs of changing suppliers. Structural and competitor analysis, discussed throughout this book, can be used to identify how a firm's suppliers will fare along these dimensions.

The second issue, vertical integration, will be postponed until Chapter 14, which examines the strategic considerations in decisions to integrate vertically. Here I assume that the firm has decided what items to purchase outside, and the question is *how to purchase them* so as to create the best structural bargaining position.

In allocating purchases among suppliers and creating bargaining power, the third and fourth issues, we can turn to structural analysis. In Chapter 1, the following conditions were identified as leading to powerful suppliers of a particular input:

- concentration of suppliers;
- lack of dependence on the customer for a substantial fraction of sales;
- switching costs facing the customer;
- a unique or differentiated product (few alternative sources);
- threat of forward integration.

The analysis of buyer selection earlier in this chapter added a number of other conditions in which the supplier will hold the power vis-à-vis the buyer:

- buyer lacks a credible threat of backward integration;
- buyer faces high information, shopping, or negotiating costs.

In purchasing, then, the goal is to find mechanisms to offset or surmount these sources of suppliers' power. In some cases this power is built into industry economics and is out of the firm's control. In many cases, however, it can be mitigated by strategy.

Spread Purchases. Purchases of an item can be spread among alternate suppliers in such a way as to improve the firm's bargaining position. The business given to each individual supplier must be large enough to cause the supplier concern over losing it—spreading purchases too widely does not take advantage of structural bargaining position. However, purchasing everything from one supplier may yield that supplier too much of an opportunity to exercise power or build switching costs. Cutting across these considerations is the purchaser's ability to negotiate volume discounts, which is partly a matter of bargaining power and partly a matter of supplier economics. Balancing these factors, the purchaser should seek to create as much supplier dependence on its business as possible and reap the maximum volume discounts without exposing itself to too great a risk of falling prey to switching costs.

Avoid Switching Costs. Good purchasing strategy, from a structural standpoint, involves the avoidance of switching costs. The common sources of switching costs have been identified earlier, and other subtle areas exist as well. Avoiding switching costs means resisting the temptation to become too dependent on a supplier for engineering assistance; insuring that employees are not coopted; avoiding suppliers' efforts to create a custom-variety or custom-engineered application without a clear cost justification that outweighs possible future exercise of leverage; and so on. This policy may involve deliberately requiring that an alternate supplier's product is used some of the time, disapproving investments in ancillary equipment that are tied to a particular supplier, and resisting supplier products that involve specialized training procedures for employees, among other things.

Help Qualify Alternate Sources. It may be necessary to encourage alternate sources to enter the business, through funding development contracts and contracts for a small part of purchases. Some purchasers have actually helped capitalize new sources or gone overseas to persuade foreign firms to come into the business. It may also be desirable to help new suppliers minimize their costs of becoming qualified sources. Mechanisms range from extreme attentiveness to finding new suppliers by the purchasing staff to subsidizing the cost of testing new suppliers' products.

Promote Standardization. All firms in an industry may be well served by promoting standardization of specifications in the industries from which they purchase inputs. This policy helps reduce suppliers' product differentiation and undercuts the erection of switching costs.

Create a Threat of Backward Integration.   Whether or not the purchaser actually desires to backward integrate into an item, its bargaining position is helped by the presence of a credible threat. This threat can be created through statements, leaked word of internal studies of the feasibility of integration, creation of contingency plans for integration with consultants or engineering firms, and so on.

Use of Tapered Integration.   When the volume of purchases allow it, a great deal of bargaining leverage can be gained through tapered integration, or partial integration into a particular item while buying some or even the majority of it from outside suppliers. This process was briefly discussed in Chapter 1 and will be examined further in Chapter 14.

The objective of all these approaches is obviously to lower the total long-run costs of purchasing. It should be recognized that using some of them may actually raise *some* aspects of narrowly defined purchasing cost. For example, maintaining alternative sources or fighting against switching costs can involve expenses that could be avoided in the short run. However, the ultimate purpose of such expenses is to improve the bargaining position of the firm and hence its long-run input costs.

A number of points emerge. First, it is important to avoid the situation in which too narrow a short-run cost-cutting orientation undermines potentially valuable purchasing strategies like those outlined above. Second, any additional costs created by such a purchasing strategy must be weighed against its long-run benefits in mitigating suppliers' bargaining power. Finally, since the cost of purchasing from different suppliers can vary, the firm should purchase from low-cost suppliers unless there are offsetting benefits in terms of long-run bargaining power.

7
Structural Analysis Within Industries

The structural analysis of an industry in Chapter 1 is based on the identification of the sources and strength of the five broad competitive forces that determine the nature of competition in the industry and its underlying profit potential. The focus of the analysis so far has been on the industry as a whole, and at this level the analysis raises numerous implications for competitive strategy. Some of these have been described in previous chapters. It is clear, however, that industry structural analysis can be used at greater depth than the industry as a whole. In many if not most industries, there are firms that have adopted very different competitive strategies, along such dimensions as breadth of product line, degree of vertical integration, and so on, and have achieved differing levels of market share. Also, some firms persistently outperform others in terms of rate of return on invested capital. IBM's return has consistently exceeded that of other mainframe computer manufacturers,[1] for example. General

[1] IBM's average rate of return on equity capital for the years 1970-75 was 19.4 percent, despite a large pool of unused cash, compared to 13.7 percent for Burroughs, 9.3 percent for Honeywell, and 4.7 percent for Control Data. See the January issue of *Forbes* annually for this and other profitability comparisons.

Motors has persistently outperformed Ford, Chrysler, and AMC. In other industries, smaller firms such as Crown Cork and Seal and National Can in the metal can industry, and Estee Lauder in cosmetics outperform larger ones.

The five broad competitive forces provide a context in which all firms in an industry compete. But we must explain why some firms are persistently more profitable than others and how this relates to their strategic postures. We must also understand how firms' differing competencies in marketing, cost cutting, management, organization, and so on relate to their strategic postures and to their ultimate performance.

This chapter will extend the concepts of structural analysis to explain differences in the performance of firms in the same industry, at the same time providing a framework for guiding the choice of competitive strategy. It will also build on and amplify the notion of generic strategies described in Chapter 2. Structural analysis *within* industries, as well as applied to industries as a whole, will prove to be a useful analytical tool in strategy formulation.

Dimensions of Competitive Strategy

Companies' strategies for competing in an industry can differ in a wide variety of ways. However, the following strategic dimensions usually capture the possible differences among a company's strategic options in a given industry:

- *specialization*: the degree to which it focuses its efforts in terms of the width of its line, the target customer segments, and the geographic markets served;
- *brand identification*: the degree to which it seeks brand identification rather than competition based mainly on price or other variables. Brand identification can be achieved via advertising, sales force, or a variety of other means;
- *push versus pull*: the degree to which it seeks to develop brand identification with the ultimate consumer directly versus the support of distribution channels in selling its product;
- *channel selection*: the choice of distribution channels ranging from company-owned channels to specialty outlets to broad-line outlets;

- *product quality*: its level of product quality, in terms of raw materials, specifications, adherence to tolerances, features, and so on;
- *technological leadership*: the degree to which it seeks technological leadership versus following or imitation. It is important to note that a firm could be a technological leader but deliberately not produce the highest quality product in the market; quality and technological leadership do not necessarily go together;
- *vertical integration*: the extent of value added as reflected in the level of forward and backward integration adopted, including whether the firm has captive distribution, exclusive or owned retail outlets, an in-house service network, and so on;
- *cost position*: the extent to which it seeks the low-cost position in manufacturing and distribution through investment in cost-minimizing facilities and equipment;
- *service*: the degree to which it provides ancillary services with its product line, such as engineering assistance, an in-house service network, credit, and so forth. This aspect of strategy could be viewed as part of vertical integration but is usefully separated for analytical purposes;
- *price policy*: its relative price position in the market. Price position will usually be related to such other variables as cost position and product quality, but price is a distinct strategic variable that must be treated separately;
- *leverage*: the amount of financial leverage and operating leverage it bears;
- *relationship with parent company*: requirements on the behavior of the unit based on the relationship between a unit and its parent company. The firm could be a unit of a highly diversified conglomerate, one of a vertical chain of businesses, part of a cluster of related businesses in a general sector, a subsidiary of a foreign company, and so on. The nature of the relationship with the parent will influence the objectives with which the firm is managed, the resources available to it, and perhaps determine some operations or functions that it shares with other units (with resulting cost implications), as has been discussed in Chapter 1;
- *relationship to home and host government*: in international industries, the relationship the firm has developed or is sub-

ject to with its home government as well as host governments in foreign countries where it is operating. Home governments can provide resources or other assistance to the firm, or conversely can regulate the firm or otherwise influence its goals. Host governments often play similar roles.

Each of these strategic dimensions can be described for a firm at differing levels of detail, and other dimensions might be added to refine the analysis; the important thing is that these dimensions provide an overall picture of the firm's position.

The scope for strategic differences along a particular dimension clearly depends on the industry. For example, in a commodity business like ammonium fertilizer, no firm has much brand identification and product quality is essentially uniform. Yet firms differ widely in backward integration, the degree to which they provide service, integration forward into dealerships, relative cost positions, and relationships to their parents.

The strategic dimensions are related. A firm with a low relative price (such as Texas Instruments in semiconductors) usually has a low-cost position and good though not superior product quality. To achieve its low costs such a firm probably has a high degree of vertical integration. The strategic dimensions for a particular firm usually form an internally consistent set, as in this example. An industry normally has firms with a number of different though internally consistent combinations of dimensions.

Strategic Groups

The first step in structural analysis within industries is to characterize the strategies of all significant competitors along these dimensions. This activity then allows for the mapping of the industry into *strategic groups*. A strategic group is the group of firms in an industry following the same or a similar strategy along the strategic dimensions. An industry could have only one strategic group if all the firms followed essentially the same strategy. At the other extreme, each firm could be a different strategic group. Usually, however, there are a small number of strategic groups which capture the essential strategic differences among firms in the industry. For example, in the major appliance industry one strategic group (with GE as the prototype) is characterized by broad product lines, heavy national advertising, extensive integration, and captive distribution and service. Another group consists of specialist producers like Maytag focusing on the high-quality, high-price segment with selective distribution. Another group (like Roper and Design and Manufacturing) produces unadvertised products for private label. One or two additional groups might be identified as well.

Note that for purposes of defining strategic groups, the strategic dimensions must include the firm's relationship to its parent. In an industry like ammonium fertilizer, for example, some firms are divisions of oil companies, some are divisions of chemical companies, some are parts of farmers' cooperatives, and the rest are independents. Each of these different types of firms is managed with somewhat differing objectives. Often relationships to the parent also translate into differences in the other dimensions of strategy—for example, all the divisions of oil companies in nitrogen fertilizer have quite similar strategies—because the relationship has a lot to do with the resources and other strengths available to the firm and the philosophy with which it is operated. The same sorts of arguments apply to the differing relationships firms may have with their home and/or host goverments, which also must be part of defining strategic groups.

Strategic groups often differ in their product or marketing approach, but not always. Sometimes, as in corn milling and the manufacture of chemicals or sugar, groups' products are identical but manufacturing, logistics, and vertical integration approaches differ. Or firms might be following strategies but have differing relationships to parent companies or host governments that affect their objectives. Strategic groups are *not* equivalent to market segments or segmentation strategies but are defined on the basis of a broader conception of strategic posture.

Strategic groups are present for a wide variety of reasons, such as firms' differing initial strengths and weaknesses, differing times of entry into the business, and historical accidents. (I will have more to say on this subject later in this chapter.) However, once groups have formed, the firms in the same strategic group generally resemble one another closely in many ways besides their broad strategies. They tend to have similar market shares and also to be affected by and respond similarly to external events or competitive moves in the industry because of their similar strategies. This latter characteristic is important in using a strategic group map as an analytical tool.

The strategic groups in an industry can be displayed on a map like the hypothetical one shown in Figure 7-1. The number of axes are obviously limited by the two-dimensional character of a printed page, which means that the analyst must select a few particularly important strategic dimensions along which to construct a map.[2] It is

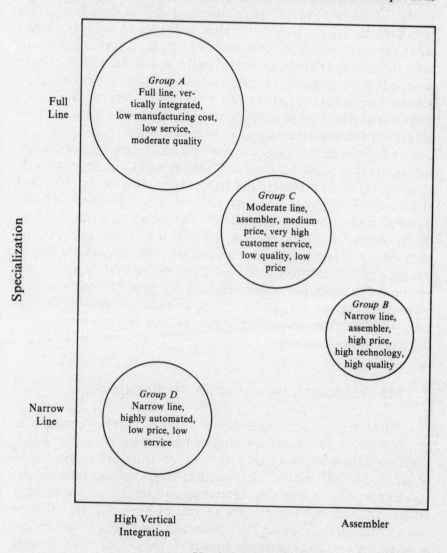

FIGURE 7-1. A Map of Strategic Groups in a Hypothetical Industry

[2]The concepts discussed below will aid in the process of doing so.

useful to represent the collective market share of the firms in each strategic group with the size of symbols for subsequent analysis.

The strategic group is an analytical device designed to aid in structural analysis. It is an intermediate frame of reference between looking at the industry as a whole and considering each firm separately. Ultimately every firm is unique, and thus classifying firms into strategic groups inevitably raises questions of judgment about what degree of strategic difference is important. These judgments must necessarily relate to structural analysis: a difference in strategy among firms is important enough to recognize in defining strategic groups if it significantly affects the structural position of the firms. I will return later to these practical considerations of mapping strategic groups and using the map as an analytical tool.

In the rare case of only one strategic group existing in an industry, the industry can be analyzed fully by using the techniques of structural analysis presented in Chapter 1. In this case the industry's structure will yield the same potential level of sustainable profitability to all firms. The actual profitability of particular firms in the industry should differ in the long run only insofar as they differ in their *ability to implement* the common strategy. If there are several strategic groups in an industry, however, the analysis is more complicated. The profit potential of firms in different strategic groups is often different, quite apart from their implementation abilities, because the five broad competitive forces will *not have equal impact on different strategic groups*.

STRATEGIC GROUPS AND MOBILITY BARRIERS

Entry barriers have been viewed so far as industry characteristics that deter new firms from coming into the industry. The major sources of entry barriers that have been identified are economies of scale, product differentiation, switching costs, cost advantages, access to distribution channels, capital requirements, and government policy. Yet although some of the sources of entry barriers will protect all firms in the industry, it is clear that overall *entry barriers depend on the particular strategic group that the entrant seeks to join*. Entering the appliance industry as a nationally branded, broad-line, vertically integrated firm will be a great deal more difficult than entering as an assembler of a narrow line of unbranded goods for small private label accounts. Differences in strategy may imply differences in product differentiation, differences in the achievement of economies of scale, differences in capital requirements, and potential differences in all the other sources of entry barriers. If barriers caused by production economies of scale exist, for example, they will be most significant in protecting the strategic group consisting of firms with large plants and extensive vertical integration. Economies of scale in distribution, if they exist in the industry, will create barriers to entry into strategic groups with captive distribution organizations. Cost advantages from accumulated experience, if they are important in the industry, create barriers protecting the groups consisting of experienced firms (although not inexperienced ones). And so on for each other source of entry barriers.

Differences in firms' relations to their parents may affect entry barriers as well. The strategic group including those firms that have a vertical relationship to their parents, for example, may enjoy superior access to raw materials or larger financial resources with which to retaliate against potential entrants than a strategic group consisting of independent competitors. Or firms who share distribution channels with another division of their parent company may reap economies of scale that their competitors cannot match, thereby deterring entry.

This view that entry barriers depend on the target strategic group carries another important implication. Entry barriers not only protect firms in a strategic group from entry by firms outside the industry but also provide *barriers to shifting strategic position from one strategic group to another*. For example, the narrow-line, unbranded appliance assembler described earlier will face many if not most of the same difficulties in entering the strategic group consisting of the broad-line, nationally branded, integrated firms as would an entirely new entrant. Factors creating entry barriers that result from competing with a particular strategy—because they affect economies of scale, product differentiation, switching costs, capital requirements, absolute cost advantages, or access to distribution—elevate the cost to other firms of adopting that strategy. This cost of adopting the new strategy can eliminate the expected gains from the change.

The same underlying economic factors leading to entry barriers can thus be framed more generally as *mobility barriers*, or factors that deter the movement of firms from one strategic position to another. The movement of a firm from a position outside the industry to a strategic group in the industry (entry) becomes one of a continuum of possibilities, using this broader concept of barriers.

Mobility barriers provide the first major reason why some firms in an industry will be persistently more profitable than others. Different strategic groups carry with them different levels of mobility barriers, which provide some firms with persistent advantages over others. The firms in strategic groups with high mobility barriers will have greater profit potential than those in groups with lower mobility barriers. These barriers also provide a rationale for why firms continue to compete with different strategies despite the fact that all strategies are not equally successful. One asks oneself why successful strategies are not quickly imitated. Without mobility barriers, firms with successful strategies would be quickly imitated by others, and firms' profitability would tend toward equality except for differences in their abilities to execute the best strategy in an operational sense. Without deterrents, for example, computer manufacturers like Control Data and Honeywell would jump at the chance to adopt IBM's strategy, with its lower costs and superior service and distribution network. The existence of mobility barriers means that some firms like IBM can enjoy systematic advantages over others, through economies of scale, absolute cost advantages, and so on, which can be overcome only by strategic breakthroughs that lead to structural change in the industry, and not merely through better execution. Finally, the presence of mobility barriers means that market shares of firms in some strategic groups in an industry can be very stable, and yet there can be rapid entry and exit (or turnover) in other strategic groups in the industry.

Just like entry barriers, mobility barriers can change; and as they do (such as if the manufacturing process becomes more capital intensive) firms often abandon some strategic groups and jump into new ones, changing the pattern of strategic groups. Mobility barriers can also be influenced by firm choices of strategy. A company in an undifferentiated product industry, for example, can attempt to create a new strategic group (with higher mobility barriers) by investing heavily in advertising to develop brand identification (like Perdue is doing in fresh chicken). Or it can try to introduce a new manufacturing process with greater economies of scale (Castle & Cooke and Ralston Purina in mushroom farming).[3] Investments in building mo-

---

[3] See "Mushrooming Business," *Forbes*, July 15, 1977.

bility barriers are generally risky, however, and to some extent trade short-term profitability for long-term profitability.

Some firms will face lower costs than others in overcoming particular mobility barriers depending on their existing strategic positions and their inventory of skills and resources. Diversified firms can also enjoy reductions in mobility barriers because of opportunities for sharing operations or functions. The implications of these factors for decisions to enter new businesses will be discussed in Chapter 16.

After mapping the strategic groups in an industry, the second step in structural analysis within an industry is to assess the height and composition of the mobility barriers protecting each group.

MOBILITY BARRIERS AND GROUP FORMATION

Strategic groups form and change in an industry for a variety of reasons. First, firms often begin with or later develop differences in skills or resources, and thus select different strategies. The well-situated firms outdistance others in the race toward the strategic groups protected by high mobility barriers as the industry develops. Second, firms differ in their goals or risk posture. Some firms may be more prone to making risky investments in building mobility barriers than others. Business units that differ in their relationship to a parent company (e.g., being vertically related, unrelated, or a free-standing firm) may differ in goals in ways that will lead to differences in strategy, as may international competitors with different situations in their other markets than domestic firms.

The historical development of an industry provides another explanation for why firms differ in their strategies. In some industries, being an early entrant provides access to strategies more costly to later entrants. Mobility barriers from scale economies, product differentiation, and other causes may also change, either as a result of firm's investments or exogenous causes. Changing mobility barriers mean that early entrants into the industry may pursue very different strategies than later entrants, some of which may not be available to later entrants. The irreversibility of many forms of investment decisions sometimes precludes early entrants from adopting the strategies of the later entrants who have the advantages of hindsight.

A related point is that the process of historical evolution of an industry tends to lead to the self-selection of different types of entrants at different times. For example, later entrants into an industry may tend to be firms with increased financial resources who can afford to wait until some of the uncertainties in the industry are resolved. Firms with few resources, on the other hand, could have been compelled to enter early when capital costs of entry were low.

Changes in the structure of the industry can either facilitate the formation of new strategic groups or work to homogenize groups. For example, as an industry increases in total size, strategies involving vertical integration, captive distribution channels, and in-house servicing may become increasingly feasible for the aggressive firm, promoting the formation of new strategic groups. Similarly, technological changes or changes in buyers' behavior can shift industry boundaries, bringing entirely new strategic groups into play.[4] Conversely, maturity in an industry, which lessens the buyer's desire for service capability or for the reassurance embodied in the manufacturer having a full product line, can work to reduce the mobility barriers that accrue to some strategic dimensions, leading to a reduction in the number of strategic groups. As a consequence of all these factors, we would expect to see the array of strategic groups and the distribution of profit rates of firms within an industry change over time.

STRATEGIC GROUPS AND BARGAINING POWER

Just as different strategic groups are protected by differing mobility barriers, they enjoy differing degrees of bargaining power with suppliers or customers. If we examine the factors leading to the presence or absence of bargaining power discussed in Chapter 1, it is apparent that they relate to some extent to the strategy adopted by the particular firm. For example, concerning bargaining power with buyers, Hewlett-Packard (HP) is in a strategic group in electronic calculators emphasizing high quality and technological leadership and focusing on the sophisticated user. Although such a strategy may limit HP's potential market share, it does expose it to less price-sensitive and less powerful buyers than the firms competing with es-

---

[4]Technological or buyer changes can increase or decrease product substitutability, and hence shift relevant industry boundaries.

sentially standardized products in the mass market, where buyers have little need for sophisticated product features. Relating this example to the terminology of Chapter 1, HP's products are more differentiated than those of the mass market competitors, its buyers are more quality-oriented, and the cost of the calculator is smaller relative to the buyers' budgets and to the value of the service they want it to perform. An example where different strategic groups have differing bargaining power with suppliers is the much greater volume of purchases and threat of backward integration that large, broad-line, national department store chains like Sears have as bargaining levers with suppliers relative to local, single-unit department stores.

Strategic groups will have differing amounts of power vis-à-vis suppliers and buyers for two categories of reasons, both illustrated in the examples above: Their strategies may yield them differing degrees of vulnerability to *common* suppliers or buyers; or their strategies may involve dealing with *different* suppliers or buyers with correspondingly different levels of bargaining power. The extent to which relative power can vary depends on the industry; in some industries all strategic groups could be in essentially the same position with respect to suppliers and buyers.

The third step in structural analysis within an industry, then, is to assess the relative bargaining power of each strategic group in the industry with its suppliers and buyers.

STRATEGIC GROUPS AND THE THREAT OF SUBSTITUTES

Strategic groups may also face differing levels of exposure to competition from substitute products if they are focusing on different parts of the product line, serving different customers, operating at different levels of quality or technological sophistication, have different cost positions, and so on. Such differences may make them more or less vulnerable to substitutes even though the strategic groups are all in the same industry.

For example, a minicomputer firm focusing on business customers, selling machines complete with software to perform a wide variety of functions, will be less vulnerable to substitution from microcomputers than a firm primarily selling to industrial buyers for repetitive process-control applications. Or a mining company with a low-cost ore source may be less vulnerable to a substitute material whose advantage is solely based on price than a mining company with a high-cost ore source that has based its strategy on a high level of customer service.

Therefore, the fourth step in structural analysis within an industry is to assess the relative position of each strategic group vis-à-vis substitute products.

STRATEGIC GROUPS AND RIVALRY AMONG FIRMS

The presence of more than one strategic group in an industry has implications for industry rivalry, or competition in price, advertising, service, and other variables. Some of the structural features that determine the strength of competitive rivalry (Chapter 1) may apply to all firms in the industry and thus provide the context in which the strategic groups interact. Broadly speaking, however, the existence of multiple strategic groups usually means that the forces of competitive rivalry are not faced equally by all firms in the industry.

The first point to be made is that the presence of several strategic groups will often affect the overall level of rivalry in the industry. Their presence will generally increase rivalry because it implies greater diversity or asymmetry among firms in the industry in the sense defined in Chapter 1. Differences in strategy and external circumstances mean that firms will have differing preferences about risk taking, time horizon, price levels, quality levels, and so on. These differences will complicate the process of firms understanding each others' intentions and reacting to them, and will thus increase the likelihood of repeated outbreaks of warfare. The industry with a complicated map of strategic groups will tend to be more competitive as a whole than one with few groups. Recent research has verified this point in a number of contexts.[5]

Not all differences in strategy are equally significant in affecting industry rivalry, however, and the process of competitive rivalry is not symmetrical. Some firms are more exposed to damaging price cutting and other forms of rivalry from other strategic groups than others. Four factors determine how strongly the strategic groups in an industry will interact in competing for customers:

- the market interdependence among groups, or the extent to which their customer targets overlap;

[5]See Hunt (1972); Newman (1978); Porter (1976, Chaps. 4, 7).

- the product differentiation achieved by the groups;
- the number of strategic groups and their relative sizes;
- the strategic distance among groups, or the extent to which strategies diverge.

The most important influence on rivalry among strategic groups is their market interdependence, or the degree to which different strategic groups are competing for the same customers or competing for customers in distinctly different market segments. When strategic groups have high market interdependence, differences in strategy will lead to the most vigorous rivalry, for example, in fertilizer where the customer (the farmer) is the same for all groups. When strategic groups are targeting very different segments, their interest in and effect on each other is much less severe. As the customers they are selling to become more distinguished, the rivalry becomes more (but not the same) as if the groups were in different industries.

The second key factor influencing rivalry is the degree of product differentiation created by the groups' strategies. If divergent strategies lead to distinct and differing brand preferences by customers, then rivalry among the groups will tend to be much less than if the product offerings are seen as interchangeable.

The more numerous and more equal in size (market share) the strategic groups, the more their strategic asymmetry generally increases competitive rivalry, other things being equal. Numerous groups imply great diversity and a high probability that one group will trigger an outbreak of warfare by attacking the position of other groups through price cutting or other tactics. Conversely, if groups are greatly unequal in size—for example, one strategic group constitutes a small share of an industry and another is a very large share—their strategic differences are likely to have little impact on the way they compete with each other, since the power of the small group to affect the large groups through competitive tactics is probably low.

The final factor, strategic distance, refers to the degree to which strategies in different groups diverge in terms of the key variables, such as brand identification, cost position, and technological leadership, as well as in external circumstances, such as relationships to parents or governments. The more the strategic distance among groups, other things being equal, the more vigorous competitive skirmishing is likely to be among the firms. Firms pursuing widely different strategic approaches tend to have quite different ideas about how to compete and a difficult time understanding each others' behavior and avoiding mistaken reactions and outbreaks of warfare. In ammonium fertilizer, as an instance, oil company participants, chemical company participants, cooperatives, and independents all have very different objectives and constraints. For example, tax benefits and unusual motives have led cooperatives to expand even when overall industry conditions were poor. Oil companies did the same thing for different reasons in the 1960s.

All four factors interrelate to determine the pattern of rivalry for customers among strategic groups in an industry. For example, the most volatile situation, likely to be associated with intense competition, is the one in which several equally balanced strategic groups, each following markedly different strategies, are competing for the same basic customer. Conversely, a situation likely to be more stable (and profitable) is one in which there are only a few large strategic groups that each compete for distinct customer segments with strategies that do not differ except along a few dimensions.

A *particular* strategic group will face rivalry from other groups based on the factors just discussed. It will be most exposed to bouts of rivalry from the other strategic groups that share market interdependence. The volatility of this rivalry will depend on the other conditions identified above. A particular group will be most exposed to rivalry from other strategic groups, for example, if they compete for the same market segments with products perceived as similar, are relatively equal in size, and follow quite different strategic approaches for getting the product to market (have high strategic distance). Achieving stability will be extremely difficult for such a strategic group, and outbreaks of aggressive warfare are likely to insure a very competitive outcome for it. However, a strategic group that has a large collective share and/or targets its efforts to distinct market segments not served by other strategic groups and achieves high product differentiation is likely to be more insulated from intergroup rivalry. The secure strategic groups that are the most insulated from rivalry will only be able to maintain profitability, however, if mobility barriers protect them from shifts in strategic position by other firms.

Thus, strategic groups affect the pattern of rivalry *within* the industry. This process is illustrated schematically by the strategic group map shown in Figure 7-2, which is similar to Figure 7-1 except that the horizontal axis is the target customer segment of the strategic group in order to measure market interdependence. The vertical axis is another key dimension of strategy in the industry. The lettered symbols are strategic groups, their size proportional to the collective market share of firms in the group. The shape of the groups is used to represent their overall strategic configuration, with differences in shape representing strategic distance. Applying the analysis presented earlier, it is clear that Group *D* will be much less affected by industry rivalry than Group *A*. Group *A* competes with similarly large Groups *B* and *C*, who use very different strategies to reach the same basic customer segment. Firms in these three groups are in constant warfare. Group *D*, on the other hand, competes for a different segment and interacts most strongly in reaching this segment with Groups *E* and *F*, who are smaller and follow similar strategies (they could be viewed as "specialist" producers following the "round" strategy or close variants to it).

The fifth step in structural analysis within an industry, then, is to assess the pattern of market interdependence among strategic groups and their vulnerability to warfare initiated by other groups.

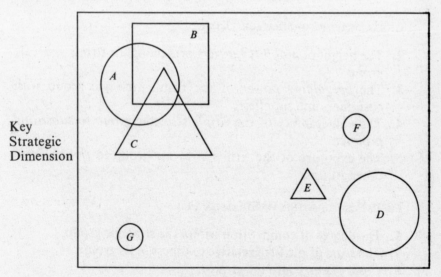

Target Customer Segment

FIGURE 7-2. Strategic Group Mapping and Intergroup Rivalry

Strategic Groups and a Firm's Profitability

We have seen that differing strategic groups can have varying situations with respect to each and every competitive force acting on an industry. We are now in a position to answer the question posed earlier; namely, what factors determine the market power and hence profit potential of individual firms in an industry, and how do these factors relate to their strategic choices?

Building on the concepts already presented, the underlying determinants of a firm's profitability are as follows:

COMMON INDUSTRY CHARACTERISTICS

1. Industry-wide elements of structure that determine the strength of the five competitive forces and that apply equally to all firms; these traits include such factors as the rate of growth of industry demand, overall potential for product differentiation, structure of supplier industries, aspects of technology, and so on, that set the overall context of competition for all firms in the industry.

CHARACTERISTICS OF STRATEGIC GROUP

2. The height of *mobility barriers* protecting the firm's strategic group.
3. The *bargaining power* of the firm's strategic group with customers and suppliers.
4. The vulnerability of the firm's strategic group to *substitute products*.
5. The exposure of the firm's strategic group to *rivalry* from other groups.

FIRM'S POSITION WITHIN ITS STRATEGIC GROUP

6. The degree of competition *within* the strategic group.
7. The *scale* of the firm relative to others in its group.
8. *Costs of entry* into the group.
9. The ability of the firm to execute or *implement* its chosen strategy in an operational sense.

Industry-wide characteristics of market structure raise or lower profit potential for all firms in the industry, but not all strategies in the industry have equal profit potential. The higher the mobility barriers protecting the strategic group, the stronger the group's bargaining position with suppliers and customers, the lower the group's vulnerability to substitute products, and the less exposed the group is to rivalry from other groups, the higher the average profit potential of firms in that group will be. Thus a second critical set of determinants of a firm's success is the position of its strategic group in the industry, which has been amplified in earlier sections.

The third category of determinants of a firm's position, which has not been discussed so far, is where the firm stands *within* its strategic group. A number of factors are crucial to this standing. First, the degree of competition within the group is important because firms in the group may compete away potential profits among themselves. This effect is more likely to occur if there are many firms in the strategic group.

Second, all firms following the same strategy are not necessarily equally positioned from a structural standpoint. Specifically, a firm's structural position may be affected by its *scale* relative to others in its strategic group. If there are any economies of scale operating that are large enough so that costs are still declining in the range of market shares held by firms in the group, then the firms that have relatively small shares will have lower profit potential. For example, although Ford and GM have relatively similar strategies and could be classified in the same strategic group, GM's greater scale allows it to reap some of the economies inherent in the strategy that Ford cannot, such as in research and development and model changeover costs. Firms like Ford have overcome scale-related mobility barriers and gotten into the strategic group, but they still face some cost disadvantages relative to a larger firm in the group.

The firm's position in its strategic group also depends on its *cost of entering* the group. The skills and resources available to the firm in entering a group may give it an advantage or disadvantage relative to others in the group. Some of these skills or resources for entry are based on the firm's position in other industries or its previous success in other strategic groups in the same industry. For example, John Deere could get into almost any strategic group in the construction equipment industry more cheaply than most firms because of its strong position in farm equipment. Or Procter and Gamble's Charmin could enter the national brand toilet tissue group more cheaply because of the combination of Charmin's past technological accomplishments coupled with Procter and Gamble's distribution strength.

The costs of entry into a group can be affected by the firm's *timing of entry* into it. In some industries it may be more expensive for late entrants into a strategic group to establish their position (e.g., higher cost of establishing an equivalent brand name; higher cost of finding good distribution channels because of foreclosure of channels by other firms). Or the situation may be reversed if newer entrants can purchase the latest equipment or use new technology. Differences in timing of entry may also translate into differences in cumulative experience and hence costs. Thus differences in timing of entry may translate into differences in sustainable profitability among members of the same strategic group.

The final factor entering into the analysis of a firm's position in its strategic group is its implementation ability. Not all firms pursuing the same strategy (thus in the same strategic group) will necessarily be equally profitable even if the other conditions that have been described are identical. Some firms are superior in their ability to organize and manage operations, develop creative advertising themes with equal budgets, make technological breakthroughs with the same expenditures on R&D, and so on. These sorts of skills are not structural advantages of the sort created by mobility barriers and the other factors discussed above, but they may well be relatively stable advantages. The firms that have superior implementation ability will be more profitable than other firms in the strategic group.

This cascading array of factors jointly determine the profit prospects of the individual firm, and at the same time, its prospects for market share. The firm will be most profitable if it is in a favorable industry, a favorable strategic group within that industry, and has a strong position in its group. New entrants do not eliminate the attractiveness of the industry because of entry barriers; the attractiveness of a strategic group is preserved by mobility barriers. The strength of a firm's position in its group is the result of its history and the skills and resources available to it.

This analysis makes it clear that *there are many different kinds of potentially profitable strategies*. Successful strategies can be based on a wide variety of mobility barriers or approaches to dealing with the competitive forces. The three generic strategies described in Chapter 2 represent the broadest difference in approach; many variations of these are possible. Much stress has recently been placed on cost position as *the* determinant of strategic position. Although cost is one approach to developing barriers, it should be clear that there are many others.

In view of the interacting nature of the considerations determining firm profitability, the profit potential of a firm is strongly affected by the competitive outcome in those strategic groups that are market interdependent and have higher mobility barriers. The strategic groups with higher mobility barriers have greater profit potential than the less protected groups if competition *within* them is not too great. However, if competition within them is fierce for some reason and their prices and profits are thereby lowered, it can also destroy the profitability of the firms in the interdependent groups less protected by mobility barriers. Lower prices (or higher costs through advertising and other forms of non-price competition) spill over via market interdependence so that less protected groups must respond, driving down their own profits. This is a risk that must be assessed in choosing a strategic group.

A good example of this process is seen in the soft drink industry. If Coke and Pepsi get into a price war or advertising battle, their profits are diminished, but not nearly so much as those of the regional and local brands who inevitably are affected because their producers are competing for the same customers. Competition among Coke, Pepsi, and the other major brands, protected by substantial mobility barriers, lowers the profit umbrella over the regional and local brands. They tend to lose not only profits but relative share.

ARE LARGE FIRMS MORE PROFITABLE THAN SMALL FIRMS?

There has been much recent discussion about strategy arguing that the firm with the largest market share will be the most profitable.[6] The previous analysis suggests that whether this is true or not depends on the circumstances. If large firms in an industry compete in strategic groups that are more protected by mobility barriers than smaller firms, in stronger positions relative to customers and suppliers, more insulated from rivalry with other groups, and so on, then

[6]See, for example, Buzzell et al. (1975).

the large firms will indeed be more profitable than smaller firms. For example, in industries like brewing and the manufacture of toiletries and television sets, where there are substantial economies of scale in manufacturing, distributing, and servicing a full product line as well as economies of scale in national advertising, then the large firms in the industry will probably be more profitable than smaller firms. On the other hand, *if* economies of scale in production, distribution, or other functions are not too great, smaller firms following specialist strategies may be able to achieve higher product differentiation or greater technological progressiveness or superior service in their particular product niches than larger firms. In such industries, smaller firms may well be more profitable than larger, broader-line firms (as in women's clothing and carpets).

It is sometimes argued that if firms with small shares are more profitable than those with large shares, it reflects a mistake in industry definition. Proponents of the dominant role of market share argue that we should define the market more narrowly, in which case "small" firms will indeed have a larger share of a specialized segment than does a broad-line firm. But if we use a narrow market definition, we should also define the market narrowly in industries where broad-line firms happen to be the most profitable. In such cases we would often find that large firms did not necessarily have the highest share of every segment but yet reaped advantages of overall scale. Ascribing the higher profits of specialized, small-share firms to specialized market definition begs the question we are seeking to answer; namely, under what industry circumstances can a firm select a specialist strategy (to take just one strategic option) without being vulnerable to economies of scale or product differentiation achieved by broader-line firms? Or under what circumstances is overall share in the industry unimportant? The answer will differ by industry, depending on the array of mobility barriers and the other structural and firm-specific features that I have outlined.

Empirical evidence suggests that the relationship between the profitability of larger share and smaller share depends on the industry. Exhibit 7-1 compares the rate of return on equity of the largest firms accounting for at least 30 percent of industry sales (leaders) to the rate of return on equity of the medium-sized firms in the same industry (followers). In this calculation small firms with assets less than $500,000 were excluded. Although some of the industries in the sample are overly broad, it is striking that followers were noticeably

EXHIBIT 7-1. Relative Profitability of Industry Leaders and Industry Followers*

Follower's Rate of Return Much Higher (4.0 or more Percentage Points) than Leader Return	Follower's Rate of Return .5 to 4.0 Percentage Points Higher than Leader's Return	Leader's Rate of Return 2.5 to 4.0 Percentage Points Higher than Follower's Return	Leader's Rate of Return Much Higher (4.0 or more Percentage Points) than Follower's Return
Meat products	Sugar	Dairy products	Wine
Liquor	Tobacco (besides cigarettes)	Grain mill products	Soft drinks
Periodicals	Knit goods	Beer	Soap
Carpets	Women's clothing	Drugs	Perfumes, cosmetics, and toilet preparations
Leather goods	Men's clothing	Jewelry	Paint
Optical, medical, and ophthalmic goods	Footwear		Cutlery, hand tools, and general hardware
	Pottery and related products		Household appliances
	Electric lighting equipment		Radio and television
	Toys and sporting goods		Photographic equipment and supplies

Source: Porter (1979).

*Includes 26 of a comprehensive sample of 38 consumer industries for the years 1963–65. In the 12 other industries not listed, average leader's group rate of return generally exceeded, and in some cases equaled, follower's group rate of return.

more profitable than leaders in 15 of 38 industries. The industries in which the followers' rates of return were higher appear generally to be those where economies of scale are either not great or absent (clothing, footwear, pottery, meat products, carpets) and/or those that are highly segmented (optical, medical and ophthalmic goods, liquor, periodicals, carpets, and toys and sporting goods). The industries in which leaders' rates of return are higher seem to be generally those with heavy advertising (soap; perfumes; soft drinks; grain mill products, i.e., cereal; cutlery) and/or research outlays and production economies of scale (radio and television, drugs, photographic equipment). This outcome is as we would expect.

STRATEGIC GROUPS AND COST POSITION

Another comparatively recent phenomenon in thinking on strategy formulation is that cost position is the only sustainable factor on which to build a competitive strategy. The firm with lowest costs, holds this view, will always be in a position to invade the territory of other areas of strategy, like differentiation, technology, or service, on which other strategic groups are based.

This view is seriously misleading, even putting aside the fact that low-cost position is by no means easy to sustain. As described most broadly in Chapter 2, in most industries there are a variety of ways to create mobility barriers or otherwise build a solid structural position. These different strategies will usually involve differing and often *conflicting* sets of functional policies. A firm attempting to achieve the greatest effectiveness at one strategy will rarely also be most effective in serving the needs met by others. Low-cost position *within the strategic group* may well be crucial, but low-cost position overall is not necessarily important or the only way to compete. Achieving low-cost position overall often involves a sacrifice in other areas of strategy, like differentiation, technology, or service, on which other strategic groups are based.

It is true, however, that strategic groups competing on bases other than low cost must be constantly aware of the differential between their costs and those of the overall low-cost strategic groups. If this differential becomes large enough, then customers may be induced to switch to the lower-cost groups despite a sacrifice in quality, service, technological progressiveness, or other areas. Relative cost position among groups is a key strategic variable in this sense.

Implications for Formulation of Strategy

Formulating competitive strategy in an industry can be viewed as *the choice of which strategic group to compete in*. This choice may involve selecting the existing group that involves the best trade-off between profit potential and the firm's costs of entering it, or it may involve the creation of an entirely new strategic group. Structural analysis within an industry points to the factors that will determine the success of a particular strategic positioning for the firm.

As described in the Introduction, the broadest guidance for the formulation of strategy is stated in terms of matching a firm's strengths and weaknesses, particularly its distinctive competence, to the opportunities and risk in its environment. The principles of structural analysis within an industry allow us to be much more concrete and specific about just what a firm's strengths, weaknesses, distinctive competence, and industry opportunities and risks are. A firm's strengths and weaknesses can be listed as follows:

Strengths	*Weaknesses*
• factors that build the mobility barriers protecting its strategic group;	• factors that lower the mobility barriers protecting its strategic group;
• factors enhancing the bargaining power of its group vis-à-vis buyers and suppliers;	• factors worsening the bargaining power of its group vis-à-vis buyers and suppliers;
• factors insulating its group from rivalry from other firms;	• factors exposing its group to rivalry from other firms;
• greater scale relative to its strategic group;	• smaller scale relative to its strategic group;
• factors allowing lower costs of entry into its strategic group than others;	• factors causing higher costs of entry into its strategic group than others;
• strong implementation abilities vis-à-vis its strategy relative to its competitors;	• weaker implementation abilities vis-à-vis its strategy relative to its competitors;
• resources and skills allowing the firm to overcome mobility barriers and move into even more desirable strategic groups.	• the lack of resources and skills that would allow the firm to overcome mobility barriers and move into more desirable strategic groups.

If the key mobility barriers into a firm's strategic group are based, for example, on its broad product line, proprietary technology, or absolute cost advantages due to experience, these sources of mobility barriers define some of the firm's key strengths. Or if the most desirable strategic group in the firm's industry is protected by mobility barriers resting on the achievement of economies of scale through a captive distribution and service organization, the lack of such a factor becomes one of the firm's key weaknesses. Structural analysis gives us a framework for systematically identifying a firm's key strengths and weaknesses relative to competitors. These strengths and weaknesses are not cast in concrete but can change as industry evolution realigns the relative position of strategic groups or as firms innovate or make investments to change their structural position.

This framework for viewing strengths and weaknesses illuminates two fundamentally different types: structural and implementational. Structural strengths and weaknesses rest on the underlying characteristics of industry structure, such as mobility barriers, determinants of relative bargaining power, and so on. As such they are relatively stable and difficult to overcome. Strengths and weaknesses in implementation, based on differences in a firm's ability to execute strategies, rest on people and managerial abilities. As such, they may be more ephemeral, though not necessarily. In any case, it is important to make a distinction between the two in analysis of strategy.

The *strategic opportunities* facing the firm in its industry can also be made more concrete by using these concepts. Opportunities can be divided into a number of categories:

- create a new strategic group;
- shift to a more favorably situated strategic group;
- strengthen the structural position of the existing group or the firm's position in the group;
- shift to a new group and strengthen that group's structural position.

Perhaps the class of opportunities with the highest payoff is in creating a *new* strategic group. Technological changes or evolution in the structure of the industry often open up possibilities for entirely new strategic groups. Even without such stimuli, the visionary firm might be able to perceive a new, favorably situated strategic group not perceived by its competitors. American Motors, for example, identified a uniquely positioned compact car in the mid-1950s, for a time overcoming serious disadvantages vis-à-vis the Big Three. Timex created a new conception of a low-price, reliable watch, coupling new manufacturing techniques with a new distribution and marketing approach. More recently, Hanes created an entirely new group in hosiery with its L'eggs strategy. Although vision is a scarce commodity, structural analysis can help direct thinking toward the areas of change that would yield the highest payoff.

Another class of potential strategic opportunity is represented by the more favorably situated strategic groups in the industry that the firm might choose to enter.

A third type of strategic opportunity is the possibility for the firm to make investments or adjustments that improve the structural position of its existing strategic group or its position within the group, for example, increase mobility barriers, improve position vis-à-vis substitute products, strengthen marketing ability, and so on. It is also possible to view such investments and adjustments as creating a new and better strategic group.

A final type of strategic opportunity is that of entering other strategic groups and increasing their mobility barriers or otherwise improving their position. Structural evolution in an industry is a powerful creator of possibilities to make this change as well as to improve the firm's position in its existing group.

The *risks* facing a firm can be identified by using the same basic concepts:

- risks of other firms entering its strategic group;
- risks of factors reducing the mobility barriers of the firm's strategic group, lowering power with customers or suppliers, worsening position relative to substitute products, or exposing it to greater rivalry;
- risks that accompany investments designed to improve the firm's position by increasing mobility barriers;
- risks of attempting to overcome mobility barriers into more desirable strategic groups or entirely new groups.

The first two can be viewed as threats to the firm's existing position, or risks of inaction, whereas the latter are risks of pursuing opportunities.

The firm's choice of strategies, or which strategic group to compete in, is a process of relating all these factors. Many, if not most, major strategic breakthroughs come about because of changing structure. Structural analysis shows how a firm's existing strategic position coupled with existing industry structure translates into performance in the marketplace. If industry structure is unchanging, then the cost of overcoming mobility barriers to move to another strategic group already occupied by other firms may well eliminate the benefits. However, if the firm can perceive an entirely new strategic position that is favorable structurally, or if it can change its position at a time when industry evolution lowers the cost of shifting, then a truly significant improvement in performance can result. The framework identified here should illuminate what to look for in such a repositioning.

The three generic strategies identified in Chapter 2 represent three broad and consistent approaches to successful strategic positioning. In the context of this chapter, they are different broad types of strategic groups that can be successful depending on the economics of the particular industry. This chapter has added a lot more flesh and blood to the analysis of the generic strategies. It is clear, based on this chapter, that the generic strategies rest on creating (in different ways) mobility barriers; favorable position with buyers, suppliers, and substitutes; and insulation from rivalry. Our extended concept of structural analysis, then, is a way of making the notion of generic strategies clearer and more operational.

The Strategic Group Map as an Analytical Tool

We are now in a position to return to a discussion of the strategic group map as an analytical tool. The map is a very useful way to graphically display competition in an industry and to see how industry changes or how trends might affect it. It is a map of "strategy space," instead of price and volume.

In mapping strategic groups, the few strategic variables used as axes of the map must be selected by the analyst. In doing so, a number of principles will prove useful. First, the best strategic variables to use as axes are those that *determine the key mobility barriers* in the industry. For example, in soft drinks the key barriers are brand identification and distribution channels, which thus serve as useful axes in a strategic group map. Second, in mapping groups it is important to select as axes variables that do not move together. For example, if all the firms with high product differentiation also have broad product lines, then both these variables should not serve as axes on the map. Rather, variables that reflect the diversity of strategic combinations in the industry should be selected. Third, the axes for a map need not be continuous or monotonic variables. For example, the target channels in the chain saw industry are servicing dealers, mass merchandisers, and sellers of private labels. Some firms focus on one of these, whereas some attempt to span the range. Servicing dealers are most distinct from private label in terms of required strategy, and mass merchandisers are somewhere in between. In mapping the industry, it is perhaps most illuminating to array firms as shown in Figure 7-3. Firms are located to reflect their mix of

FIGURE 7-3. Illustrative Map of the U.S. Chain Saw Industry

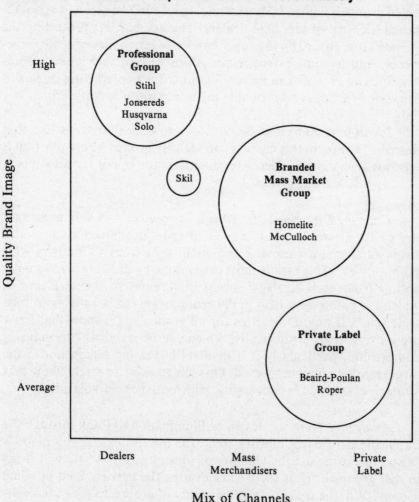

channels. A final principle is that an industry can be mapped several times, using various combinations of strategic dimensions, to help the analyst see the key competitive issues. Mapping is a tool to help diagnose competitive relationships, and there is no necessarily right approach.

Having constructed a strategic group map of an industry, a number of analytical steps can be illuminating:

Identifying Mobility Barriers.   The mobility barriers that protect each group from attacks from other groups can be identified. For example, the key barriers protecting the high quality/dealer-oriented group in Figure 7-3 are technology, brand image, and an established network of servicing dealers. The key barriers protecting the private label group, on the other hand, are economies of scale, experience, and to some extent relationships with private label customers. Such an exercise can be very illuminating in predicting threats to the various groups and probable shifts in position among firms.

Identifying Marginal Groups.   A structural analysis like that described earlier in this chapter can identify groups whose position is tenuous or marginal. These are candidates for exit or for attempts at moving into another group.

Charting Directions of Strategic Movement.   A very important use of the strategic group map is to chart the directions in which firms' strategies are moving and might shift from an industry-wide point of view. This task is most easily done by drawing arrows emanating from each strategic group that represent the direction in which the group (or a firm in the group) seems to be moving in strategic space, if any. Doing this for all groups might show that firms are moving apart strategically, which can be stabilizing to industry competition, particularly if it involves increasing separation of the target market segments served. Or such an exercise might show that strategic positions are converging, which can be very volatile.

Analyzing Trends.   It can be illuminating to think through the implications of each industry trend for the strategic group map. Is the trend closing off the viability of some groups? Where will firms in that group shift? Is the trend elevating the barriers held by some groups? Will the trend reduce the ability of groups to separate themselves along some dimension? All these factors can lead to predictions about industry evolution.

Predicting Reactions.   The map can be used to predict reactions of the industry to an event. Firms in a group tend to react symmetrically to disturbances or trends given the similarity of their strategies.

8
Industry Evolution

Structural analysis gives us a framework for understanding the competitive forces operating in an industry that are crucial to developing competitive strategy. It is clear, however, that industries' structures change, often in fundamental ways. Entry barriers and concentration have gone up significantly in the U.S. brewing industry, for example, and the threat of substitutes has risen to put a severe squeeze on acetylene producers.

Industry evolution takes on critical importance for formulation of strategy. It can increase or decrease the basic attractiveness of an industry as an investment opportunity, and it often requires the firm to make strategic adjustments. Understanding the process of industry evolution and being able to predict change are important because the cost of reacting strategically usually increases as the need for change becomes more obvious and the benefit from the best strategy is the highest for the first firm to select it. For example, in the early postwar farm equipment business, structural change elevated the importance of a strong exclusive dealer network backed by company support and credit. The firms that recognized this change first had their pick of dealers to choose from.

This chapter will present analytical tools for predicting the evolutionary process in an industry and understanding its significance for the formulation of competitive strategy. The chapter begins by describing some basic concepts in the analysis of industry evolution.

Next I will identify the driving forces that are at the root of industry change. Finally, some important economic relationships in the evolutionary process will be described and strategic implications explored.

Basic Concepts in Industry Evolution

The starting point for analyzing industry evolution is the framework of structural analysis in Chapter 1. Industry changes will carry strategic significance if they promise to affect the underlying sources of the five competitive forces; otherwise changes are important only in a tactical sense. The simplest approach to analyzing evolution is to ask the following question: Are there any changes occuring in the industry that will affect each element of structure? For example, do any of the industry trends imply an increase or decrease in mobility barriers? An increase or decrease in the relative power of buyers or suppliers? If this question is asked in a disciplined way for each competitive force and the economic causes underlying it, a profile of the significant issues in the evolution of an industry will result.

Although this industry-specific approach is the place to start, it may not be sufficient, because it is not always clear what industry changes are occurring currently, much less which changes might occur in the future. Given the importance of being able to predict evolution, it is desirable to have some analytical techniques which will aid in anticipating the pattern of industry changes that we might expect to occur.

PRODUCT LIFE CYCLE

The grandfather of concepts for predicting the probable course of industry evolution is the familiar product life cycle. The hypothesis is that an industry[1] passes through a number of phases or stages—introduction, growth, maturity, and decline—illustrated in Figure 8-1. These stages are defined by inflection points in the rate of growth of industry sales. Industry growth follows an S-shaped curve

---

[1] There is some controversy about whether the life cycle applies only to individual products or to whole industries. The view that it applies to industries is summarized here.

because of the process of innovation and diffusion of a new product.[2] The flat introductory phase of industry growth reflects the difficulty of overcoming buyer inertia and stimulating trials of the new product. Rapid growth occurs as many buyers rush into the market once the product has proven itself successful. Penetration of the product's potential buyers is eventually reached, causing the rapid growth to stop and to level off to the underlying rate of growth of the relevant buyer group. Finally, growth will eventually taper off as new substitute products appear.

As the industry goes through its life cycle, the nature of competition will shift. I have summarized in Figure 8-2 the most common predictions about how an industry will change over the life cycle and how this should affect strategy.

The product life cycle has attracted some legitimate criticism:

1. The duration of the stages varies widely from industry to industry, and it is often not clear what stage of the life cycle an industry is in. This problem diminishes the usefulness of the concept as a planning tool.

2. Industry growth does not always go through the S-shaped pattern at all. Sometimes industries skip maturity, passing straight from growth to decline. Sometimes industry growth revitalizes after a period of decline, as has occurred in the motorcycle and bicycle industries and recently in the radio broadcasting industry. Some industries seem to skip the slow takeoff of the introductory phase altogether.

FIGURE 8-1.   Stages of the Life Cycle

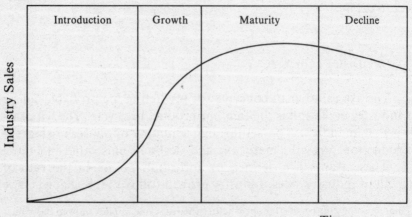

[2]Kotler (1972), pp. 432–433; see also Polli and Cook (1969), pp. 385–387.

FIGURE 8-2. Predictions of Product Life Cycle Theories About Strategy, Competition, and Performance

	Introduction	Growth	Maturity	Decline
Buyers and Buyer Behavior	High income purchaser[j,k,l]; Buyer interia[a]; Buyers must be convinced to try the product[a,j]	Widening buyer group[j]; Consumer will accept uneven quality[i]	Mass market[l]; Saturation[a]; Repeat buying[a,j]; Choosing among brands is the rule[a]	Customers are sophisticated buyers of the product[i]
Products and Product Change	Poor quality[l]; Product design and development key[g]; Many different product variations; no standards[k]; Frequent design changes[j,k]; Basic product designs[l]	Products have technical and performance differentiation[h]; Reliability key for complex products[g]; Competitive product improvements[l]; Good quality[l]	Superior quality[l]; Less product differentiation[b,f,i]; Standardization[f,k]; Less rapid product changes—more minor annual model changes[i,j]; Trade-ins become significant[j]	Little product differentiation[h,i]; Spotty product quality[l]
Marketing	Very high advertising/sales (a/s)[b,h]; Creaming price strategy[k]; High marketing costs[j]	High advertising,[b] but lower percent of sales than introductory[b,h]; Most promotion of ethical drugs[c]; Advertising and distribution key for nontechnical products[g]	Market segmentation[a,j,l]; Efforts to extend life cycle[d,i]; Broaden line[j]; Service and deals more prevalent[a,j]; Packaging important[a]; Advertising competition[a]; Lower a/s[a,b]	Low a/s and other marketing[b,j]

FIGURE 8-2 Continued

	Introduction	Growth	Maturity	Decline
Manufacturing and Distribution	Overcapacity[l] Short production runs[j,k] High skilled-labor content[k] High production costs[j] Specialized channels[l]	Undercapacity[l] Shift toward mass production[j,k] Scramble for distribution[j] Mass channels[l]	Some overcapacity[a] Optimum capacity[l] Increasing stability of manufacturing process[e] Lower labor skills[k] Long production runs with stable techniques[k] Distribution channels pare down their lines to improve their margins[j] High physical distribution costs due to broad lines[j] Mass channels[l]	Substantial overcapacity[a,l] Mass production[h] Specialty channels[l]
R&D	Changing production techniques[k]			
Foreign Trade	Some exports[k]	Significant exports[k] Few imports[k]	Falling exports[k] Significant imports[k]	No exports[k] Significant imports[k]
Overall Strategy	Best period to increase market share[e] R&D, engineering are key functions[i]	Practical to change price or quality image[i] Marketing the key function[i]	Bad time to increase market share Particularly if low-share company[e] Having competitive costs becomes key[j] Bad time to change price image or quality image[i] "Marketing effectiveness" keys[g]	Cost control keys[g,i]

FIGURE 8-2 Continued

	Introduction	Growth	Maturity	Decline
Competition	Few companies[a,j,k,l]	Entry[a] Many competitors[a,d,j,l] Lots of mergers and casualties[l]	Price competition[a,i,j,k] Shakeout[j,k] Increase in private brands[d,e]	Exits[a] Fewer competitors[j,l]
Risk	High risk[a]	Risks can be taken here because growth covers them up[j]	Cyclicality sets in[j]	
Margins and Profits	High prices and margins[b,j,l] Low profits[g,j] Price elasticity to individual seller not as great as in maturity[k]	High profits[b,j,l] Highest profits[h] Fairly high prices[b] Lower prices than introductory phase[j] Recession resistant[j] High P/E's[j] Good acquisition climate[j]	Falling prices[b,j,l] Lower profits[l] Lower margins[b,l] Lower dealer margins[i,j] Increased stability of market shares and price structure[e] Poor acquisition climate —tough to sell companies[j] Lowest prices and margins[l]	Low prices and margins[a] Falling prices[b,j] Prices might rise in late decline[j,l]

[a]Levitt (1965).
[b]Buzzell (1966).
[c]Cox (1967).
[d]Buzzell et al. (1972).
[e]Catry and Chevalier (1974).
[f]Dean (1950).
[g]Clifford (1965).
[h]Forrester (1959).
[i]Patton (1959).
[j]Staudt, Taylor, and Bowersox (1976).
[k]Wells (1972).
[l]Smallwood (1973).

3. Companies can *affect* the shape of the growth curve through product innovation and repositioning, extending it in a variety of ways.[3] If a company takes the life cycle as given, it becomes an undesirable self-fulfilling prophesy.

4. The nature of competition associated with each stage of the life cycle is *different* for different industries. For example, some industries start out highly concentrated and stay that way. Others, like bank cash dispensers, are concentrated for a significant period and then become less so. Still others begin highly fragmented; of these some consolidate (automobiles) and some do not (electronic component distribution). The same divergent patterns apply to advertising, R&D expenditures, degree of price competition, and most other industry characteristics. Divergent patterns such as these call into serious question the strategic implications ascribed to the life cycle.

The real problem with the product life cycle as a predictor of industry evolution is that it attempts to describe *one* pattern of evolution that will invariably occur. And except for the industry growth rate, there is little or no underlying rationale for why the competitive changes associated with the life cycle will happen. Since actual industry evolution takes so many different paths, the life cycle pattern does not always hold, even if it is a common or even the most common pattern of evolution. Nothing in the concept allows us to predict when it will hold and when it will not.

A FRAMEWORK FOR FORECASTING EVOLUTION

Instead of attempting to describe industry evolution, it will prove more fruitful to look underneath the process to see what really drives it. Like any evolution, industries evolve because some forces are in motion that create incentives or pressures for change. These can be called *evolutionary processes*.

Every industry begins with an *initial structure*—the entry barriers, buyer and supplier power, and so on which exist when the industry comes into existence. This structure is usually (though not always) a far cry from the configuration the industry will take later in its development. The initial structure results from a combination of underlying economic and technical characteristics of the industry, the initial constraints of small industry size, and the skills and re-

[3]For a discussion of these methods, see Levitt (1965).

sources of the companies that are early entrants. For example, even an industry like automobiles with enormous possibilities for economies of scale started out with labor-intensive, job-shop production operations because of the small volumes of cars produced during the early years.

The evolutionary processes work to push the industry toward its *potential structure*, which is rarely known completely as an industry evolves. Imbedded in the underlying technology, product characteristics, and nature of present and potential buyers, however, there is a range of structures the industry might possibly achieve, depending on the direction and success of research and development, marketing innovations, and the like.

It is important to realize that instrumental in much industry evolution are the investment decisions by both existing firms in the industry and new entrants. In response to pressures or incentives created by the evolutionary process, firms invest to take advantage of possibilities for new marketing approaches, new manufacturing facilities, and the like, which shift entry barriers, alter relative power against suppliers and buyers, and so on. The luck, skills, resources, and orientation of firms in the industry can shape the evolutionary path the industry will actually take. Despite potential for structural change, an industry may not actually change because no firm happens to discover a feasible new marketing approach; or potential scale economies may go unrealized because no firm possesses the financial resources to construct a fully integrated facility or simply because no firm is inclined to think about costs. Because innovation, technological developments, and the identities (and resources) of the particular firms either in the industry or considering entry into it are so important to evolution, industry evolution will not only be hard to forecast with certainty but also an industry can potentially evolve in a variety of ways at a variety of different speeds, depending on the luck of the draw.

Evolutionary Processes

Although initial structure, structural potential, and particular firms' investment decisions will be industry-specific, we can generalize about what are the important evolutionary processes. There are some predictable (and interacting) dynamic processes that occur in every industry in one form or another, though their speed and direction will differ from industry to industry:

- long-run changes in growth;
- changes in buyer segments served;
- buyers' learning;
- reduction of uncertainty;
- diffusion of proprietary knowledge;
- accumulation of experience;
- expansion (or contraction) in scale;
- changes in input and currency costs;
- product innovation;
- marketing innovation;
- process innovation;
- structural change in adjacent industries;
- government policy change;
- entries and exits.

Each evolutionary process will be described, with attention to its determinants, its relationship to other processes, and its strategic implications.

LONG-RUN CHANGES IN GROWTH

Perhaps the most ubiquitous force leading to structural change is a change in the long-run industry growth rate. Industry growth is a key variable in determining the intensity of rivalry in the industry, and it sets the pace of expansion required to maintain share, thereby influencing the supply and demand balance and the inducement the industry offers to new entrants.

There are five important external reasons why long-run industry growth changes:

DEMOGRAPHICS

In *consumer goods*, demographic changes are one key determinant of the size of the buyer pool for a product and thereby the rate of growth in demand. The potential customer group for a product may be as broad as all households, but it usually consists of buyers characterized by particular age groups, income levels, educational levels, or geographic locations. As the total growth rate of the population, its distribution by age group and income level, and demographic factors change, these translate directly into alterations in demand. A particularly vivid current example of this situation is the adverse effect of the reduced U.S. birthrate on demand for baby products of all types, whereas products catering to the 25-to-35-year-old age group are currently enjoying the effects of the post-World War II baby boom. Demographics also represent a potential problem for the recording and candy industries, which have traditionally sold most heavily to the pre-20-year-old age group, which is currently shrinking.

Part of the effect of demographic changes is caused by *income elasticity*, which refers to the change in a buyer's demand for a product as his/her income rises. For some products (mink golf club covers), demand tends to rise disproportionately with buyers' income. For other products, demand rises less than proportionally as incomes rise, or even falls. It is important from a strategic point of view to identify where an industry's product lies in this spectrum, because it is critical to forecasting long-run growth as general income levels of buyers change both in a firm's home country and in potential international markets. Sometimes industries can shift their products up or down the scale of income elasticity through product innovation, however, so the effects of income elasticity are not necessarily a foregone conclusion.

For *industrial products*, the effect of demographic changes on demand is based on the life cycle of customer industries. Demographics affect consumers' demand for end products, which filters back to affect the industries supplying inputs toward those end products.

Firms can attempt to cope with adverse demographics by widening the buyer group for their product through product innovations, new marketing approaches, additional service offerings, and so on. These approaches can in turn affect industry structure by raising economies of scale, exposing the industry to fundamentally different buyer groups with different bargaining power, and so forth.

TRENDS IN NEEDS

Demand for an industry's product is affected by changes in the lifestyle, tastes, philosophies, and social conditions of the buyer population which any society tends to experience over time. For example, in the late 1960s and early 1970s there were such shifts in the United States as a return to "nature," increased leisure time, more casual dress, and nostalgia. These trends boosted demand for back-packs, blue jeans, and other products. The recent "back to basics" movement in education is creating new demand for standardized reading and writing tests, to give another example. There have also been social trends such as an increase in the crime rate, the changing role of women, and increased health consciousness that have in-creased demand for some products (bicycles, day care) and reduced demand for others.

Trends in needs like these not only directly affect demand but also affect the demand for industrial products indirectly through in-tervening industries. Trends in needs affect the demand in particular industry segments as well as total industry demand. Needs may be newly created or just made more intense by social trends. For exam-ple, property theft has increased quite dramatically in the last twenty years, greatly increasing the demand for security guards, locks, safes, and alarm systems. The rising expected losses due to theft have justified greater spending to prevent it.

Finally, changes in government regulation can increase or de-crease needs for products. For example, demand for pinball and slot machines is growing as a result of impending and already passed leg-islation that legalizes gambling.[4]

Change in the Relative Position of Substitutes

Demand for a product is affected by the cost and quality, broadly defined, of substitute products. If the cost of a substitute falls in relative terms, or if its ability improves to satisfy the buyer's needs, industry growth will be adversely affected (and vice versa). Examples are the inroads that television and radio have made on the demand for live concerts by symphony orchestras and other perform-ing groups; the growth in demand for magazine advertising space as television advertising rates climb sharply and prime advertising tele-vision time becomes increasingly scarce; and the depressing effect of rising prices on the demand of such products as chocolate candy and soft drinks relative to their substitutes.

In predicting long-run change in growth, a firm must identify all the substitute products that can meet the needs its product satis-fies. Then technological and other trends that will affect the cost or quality of each of these substitutes should be charted. Comparing these with the analogous trends for the industry will yield predictions

[4]See *Dun's*, February 1977.

about future industry growth rates and identify critical ways in which substitutes are gaining, thereby providing leads for strategic action.[5]

Changes in the Position of Complementary Products

The effective cost and quality of many products to the buyer depends on the cost, quality, and availability of complementary products, or products used jointly with them. For example, in many areas of the United States mobile homes are primarily sited in mobile home parks. In the last decade there has been a chronic shortage of these parks, which has limited demand for mobile homes. Similarly, demand for stereophonic records was strongly affected by the availability of stereophonic audio equipment, which in turn was affected by the cost and reliability of this equipment.

Just as it is important to identify substitutes for an industry's product it is important to identify complements comprehensively. Complementary products should be viewed broadly. For example, credit at prevailing interest rates is a complementary product to purchases of durable goods. Specialized personnel are a complementary product to many technically oriented goods (e.g., computer programmers to computers and mining engineers to coal mining). Charting trends in cost, availability, and quality of complementary products will yield predictions about long-run growth for an industry's product.

Penetration of the Customer Group

Most very high industry growth rates are the result of increasing penetration, or sales to new customers rather than to repeat customers. Eventually, however, it is a fact of life that an industry must reach essentially complete penetration. Its growth rate is then determined by replacement demand. Renewed periods of adding new customers can sometimes be stimulated by product or marketing changes, which broaden the scope of the customer base or stimulate rapid replacement. However, all very high growth rates eventually come to an end.

Once penetration is reached the industry is selling primarily to repeat buyers. There may well be major differences betweeen selling to repeat and first-time buyers that have important consequences for

[5]Government policies can affect a product's position vis-à-vis substitutes in areas like safety regulation (that raises costs), subsidies, and so on.

industry structure. The key to achieving industry growth when selling to repeat buyers is either stimulating rapid replacement of the product or increasing per capita consumption. Since replacement is determined by physical, technological, or design obsolescence as perceived by the buyer, strategies to maintain growth after penetration will hinge on affecting these factors. For example, replacement demand for clothing is stimulated by annual and even seasonal style changes. And the classic story of General Motors' ascendency over Ford is an example of how model changes stimulated demand after market saturation for the basic (one color: black) automobile occurred.

Whereas penetration most often means that industry demand will level off, for *durable goods*, achieving penetration can lead to an abrupt drop in industry demand. After most potential customers have purchased the product, its durability implies that few will buy replacements for a number of years. If industry penetration has been rapid, this situation may translate into several very lean years for industry demand. For example, industry sales of snowmobiles, which underwent very rapid penetration, fell from 425,000 units per year in the peak year (1970-1971) to 125,000 to 200,000 units per year in 1976-1977.[6] Recreational vehicles underwent a similar though not quite so dramatic decline. The relation between the growth rate after penetration and growth before penetration will be a function of how fast penetration has been reached and the average time before replacement, and this figure can be calculated.

The decline in industry sales for durables means that manufacturing and distributing capacity will inherently overshoot demand. As a result, a serious decline in profit margins usually occurs, and some producers may exit. Another characteristic of the demand for durable goods is that growth fueled by penetration can overshadow cyclicality despite the fact that the product is inherently sensitive to the business cycle. An industry approaching penetration will thus have its first deep cycle, exacerbating the problem of overshooting.

PRODUCT CHANGE

The five external causes of industry growth have presupposed no change in the products offered by the industry. Product innova-

[6]"A Smoother Trail for Snowmobile Makers," *Business Week*, December 13, 1976.

tion by the industry, however, can allow it to serve new needs, can improve the industry's position vis-à-vis substitutes, and can eliminate or reduce the necessity of scarce or costly complementary products. Thus product innovation can improve an industry's circumstances relative to the five external causes of growth, and thereby increase the industry's growth rate. Product innovations have played a major part in fueling the rapid growth of motorcycles, bicycles, and chain saws, for example.

CHANGES IN BUYER SEGMENTS SERVED

The second important evolutionary process is change in the buyer segments served by the industry. For example, early electronic calculators were sold to scientists and engineers, only later to students and bill payers. Light aircraft were initially sold to the military and later to private and commercial users. Related to this is the possibility that additional segmentation of *existing* buyer segments can take place by creating different products (broadly defined) and marketing techniques for them. A final possibility is that certain buyer segments are no longer served.

The significance of new buyer segments for industry evolution is that the requirements for serving these new buyers (or eliminating requirements for serving obsolete segments) can have a fundamental impact on industry structure. For example, although early buyers of the product may not have required credit and field servicing, later buyers might. If the provision of credit and in-house service creates potential economies of scale and raises capital requirements, then entry barriers will rise significantly.

A good example is provided by changes occurring in the optical character reader business in the late 1970s. This industry and its leader, Recognition Equipment, have been producing large, expensive optical scanning machines to sort checks, credit cards, and mail. Each machine has been custom-made, requiring special engineering and produced on a job-shop basis. In recent years, however, small wands for use with retail point-of-sale terminals have been developed. In addition to opening up a vast potential market, the wands are amenable to high-volume, standardized manufacturing and will be purchased in large quantities by individual buyers. This development promises to change economies of scale, capital requirements, marketing methods, and many other aspects of industry structure.

Analysis of industry evolution, then, should include an identification of all potential new buyer segments and their characteristics.

LEARNING BY BUYERS

Through repeat purchasing, buyers accumulate knowledge about a product, its use, and the characteristics of competing brands. Products have a tendency to *become more like commodities* over time as buyers become more sophisticated and purchasing tends to be based on better information. Thus there is a natural force reducing product differentiation over time in an industry. Learning about the product may lead to increasing demands by buyers for warranty protection, service, improved performance characteristics, and so forth.

An example is the aerosol packaging industry. Aerosol packaging first came into use in consumer goods in the 1950s. The package, an extremely important part of marketing many consumer goods, often represents an important cost item to the marketing company. In the early years of aerosol packaging, consumer marketers were unfamiliar with how to design aerosol applications, how aerosol containers were filled, and how best to market aerosol products. A contract aerosol filling industry sprang up to assemble and fill aerosol packages, and this industry also played a major role in assisting consumer marketing companies find new aerosol applications, solve production problems, and so on. Over time, however, consumer marketers learned a great deal about aerosols and began developing their own applications and marketing programs, in some cases actually initiating integration backward. Contract fillers found it increasingly difficult to differentiate their services, and their role became increasingly one of supplying commodity aerosol containers. As a result, contract fillers' profit margins were severely squeezed, and many left the industry.

A buyer's learning tends to progress at different rates for different products, depending on how important the purchase is and the buyer's technical expertise. Smart or interested (because it is an important product) buyers tend to learn faster.

Offsetting buyer's experience is change in the product or in the way it is sold or used, such as new features, new additives (hexachlorophine), style changes, new advertising appeals, and the like. This development nullifies some of the buyer's accumulated knowledge and hence enhances the possibilities for continued product differentiation. Such possibilities are also enhanced by expanding the customer base to new buyers inexperienced with the product, particularly those whose purchasing characteristics tend to make them learn slowly.

REDUCTION OF UNCERTAINTY

Another type of learning that affects industry structure is reduction of uncertainty. Most new industries are initially characterized by a great deal of uncertainty about such things as the potential size of the market, optimal product configuration, nature of potential buyers and how they can best be reached, and whether technological problems can be overcome. This uncertainty often leads firms to a high degree of experimentation, with many different strategies adopted representing different bets about the future. Rapid growth provides slack to allow these differing strategies to coexist for long periods of time.

Over time, however, there is a continual process by which uncertainties are resolved. Technologies are proven or disproven, buyers are identified, and indications are gleaned from the industry's growth about its potential size. Hand in hand with such reduction of uncertainty is a process of imitation of successful strategies and the abandonment of poor ones.

Reduction of uncertainty may also attract *new types of entrants* into the industry. Reduced risk may attract larger, established firms with lower-risk profiles than the newly created companies so common in emerging industries. As it becomes clear that an industry's potential is large and technological hurdles can be overcome, bigger firms may find it worth their while to enter—which has happened in recreational vehicles, video games, solar heating, and many other industries. Of course events can create new uncertainties in an industry, but like buyers' learning, reduction of uncertainty will be continually operating to resolve existing doubts.

Strategically, reduction of uncertainty and imitation suggest that a firm cannot rely on uncertainty alone to protect it from its rivals or from new entrants very long. Depending on mobility barriers, the imitation of successful strategies can be more or less difficult. To protect its position a firm must strategically prepare either to defend its position against imitators and new entrants or adjust its approach if its early bets about the appropriate strategy prove wrong.

DIFFUSION OF PROPRIETARY KNOWLEDGE

Product and process technologies developed by particular firms (or suppliers or other parties) tend to become less proprietary. Over time, a technology becomes more established and knowledge about it more widespread. Diffusion occurs through a variety of mechanisms. First, firms can learn from physical inspection of competitors' proprietary products and from information gleaned from a variety of sources about the size, location, organization, and other characteristics of competitors' operations. Suppliers, distributors, and customers are all conduits for such information and often have strong interest in promoting diffusion for their own purposes (e.g., creating another strong supplier). Second, proprietary information is also diffused as it becomes embodied in capital goods produced by outside suppliers. Unless firms in the industry make their own capital goods or protect the information they give to suppliers, the technology may become purchasable by competitors. Third, personnel turnover increases the number of people who have the proprietary information and may provide a direct conduit for the information to other firms. Spin-off firms founded by technical personnel who have left pioneering companies are common, as is the practice of hiring away personnel. Finally, specialized personnel who are expert in the technology invariably become more numerous from sources such as consulting firms, suppliers, customers, response of university technical schools, and so on.

In the absence of patent protection, therefore, proprietary advantages will tend to erode, as hard as it is for some firms to accept this fact. Thus any mobility barriers built on proprietary knowledge or specialized technology tend to erode over time, as do those caused by shortages of qualified, specialized personnel. These changes make it easier not only for new competitors to spring up but also for suppliers or customers to vertically integrate into the industry.

Returning to the previously discussed aerosol example, over time the new aerosol technology became better and better known. Since the production volume needed to achieve efficient scale in aerosol packaging was relatively small, many large consumer marketing companies could support their own captive filling operations.

As knowledge about the technology and specialized personnel became more common, many of these companies vertically integrated into aerosol filling or could threaten to do so. This development left the contract filler in the role of meeting emergency demand and in a very adverse bargaining situation. The response of many contract fillers was to invest in improving filling technology and to invent new aerosol applications to restore their technological advantage. This strategy proved to be increasingly difficult, and the contract fillers' position weakened substantially over time.

The rate of diffusion of proprietary technology will depend on the particular industry. The more complex the technology, the more specialized the required technical personnel, the greater the critical mass of research personnel required, or the greater the economies of scale in the research function, the slower proprietary technology will tend to diffuse. When heavy capital requirements and economies of scale in R&D confront imitators, proprietary technology can provide a lasting mobility barrier.

One key offsetting force to diffusion of proprietary technology is patent protection, which legally inhibits diffusion. However, this protection is unreliable in preventing diffusion since patents can be sidestepped by similar inventions. The other offsetting force to diffusion is the continual creation of new proprietary technology through research and development. New knowledge will provide companies with additional periods of proprietary advantages. However, continual innovation may not pay if the diffusion period is short and buyers' loyalties to pioneering firms are not very strong.

Two of many possible patterns of mobility barriers arising from proprietary technology are illustrated in Figure 8-3. Economies of scale in research were initially low in both industries since the initial, crude, breakthrough innovations that created the product could be made by small groups of research personnel. This situation is relatively common, having occurred in such industries as minicomputers, semiconductors, and others. Proprietary technology provided a modest initial mobility barrier in such an industry, but one that was soon eroded by diffusion. In one industry, the complex technology led to increasing economies of scale in the research function. In the other, there was little opportunity for continued technological innovation and hence little need for further research on a significant scale. In the first industry, then, mobility barriers from proprietary technology quickly rose again to a level higher than the initial one. Eventually they tailed off as opportunities for further innovation

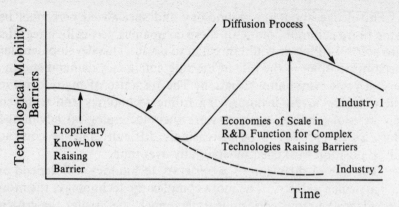

FIGURE 8-3. Illustrative Pattern of Technological Barriers and Industry Evolution

waned and diffusion took over. In the other industry, mobility barriers from proprietary technology quickly sunk to a low level. Thus one industry would probably have a profitable maturity phase, whereas the other would be dependent on other sources of barriers to prevent profit erosion to the competitive level. In the aerosol example, the nature of the technology did not allow the secondary increase in entry barriers.

From a strategic point of view, the diffusion of knowledge about technology means that to maintain position (1) existing know-how and specialized personnel must be protected, which is very difficult to do in practice;[7] (2) technological development must occur to maintain the lead; or (3) strategic position must be shored up in other areas. Planning for the defense of strategic position against technological diffusion takes on high priority if a firm's existing position is heavily dependent on technological barriers.

ACCUMULATION OF EXPERIENCE

In some industries, whose characteristics were identified in Chapter 1, unit costs decline with experience in manufacturing, distributing, and marketing the product. The significance of the learning curve for industry competition is dependent upon whether firms

---

[7]Some firms have been successful through defensive innovation and patenting. If the firm can discover and patent the best alternative technologies as well as the one they use, the difficulty of the entrant is greatly increased. Such strategies have been followed by Bulova with the Accutron watch and Xerox with Xerography.

with more experience can establish significant and sustainable leads over others. For these leads to persist, firms that are behind must be unable to catch up by copying the methods of leaders, buying new and more efficient machinery the leaders may have pioneered, and so on. If firms that are behind can leapfrog, the leaders may be at a disadvantage from bearing the expense of research, experimentation, and introduction of new methods and equipment in the first place. The tendency for proprietary technology to diffuse works against the learning curve to some extent.

When experience can be kept proprietary, it can be a potent force in industry change. If the firm is not gaining experience the fastest, it must prepare strategically to either practice rapid imitation or build strategic advantages in other areas besides cost. Doing the latter requires the firm to adopt generic strategies of differentiation or focus.

EXPANSION (OR CONTRACTION) IN SCALE

A growing industry is, by definition, increasing its total scale. This growth is usually accompanied by increases in the absolute size of the leading firms in the industry, and firms gaining market share must be increasing in size even more rapidly. Increasing scale in industry and firm has a number of implications for industry structure. First, it tends to widen the set of available strategies in ways that often lead to increased economies of scale and capital requirements in the industry. For example, it may allow larger firms to substitute capital for labor, adopt production methods subject to greater economies of scale, establish captive distribution channels or a captive service organization and utilize national advertising. Increasing scale also can make it feasible for an outsider to enter the industry with substantial competitive advantages by being the first to adopt such changes.[8]

The way in which increasing scale operates on industry structure is illustrated by light aircraft in the 1960s and early 1970s. In this industry, growth allowed Cessna (the industry leader) to shift its production process from job shop to quasi-mass production. This change resulted in a cost advantage for Cessna because it reaped economies of scale in mass production as yet unavailable to its major competitors. If Cessna's two leading competitors also reach the scale

[8]Contraction of industry scale has the reverse effects.

to begin more capital-intensive mass production, barriers to entry into the industry by outsiders will increase markedly.

Another consequence of industry growth is that strategies of vertical integration tend to become more feasible, and increased vertical integration tends to elevate barriers. Increasing industry scale also means that suppliers to the industry are selling it larger volumes of goods, and the industry's customers as a group are purchasing larger quantities. To the extent that *individual* suppliers or buyers are increasing their sales or purchases as well, there may be temptations for them to begin forward or backward integration into the industry. Whether or not integration actually occurs, the bargaining power of suppliers or buyers will go up.

There may also be a tendency for large industry scale to attract new entrants, who can make it tougher for existing leaders, particularly if the entrants are large, established firms. Many large firms will enter a market only after it has reached a significant absolute size (to justify the fixed costs of entry and make a material contribution to their overall sales), even though they have been probable potential entrants right from the industry's birth as a result of skills or assets they bring from their existing businesses. For example, in the recreational vehicle industry the initial entrants were new firms started from scratch and relatively small diversifying mobile home producers whose production process was similar to that of making recreational vehicles. As the industry got large enough, big farm equipment and automotive companies began to enter. These firms had ample resources for competing in recreational vehicles drawn from their existing operations, but they left it to the smaller firms to develop the market and prove that a significant market existed before they entered.

CHANGES IN INPUT COSTS AND EXCHANGE RATES

Every industry uses a variety of inputs to its manufacturing, distribution, and marketing process. Changes in the cost or quality of these inputs can affect industry structure. The important classes of input costs subject to change are the following:

- wage rates (encompassing the full costs of labor);
- material costs;
- cost of capital;

- communication costs (including media);
- transportation costs.

The most straightforward effect is in increasing or decreasing the cost (and price) of the product, thereby affecting demand. For example, the cost of producing movies has risen quite markedly in recent years. This rise is squeezing independent producers relative to well-financed movie companies, particularly since movie tax shelters have been circumscribed by 1976 tax legislation. This development has cut a major avenue of financing for independent producers.

Changes in wage rates or capital costs may change the shape of the industry's cost curve, altering economies of scale or promoting substitution of capital for labor. Escalating labor costs in service calls and deliveries are fundamentally affecting strategy in many industries. Changes in the cost of communication or transportation can promote reorganization of production, which affects entry barriers. Changes in communication costs may lead to use of different cost-effective selling media (and thereby changes in the level of product differentiation), changed distribution arrangements, and so on. In addition, changes in transportation costs can shift geographic market boundaries, which either increases or decreases the effective number of competitors in the industry.

Exchange rate fluctuations can also have a profound effect on industry competition. The devaluation of the dollar against the yen and many European currencies, for example, has triggered significant shifts in position in many industries since 1971.

PRODUCT INNOVATION

A major source of industry structural change is technological innovations of various types and origins. Innovation in product is one important type. Product innovation can widen the market and hence promote industry growth and/or it can enhance product differentiation. Product innovation also can have indirect effects. The process of rapid product introduction, and associated needs for high marketing costs, may itself create mobility barriers. Innovations may require new marketing, distribution, or manufacturing methods that change economies of scale or other mobility barriers. Significant product change can also nullify buyer experience and hence impact purchasing behavior.

Product innovations can come from outside or inside the industry. Color television was pioneered by RCA, a leader in black and white television. However, electronic calculators were introduced by electronics companies and not mechanical calculator or slide rule producers. Thus forecasting product innovations involves examining possible external sources. Many innovations flow vertically, originated by customers and suppliers, where the industry is an important customer or source of inputs.

An example of the influence of product innovation on structure is the introduction of the digital watch. Economies of scale in producing digital watches are greater than those in producing most conventional watch varieties. Competing in digital watches also requires large capital investments and an entirely new technological base compared to conventional watches. Thus mobility barriers and other aspects of the structure of the watch industry are changing rapidly.

MARKETING INNOVATION

Like innovations in product, those in marketing can influence industry structure directly through increasing demand. Breakthroughs in the use of advertising media, new marketing themes or channels, and so forth can allow reaching new consumers or reducing price sensitivity (raising product differentiation). For example, movie companies have boosted demand by advertising movies on television. The discovery of new channels of distribution can similarly widen demand or raise product differentiation; innovations in marketing that make it more efficient can lower the cost of the product.

Innovations in marketing and distribution also have effects on other elements of industry structure. New forms of marketing can be subject to increased or decreased economies of scale and hence affect mobility barriers. For example, the shift in marketing wine from low-key magazine advertising to network television has raised the mobility barriers in the wine industry. Marketing innovations can also shift power relative to buyers, and affect the balance of fixed and variable costs and hence the volatility of rivalry.

PROCESS INNOVATION

The final class of innovation that can change industry structure is that in the manufacturing process or methods. Innovations can make the process more or less capital intensive, increase or decrease economies of scale, change the proportion of fixed costs, increase or decrease vertical integration, affect the process of accumulating experience, and so on—all of which affect industry structure. Innovations that increase scale economies or extend the experience curve beyond the size of national markets can lead to industry globalization (see Chapter 13).

An example of the way in which interacting evolutionary processes can trigger manufacturing changes is found in changes occurring in the computer service bureau business in 1977. Computer service bureaus provide computer power and a library of programs to a wide variety of users, including those in business, education, and financial institutions. Traditionally service bureaus have been local or regional organizations serving primarily smaller businesses with simple computer packages in areas like accounting and payroll. However, a substitute product, the minicomputer, has made cheap computer power easily accessible to even small organizations. As a result, forces have been set in motion which are promoting the development of large regional and national service bureaus. First, more sophisticated programs are being developed to differentiate the service bureau from the minicomputer, which require substantial investments. The economies of spreading such investments over a large number of users are promoting concentration. Second, pressure to offer computer power at low cost is putting a premium on efficient use of facilities. This development is adding to the impetus toward national companies to take advantage of time zone changes to make use of off-hours capacity. Third, computer technology continues to increase in complexity, raising technological barriers to establish a service bureau at least in the short run. So all these forces built up in the evolutionary process have led to a change in the manufacturing process of the leading service bureaus.

Manufacturing innovations that change structure can come from outside the industry as well as from within. Developments in computerized machine tools and other manufacturing equipment by equipment suppliers, for example, may lead to increased scale economies in production in an industry. The 1950s innovations by fiberglass producers that led to the use of fiberglass in boats greatly reduced the difficulty of designing and building pleasure boats. This reduction in entry barriers triggered the entry of a large number of new companies into the industry with disastrous consequences for profits, many failing between 1960 and 1962 as the industry underwent a shake-out. In the metal container industry, suppliers of steel expended substantial resources to help defend steel cans against the inroads of the aluminum can through innovations reducing the gauge of steel and techniques for lower-cost can manufacture. All these examples suggest that the firm must broaden its view of technological change beyond industry boundaries.

STRUCTURAL CHANGE IN ADJACENT INDUSTRIES

Since the structure of suppliers' and customers' industries affects their bargaining power with an industry, changes in their structure have potentially important consequences for industry evolution. For example, there has been substantial chain-store development in the retailing of clothing and hardware in the 1960s and 1970s. As the structure of retailing has become concentrated, the retailers' bargaining power with their supplying industries has increased. Apparel makers are getting squeezed by retailers, who are ordering closer and closer to the selling season and demanding other concessions. Manufacturers' marketing and promotional strategies have had to adjust, and concentration in apparel manufacturing is forecast to increase. The mass merchandising revolution in retailing generally has had similar effects on many other industries (watches, small appliances, toiletries).

Whereas changes in the concentration or vertical integration of adjacent industries attract the most attention, more subtle changes in the methods of competition in the adjacent industries can often be just as important in affecting evolution. For example, in the 1950s and early 1960s record retailers dropped the policy of allowing consumers to play records in the store. The effects of this change in the adjacent recording industry proved to be profound. Since the consumer could no longer sample records in the store, what radio stations played became critical to record sales. However, because advertising rates were becoming increasingly tied to sustained audience size, radio stations were shifting to the "Top 40" format, that is, repeatedly playing only the leading songs. It became extremely difficult to get a new, unproven record aired on the radio. The change in retailing created a powerful new element for the recording industry—radio stations—which changed the strategic requirements for success. It also forced the recording industry to purchase advertising time for new record releases on radio stations, the only sure way to assure that new recordings were played, and generally increased barriers into the recording industry.

The importance of changes in the structure of adjacent industries points to the need to diagnose and prepare for structural evolution in supplying and buying industries, just as in the industry itself.

GOVERNMENT POLICY CHANGE

Government influences can have a significant and tangible impact on industry structural change, the most direct through full-blown regulation of such key variables as entry into the industry, competitive practices, or profitability. For example, pending national health insurance legislation with cost-plus reimbursement will fundamentally affect profit potential in the proprietary hospital and clinical laboratory industries. Requirements for licensing, an intermediate form of government regulation, tend to restrict entry and thereby provide an entry barrier protecting existing firms. Changes in government pricing regulation also can have a fundamental impact on industry structure. A current example is the profound consequences that have accompanied the shift from legally fixed commissions to negotiated commissions in securities transactions. Fixed commissions created a price umbrella for securities firms and shifted competition from price to service and research. Ending fixed commissions has shifted competition to price and resulted in mass exit from the industry, either through outright failure or mergers. Mobility barriers in the new environment are dramatically increased. Government actions can also dramatically increase or decrease the likelihood of international competition (see Chapter 13).

Less direct forms of government influence on industry structure occur through the regulation of product quality and safety, environmental quality, and tariffs or foreign investments. The effect of many new product quality and environmental regulations, though they surely achieve some desirable social objectives, is to raise capital requirements, elevate economies of scale through the imposition of research and testing requirements, and otherwise worsen the position of smaller firms in an industry and raise barriers facing new firms.

An example of the impact of quality regulation is in the security guard industry. Criticism has mounted over the lack of training that companies give their guards in the use of weapons, arrest techniques, and so on, and legislation to require mandatory training of a specified duration is on the horizon. Although such a requirement will be easily met by the larger companies, many smaller companies may be severely hurt by the increased overhead and the need to compete for higher skilled employees.

ENTRY AND EXIT

Entry clearly affects industry structure, particularly entry by established firms from other industries. Firms enter an industry because they perceive opportunities for growth and profits that exceed the costs of entry (or of surmounting mobility barriers).[9] Based on case studies of many industries, industry growth seems to be the most important signal to outsiders that there are future profits to be made, even though this can often be a poor assumption. Entry also follows particularly visible indications of future growth, such as regulatory changes, product innovations, and so on. For example, the energy crisis and recent proposed legislation to provide federal subsidy have evoked rapid entry into solar heating even though demand for solar heating is still quite low.

The entry into an industry (by either acquisition or internal development) of an established firm is often a major driving force for industry structural change.[10] Established firms from other markets generally have skills or resources that can be applied to change competition in the new industry; in fact this often provides a major motivation for their entry decision. Such skills and resources are very often different from those of existing firms, and their application in many cases changes the industry's structure. Also, firms in other markets may be able to perceive opportunities to change industry structure better than existing firms because they have no ties to historical strategies and may be in a position to be more aware of technological changes occurring outside the industry that can be applied to competing in it.

An example will serve to illustrate. In 1960, the U.S. wine industry was composed primarily of small family firms producing pre-

[9]The decision to enter a new industry is discussed in detail in Chapter 16.

[10]Entry into the domestic market of foreign firms already in the industry elsewhere in the world can also have major structural repercussions: The competitive norms may be very different in foreign markets, and strategic approaches may be very different as well.

mium wines and selling them in regional markets. There was little advertising or promotion, few firms had national distribution, and the competitive focus of most firms in the industry was clearly on the production of fine wines.[11] Profits in the industry were modest. In the mid-1960s, however, a number of large consumer marketing companies (e.g., Heublein, United Brands) either entered the industry through internal development or purchased existing wine producers. They began investing heavily in consumer advertising and promotion for both low-cost and premium brands. Since several of these firms had national distribution through liquor stores because they produced other alcoholic beverages, they rapidly expanded distribution for their brands nationally. Frequent introduction of new brand names became the rule in the industry, and many new products were introduced at the low end of the quality spectrum, which old-line companies had generally downplayed while they developed a name for U.S. wines. The profitability of the industry leaders was excellent. Thus the entry of a different type of firm into the U.S. wine industry has caused or at least speeded up a significant structural change in the industry, and one which the early family-controlled participants in the industry had neither the skills, the resources, nor the inclination to cause themselves.

Exit changes industry structure by reducing the number of firms and possibly increasing the dominance of the leading ones. Firms exit because they no longer perceive the possibility of earning returns on their investment that exceed the opportunity cost of capital. The exit process is impeded by exit barriers (Chapter 1), which worsen the position of remaining, healthier firms and may lead to price warfare and other competitive outbreaks. Increases in concentration and the ability of an industry's profitability to climb in response to industry structural shifts also will be impeded by the presence of exit barriers.

The evolutionary processes are a tool for predicting industry changes. Each evolutionary process is the basis of a key strategic question. For example, the potential impact of government regulatory change on an industry's structure means that a company must ask itself, "Are there any government actions on the horizon that may influence some element of the structure of my industry? If so, what does the change do for my relative strategic position, and how

---

[11]The only important exception was Gallo, which as a result was to play a major role in the industry.

can I prepare to deal with it effectively now?'' A similar question can be formulated for each of the other evolutionary processes discussed above. The set of questions that result should be asked on a repeated basis, perhaps even formally through the strategic planning process.

Furthermore, each evolutionary process identifies a number of key strategic *signals*, or pieces of key strategic information, for which the firm must constantly scan its environment. The entry of an established firm from another industry, a key development affecting a substitute product, and so on should cause a red light to go in the minds of executives charged with maintaining the strategic health of a business. This red light should trigger a chain of analysis to predict the significance of the change for the industry and the appropriate response.

Finally, it is important to note that learning, experience, increasing market size, and several other of the processes discussed above will be operating *even if there are no important distinct events to signal this*. The implication is that regular attention should be given to structural changes that may be resulting from these hidden processes.

Key Relationships in Industry Evolution

In the context of this analysis, *how* do industries change? They do not change in a piecemeal fashion, because an industry is an *interrelated system*. Change in one element of an industry's structure tends to trigger changes in other areas. For example, an innovation in marketing might develop a new buyer segment, but serving this new segment may trigger changes in manufacturing methods, thereby increasing economies of scale. The firms reaping these economies first will also be in a position to start backward integration, which will affect power with suppliers—and so on. One industry change, therefore, often sets off a chain reaction leading to many other changes.

It should be clear from the discussion in this chapter that whereas industry evolution is always occurring in nearly every business and requires a strategic response, there is no one way in which industries evolve. Any single model for evolution such as the product life cycle should therefore be rejected. However, there are some particularly important relationships in the evolutionary process that I will examine in this section.[12]

WILL THE INDUSTRY CONSOLIDATE?

It seems to be an accepted fact that industries tend to consolidate over time, but as a general statement, it simply is not true. In a broad sample of 151 4-digit U.S. manufacturing industries in the 1963-1972 time period, for example, 69 increased in 4-firm concentration more than 2 percentage points, whereas 52 decreased more than 2 percentage points over the same period. The question of whether consolidation will occur in an industry exposes perhaps the most important interrelationship among elements of industry structure—that involving competitive rivalry, mobility barriers, and exit barriers.

Industry Concentration and Mobility Barriers Move Together. If mobility barriers are high or especially if they increase, concentration almost always increases. For example, concentration has increased in the U.S. wine industry. In the standard-quality segment of the market, which represents much of the volume, the strategic changes described earlier in this chapter have greatly increased barriers to mobility (high advertising, national distribution, rapid brand innovation, etc). As a result, the larger firms have gotten further ahead of smaller ones, and few new firms have entered to challenge them.

No Concentration Takes Place if Mobility Barriers Are Low or Falling. Where barriers are low, unsuccessful firms that exit will be replaced by new firms. If a wave of exit has occurred because of an economic downturn or some other general adversity, there may be a temporary increase in industry concentration. But at the first signs that profits and sales in the industry are picking up, new entrants will appear. Thus a shake-out when an industry reaches maturity does not necessarily imply long-run consolidation.

[12]Industry evolution has implications for the optimal timing of entry into an industry; they are discussed in Chapter 10.

Exit Barriers Deter Consolidation. Exit barriers keep companies operating in an industry even though they are earning subnormal returns on investment. Even in an industry with relatively high mobility barriers, the leading firms cannot count on reaping the benefits of consolidation if high exit barriers hold unsuccessful firms in the market.

Long-run Profit Potential Depends on Future Structure. In the period of very rapid growth early in the life of an industry (especially after initial product acceptance has been achieved), profit levels are usually high. For example, growth in sales of skiing equipment were in excess of 20 percent per year in the late 1960s, and nearly all firms in the industry enjoyed strong financial results. When growth levels off in an industry, however, there is a period of turmoil as intensified rivalry weeds out the weaker firms. All firms in the industry may suffer financially during this adjustment period. Whether or not the remaining firms will enjoy above-average profitability will depend on the level of mobility barriers, as well as the other structural features of the industry. If mobility barriers are high or have increased as the industry has matured, the remaining firms in the industry may enjoy healthy financial results even in the new era of slower growth. If mobility barriers are low, however, slower growth probably means the end of above-average profits for the industry. Thus mature industries may or may not be as profitable as they were in their developmental period.

CHANGES IN INDUSTRY BOUNDARIES

Structural change in an industry is often accompanied by changes in industry boundaries. As discussed in Chapter 1, industry boundaries are a judgmental placement of the dotted line in Figure 8-4.

Industry evolution has a strong tendency to shift these boundaries. Innovations in the industry or those involving substitutes may effectively enlarge the industry by placing more firms into direct competition. Reduction in transportation cost relative to timber cost, for example, had made timber supply a world market rather than one restricted to continents. Innovations increasing the reliability and lowering the cost of electronic surveillance devices have put them into effective competition with security guard services. Struc-

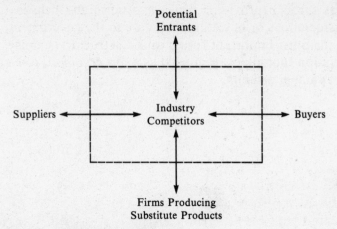

FIGURE 8-4.   Industry Boundaries

tural changes making it easier for suppliers to integrate forward into the industry may well mean that suppliers effectively become competitors. Or buyers purchasing private label goods in large quantities and dictating product design criteria may become effective competitors in the manufacturing industry (Sears-Roebuck). Part of the analysis of the strategic significance of industry evolution is clearly an analysis of how industry boundaries may be affected.

FIRMS CAN INFLUENCE INDUSTRY STRUCTURE

As described briefly in Chapter 1 and highlighted here, industry structural change can be influenced by firms' strategic behavior. If it understands the significance of structural change for its position, the firm can seek to influence industry change in ways favorable to it, either through the way it reacts to strategic changes of competitors or in the strategic changes it initiates.

Another way a company can influence structural change is to be very sensitive to external forces that can cause the industry to evolve. With a head start, it is often possible to direct such forces in ways appropriate to the firm's position. For example, the specific form of regulatory changes can be influenced; the diffusion of innovations coming from outside the industry can be altered by the form that licensing or other agreements with innovating firms take; positive action can be initiated to improve the cost or supply of complementary products through providing direct assistance and help in forming trade associations or in stating their case to the government; and so on for the other important forces causing structural change. Industry evolution should not be greeted as a *fait accompli*, to be reacted to, but as an opportunity.

II
Generic Industry Environments

Part II builds on the foundation of analytical techniques for formulating competitive strategy (in Part I) to consider the more specific analysis of strategy in important types of industry environments. Industry environments differ most strongly in their fundamental strategic implications along a number of key dimensions:

- industry concentration;
- state of industry maturity;
- exposure to international competition.

In Part II, I select a number of generic industry environments based on these dimensions for in-depth consideration. In each of these environments, the crucial aspects of industry structure, key strategic issues, characteristic strategic alternatives, and strategic pitfalls are identified.

Five important generic environments are singled out for consideration in Part II. Chapter 9 examines competitive strategy in fragmented industries, or industries where the level of industry concentration is low. Chapters 10, 11, and 12 consider strategy formulation in industries at fundamentally differing states of maturity: Chapter 10 examines the emerging or new industry; Chapter 11, the industry undergoing the difficult transition from rapid growth to maturity; and Chapter 12, the unique problems of the industry that is declining. Finally, Chapter 13 examines strategy formulation in global industries, an increasingly common industry setting in the 1980s.

The environments examined in Part II are all based on *one* key structural dimension of the industry, and each chapter develops the implications for competitive strategy of this one dimension. Although some of the chapters examine environments that are mutually exclusive (an industry might be emerging or declining but not both, for example), some of the industry environments may not be. For example, a global industry might also be fragmented or be undergoing transition to maturity.

The reader should begin by characterizing the environment of the particular industry being studied into the framework of Part II. In industries that fall into more than one of the environments examined, the problem of setting competitive strategy is one of reconciling the strategic implications flowing from each of the important aspects of the industry's structure.

9
Competitive Strategy In Fragmented Industries

An important structural environment in which many firms compete is the fragmented industry, that is, an industry in which no firm has a significant market share and can strongly influence the industry outcome. Usually fragmented industries are populated by a large number of small- and medium-sized companies, many of them privately held. There is no single precise quantitative definition of a fragmented industry, and such a definition is probably unnecessary for purposes of discussing the strategic issues in this important environment. The essential notion that makes these industries a unique environment in which to compete is the absence of market leaders with the power to shape industry events.

Fragmented industries are found in many areas of an economy, whether in the United States or some other country, and are common in areas such as the following:

- services;
- retailing;
- distribution;
- wood and metal fabrication;
- agricultural products;
- "creative" businesses.

Some fragmented industries, such as computer software and television program syndication, are characterized by products or services that are differentiated, whereas others, such as oil tanker shipping, electronic component distribution, and fabricated aluminum products, involve essentially undifferentiated products. Fragmented industries also vary greatly in their technological sophistication, ranging from high technology businesses like solar heating to garbage collection and liquor retailing. Exhibit 9-1 lists the U.S. manufacturing industries in which the share of the industry accounted for by the top four firms was 40 percent or less in 1972. Although this list leaves out distribution, services, and many other industries that do not fall into the manufacturing sector or have not yet emerged as census industries, it does provide an illustration of how broad the array of fragmented businesses is.

This chapter will examine the special problems of formulating competitive strategy in fragmented industries, seen as one important generic industry environment. As with the other chapters in Part II, this chapter is not intended as an exhaustive primer for competing in any particular fragmented industry. The full range of analytical techniques and concepts presented elsewhere in this book should be combined with the concepts in this chapter to draw conclusions about competitive strategy in any particular industry.

The chapter is divided into a number of sections. First, I will consider the reasons why industries are fragmented, because understanding this is essential to strategy formulation. Second, I will

EXHIBIT 9-1. Illustrative Fragmented Industries in U.S. Manufacturing, 1972

Industry (4-digit)	Total Market Share of Top 4 Firms (%)	Total Market Share of Top 8 Firms (%)
Meat-packing	22	37
Sausages and other prepared meats	19	26
Poultry dressing	17	26
Poultry and egg processing	23	36
Condensed and evaporated milk	39	58
Ice cream and frozen desserts	29	40
Fluid milk	18	26
Canned fruits and vegetables	20	31

EXHIBIT 9-1.   Continued

Industry (4-digit)	Total Market Share of Top 4 Firms (%)	Total Market Share of Top 8 Firms (%)
Dehydrated fruits, vegetables, soups	33	51
Frozen fruits and vegetables	29	43
Flour and other grain mill products	33	53
Bread, cake, and related products	29	39
Confectionary products	32	42
Animal and marine fats and oils	28	37
Fresh and frozen packaged fish	20	32
Narrow fabric mills	20	31
Knit outerwear mills	16	26
Finishing plants, cotton	27	41
Tufted carpets and rugs	20	33
Yarn mills, except wool	21	31
Throwing and winding mills	35	51
Lace goods	34	51
Paddings and upholstery filling	28	40
Cordage and twine	36	56
Men's and boys' suits and coats	19	31
Men's and boys' dress shirts and nightwear	22	31
Men's and boys' neckwear	26	36
Men's and boys' separate trousers	29	41
Women's and misses' blouses and waists	18	26
Women's and misses' dresses	9	13
Women's and misses' suits and coats	13	18
Women's and children's underwear	15	23
Children's dresses and blouses	17	26
Children's coats and suits	18	31
Fur goods	7	12
Robes and dressing gowns	24	39
Waterproof outer garments	31	40
Leather and sheep-lined clothing	19	32
Apparel belts	21	32
Curtains and draperies	35	43
Canvas and related products	23	29
Sawmills and planing mills, general	18	23

EXHIBIT 9-1. Continued

Industry (4-digit)	Total Market Share of Top 4 Firms (%)	Total Market Share of Top 8 Firms (%)
Wood kitchen cabinets	12	19
Mobile homes	26	37
Prefabricated wood buildings	33	40
Upholstered household furniture	14	23
Metal household furniture	13	24
Mattresses and bedsprings	24	31
Wood office furniture	25	38
Folding paperboard boxes	23	35
Corrugated and solid fiber boxes	18	32
Periodicals	26	38
Book publishing	19	31
Book printing	24	36
Commercial printing, letterpress	14	19
Commercial printing, lithographic	4	8
Typesetting	5	8
Photoengraving	13	19
Paints and allied products	22	34
Fertilizers, mixing only	24	38
Adhesives and sealants	19	31
Paving mixtures and blocks	15	23
Lubricating oils and greases	31	44
Leather tanning and finishing	17	28
Leather gloves and mittens	35	50
Women's handbags and purses	14	23
Cement, hydraulic	26	46
Brick and structural clay tile	17	26
Concrete blocks and bricks	5	8
Ready-mixed concrete	6	10
Steel wire and related products	18	30
Steel pipe and tubes	23	40
Aluminum foundries	23	30
Brass, bronze, and copper foundries	20	28
Plumbing fittings and brass goods	26	42
Heating equipment, except electric	22	31
Fabricated structural metal	10	14
Metal doors, sash, and trim	12	19
Fabricated platework (boiler shops)	29	35
Sheet metalwork	9	15

EXHIBIT 9-1. Continued

Industry (4-digit)	Total Market Share of Top 4 Firms (%)	Total Market Share of Top 8 Firms (%)
Conveyors and conveying equipment	22	32
Machine tools, metal forming types	18	33
Special dies, tools, jigs, and fixtures	7	10
Architectural metalwork	14	21
Screw machine products	6	9
Bolts, nuts, rivets, and washers	16	25
Iron and steel forgings	29	40
Plating and polishing	5	8
Metal coating and allied services	15	23
Valves and pipe fittings	11	21
Wire springs	26	38
Fabricated pipe and fittings	21	32
Machine tool accessories	19	30
Food products machinery	18	27
Textile machinery	31	46
Paper industries machinery	32	46
Pumps and pumping equipment	17	27
Blowers and fans	26	37
Industrial furnaces and ovens	30	43
Radio and TV communication equipment	19	33
Truck and bus bodies	26	34
Boat building and repairing	14	23
Engineering and scientific instruments	22	33
Jewelry, precious metal	21	26
Dolls	22	34
Games, toys, and children's vehicles	35	49
Sporting and athletic goods, N.E.C.	28	37
Costume jewelry	17	27
Artificial flowers	33	44
Buttons	31	47
Signs and advertising displays	6	10
Burial caskets	25	34

Source: U.S. Bureau of the Census, *1972 Census of Manufactures,* "Concentration Ratios in Manufacturing," Table 5.

discuss some approaches to stimulating structural change that can overcome industry fragmentation. Third, where overcoming fragmentation is unworkable, I will examine some of the alternatives for coping with a fragmented structure. Related to this discussion, some traps companies fall into in competing in fragmented industries will be identified. Finally, I will present a basic analytical framework for the formulation of competitive strategy in fragmented industries, drawing on the earlier sections of this chapter.

What Makes an Industry Fragmented?

Industries are fragmented for a wide variety of reasons, with greatly differing implications for competing in them. Some industries are fragmented for historical reasons—because of the resources or abilities of the firms historically in them—and there is no fundamental economic basis for fragmentation. However, in many industries there are underlying economic causes, and the principal ones seem to be as follows:

Low Overall Entry Barriers.   Nearly all fragmented industries have low overall entry barriers. Otherwise they could not be populated by so many small firms. However, although a prerequisite to fragmentation, low entry barriers are usually not *sufficient* to explain it. Fragmentation is nearly always accompanied by one or more of the other causes discussed below.

Absence of Economies of Scale or Experience Curve.   Most fragmented industries are characterized by the absence of significant scale economies or learning curves in any major aspect of the business, whether it be manufacturing, marketing, distribution, or research. Many fragmented industries have manufacturing processes characterized by few if any economies of scale or experience cost declines, because the process is a simple fabrication or assembly operation (fiberglass and polyurethane molding), is a straightforward warehousing operation (electronic component distribution), has an inherently high labor content (security guards), has a high personal service content, or is intrinsically hard to mechanize or routinize. In an industry like lobster fishing, for example, the unit of production is the individual boat. Having multiple boats does little to lower fishing costs because all boats are essentially fishing in the same waters with the same chance of a good catch. Thus there are many, many small operators with roughly equal costs. Until recently, mushroom farming has been similarly resistant to cost savings through scale or learning. Finicky mushrooms have been grown in caves by many small operators who know the "black art" required. Recently this situation has started to change, however, as will be discussed further.

High Transportation Costs.   High transportation costs limit the size of an efficient plant or production location despite the presence of economies of scale. Transportation costs balanced against economies of scale determine the radius a plant can economically service. Transportation costs are high in such industries as cement, fluid milk, and highly caustic chemicals. They are effectively high in many service industries because the service is "produced" at the customer's premises or the customer must come to where the service is produced.

High Inventory Costs or Erratic Sales Fluctuations.   Although there may be intrinsic economies of scale in the production process, they may not be reaped if inventory carrying costs are high and sales fluctuate. Here production has to be built up and down, which works against the construction of large-scale, capital-intensive facilities and operating them continuously. Similarly, if sales are very erratic and fluctuate over a wide range, then the firm with large-scale facilities may not have advantages over the smaller, more nimble firm, even if the large firm's production operations are more efficient in a fully loaded state. Small-scale, less specialized facilities or distribution systems are usually more flexible in absorbing output shifts than large, more specialized ones, even though they may have higher operating costs at a steady operating rate.

No Advantages of Size in Dealing with Buyers or Suppliers. The structure of the buyer groups and supplier industries is such that a firm gains no significant bargaining power in dealing with these adjacent businesses from being large. Buyers, for example, might be so large that even a large firm in the industry would only be marginally better off in bargaining with them than a smaller firm. Sometimes powerful buyers or suppliers will be powerful enough to actually keep companies in the industry small, through intentionally spreading their business or encouraging entry.

Diseconomies of Scale in Some Important Aspect. Diseconomies of scale can stem from a variety of factors. Rapid product changes or style changes demand quick response and intense coordination among functions. Where frequent new product introductions and style changes are essential to competition, allowing only short lead times, a large firm may be less efficient than a smaller one—which seems to be true in women's clothing and other industries in which style plays a major role in competition.

If maintaining a *low overhead* is crucial to success, this factor can favor the small firm under the iron hand of an owner-manager, unencumbered by pension plans and other corporate trappings and less subject to scrutiny by government regulators than the larger firm.

A highly *diverse product line* requiring customization to individual users requires a great deal of user-manufacturer interface on small volumes of product and can favor the small firm over the larger one. The business forms industry may be an example of one in which such product diversity has led to fragmentation. The top two North American business form producers hold only about a 35 percent share of the market.

Although there are exceptions, if *heavy creative content* is required, it is often difficult to maintain the productivity of creative personnel in a very large company. One sees no dominant firms in industries such as advertising and interior design.

If *close local control* and supervision of operations is essential to success the small firm may have an edge. In some industries, particularly services like nightclubs and eating places, an intense amount of close, personal supervision seems to be required. Absentee management works less effectively in such businesses, as a general rule, than an owner-manager who maintains close control over a relatively small operation.[1]

Smaller firms are often more efficient where *personal service* is the key to the business. The quality of personal service and the customer's perception that individualized, responsive service is being provided often seem to decline with the size of the firm once a threshold is reached. This factor seems to lead to fragmentation in such industries as beauty care and consulting.

Where a *local image and local contacts* often are keys to the business the large firm can be at a disadvantage. In some industries like aluminum fabricating, building supply, and many distribution

---

[1]A related situation is one in which the business requires long or unusual hours, such as agricultural supply dealers selling a large percentage of the year's volume of products like fertilizer and seed in a matter of a few frenetic weeks. It is difficult to get anyone but an owner-manager to make the required sacrifices.

businesses, a local presence is essential to success. Intense business development, contact building, and sales effort on a local level are necessary to compete. In such industries a local or regional firm can often outperform a larger firm provided it faces no significant cost disadvantages.

Diverse Market Needs.   In some industries buyers' tastes are fragmented, with different buyers each desiring special varieties of a product and willing (and able) to pay a premium for it rather than accept a more standardized version. Thus the demand for any particular product variety is small, and adequate volume is not present to support production, distribution, or marketing strategies that would yield advantages to the large firm. Sometimes fragmented buyers' tastes stem from regional or local differences in market needs, for example, in the fire engine industry. Every local fire department wants its own customized fire engine with many expensive bells, whistles, and other options. Thus nearly every fire engine sold is unique. Production is job shop and almost purely assembly, and there are literally dozens of fire engine manufacturers, none of whom has a major market share.

High Product Differentiation, Particularly if Based on Image. If product differentiation is very high and based on image, it can place limits on a firm's size and provide an umbrella that allows inefficient firms to survive. Large size may be inconsistent with an image of exclusivity or with the buyer's desire to have a brand all his or her own. Closely related to this situation is one in which key suppliers to the industry value exclusivity or a particular image in the channel for their products or services. Performing artists, for example, may prefer dealing with a small booking agency or record label that carries the image they desire to cultivate.

Exit Barriers.   If there are exit barriers, marginal firms will tend to stay in the industry and thereby hold back consolidation. Aside from economic exit barriers, managerial exit barriers appear to be common in fragmented industries. There may be competitors with goals that are not necessarily profit-oriented. Certain businesses may have a romantic appeal or excitement that attracts competitors who want to be in the industry despite low or even nonexistent profitability. This factor seems to be common in such industries as fishing and talent agencies.

Local Regulation. Local regulation, by forcing the firm to comply with standards that may be particularistic, or to be attuned to a local political scene, can be a major source of fragmentation in an industry, even where the other conditions do not hold. Local regulation has probably been a contributing factor to fragmentation in industries like liquor retailing and personal services such as dry cleaning and fitting eyeglasses.

Government Prohibition of Concentration. Legal restrictions prohibit consolidation in industries such as electric power and television and radio stations, and McFadden Act restrictions on branch banking across state lines are impeding consolidation in electronic funds transfer systems.

Newness. An industry can be fragmented because it is new and no firm or firms have yet developed the skills and resources to command a significant market share, even though there are no other impediments to consolidation. Solar heating and fiber optics may well have been in this state in 1979.

It takes the presence of only one of these characteristics to block the consolidation of an industry. If none of them are present in a fragmented industry, then this is an important conclusion, as will be discussed below.

Overcoming Fragmentation

Overcoming fragmentation can be a very significant strategic opportunity. The payoff to consolidating a fragmented industry can be high because the costs of entry into it are by definition low, and there tend to be small and relatively weak competitors who offer little threat of retaliation.

I have stressed earlier in this book that an industry must be viewed as an interrelated system, and this fact applies to fragmented industries as well. An industry can be fragmented because of only one of the factors listed in the previous section. If this fundamental block to consolidation can be somehow overcome, this often triggers a process by which the entire structure of the industry changes.

The beef cattle industry provides a good example of how a fragmented industry can change in structure. The industry has historically been characterized by a large number of small ranchers grazing cattle on rangelands and transporting them to a meat-packer for processing. Raising cattle has traditionally involved few economies of scale; if anything, there could well be diseconomies of controlling a very large herd and moving it from area to area. However, technological developments have led to the wider use of the feedlot as an alternative process for fattening cattle. Under carefully controlled conditions, the feedlot has proven to be a far cheaper way to put weight on animals. Constructing feedlots requires large capital outlays, though, and there appear to be significant economies of scale in their operation. As a result, some large beef growers, such as Iowa Beef and Monfort, are emerging and the industry is concentrating. These large growers are beginning to be large enough to backward integrate into processing of feeds and to forward integrate into meat processing and distribution. The latter has led to the development of brand names. In this industry the fundamental cause of fragmentation was the production technology utilized for fattening cattle. Once this impediment to consolidation was removed, a process of structural change was triggered which has encompassed many elements of industry structure going far beyond feedlots alone.

COMMON APPROACHES TO CONSOLIDATION

Overcoming fragmentation is predicated on changes that unlock the fundamental economic factors leading to the fragmented structure. Some common approaches to overcoming fragmentation are as follows:

Create Economies of Scale or Experience Curve. As in the beef cattle industry, if technological change leads to economies of scale or a significant experience curve, then consolidation can occur. Economies of scale created in one part of the business can sometimes outweigh diseconomies in another.

In manufacturing, innovations leading to mechanization and greater capital intensity have led to consolidation in the industry supplying laboratory animals for medical research and in the mushroom farming industry mentioned earlier in this chapter. In laboratory animals, Charles River Breeding Laboratories has pioneered the use of large, costly breeding facilities where sanitary conditions and all aspects of the animals' environment and diet are carefully controlled. Such facilities yield a superior animal for research and also unlock the fundamental cause of fragmentation in the industry. In mushroom farming, a few large companies have entered the industry and pioneered sophisticated processes for controlled mushroom growth by using conveyors, climate controls, and other devices that reduce labor costs and boost yields. These processes involve significant economies of scale, capital outlays, and technological sophistication and have provided a basis for consolidation to occur in the industry.

Innovations that create economies of scale in marketing can also lead to industry consolidation. For example, the widespread adoption of network television as the primary means of marketing toys has been accompanied by significant industry consolidation. The emergence of the exclusive, full-line dealer offering financing and service has brought about consolidation among earthmoving equipment manufacturers, with Caterpillar Tractor the major beneficiary.

The same basic arguments apply to creating scale economies in other functions, such as in distribution, service, and elsewhere.

Standardize Diverse Market Needs. Product or marketing innovations can standardize heretofore diverse market needs. For example, the creation of a new product might coalesce buyers' tastes; a design change might dramatically lower the cost of a standardized variety, leading buyers to judge the standardized product a better value than the expensive, custom variety. Modularizing a product might allow components to be produced in large volumes and thereby reap economies of scale or experience cost declines while maintaining the heterogeneity of final products. The potential for such innovations is clearly limited by the underlying economic characteristics of the industry, but in many industries the limiting factor to consolidation has seemed to be ingenuity and creativity in finding ways to deal with the causes of fragmentation.

Neutralize or Split Off Aspects Most Responsible for Fragmentation. Sometimes the causes of industry fragmentation are centered in one or two areas, such as diseconomies of scale in production or fragmented buyer tastes. One strategy for overcoming fragmentation is to somehow separate those aspects from the rest of the business. Two striking examples of this are campgrounds and fast food. Both these businesses rely on the need for tight local control and maintaining good service. They must also intrinsically consist of small individual locations, because any potential economies of scale in campground or fast-food facilities are offset by the need to locate near customers, or near the many major highways and vacation spots. Both the campground and fast-food industries have been historically fragmented, with thousands and thousands of small, owner-managed operations. Yet there are significant economies of scale in marketing and purchasing in both these businesses, particularly if national saturation can be achieved which allows the use of national advertising media. In both industries, fragmentation was overcome by franchising the individual locations to owner-managers, who operated under the mantle of a national organization which marketed the brand name and provided central purchasing and other services. Close control and maintenance of service are insured, as well as the benefits of economies of scale. This concept has spawned such giants as KOA in campgrounds and McDonald's, Pizza Hut, and many others in fast food. Another industry in which franchising is unlocking fragmentation today is real estate brokerage. Century 21 is rapidly expanding share in this highly fragmented industry by franchising local firms, allowing them to operate autonomously with their local names but doing so under the umbrella of the nationally advertised Century 21 name.

When the causes of fragmentation center around the production or service delivery process, as in the examples above, overcoming fragmentation requires decoupling production from the rest of the business. If buyer segments are numerous or where extreme product differentiation leads to preferences for exclusivity, it may be possible—through the use of multiple, scrupulously disassociated brand names and styles of packaging—to overcome the constraints placed on market share. Another case is that in which an artist or other customer or supplier wants to deal with a smaller, more personalized organization with a particular image or reputation. In the record industry, this desire has been dealt with by the use of multiple in-house labels and contracts with associated labels, all of which use the same record pressing, marketing, promotion, and distribution organization. Each label is set up independently and strives to create the personal touch for its artists. Yet the overall market share of the parent company can be significant, as in the case of CBS and Warner Brothers, each with about 20 percent of the market.

This basic approach to overcoming fragmentation recognizes that the root cause of the fragmentation cannot be altered. Rather, the strategy is to neutralize the parts of the business subject to fragmentation to allow advantages of share in other aspects to come into play.

Make Acquisitions for a Critical Mass. In some industries there may ultimately be some advantages to holding a significant share, but it is extremely difficult to build share incrementally because of the causes of fragmentation. For example, if local contacts are important in selling, it is difficult to invade the territory of other firms in order to expand. But if the firm can develop a threshold share, it can begin to reap any significant advantages of scale. In cases such as this, a strategy of making many acquisitions of local companies can be successful, provided the acquisitions can be integrated and managed.

Recognize Industry Trends Early. Sometimes industries consolidate naturally as they mature, particularly if the primary source of fragmentation was the newness of the industry; or exogenous industry trends can lead to consolidation by altering the causes of fragmentation. For example, computer service bureaus are facing increasing competition from minicomputers and microcomputers. This new technology means that even the small- and medium-sized firm can afford to have its own computer. Thus, service bureaus increasingly have had to service the large, multilocation company to continue their growth and/or to offer sophisticated programming and other services in addition to just computer time. This development has increased the economies of scale in the service bureau industry and is leading to consolidation.

In the service bureau example, the threat of substitute products triggered consolidation by shifting buyers' needs, and thereby stimulating changes in service that were increasingly subject to economies of scale. In other industries, changes in buyers' tastes, changes in the structure of distribution channels, and innumerable other industry trends may operate, directly or indirectly, on the causes of fragmentation. Government or regulatory changes can force consolidation by raising standards in the product or manufacturing process beyond the reach of small firms through the creation of economies of scale. Recognizing the ultimate effect of such trends, and positioning the company to take advantage of them, can be an important way of overcoming fragmentation.

INDUSTRIES THAT ARE "STUCK"

So far I have concentrated on industries whose fragmentation is rooted in industry economics and on ways of overcoming fragmentation that address these root causes. Yet a critical point to recognize for purposes of strategy is that many industries are fragmented, not for fundamental economic reasons, but because they are "stuck" in a fragmented state. Industries become stuck for a number of reasons.

Existing Firms Lack Resources or Skills. Sometimes the steps required to overcome fragmentation are evident, but existing firms lack the resources to make the necessary strategic investments. For example, there may be potential economies of scale in production, but firms lack the capital or expertise to construct large-scale facilities or to make required investments in vertical integration. Firms may also lack the resources or skills to develop in-house distribution channels, in-house service organizations, specialized logistical facilities, or consumer brand franchises that would promote industry consolidation.

Existing Firms Are Myopic or Complacent. Even though firms have the resources to promote industry consolidation, they may be emotionally tied to traditional industry practices that support the fragmented structure or otherwise unable to perceive opportunities for change. This fact, possibly combined with the lack of resources, may partly explain the historical fragmentation of the U.S. wine industry. Producers had long been production-oriented and had made apparently little effort to develop national distribution or consumer brand recognition. A number of large consumer goods and liquor companies bought their way into the industry in the mid-1960s and reversed this orientation.

Lack of Attention by Outside Firms. If the previous two conditions are present, some industries remain fragmented for long periods of time, despite presenting ripe targets for consolidation, because of lack of attention by outside firms. No outsiders perceive the opportunity to infuse resources and a fresh perspective into the industry to promote consolidation. Industries that escape attention (and offer ripe prospects for entry) tend to be those off the beaten track (manufacture of labels, mushroom farming) or those lacking glamour or any apparent excitement (manufacture of air filters and grease filters). They may also be too new or too small to be of interest to major established firms which have the resources to overcome fragmentation.

If a firm can spot an industry in which the fragmented structure does *not* reflect the underlying economics of competition, this can provide a most significant strategic opportunity. A company can enter such an industry cheaply because of its initial structure. Since there are no underlying economic causes of fragmentation, none of the investment costs or risks of innovations to change underlying economic structure need be borne.

Coping with Fragmentation

In many situations, industry fragmentation is indeed the result of underlying industry economics that cannot be overcome. Fragmented industries are characterized not only by many competitors but also by a generally weak bargaining position with suppliers and buyers. Marginal profitability can be the result. In such an environment, strategic *positioning* is of particularly crucial significance. The strategic challenge is to cope with fragmentation by becoming one of the most successful firms, although able to garner only a modest market share.

Since every industry is ultimately different, there is no generalized method for competing most effectively in a fragmented industry. However, there are a number of possible strategic alternatives for coping with a fragmented structure that should be considered when examining any particular situation. These are specific approaches to pursuing the low cost, differentiate, or focus generic strategies described in Chapter 2 in the peculiar environment of the fragmented industry. Each is directed at either better matching the firm's strategic posture to the particular nature of competition in fragmented industries or neutralizing the intense competitive forces that are usually the rule in these industries.

Tightly Managed Decentralization. Since fragmented industries often are characterized by the need for intense coordination, local management orientation, high personal service, and close control, an important alternative for competition is tightly managed decentralization. Rather than increasing the scale of operations at one or a few locations, this strategy involves deliberately keeping individual operations small and as autonomous as possible. This approach is supported by tight central control and performance-oriented compensation for local managers. This strategy is being practiced with great success by Indal in the aluminum extrusion and fabricating industry in Canada, by several growing chains of small- and medium-sized newspapers that have sprung up in the United States over the past decade, and by the highly successful Dillon Companies in the food retailing industry, just to name a few examples. Dillon, for instance, has a strategy of acquiring a group of small, regional grocery chains and keeping them autonomous, each with its own name, buying group, and so on. This system is reinforced with central control and a strong promotion-from-within policy. The strategy has avoided the homogenizing of individual units and resulting insensitivity to local conditions that plague some food chains, and as a by-product, has kept unionization low.

The essential notion of this type of strategy is to recognize and cater to the causes of fragmentation but to add a degree of professionalism to the manner in which local managers operate.

"Formula" Facilities. Another alternative, related to the previous one, is to view the key strategic variable in the business as the building of efficient, low-cost facilities at multiple locations. This strategy involves designing a standard facility, whether it be a plant or a service establishment, and polishing to a science the process of constructing and putting the facility into operation at minimum cost. The firm thereby lowers its investment relative to competitors and/or provides a more attractive or efficient location from which to do business. Some of the most successful mobile home producers, such as Fleetwood, Inc., have followed this strategy.

Increased Value Added. Many fragmented industries produce products or services that are commodities or otherwise difficult to differentiate; many distribution businesses, for example, stock similar if not identical product lines to their competitors'. In cases such as these, an effective strategy may be to increase the value added of the business by providing more service with sale, by engaging in some final fabrication of the product (like cutting to size or punching holes), or by doing subassembly or assembly of components before they are sold to the customer. Enhanced product differentiation, and thereby higher margins, that cannot be achieved on the basic product or service may be achievable through such activities. This concept has been successfully implemented by a number of metal distributors who have positioned themselves as "metal service centers," engaging in simple fabrication operations and providing a great deal of advice to the customer in what had historically been a purely pass-through business. Some electronic component distributors have similarly been successful in subassembly of connectors from individual components or assembling kits.

Value added can also sometimes be enhanced by forward integration from manufacturing into distribution or retailing. This step may neutralize buyers' power or allow greater product differentiation by better controlling the conditions of sale.

Specialization by Product Type or Product Segment. When industry fragmentation results from or is accompanied by the presence of numerous items in the product line, an effective strategy for achieving above-average results can be to specialize on a tightly constrained group of products. This approach is one variant of the focus strategy described in Chapter 2. It can allow the firm to achieve some bargaining power with suppliers by developing a significant volume of their products. It may also allow the enhancement of product differentiation with the customer as a result of the specialist's perceived expertise and image in the particular product area. The focused strategy allows the firm to be better informed about the product area and potentially to invest in its ability to educate customers and to provide services relating to the particular area. The cost of such a strategy of specialization may be some limitation in the growth prospects for the firm.

An intriguing example of product specialization coupled with increasing value added is provided by Ethan Allen, a highly successful participant in the fragmented U.S. furniture industry. Ethan Allen has specialized in early American furniture offering a line that allows the consumer to draw together individual items into professionally designed rooms:

> We are selling what you can do with the product, not the product itself. We offer the middle-class a service that only the rich could afford.[2]

The integrated concept allows Ethan Allen to charge up to a 20 percent premium for its products, which is plowed into heavy television advertising. The company also sells only through a unique network of independent, exclusive retail outlets, which allows it to enhance differentiation and avoid the hard bargaining of department stores and discount houses. Although the firm's market share is only about 3 percent, its profitability is well above average.

Specialization by Customer Type.   If competition is intense because of a fragmented structure, a firm can potentially benefit by specialization on a particular category of customer in the industry— perhaps the customers with the least bargaining leverage because they purchase small annual volumes or because they are small in absolute size. Or the firm might specialize in the customers who are the least price sensitive[3] or who most need the value added the firm can provide along with the basic product or service. Like product specialization, customer specialization may limit growth prospects for the firm in return for offering higher profitability.

Specialization by Type of Order.   Regardless of the customer, the firm can specialize in a particular type of order to cope with intense competitive pressure in a fragmented industry. One approach is to service only small orders for which the customer wants immediate delivery and is less price sensitive. Or the firm can service only custom orders to take advantage of less price sensitivity or to build switching costs. Once again, the cost of such specialization may be some limitation in volume.

A Focused Geographic Area.   Even though a significant industry-wide share is out of reach or there are no national economies of scale (and perhaps even diseconomies), there may be substantial economies in blanketing a given geographic area by concentrating facilities, marketing attention, and sales activity. This policy can economize on the use of the sales force, allow more efficient adver-

---

[2]"Nat Ancell's Unique Selling Proposition," *Forbes*, December 25, 1978.
[3]See Chapters 1 and 6 for a discussion of the characteristics that affect the bargaining power of buyers and their price sensitivity.

tising, allow a single distribution center, and so on. Having bits and pieces of business in a number of areas, on the other hand, accentuates the problems of competing in a fragmented industry. The blanketing strategy has been quite effective for food stores, which remain a fragmented industry despite the presence of some large national chains.

Bare Bones/No Frills.   Given the intensity of competition and low margins in many fragmented industries, a simple but powerful strategic alternative can be intense attention to maintaining a bare bones/no frills competitive posture—that is, low overhead, low-skilled employees, tight cost control, and attention to detail. This policy places the firm in the best position to compete on price and still make an above-average return.

Backward Integration.   Although the causes of fragmentation can preclude a large share of the market, selective backward integration may lower costs and put pressure on competitors who cannot afford such integration. Of course, the decision to integrate should be made only after a complete analysis, which is discussed in Chapter 14.

Potential Strategic Traps

The unique structural environment of the fragmented industry offers a number of characteristic strategic traps. Some common traps, which should serve as red flags in the analysis of strategic alternatives in any particular fragmented industry, are as follows:

Seeking Dominance.   The underlying structure of a fragmented industry makes seeking dominance futile unless that structure can be fundamentally changed. Barring this, a company trying to gain a dominant share of a fragmented industry is usually doomed to failure. The underlying economic causes of fragmentation usually insure that the firm exposes itself to inefficiencies, loss of product differentiation, and whims of suppliers and customers as it increases its share. Trying to be all things to all people generally maximizes vulnerability to the competitive forces in a fragmented industry, although it may be an extremely successful strategy in other industries in which there are cost advantages to volume production and other economies.

An example of a company that learned this lesson the hard way was Prelude Corporation, which had the stated goal of being the "General Motors of the lobster industry."[4] It built a large fleet of expensive, high-technology lobster boats; established in-house maintenance and docking facilities; and vertically integrated into trucking and restaurants. Unfortunately, the economics were such that its vessels had no significant advantage in catching lobsters over other fishermen, and its high overhead structure and heavy fixed costs maximized the company's vulnerability to the inherent fluctuations of the catch in the industry. The high fixed costs also led to undercutting on price by small fishermen who did not measure their businesses against corporate ROI targets but seemed satisfied with a much lower return. The result was a financial crisis and eventual cessation of operations. Nothing in the Prelude strategy addressed the causes of fragmentation in its industry, and hence its strategy of dominance was futile.

Lack of Strategic Discipline. Extreme strategic discipline is nearly always required for effective competition in fragmented industries. Unless the cause of fragmentation can be overcome, the competitive structure of fragmented industries generally requires focus or specialization on some tight strategic concept like those articulated in the previous section. Implementing these may well require the courage to turn away some business, as well as to go against the conventional wisdom of how things are done in the business generally. An undisciplined or opportunistic strategy may work in the short run, but it usually maximizes the exposure of the firm to the intense competitive forces common in fragmented industries in the longer run.

Overcentralization. The essence of competition in many fragmented industries is personal service, local contacts, close control of operations, ability to react to fluctuations or style changes, and so on. A centralized organizational structure is counterproductive in most cases, because it slows response time, lowers the incentives of those at the local level, and can drive away skilled individuals necessary to perform many personal services. Whereas centralized control

---

[4]For an extended description of Prelude see *Prelude Corporation*, Harvard Business School, ICCH #4-373-052, 1968.

is often useful and even essential in managing a multiunit enterprise in a fragmented industry, centralized structure can be a disaster.

Similarly, the economic structure of fragmented industries is often such that a centralized production or marketing organization is subject to no economies of scale, or even diseconomies. Thus centralization in these areas weakens rather than strengthens the firm.

Assumption that Competitors Have the Same Overhead and Objectives.   The peculiar nature of fragmented industries often means that there are many small, privately held firms. Also, owner-managers may have noneconomic reasons for being in the business. Under these circumstances, the assumption that these competitors will have an overhead structure or objectives of a corporation is a serious error. They often work out of homes, use family labor, and avoid regulatory costs and the need to offer employee benefits. Even though such competitors may be "inefficient," it does not mean that their costs are high relative to those of a corporation in the same business. Similarly, such competitors may be satisfied with much different (and lower) levels of profitability than a corporation, and they may be much more interested in keeping up volume and providing work for their employees than profitability per se. Thus their reactions to price changes and to other industry events may be a lot different than the "normal" company.

Overreactions to New Products.   In a fragmented industry the large number of competitors almost always insures that the buyer will exercise a great deal of power and be able to play one competitor against the other. In such a setting, products early in their life can often appear as salvations to an otherwise intense competitive situation. With rapidly growing demand and buyers generally unfamiliar with the new product, price competition may be modest and buyers may be clamoring for education and service from the firm. This is such a welcomed relief in the fragmented industry that firms make major investments in gearing up to respond. At the first signs of maturity, however, the fragmented structure catches up with demand and the margins that were there to support these investments disappear. Thus there is a risk of overreacting to new products in ways that will raise costs and overhead and put the firm at a competitive disadvantage in the price competition that is a fact of life in many fragmented industries. Although coping with new products is a difficult problem in all industries, it seems especially difficult in fragmented businesses.

Formulating Strategy

Collecting the ideas that have been discussed earlier, we are in a position to outline a broad analytical framework for formulating competitive strategy in fragmented industries (see Figure 9-1). *Step one* is to conduct a full industry and competitor analysis to identify the sources of the competitive forces in the industry, the structure within the industry, and the positions of the significant competitors. With this analysis as background, *step two* is to identify the causes of fragmentation in the industry. It is essential that the list of causes be complete and that their relationship to the economics of the industry be established. If there is no underlying economic basis for the fragmentation, this is an important conclusion, as has been discussed.

Step three is to examine the causes of industry fragmentation one by one in the context of the industry and competitor analysis in step one. Can any of these sources of fragmentation be overcome through innovation or strategic change? Is the infusion of resources or a fresh perspective all that is necessary? Will any of the sources of fragmentation be altered directly or indirectly by industry trends?

Step four depends on a positive answer to one of the preceding questions. If fragmentation can be overcome, the firm must assess whether or not the implied future structure of the industry will yield attractive returns. To answer this question the firm must predict the new structural equilibrium in the industry once consolidation occurs and must then reapply structural analysis. If the consolidated indus-

FIGURE 9-1   Steps for Formulating Competitive Strategy in Fragmented Industries

Step One	What is the structure of the industry and the positions of competitors?
Step Two	Why is the industry fragmented?
Step Three	Can fragmentation be overcome? How?
Step Four	Is overcoming fragmentation profitable? Where should the firm be positioned to do so?
Step Five	If fragmentation is inevitable, what is the best alternative for coping with it?

try does promise attractive returns, the final question is, What is the best, defendable position for the firm to adopt to take advantage of industry consolidation?

If the chances of overcoming fragmentation analyzed in step three are unfavorable, *step five* is to select the best alternative for coping with the fragmented structure. This step will involve a consideration of the broad alternatives presented above, as well as others that may be appropriate to the particular industry, in light of the particular resources and skills of the firm.

Besides providing a series of analytical processes to go through periodically, these steps also direct attention to the key pieces of data in analyzing fragmented industries and in competing in them. The causes of fragmentation, predictions about the effects of innovation on these causes, and identification of industry trends that might alter the causes of fragmentation become essential requirements for environmental scanning and technological forecasting.

10
Competitive Strategy in Emerging Industries

Emerging industries are newly formed or re-formed industries that have been created by technological innovations, shifts in relative cost relationships, emergence of new consumer needs, or other economic and sociological changes that elevate a new product or service to the level of a potentially viable business opportunity. Emerging industries are being created all the time; some of the many creations of the 1970s include solar heating, video games, fiber optics, word processing, bio-separation media, personal computers, and smoke alarms. From a strategic standpoint, the problems of an emerging industry are also present when an old business experiences a fundamental change in its competitive rules coupled with growth in scale by orders of magnitude, caused by the sorts of environmental changes just described. For example, bottled water has been around for many years, but the ascendance of Perrier is symptomatic of a growth and redefinition of the business that are fundamental. When such growth and redefinition have occurred, an industry must confront strategic issues that do not differ substantially from those of an industry beginning anew.

The essential characteristic of an emerging industry from the viewpoint of formulating strategy is that there are no rules of the game. The competitive problem in an emerging industry is that all the rules must be established such that the firm can cope with and prosper under them. The absence of rules is both a risk and a source of opportunity; in any case it must be managed.

This chapter will examine the problems of competitive strategy in this important structural environment, building on the analytical base developed in Part I. First the structural and competitor characteristics of emerging industries will be outlined, to highlight the competitive environment in such a setting. Next, I will identify the characteristic problems encountered in the development of a new industry, that limit its growth and are central to the jockeying for position among competitors. The factors that determine the buyers or buyer segments that will be early buyers, or "early adopters," of the new industry's product will be identified. Identifying these buyers is crucial, not only for formulating competitive strategy directly, but also for forecasting industry development since early adopters can have a major impact on the way in which an industry designs, produces, delivers, and markets its product.

Having identified some key aspects of the environment in emerging industries, I will then consider some important strategic choices that firms in them must face and some strategic alternatives that can be successful in coping with them. Finally, some analytical tools for forecasting the future of emerging industries will be presented, along with principles for selecting emerging industries that offer favorable prospects as candidates for entry.

The Structural Environment

Although emerging industries can differ a great deal in their structures, there are some common structural factors that seem to characterize many industries in this stage of their development. Most of them relate either to the absence of established bases for competition or other rules of the game or to the initial small size and newness of the industry.

COMMON STRUCTURAL CHARACTERISTICS

Technological Uncertainty. There is usually a great deal of uncertainty about the technology in an emerging industry: What product configuration will ultimately prove to be the best? Which production technology will prove to be the most efficient? For example, in smoke alarms there is continued uncertainty over whether photoelectric or ionization detectors will win out as the favored alternative; both are currently being produced by different companies.[1] The Philips and RCA approaches to video disc technology are contending for adoption as the industry standard, as did alternative approaches to television set technology in the 1940s. Alternative production technologies may also be present, all of which have been untried on a large-scale basis. In the manufacture of optical fibers, for example, there are at least five different processes backed by different industry participants.

Strategic Uncertainty. Related to the technological uncertainty, but broader in cause, are a wide variety of strategic approaches often being tried by industry participants. No "right" strategy has been clearly identified, and different firms are groping with different approaches to product/market positioning, marketing, servicing, and so on, as well as betting on different product configurations or production technologies. For example, solar heating firms are taking a wide variety of stances with respect to supplying components versus systems, market segmentation, and distribution channels. Closely related to this problem, firms often have poor information about competitors, characteristics of customers, and industry conditions in the emerging phase. No one knows who all the competitors are, and reliable industry sales and market share data are often simply unavailable, for example.

High Initial Costs but Steep Cost Reduction. Small production volume and newness usually combine to produce high costs in the emerging industry relative to those the industry can potentially achieve. Even for technologies for which the learning curve will soon level off, there is usually a very steep learning curve operating. Ideas come rapidly in terms of improved procedures, plant layout, and so on, and employees achieve major gains in productivity as job familiarity increases. Increasing sales make major additions to the scale and total accumulated volume of output produced by firms. These factors are accentuated if, as is common, the technology in the

[1]Abernathy usefully terms this the absence of a "dominant design" for the product or service. See Abernathy (1978).

emerging phase of the industry is more labor intensive than it may ultimately become.

The result of a steep learning curve is that the initially high costs are declining at a very high proportional rate. If the gains due to learning are combined with increasing opportunities to reap economies of scale as the industry grows, the cost declines will be even more rapid.

Embryonic Companies and Spin-Offs. The emerging phase of the industry is usually accompanied by the presence of the greatest proportion of newly formed companies (to be contrasted with newly formed units of established firms) that the industry will ever experience. Witness the many new firms populating such contemporary emerging industries as personal computers and solar heating and which characterized the early automobile industry (Packard, Hudson, Nash, and dozens of others) and early minicomputer industry (e.g., Digital Equipment, Data General, Computer Automation). Without established rules of the game or scale economies as deterrents, newly formed companies are in a position to get into emerging industries (this situation will be discussed further).

Related to the presence of newly formed companies is that of many spin-off firms, or firms created by personnel leaving firms in the industry to create their own new firms. Digital Equipment spawned a number of spin-offs in minicomputers (e.g., Data General) as did Varian Associates (e.g., General Automation), and Honeywell, and we could cite many other industries in which spin-offs were numerous. The phenomenon of spin-offs is related to a number of factors. First, in an environment of rapid growth and perceived opportunity, the rewards of equity participation may seem attractive when compared to a salary at an established company. Second, because of the fluidity of technology and strategy in the emerging phase, employees of established firms are often in a good position to think up new and better ideas, taking advantage of their proximity to the industry. Sometimes they leave in order to increase their potential rewards, but not infrequently spin-offs occur because the employee with a new idea confronts an unwillingness of his superior to try it, perhaps because it undermines much of the investment the firm has made in the past. Data General was formed, so industry observers tell it, when Edson de Castro and a handful of other Digital Equipment employees could not sell Digital on a new product idea they believed had high potential. Provided industry structure does not provide substantial entry barriers to newly created firms, spin-offs can be a common phenomenon in emerging industries.

First-Time Buyers.   Buyers of the emerging industry's product or service are inherently first-time buyers. The marketing task is thus one of inducing substitution, or getting the buyer to purchase the new product or service instead of something else. The buyer must be informed about the basic nature and functions of the new product or service, be convinced that it can actually perform these functions, and be persuaded that the risks of purchasing it are rationally borne given the potential benefits. Right now, for example, solar heating companies are struggling to persuade homeowners and homebuyers that the cost savings of solar heating are real, that systems will perform reliably, and that they need not wait for further government tax incentives to commit to the new technology. I will have much more to say later about the factors prompting buyers to commit themselves early to a new product or service.

Short Time Horizon.   In many emerging industries the pressure to develop customers or produce products to meet demand is so great that bottlenecks and problems are dealt with expediently rather than as a result of an analysis of future conditions. At the same time, industry conventions are often born out of pure chance: Confronted with the need to set a pricing schedule, for example, one firm adopts a two-tiered price that the marketing manager used in his previous firm, and the other firms in the industry imitate for lack of a ready alternative. In both these ways "conventional wisdom," which was discussed in Chapter 3, is created.

Subsidy.   In many emerging industries, especially those with radical new technology or that address areas of societal concern, there may be subsidization of early entrants. Subsidy may come from a variety of government and nongovernment sources; heavy subsidies in solar energy and conversion of fossil fuels into gas are particularly prominent examples of the early 1980s. Subsidies can be awarded directly to firms in the form of grants, or can operate indirectly through tax incentives, subsidizing buyers, and so on. Subsidies often add a great degree of instability to an industry, which is made dependent on political decisions that can be quickly reversed or modified. While subsidies are obviously beneficial to industry development in some respects, they often deeply involve government bodies in an industry, which can be a mixed blessing. Yet the need to overcome startup difficulties leads many emerging industries to seek subsidies; aquaculturists are actively lobbying for them in 1980.

EARLY MOBILITY BARRIERS

In an emerging industry, the configuration of mobility barriers is often predictably different from that which will characterize the industry later in its development. Common early barriers are the following:

- proprietary technology;
- access to distribution channels;
- access to raw materials and other inputs (skilled labor) of appropriate cost and quality;
- cost advantages due to experience, made more significant by the technological and competitive uncertainties;
- risk, which raises the effective opportunity cost of capital and thereby effective capital barriers.

As discussed in Chapter 8, some of these barriers—such as proprietary technology, access to distribution, learning effects, and risk—have a strong tendency to decline or disappear in importance as the industry develops. Although there are exceptions, early mobility barriers are usually *not* brand identification (it is just being created), economies of scale (the industry is too small to allow them), or capital (today's large firms can generate prodigious capital for a low-risk investment).

The nature of the early barriers is a key reason why we observe newly created companies in emerging industries. The typical early barriers stem less from the need to command massive resources than from the ability to bear risk, be creative technologically, and make forward-looking decisions to garner input supplies and distribution channels. These same sorts of barriers also help explain why established companies are often not the first firms into new industries, even if they have obvious strengths, but climb on the bandwagon later. Established companies may place a higher opportunity cost on capital and are often ill-prepared to take the technological and product risks necessary in the early phases of industry development. For example, the toy companies were relatively late entrants into video games despite some obvious strengths like knowledge of customers, brand names, and distribution. The dizzying technological change appears to have been too intimidating. Similarly, the traditional vacuum tube firms were late entrants into semiconductor manufacture, and the electric coffee percolator manufacturers were beaten in automatic drip coffee makers by new firms such as Mr. Coffee. There may be some advantages to late entry, however, that will be discussed later.

Problems Constraining Industry Development

Emerging industries usually face limits or problems, of varying severity, in getting the industry off the ground. These stem from the newness of the industry, its dependence for growth on other outside economic entities, and externalities in its development that result from its need to induce substitution by buyers to its product.

Inability to Obtain Raw Materials and Components. The development of an emerging industry requires that new suppliers be established or existing suppliers expand output and/or modify raw materials and components to meet the industry's needs. In the process, severe shortages of raw materials and components are very common in emerging industries. For example, acute shortages of color picture tubes in the mid-1960s was a major strategic factor affecting industry participants. Video game chips, particularly those for single-chip games pioneered by General Instrument, were very scarce and all but unavailable to new entrants for over a year after their introduction.

Period of Rapid Escalation of Raw Materials Prices. Confronted with burgeoning demand and inadequate supply, prices for key raw materials often skyrocket in the early phases of an emerging industry. This situation is partly simple economics of supply and demand and partly the result of suppliers realizing the value of their products to the desperate industry. As suppliers expand (or industry participants integrate to ease bottlenecks), however, prices for raw materials can fall off just as sharply. This fall-off will not happen when supplies of raw materials cannot expand easily, such as in mineral bearing lands and skilled labor.

Absence of Infrastructure. Emerging industries are often faced with difficulties like those of material supply caused by the lack of appropriate infrastructure: distribution channels, service facilities, trained mechanics, complementary products (e.g., appropriate campsites for recreational vehicles; coal supplies for coal gasification technology), and the like.

Absence of Product or Technological Standardization. Inability to agree on product or technical standards accentuates problems in the supply of raw materials or complementary products, and can impede cost improvements. The lack of agreement is usually caused by the high level of product and technological uncertainty that still remains in an emerging industry.

Perceived Likelihood of Obsolescence. An emerging industry's growth will be impeded if buyers perceive that second- or third-generation technologies will significantly make obsolete currently available products. Buyers will wait instead for the pace of technological progress and cost reduction to slow down. This phenomenon has been present in such industries as digital watches and electronic calculators.

Customers' Confusion. Emerging industries are often beset by customers' confusion, which results from the presence of a multiplicity of product approaches, technological variations, and conflicting claims and counterclaims by competitors. All these are symptomatic of technological uncertainty and the resulting lack of standardization and general technical agreement by industry participants. Such confusion can limit industry sales by raising the new buyers' perceived risk of purchase. For example, the conflicting claims being made by ionization versus photoelectric smoke alarm manufacturers are believed by some observers to be causing buyers to postpone purchases. An article summarizes a similar problem for the solar heating industry in 1979:

> But also important for the industry's future health will be its degree of success in matching equipment performance to customer

expectation. "Overenthusiasm, ignorance and selfish interests are endangering the success of applying a great energy source to America's needs," said Loff at the Denver solar conference. While Loff emphasized that inaction on the tax incentives was a root cause of industry malaise, he also blamed uninformed "solar messiahs, problems and failures with solar heating systems in buildings, and . . . irresponsible claims of suppliers."[2]

Erratic Product Quality. With many newly established firms, lack of standards, and technological uncertainty, product quality is often erratic in emerging industries. This erratic quality, even if caused by only a few firms, can negatively affect the image and credibility of the *entire industry*. Video game defects, such as the burning of television picture tubes, have set back early growth in much the same way as the erratic performance of digital watches (and of newly established franchised automobile tune-up centers) has led to customers' suspicion.

Image and Credibility with the Financial Community. As a result of newness, the high level of uncertainty, customer confusion, and erratic quality, the emerging industry's image and credibility with the financial community may be poor. This result can affect not only the ability of firms to secure low-cost financing but also the ability of buyers to obtain credit. Although difficulty in financing is probably the most common situation, some industries (usually high-technology businesses or "concept" companies) seem to be an exception. In industries like minicomputers and data transmission, even newly started firms have enjoyed a status as darlings of Wall Street, with very high multiples and effectively cheap money.[3]

Regulatory Approval. Emerging industries often face delays and red tape in gaining recognition and approval by regulatory agencies if they offer new approaches to needs currently served by other means and subject to regulation. For example, modular housing was severely crippled by inflexibility in building codes, and new medical products now face long periods of mandatory precertification testing. On the other hand, government policy can put an emerging in-

---

[2]"The Coming Boom in Solar Energy," *Business Week*, October 9, 1978.
[3]See Fruhan (1979) for other examples.

dustry on the map almost overnight, as it has by mandating smoke alarms.

If the emerging industry is outside a traditionally regulated sphere, regulation sometimes comes abruptly and can slow the industry's progress. For example, mineral water was traditionally ignored by regulators until the industry greatly expanded in the mid-1970s. Having reached significant size, however, mineral water producers are being drowned in regulations about labeling and health.[4] The same phenomenon occurred in bicycles and chain saws; once a growth boom increased the size of the industry, regulators took notice.

High Costs.   Because of many of the structural conditions described earlier, the emerging industry is often faced with unit costs much higher than firms know they will eventually be. This situation sometimes requires firms initially to price below cost or severely limit industry development. The problem is starting up the cost-volume cycle.

Response of Threatened Entities.   Some entity is almost always threatened by the advent of an emerging industry. It may be the industry producing a substitute product, labor unions, distribution channels with ties to the old product and preferring the certainty of dealing with it, and so on. For example, most electric utilities are lobbying against solar energy subsidies because they believe solar power will not relieve needs for peak load electrical capacity. Construction unions fought bitterly against modular housing.

The threatened entity can fight the emerging industry in a number of ways. One is in the regulatory or political arena; another is at the collective bargaining table. In the case of an industry threatened by substitution, its response can take the form of foregoing profits by lowering prices (or raising costs such as marketing) or making R&D investments aimed at making the threatened product or service more competitive. Figure 10-1 illustrates the latter choice.[5] If the threatened industry chooses to invest to try to bring its quality-adjusted costs down, it is clear that the target at which learning and scale-related cost reductions in the emerging industry must shoot is a moving one.

4"Mineral Water Could Drown in Regulation," *Business Week*, June 11, 1979.
5This diagram was suggested by John Forbus of McKinsey & Company.

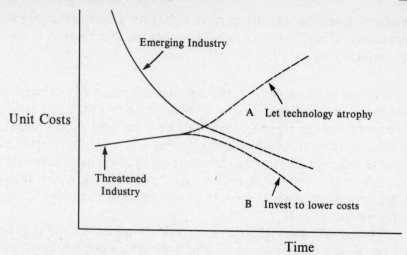

FIGURE 10-1.   Response of Threatened Industry to Substitution

The propensity of the threatened industry to forego profits in pricing or aggressively investing in cost reduction to hold volume will be a direct function of the *exit barriers* (see Chapters 1 and 12) in the threatened industry. If they are high because of specialized assets, high perceived strategic importance, emotional ties, or other causes, then the emerging industry may well face determined and even desperate efforts by the threatened industry to stem its growth.

Early and Late Markets[6]

One of the crucial questions for strategic purposes in an emerging industry is often the assessment of which markets for the new industry's product will open up early and which will come later. This assessment not only helps focus product development and marketing efforts but also is essential to forecasting structural evolution, since the early markets often exert a major influence on the manner in which an industry develops.

Markets, market segments, and even particular buyers within market segments may have greatly different receptivity to a new

[6]The ideas in this section have benefited greatly from work by Margaret O. Lawrence, then research assistant in Business Policy at the Harvard Business School.

product. A number of criteria seem to be crucial in determining this receptivity, some of which can be influenced or overcome by firms in the emerging industry.[7]

Nature of the Benefit. Perhaps the single most important determinant of the receptivity of the buyer to a new product or service is the nature of the expected benefit. We can imagine a continuum of benefits ranging from a new product that offers a *performance* advantage unachievable through other means to one that offers solely a *cost* advantage. Intermediate cases are those offering an advantage in performance but one that could be replicated through other means at higher cost.

The earliest markets purchasing a new product, other things being equal, are usually those in which the advantage is one of performance. This situation occurs because the achievement of a cost advantage *in practice* is often viewed with suspicion when buyers confront the newness, uncertainty, and often erratic performance of the emerging industry, among other factors to be discussed later. Whether the benefit from the new product is one of cost or performance, however, the receptivity of the buyer depends on a number of other aspects of the nature of the benefit it offers:

PERFORMANCE ADVANTAGE

- How large is the performance advantage for the particular buyers? Buyers will differ in this regard because of differences in their situations.
- How obvious is the advantage?
- How pressing is the need for the buyer to improve along the dimension offered by the new product?
- Does the performance advantage improve the competitive position of the buyer?
- How strong is competitive pressure to compel changeover? Performance advantages that help counter a threat to the buyer's business or are defensive in nature usually stimulate adoption before those that offer a chance to improve competitively on an offensive basis.
- How price and/or cost sensitive is the buyer, if the added performance entails higher cost?

[7]These criteria can also be applied to forecasting early markets for a new product variety in an established industry.

Cost Advantage

- How large is the cost advantage for the particular buyer?
- How obvious is the advantage?
- Can a lasting competitive advantage be gained from lowering costs?
- How much competitive pressure compels changeover?
- How cost-oriented is the prospective buyer's business strategy?

In some cases, buyers are compelled by regulatory fiat (or by fiat from other entitites, like insurance companies in order to qualify for insurance) to purchase a new product that serves a particular function. In such cases buyers usually will purchase the lowest cost alternative that meets the technical requirements.

State of the Art Required to Yield Significant Benefits. A second key factor in determining whether buyers will adopt the new product early is the technological performance their application demands of the product. Some buyers may be able to achieve valuable benefits even with rudimentary versions of the new product, whereas others will require more sophisticated varieties. For example, scientists in the laboratory were satisfied with relatively high-cost and low-speed minicomputers to solve data processing problems for which no real alternatives existed. Conversely, accounting and control applications required lower-cost and more sophisticated versions, and these applications developed later.

Cost of Product Failure. Buyers who face a relatively high cost of product failure will usually be slower in adopting a new product than ones whose risk is lower. Buyers whose use for the new product involves plugging it into an integrated system often face very high failure costs, as do buyers who pay particularly high penalties for interrupted service of the product for some reason. The cost of failure also depends on the resources of the buyers. For example, wealthy individuals are probably less concerned that their newly purchased snowmobile does not work or does not provide the claimed benefits than are individuals for whom the purchase will effectively negate possibilities for acquiring other leisure-time products.

Introduction or Switching Costs. The costs of introducing a new product or of substituting the new product for an existing one will differ for different buyers. These costs are analogous to switching costs, which are discussed in Chapters 1 and 6, and include the following:

- costs of retraining employees;
- costs of acquiring new ancillary equipment;
- write-offs due to undepreciated investment (net of salvage value) in old technology;
- capital requirements for changeover;
- engineering or R&D costs of changeover;
- costs in modifying interrelated stages of production or related aspects of the business.

Changeover costs can be subtle. For example, when adopting the new coal gasification technology instead of purchasing gas from a utility, a prospective buyer often must cope with changes in the chemical properties of the gas. For some buyers this affects the performance of the gas in their downstream manufacturing operations and requires investments in modification there.

Changeover costs are often influenced by the pace of changeover, when the pace is discretionary, and also by such factors as

- whether the new product is serving a *new function* or replacing an existing product; replacement often involves the added cost of retraining, undepreciated investment, and so on;
- length of redesign cycles; it is usually easier to substitute a new product during a period of normal redesign than if the substitution requires an unscheduled redesign.

Support Services. Closely related to changeover costs in influencing timing of adoption are the requirements the buyer faces for support services (e.g., engineering, repair) to cope with the new product, relative to the capability of the buyer. For example, if the new product requires skilled operators or service technicians, it is likely to be adopted first by buyers who either have such resources already or have experience in dealing with them.

Cost of Obsolescence. For particular buyers, the degree to which successive generations of technology in the emerging industry will make early versions of the product obsolete varies. Some buyers can obtain all the benefits they really need from the first generation, whereas others will be forced to acquire successive generations of the new product to remain competitive. Depending on their changeover costs (discussed above), the latter buyers may be more or less willing to buy early.

Asymmetric Government, Regulatory, or Labor Barriers. The degree to which regulatory barriers to adopting the new product are present may differ for various buyers. Food and pharmaceutical producers are closely monitored concerning any change in their manufacturing operations, for example, whereas firms in many other industries can change their processes freely. The same asymmetry can apply to inertia created by labor agreements.

Resources to Change. Buyers will differ with respect to the resources they have available for changeover to the new product, including capital, engineering, and R&D personnel.

Perception of Technological Change. Buyers may differ in their comfort with and experience in technological change. In businesses characterized by rapid technological progress and possessing a high degree of technological sophistication, a new product can seem a great deal less threatening than in a very stable, low-technology industry. Related to this factor, technological change in some industries is viewed as an opportunity to improve strategic position, whereas in others it has always been a threat. The former are more likely to be the early buyers of a new product than the latter, other things being equal.

Personal Risk to the Decision Maker. Buyers will be slowest to adopt a new product when the responsible decision maker faces the greatest perceived risk if the decision to adopt proves incorrect in the near to medium term. This perceived personal risk may vary a great deal, depending on the ownership or power structure of the buyer.

Strategic Choices

Formulation of strategy in emerging industries must cope with the uncertainty and risk of this period of an industry's development. The rules of the competitive game are largely undefined, the structure of the industry unsettled and probably changing, and competitors hard to diagnose. Yet all these factors have another side—the emerging phase of an industry's development is probably the period when the strategic degrees of freedom are the greatest and when the leverage from good strategic choices is the highest in determining performance.

Shaping Industry Structure.   The overriding strategic issue in emerging industries is the ability of the firm to shape industry structure. Through its choices, the firm can try to set the rules of the game in areas like product policy, marketing approach, and pricing strategy. Within the constraints set by the underlying economics of the industry and its resources, the firm should seek to define the rules in the industry in a manner that will yield it the strongest position in the long run.

Externalities in Industry Development.   In an emerging industry, a key strategic issue is the balance the firm strikes between industry advocacy and pursuing its own narrow self-interest. Because of potential problems with industry image, credibility, and confusion of buyers (outlined in Section II in this chapter), in the emerging phase the firm is in part dependent on others in the industry for its own success. The overriding problem for the industry is inducing substitution and attracting first-time buyers, and it is usually in the firm's interest during this phase to help promote standardization, police substandard quality and fly-by-night producers, and present a consistent front to suppliers, customers, government, and the financial community. Industry conferences and associations can be a useful device, as can the avoidance of strategies that degrade competitors. For example, in the hospital management industry that has grown up since 1970, all the participants are critically dependent on the industry's image of professionalism and its credibility with lenders. Firms in this industry have had a practice of actually praising the industry and their competitors by name.

This need for industry cooperation during the emerging period often seems to raise an internal dilemma for firms, who are driven toward pursuing their own market position, often to the detriment of industry development. A firm may resist standardization on products, needed to aid ease of repair and promote customers' confidence, because it wants to maintain uniqueness or garner the advantage of having its particular product variety adopted as standard. There is a fine line of judgment that determines whether or not such an approach is optimal in the long run. Some firms in the smoke alarm industry, for example, are advocating industry standards that will hurt other firms. At the same time, buyers' confusion is continuing about just what kind of alarm is best. The question is whether the industry is developed enough for such confusion to be a significant problem for future industry growth.

It is probably a valid generalization that the balance between industry outlook and firm outlook must shift in the direction of the firm as the industry begins to achieve significant penetration. Sometimes firms who have taken very high profiles as industry spokespersons, much to their and the industry's benefit, fail to recognize that they must shift their orientation. As a result, they can be left behind as the industry matures.

Another implication of externalities in industry development is the possibility that a firm may have to compete initially with a strategy it ultimately does not want to follow or participate in market segments it plans to drop out of in the long run. These "temporary" actions may be necessary to develop the industry, but once it is developed the firm is free to seek its optimal position. For example, Corning Glass Works has been forced to invest in research on connectors, splicing techniques, and light sources for fiber optic applications— even though in the long run Corning seems to want to be a fiber and cable supplier only—because the quality of available equipment and techniques has been an impediment to the development of fiber optics generally. Such investments outside the firm's ideal long-run position are part of the cost of pioneering.

Changing Role of Suppliers and Channels. Strategically, the firm in an emerging industry must be prepared for a possible shift in the orientation of its suppliers and distribution channels as the industry grows in size and proves itself. Suppliers may become increasingly willing (or can be forced) to respond to the industry's special needs in terms of varieties, service, and delivery. Similarly, distribution channels may become more receptive to investing in facilities, advertising, and so forth in partnership with the firms. Early exploitation of these changes in orientation can give the firm strategic leverage.

Shifting Mobility Barriers. As outlined above in this chapter, the early mobility barriers may erode quickly in an emerging industry, often to be replaced by very different ones as the industry grows in size and as the technology matures. This factor has a number of implications. The most obvious is that the firm must be prepared to find new ways to defend its position and must not rely solely on things like proprietary technology and a unique product variety on which it has succeeded in the past. Responding to shifting mobility barriers may involve commitments of capital that far exceed those that have been necessary in the early phases.

Another implication is that the *nature of entrants* into the industry may shift to more established firms attracted to the larger and increasingly proven (less risky) industry, often competing on the basis of the newer forms of mobility barriers, like scale and marketing clout. The firm in an emerging industry must forecast the nature of probable potential entrants based on its assessment of present and future barriers, coupled with the attraction the industry will hold to various types of firms and their ability to hurdle the barriers cheaply.

Another implication related to increasing industry size and technological maturity is that customers or suppliers may *integrate* into the industry—which has occurred in such industries as aerosol packaging, recreational vehicles, and electronic calculators. The firm must be prepared to secure supplies and markets if integration occurs or stop integration moves by the way in which it competes.

TIMING ENTRY

A crucial strategic choice for competing in emerging industries is the appropriate timing of entry. Early entry (or pioneering) involves high risk but may involve otherwise low entry barriers and can offer a large return. Early entry is appropriate when the following general circumstances hold:

- Image and reputation of the firm are important to the buyer, and the firm can develop an enhanced reputation by being a pioneer.
- Early entry can initiate the learning process in a business in which the learning curve is important, experience is difficult to imitate, and it will not be nullified by successive technological generations.
- Customer loyalty will be great, so that benefits will accrue to the firm that sells to the customer first.
- Absolute cost advantages can be gained by early commitment to supplies of raw materials, distribution channels, and so on.

Early entry is especially risky in the following circumstances:

- Early competition and market segmentation are on a basis different to that which will be important later in industry development. The firm, therefore, builds the wrong skills and may face high costs of changeover.
- Costs of opening up the market are great, including such things as customer education, regulatory approvals, and technological pioneering, and the benefits of opening up the market cannot be made proprietary to the firm.
- Early competition with small, newly started firms will be costly, but these firms will be replaced by more formidable competition later.
- Technological change will make early investments obsolete and allow firms entering later to have an advantage by having the newest products and processes.

Tactical Moves. The problems limiting development of an emerging industry suggest some tactical moves that may improve the firm's strategic position:

- Early commitments to suppliers of raw materials will yield favorable priorities in times of shortages.
- Financing can be timed to take advantage of a Wall Street love affair with the industry if it happens, even if financing is ahead of actual needs. This step lowers the firm's cost of capital.

COPING WITH COMPETITORS

Coping with competitors in an emerging industry may be a difficult problem, particularly for firms that have been pioneers and have enjoyed major market shares. The proliferation of newly formed entrants and spin-offs may cause resentments, and the firm must confront the external factors described previously which make it in part dependent on competitors for the development of the industry.

One common problem in emerging industries is that pioneers expend excessive resources defending high market shares and responding to competitors who may have little chance of becoming market forces in the long run. This can be partly an emotional reaction. Although it may sometimes be appropriate to respond to competitors vigorously in the emerging phase, it is more likely that the firm's efforts are best spent in building its own strengths and in developing the industry. It may even be appropriate to *encourage* the entry of certain competitors, perhaps through licensing or other means. Given the characteristics of the emerging phase, the firm often benefits from having other firms aggressively selling the industry's product and aiding in technological development. The firm may also want competitors who are known quantities, rather than preserving a large share for itself but inviting entry by major established firms as the industry matures. It is difficult to generalize about the appropriate strategy, but only in rare cases will it be feasible and profitable to defend a near monopoly market share as the industry grows rapidly, even though the firm has one initially.

Techniques for Forecasting

The overriding aspect of emerging industries is great uncertainty, coupled with the certainty that change will occur. Strategy cannot be formulated without an explicit or implicit forecast of how the structure of the industry will evolve. Unfortunately, however, the number of variables that enter into such a forecast is usually staggering. As a result, an approach for reducing the complexity of the forecasting process is highly desirable.

The device of *scenarios* is a particularly useful tool in emerging industries. Scenarios are discrete, internally consistent views of how the world will look in the future, which can be selected to bound the probable range of outcomes that might feasibly occur. Scenarios can be used for forecasting in emerging industries as shown in Figure 10-2. The starting point for forecasting is estimating the future evolution of product and technology, in such terms as cost, product variety, and performance. The analyst should select a small number of internally consistent product/technology scenarios that encompasses the range of possible outcomes. For each of these scenarios, the analyst then creates a scenario of which markets will open up and what their size and characteristics will be. Here the first feedback loop occurs, since the nature of the markets that open up early can shape the way in which the products and technology evolve. The analyst must

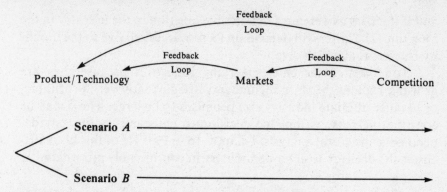

FIGURE 10-2.   Forecasting in an Emerging Industry

attempt to build this interaction in an iterative way into the scenarios.

The next step is to develop the implications for competiton for each product/technology/market scenario and then forecast the probable success of different competitors. This process may well involve forecasting the entry of new firms, and accomplishing it will involve further feedbacks, because the nature and resources of competitors can influence the direction an industry takes in its development.

Having developed the scenarios as outlined, the firm is in a position to examine its position, assessing which scenario it will bet on or how it will behave strategically if each scenario actually occurs. The firm may choose to try to *cause* the most advantageous scenario to occur if it has resources; or it may be forced by limited resources or great uncertainty to maintain flexibility. In any case, the firm will benefit by identifying explicitly the *key events* which will signal whether one scenario or another is actually occurring, in order to create an agenda for its strategic planning and technological monitoring.

Which Emerging Industries to Enter

The choice of which emerging industry to enter is dependent on the outcome of a predictive exercise such as the one described above. An emerging industry is attractive if its ultimate structure (not its *initial* structure) is one that is consistent with above-average returns and if the firm can create a defendable position in the industry in the long run. The latter will depend on its resources relative to the mobility barriers that will evolve.

Too often firms enter emerging industries because they are growing rapidly, because incumbents are currently very profitable, or because ultimate industry size promises to be large. These may be contributing reasons, but the decision to enter must ultimately depend on a structural analysis. Chapter 16 in Part III of this book discusses the decision to enter an industry in considerably more detail.

11
The Transition to Industry Maturity

As part of their evolutionary process, many industries pass from periods of rapid growth to the more modest growth of what is commonly called industry maturity. Snowmobiles, hand calculators, tennis courts and equipment, and integrated circuits are just a few of the industries going through such a process in the mid- and late 1970s. As discussed in Chapter 8, industry maturity does not occur at any fixed point in an industry's development, and it can be delayed by innovations or other events that fuel continued growth for industry participants. Moreover, in response to strategic breakthroughs, mature industries may regain their rapid growth and thereby go through more than one transition to maturity. With these important qualifications in mind, however, let us consider the case in which a transition to maturity is occurring and possibilities for forestalling such a transition have been exhausted.

When it occurs, the transition to maturity is nearly always a critical period for companies in an industry. It is a period during which fundamental changes often take place in companies' competitive environment, requiring difficult strategic responses. Firms sometimes have trouble perceiving these environmental changes clearly; even when they are perceived, responding to them can require changes in strategy that firms balk at making. Moreover, the impact of transition to maturity extends beyond strategic considerations, holding implications for the organizational structure of the firm and the role of its leadership. These administrative implications are at the heart of some of the difficulties in making the required strategic adjustments.

This chapter will examine some of these issues, drawing on the analytical base in Part I of this book. It will focus on identifying the strategic and administrative problems raised by the transition rather than on an analysis of the process itself. Industry evolution itself is treated in more depth in Chapter 8.

Industry Change during Transition

Transition to maturity can often signal a number of important changes in an industry's competitive environment. Some of the probable tendencies for change are as follows:

1. *Slowing growth means more competition for market share.* With companies unable to maintain historical growth rates merely by holding market share, competitive attention turns inward toward attacking the shares of the others. This situation occurred in 1978 in the dishwasher business, which was becoming saturated, when both GE and Maytag began to attack Hobart aggressively in the higher-price segments of the market. Increased competition for market share requires a fundamental reorientation in a company's perspective and a completely new set of assumptions about how competitors will behave and react. Competitor analysis like that described in Chapters 3 and 4 must be repeated. Knowledge of competitors' characteristics and their reactions that has been gained in the past must be reassessed, if not discarded. Not only are competitors probably going to be more aggressive, but also the likelihood of misperceptions and "irrational" retaliation is great. Outbreaks of price, service, and promotional warfare are common during transition to maturity.

2. *Firms in the industry increasingly are selling to experienced, repeat buyers.* The product is no longer new but an established, legitimate item. Buyers are often increasingly knowledgeable and experienced, having already purchased the product, sometimes repeatedly.

The buyers' focus shifts from deciding whether to purchase the product at all to making choices among brands. Approaching these differently oriented buyers requires a fundamental reassessment of strategy.

3. *Competition often shifts toward greater emphasis on cost and service.* As a result of slower growth, more knowledgeable buyers, and usually greater technological maturity, competition tends to become more cost- and service-oriented. This development shifts the requirements for success in the industry and may require a dramatic reorientation of the "way of life" in a company used to competing on other grounds. The added pressure on costs may also increase requirements for capital by forcing the firm to acquire the most modern facilities and equipment.

4. *There is a topping-out problem in adding industry capacity and personnel.* As the industry adjusts to slower growth, the rate of capacity addition in the industry must slow down as well or overcapacity will occur. Thus companies' orientations toward adding capacity and personnel must fundamentally shift and be disassociated from the euphoria of the past. A firm is confronted with the need to monitor competitors' capacity additions closely and to time its capacity additions with precision. Rapid growth will no longer quickly cover mistakes by rapidly eliminating excess capacity.

These shifts in perspective rarely occur in maturing industries, and overshooting of industry capacity relative to demand is common. Overshooting leads to a period of overcapacity, accentuating the tendency during transition toward price warfare. The greater the size of efficient increments of capacity in the industry, the more difficult the topping-out problem. It is also more difficult if the personnel to be added are highly skilled and require long periods to locate and train.

5. *Manufacturing, marketing, distributing, selling, and research methods are often undergoing change.* These changes are caused by increased competition for market share, technological maturity, and buyer sophistication. (Some of the possible changes have been discussed in Chapter 8.)The firm is faced with the need for either a fundamental reorientation of its functional policies or some strategic action that will make reorientation unnecessary. If the firm must respond to such changes in functional policy, capital resources and new skills are almost always required. Adoption of new manufacturing methods may accentuate the problems of overcapacity discussed above.

6. *New products and applications are harder to come by*. Whereas the growth phase may have been one of rapid discovery of new products and applications, the ability to continue product change generally becomes increasingly limited, or the costs and risks greatly increase, as the industry matures. This change requires, among other things, a reorientation of attitude toward research and new product development.

7. *International competition increases*. As a consequence of technological maturity, often accompanied by product standardization and increasing emphasis on costs, transition is often marked by the emergence of significant international competition. The forces leading to internationalization of an industry are discussed in detail in Chapter 13, as are some of the key implications of global competition. International competitors often have different cost structures and different goals than domestic firms and a home market base from which to operate. Significant exports or foreign investment by domestic firms usually predates transition to maturity in a large market like the United States.

8. *Industry profits often fall during the transition period, sometimes temporarily and sometimes permanently*. Slowing growth, more sophisticated buyers, more emphasis on market share, and the uncertainties and difficulties of the required strategic changes usually mean that industry profits fall in the short run from the levels of the pretransition growth phase. Some firms may be more affected than others, the firms with smaller share usually the most. Falling profits reduce cash flow during a period when it may be sorely needed. They also tend to send stock prices tumbling for publicly held companies and increase the difficulty of raising debt financing. Whether or not profits will rebound depends on the level of mobility barriers and other elements of industry structure which have been discussed in Part I.

9. *Dealers' margins fall, but their power increases*. For the same reasons that industry profits are often depressed, dealers' margins may be squeezed, and many dealers may drop out of the business—often *before* the effect on manufacturers' profits is noticeable. This factor may be seen recently among dealers of television receivers and recreational vehicles. Such trends tighten competition among industry participants for dealers, who may have been easy to find and hold in the growth phase but not upon maturity. Thus, dealers' power may increase markedly.

Some Strategic Implications of Transition

The changes that often accompany transition to maturity represent possible changes in the basic structure of the industry. Each major element of industry structure often is changing: overall mobility barriers, the relative significance of various barriers, the intensity of rivalry (it usually increases), and so on. Structural change nearly always means that firms must respond strategically, because it implies that the fundamental nature of competition changes correspondingly in the industry.

Some characteristic strategic issues often arise in transition. These are presented as issues to examine rather than generalizations that will apply to all industries; like humans, all industries mature a little differently. Many of these approaches can be a basis for the entry of new firms into an industry even though it is mature.

OVERALL COST LEADERSHIP VERSUS DIFFERENTIATE VERSUS FOCUS—THE STRATEGIC DILEMMA MADE ACUTE BY MATURITY

Rapid growth tends to mask strategic errors and allow most, if not all, companies in the industry to survive and even to prosper financially. Strategic experimentation is high, and a wide variety of strategies can coexist. Strategic sloppiness is generally exposed by industry maturity, however. Maturity may force companies to confront, often for the first time, the need to choose among the three generic strategies described in Chapter 2. It becomes a matter of survival.

SOPHISTICATED COST ANALYSIS

Cost analysis becomes increasingly important in maturity to (1) rationalize the product mix and (2) price correctly.

RATIONALIZING THE PRODUCT MIX

Although a broad product line and frequent introduction of new varieties and options may have been possible during growth, and often necessary and desirable for industry development, this situation may no longer be viable in the mature setting. Cost competition and fights for market share are too demanding. As a result, a quantum improvement in the sophistication of product costing is necessary to allow pruning of unprofitable items from the line and to focus attention on items either that have some distinctive advantage (technology, cost, image, etc.) or whose buyers are "good" buyers.[1] Average costing for groups of products, or the loading of average overhead for costing purposes, becomes inadequate for evaluating the product line and possible additions to it. The need to rationalize the product line sometimes creates the need to install computerized costing systems, which had not been of high priority during the industry's developmental years. Such line pruning has been crucial to RCA's success with Hertz, for example.

CORRECT PRICING

Related to product line rationalization is the change in pricing methodology that is often necessary in maturity. Although average-cost pricing, or pricing the line as a whole rather than as individual items, may have been sufficient in the growth era,[2] maturity often requires increased capability to measure costs on individual items and to price accordingly. Implicit cross-subsidization within the product line through average-cost pricing hides products whose markets cannot support their true costs and gives away profits in those situations in which buyers are not price sensitive. Cross-subsidization also invites price cutting or new product introductions by competitors against the items priced artificially high. Competitors who lack the costing sophistication to price rationally, and hence who retard the adjustment of prices on unrealistically low-priced items, are sometimes a problem in mature industries.

Sometimes other aspects of pricing strategy can and should be changed in maturity. For example, Mark Controls has achieved great success in the tough valve business by eliminating unprofitable lines and also by renegotiating contracts with buyers to include escalator clauses for inflation. Contracts in the industry traditionally had been fixed price, and inflation adjustments were not critical to raising prices in the growth phase; no other firm had ever had to negotiate escalator clauses. However, they have proved to be of great

[1] See Chapter 6.

[2] Average-cost pricing may have been desirable to develop the full product line and establish a market position.

benefit in the mature phase, when making price increases stick has become increasingly difficult.

We might summarize this and the other points in this section by saying that an enhanced level of "financial consciousness" along a variety of dimensions is often necessary in maturity, whereas in the developmental period of the industry areas such as new products and research may have rightly held center stage. Raising financial consciousness may be more or less difficult in the industry depending on the training and orientation of management. In the Mark Controls case, for example, it took a financially oriented outsider to initiate financial innovations in an industry dominated by established family firms.

PROCESS INNOVATION AND DESIGN FOR MANUFACTURE

The relative importance of process innovations usually increases in maturity, as does the payoff for designing the product and its delivery system to facilitate lower-cost manufacturing and control.[3] Japanese industry has put a great premium on this factor, to which many attribute its success in industries such as television receivers. Designing for manufacture has also been key to Canteen Corporation's improvements in position in the maturing industrial food service business. Canteen has moved from allowing local cooks latitude in the preparation of meals toward common dish formulations nationwide. This change has improved the consistency of the quality of meals, allowed easier shifting of cooks among locations, facilitated easier control of operations, and led to other cost-savings and productivity improvements.[4]

INCREASING SCOPE OF PURCHASES

Increasing purchases of existing customers may be more desirable than seeking new customers. Incremental sales to existing customers can sometimes be increased by supplying peripheral equipment and service, upgrading the product line, widening the line, and so on. Such a strategy may take the firm out of the industry into related industries. This strategy is often less costly than finding new

[3]For an intriguing study documenting this situation, see Abernathy (1978).
[4]For a brief description, see *Business Week*, August 15, 1977.

customers. In a mature industry, winning new customers usually means battling for market share with competitors and is consequently quite expensive.

This strategy has been or is being practiced successfully by such firms as Southland Corp. (7-Eleven Stores), Household Finance Corporation (HFC), and Gerber Products. Southland is adding fast food, self-service gas, pinball machines, and other lines to its stores to capture a bigger share of its customers' dollars and to increase impulse buying and avoid the cost of establishing new locations. Similarly, HFC is adding new services, such as tax preparation, larger loans, and even banking, to broaden the product line it can sell to its very large customer base. Gerber's strategy of "more bucks per baby" is another variation of the same approach. Gerber has added infant clothes and other infant products to its dominant baby-food line.

BUY CHEAP ASSETS

Sometimes assets can be acquired very cheaply as a result of the company distress that is caused by transition to maturity. A strategy of acquiring distressed companies or buying liquidated assets can improve margins and create a low-cost position if the rate of technological change is not too great. This strategy has been employed successfully by little-known Heilman in the brewing industry. Despite increasing concentration at the top of the industry, Heilman grew at 18 percent per year from 1972–1976 (to $300 million in sales in 1976), with a return on equity in excess of 20 percent, by acquiring regional brewers and used equipment at bargain prices. Industry leaders have been blocked from acquisitions by the antitrust laws and have been forced to build large new plants at current prices. White Consolidated also employs a variant of this strategy. It specializes in purchasing distressed companies, such as Sundstrand's machine tool business and Westinghouse's appliance business, at prices below book value and then reducing overhead. In many cases this strategy results in a profitable going concern.

BUYER SELECTION

As buyers become more knowledgeable and competitive pressures increase in maturity, buyer selection can sometimes be a key to continued profitability. Buyers who may not have exercised their bargaining power in the past, or had less power because of limited product availability, will usually not be bashful about exercising their power in maturity. Identifying "good" buyers and locking them in, as discussed in Chapter 6, becomes crucial.

DIFFERENT COST CURVES

There is often more than one cost curve possible in an industry. The firm that is *not* the overall cost leader in a mature market can sometimes find new cost curves which may actually make it a lower-cost producer for certain types of buyers, product varieties, or order sizes. This step is key to implementing the generic strategy of focus described in Chapter 2. Consider Figure 11-1, for example:

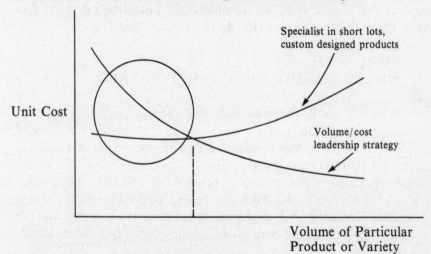

FIGURE 11-1. Alternative Cost Curves

The firm explicitly designing its manufacturing process for flexibility, rapid setups, and short lots (general purpose, computer-controlled machines, for example) may well enjoy cost advantages over the high-volume producer for servicing custom orders or small lots. A viable strategy in such a situation is to focus on orders in the circled area of Figure 11-1. Cost curve differences allowing such a strategy may be based on small orders, custom orders, particular small-volume product varieties, and others. Wickham Skinner has described how such manufacturing strategies can be implemented in his concept of the "focused factory."[5]

COMPETING INTERNATIONALLY

A firm may escape maturity by competing internationally where the industry is more favorably structured. This straightforward approach has been practiced, for example, by Crown Cork and Seal in metal containers and crowns, and Massey-Ferguson in farm implements. Sometimes equipment that is obsolete in the home market can be used quite effectively in international markets, greatly lowering the costs of entry there. Or industry structure may be a great deal more favorable internationally, with less sophisticated and powerful buyers, fewer competitors, and the like. The drawbacks to this strategy are the familiar risks of international competition and the fact that it may only postpone maturity rather than deal with it.

SHOULD TRANSITION BE ATTEMPTED AT ALL?

It should not be taken as given that the strategic shifts required to compete successfully in a maturing industry should be attempted at all, in view of the substantial and perhaps new types of resources and skills that may be required. The choice depends not only on resources but also on the number of other firms who have the capability to keep playing in the industry, the expected duration of the turmoil in the industry while adjustments to maturity are made, and the future prospects for industry profits (which depend on future industry structure).

For some companies, a disinvestment strategy may be better than making further reinvestments with an uncertain payout—which is what Dean Foods has done in fluid milk. Emphasis at Dean has been on cost cutting and highly selective investments in cost-saving equipment rather than on expansion of market position.

Industry leaders may or may not be in the best position to make the adjustments required by transition if they have substantial inertia built into their strategies and strong ties to the strategic requirements of the growth phase of the industry's development. The flexibility of a smaller firm may prove advantageous in transition,

[5]Skinner (1974).

provided the resources needed to adjust are available. The small firm may also be able to segment the market easier. Similarly, a new firm entering the industry during the transition phase, possessing financial and other resources but no ties to the past, is often able to establish a strong position. The turmoil caused by the transition period yields opportunities for the potential entrant provided long-run industry structure is favorable.

Strategic Pitfalls in Transition

In addition to failure to recognize the strategic implications of transition described above, there is the tendency for firms to fall prey to some characteristic strategic pitfalls:

1. *A company's self-perceptions and its perception of the industry.* Companies develop perceptions or images of themselves and their relative capabilities ("we are the quality leader"; "we provide superior customer service"), which are reflected in the implicit assumptions that form the basis of their strategies (see Chapter 3). These self-perceptions may be increasingly inaccurate as transition proceeds, buyers' priorities adjust, and competitors respond to new industry conditions. Similarly, firms have assumptions about the industry, competitors, buyers, and suppliers which may be invalidated by transition. Yet altering these assumptions, built up through actual past experience, is sometimes a difficult process.

2. *Caught in the middle.* The problem of being caught in the middle described in Chapter 2 is particularly acute in transition to maturity. Transition often squeezes out the slack that has made this strategy viable in the past.

3. *The cash trap—investments to build share in a mature market.* Cash should be invested in a business only with the expectation of being able to remove it later. In a mature, slow-growing industry, the assumptions required to justify investing new cash in order to build market share are often heroic. Maturity of the industry works against increasing or maintaining margins long enough to recoup cash investments down the road, by making the present value of cash inflows justify the outflows. Thus businesses in maturity can be cash traps, particularly when a firm is not in a strong market position but is attempting to build a large market share in a maturing market. The odds are against it.

A related pitfall is placing heavy attention on revenues in the maturing market instead of on profitability. This strategy may have been desirable in the growth phase, but it usually faces diminishing returns in maturity. Hertz may very well have had this problem in the late 1960s, offering RCA much opportunity for achieving a profit turnaround in the mid-1970s.

4. *Giving up market share too easily in favor of short-run profits.* In the face of the profit pressures in transition, there seems to be a tendency for some companies to try to maintain the profitability of the recent past—which is done at the expense of market share or by foregoing marketing, R&D, and other needed investments, which in turn hurts future market position. Unwillingness to accept lower profits during transition can be seriously shortsighted if economies of scale will be significant in the mature industry. A period of lower profits may be inevitable while industry rationalization occurs, and a cool head is necessary to avoid overreaction.

5. *Resentment and irrational reaction to price competition ("we will not compete on price").* It is often difficult for firms to accept the need for price competition after a period in which it has not been necessary, and therefore, when avoiding it may have been a sacred rule. Some managements even view price competition as unseemly or beneath their dignity. This can be a dangerous reaction to transition, when a firm willing to price aggressively may be able to take share that will be crucial to establishing a low-cost position for the long run.

6. *Resentment and irrational reaction to changes in industry practices ("they are hurting the industry").* Changes in industry practices, such as marketing techniques, production methods, and the nature of distributor contracts are often an inevitable part of transition. They may be important to the industry's long-run potential, but there is often resistance to them. Substitutions of machines for hand methods are resisted, as they have been in some sporting goods businesses, and firms are unwilling to begin aggressively marketing their products ("marketing does not work in this industry; it requires personal selling"). And so on. Such resistance can put a firm seriously behind in adapting to the new competitive environment.

7. *Overemphasis on "creative," "new" products rather than improving and aggressively selling existing ones.* Although past success in the early and growth phases of an industry may have been built on research and on new products, the onset of maturity often

means that new products and applications are harder to come by. It is usually appropriate that the focus of innovative activity should change, putting standardization rather than newness and fine tuning at a premium. Yet this development is not satisfying to some companies and is often resisted.

8. *Clinging to "higher quality" as an excuse for not meeting aggressive pricing and marketing moves of competitors.* High quality can be a crucial company strength, but quality differentials have a tendency to erode as an industry matures (see Chapter 8). Even if they remain, more knowledgeable buyers may be willing to trade quality for lower prices in a mature business where they have purchased the products before. Yet it is difficult for many companies to accept the fact that they do not possess the highest quality product or that their quality is unnecessarily high.

9. *Overhanging excess capacity.* As a result of capacity overshooting demand, or because of capacity increases that inevitably accompany the plant modernization required to compete in the mature industry, some firms may have some excess capacity. Its mere presence creates both subtle and unsubtle pressures to utilize it, and it can be used in ways that will undermine the firm's strategy. For example, overhanging capacity can push a firm into the middle, in the terminology of Chapter 2, rather than maintaining a more focused approach. Or it can lead to managerial pressures to fall into the cash trap. It is often desirable to sell off or scrap excess capacity rather than hold it. Obviously, however, capacity should not be sold to anyone who will use it in the same business.

Organizational Implications of Maturity

We tend to think of requirements for organizational change as resulting from major shifts in strategy and from evolution in the size and diversification of a company. The necessary fit between organizational structure and a firm's strategy holds equally true in industry maturity, and the transition to maturity can be one of the critical points in the development of an organizational structure and systems. Particularly in the area of control and motivational systems, there are some subtle adjustments that must take place.

On the strategic level, we have discussed how a firm must be prepared to adjust its key competitive priorities to the often differing requirements of industry maturity. More attention to costs, customer service, and true marketing (as opposed to selling) may be required. Reduced attention to introducing new products versus refining old ones may be necessary. Less "creativity" and more attention to detail and pragmatism is often what is needed in the mature business.

These shifts in competitive focus obviously require changes in organizational structure and systems to support them. Systems designed to highlight and control different areas of the business are necessary. Tighter budgeting, stricter control, and new performance-based incentive systems may well be required in the mature business, all more formal than those used previously.[6] Control of financial assets such as inventory and accounts receivable may take on greater importance. All these sorts of changes have been key to successful company turnarounds in industries such as nursing homes and recreational vehicles that have recently gone through transition.

More coordination across functions and among manufacturing facilities must often occur for the company to be cost competitive. For example, industry maturity means that regional plants heretofore operating independently may well have to be tied together and better coordinated, requiring not only new systems and procedures but also major changes in the plant managers' jobs.

There can sometimes be resistance to changes along these lines. The company that has prided itself on pioneering and on a high-quality product may find it very difficult to engage in "distasteful" price competition and in aggressive marketing, as was discussed previously. Competition along these dimensions is often resented deep down in the organization, all the way to the shop floor and the sales force. Sacrificing quality for costs and close monitoring of costs are resisted. Furthermore, new reporting requirements, new controls, new organizational relationships, and other changes are sometimes seen as a loss in personal autonomy and as a threat. A company must be prepared to reeducate and remotivate personnel at all levels as it enters the maturity stage.

---

[6]In the transition from an entrepreneurally managed to a more professionally managed company, organization and systems must become more rationalized, formal, and impersonal. Whereas this transition is difficult in itself, it is important to note that the organizational transition required to cope with industry maturity may also involve a *different* structure and *different* focal points for the key managerial systems, as a result of the changes in the competitive environment brought on by maturity. If these two transitions have to occur simultaneously in a company, it raises a serious challenge.

General management must also be aware of subtle changes in the motivational climate in the organization that can accompany transition to industry maturity. In the growth period which preceded transition, opportunities for advancement have usually been great, excitement has been high for the participants in the rapidly growing enterprise, and intrinsic job satisfaction has obviated the need for much in the way of formal internal mechanisms to build company loyalty. Yet in the more mature competitive environment, there is less growth, less glamour, less excitement, and the spirit of pioneering and uniqueness tends to fade. This development raises a number of extremely difficult problems for general management.

1. *Scaled down expectations for financial performance.* The standards for acceptable growth and profits must often be reduced in managers' minds. If managers try to meet the old standards, they may take actions that are extremely dysfunctional for the long-run health of the company in the mature market unless it has an extremely strong market position. The scaling-down process is difficult because a strong tradition of achieving financial results may have been built up through past successes by the organization. I hasten to add that general management of the organization is subject to the same problems in revising its own expectations.

2. *More discipline from the organization.* All the common environmental changes in a mature industry previously described allow less slack and require greater discipline from the organization in executing its chosen strategy. This need extends to all layers of the organization in tangible and intangible ways.

3. *Scaled-down expectations for advancement.* Past rates of personal advancement are unlikely to be possible in the more mature environment. Yet managers may have learned to define success in terms of advancement at the old pace. Many managers may leave during the transition process for these reasons, and the pressure the organization places on the general manager can be great. The challenge for general management is to find new ways to motivate and reward personnel. The pressure of transition in this area leads some companies to diversify to provide the growth and advancement possibilities of those of the past. Diversifying *solely* for this reason can be a serious error.

4. *More attention on the human dimension.* In the process of adapting to the new climate of the mature industry, and the shifting strategic priorities implied, there will usually be a need to place more attention internally on the human dimension. Organizational mecha-

nisms are required to build more company identification and loyalty, and more subtle motivational devices must be developed than those that have sufficed during the rapid growth phase. Support and encouragement internally are needed to replace the external stimuli and rewards of the past and to provide a backstop for the difficult internal adjustments in organizational climate that may be required.

5. *Recentralization.* The pressures industry maturity places on cost control may sometimes require the reversal of previous moves to create autonomous profit centers, at the plant level and elsewhere. This is particularly true if the profit center organization was designed to facilitate the addition of new products or to open up new markets as the industry developed.

A shift back to a more functional organization increases central control, can eliminate substantial overhead, and can enhance the possibilities for coordination among units. Coordination may become more important than entrepreneurship in the mature business. Crown Cork and Seal achieved a dramatic turnaround by using this approach, troubled Texfi is now attempting it in its textiles,[7] and Burger King is using it to take on McDonald's.

Industry Transition and the General Manager

Industry transition to maturity, especially when it requires many of the strategic adjustments described above, often signals a new "way of life" in a company. The excitement of rapid growth and pioneering are replaced by the need to control costs, compete on price, market aggressively, and so on. This change in the way of life has important implications for the general manager.

The *atmosphere* of the company may well change in ways the general manager may find undesirable. He or she cannot provide as much opportunity and advancement for personnel and must increasingly measure performance closely through detailed and formal systems. The old informality and personal friendships may be hard to maintain in such an environment. The *skills* required of the general manager shift as the key requirements of the organization shift. Tight cost control, cross-functional coordination, marketing, and so on may be very different skills than those required to build the orga-

[7] *Business Week*, August 15, 1977.

nization in a rapidly growing industry. These new skills are both strategic and administrative, and thus the adaptation is doubly difficult.[8] Finally, the *mood* or feeling of excitement and pioneering the general manager has felt in the past may give way to one of increasing pressure to keep up and concern for survival. Often a sort of malaise appears.

Thus transition to maturity is often a difficult period for a general manager, particularly for the founding entrepreneur but not exclusively so. Some unfortunate but common outcomes are as follows:

- Denies transition: The general manager fails to recognize and accept the changes required or lacks the required skills. As a result, the historical strategy and organizational arrangements are doggedly continued. This sort of rigidity is a common reaction to strategic difficulty not only during transition but also in other adverse company situations.[9]
- Leaves active management: Recognizing that either the new way of life in the company is no longer satisfactory or that his or her managerial skills are inadequate for the new environment, the general manager relinquishes control.

The implication of industry transition for the general manager carries an important message not only for the general manager himself but also for the corporate management of diversified companies. The standards for measuring business unit managers usually need to change in a mature business, as do the skills and orientation of the general manager. It may be, for these reasons, that rotation of managers is appropriate as a division enters maturity. There is a tendency in diversified companies to apply the same standards to division managers regardless of their fundamentally different strategic situations and to expect managers skilled in one setting to manage well in another. Attention to the managerial implications of transition to maturity is one way to avoid these difficulties.

---

[8]In the classic transition from an entrepreneurally to professionally managed company, the adaptation in skills required of the general manager is largely along organizational and administrative lines only.

[9]See Porter (1976b).

12
Competitive Strategy in Declining Industries

For purposes of strategic analysis, declining industries are treated here as those that have experienced an absolute decline in unit sales over a sustained period.[1] Thus, decline cannot be ascribed to the business cycle or to other short-term discontinuities, such as strikes or material shortages, but represents a true situation in which end-game strategies must be developed. There have always been industries in decline, but the prevalence of this difficult structural environment has probably increased with slower world economic growth, product substitution resulting from rapid cost inflation, and continued technological change in areas like electronics, computers, and chemicals.

Although deceptively familiar as a phase of the product life cycle, declining industries have not received much study. The decline phase of a business is characterized in the life-cycle model as one of shrinking margins, pruning product lines, falling R&D and advertising, and a dwindling number of competitors. The accepted strategic prescription for decline is a "harvest" strategy, that is, eliminating investment and generating maximum cash flow from the business,

[1]This chapter has benefited greatly from work by Kathryn Rudie Harrigan, my student at Harvard and now Assistant Professor of Business at the University of Texas at Dallas.

followed by eventual divestment. The product portfolio models in common use for planning today yield the same advice for declining industries: Do not invest in slow or negative-growth, unfavorable markets but pull cash out.

However, in-depth study of a wide spectrum of declining industries suggests that the nature of competition during decline as well as the strategic alternatives available to firms for coping with decline are a great deal more complex. Industries differ markedly in the way competition responds to decline; some industries age gracefully, whereas others are characterized by bitter warfare, prolonged excess capacity, and heavy operating losses. Successful strategies vary just as widely. Some firms have reaped high returns from strategies actually involving heavy reinvestment in a declining industry that make their businesses better cash cows later. Others have avoided losses subsequently borne by their competitors by exiting before the decline was generally recognized, and not harvesting at all.

This chapter will apply the analytical tools of Part I to the peculiar environment of declining industries, in cases where the decline itself is beyond the control of incumbent firms.[2] First I will describe the structural conditions that determine the nature of competition during the decline phase and the hospitability of the industry to those firms that remain. Next I will identify in some detail the generic strategic alternatives (end-game strategies) available to the firm in decline. The chapter will conclude with some principles for choosing a strategy.

Structural Determinants of Competition in Decline

In the context of the analysis in Chapter 1, a number of structural factors take on a particular importance in determining the nature of competition in the decline phase of an industry. Shrinking industry sales make this phase potentially volatile. However, the extent to which the incipient competitive pressure erodes profitability depends on some key conditions, which influence how easily capaci-

[2]Decline may sometimes be reversed through innovations, cost reduction, and shifts in other circumstances. Some approaches to staving off decline are discussed in Chapter 8. Our focus in this chapter is on industries in which available remedies have been exhausted and the strategic problem thus becomes coping with decline.

ty will leave the industry and how bitterly the remaining firms will try to stem the tide of their own shrinking sales.

CONDITIONS OF DEMAND

The process by which demand declines and the characteristics of the market segments that remain have a major influence on competition in the decline phase.

UNCERTAINTY

The degree of uncertainty perceived by competitors (whether rationally or not) about whether demand will continue to decline is one of the most potent factors affecting end-game competition. If firms believe that demand might revitalize or level off, they will probably try to hold onto their positions and remain in the industry. Their efforts to maintain position despite shrinking sales will have a high probability of leading to bitter warfare. This situation has been occurring in the rayon industry, where there have been continued and probably justified hopes that rayon's losses to nylon and steel in the tire cord market, and losses to other fibers in the textile market, could be reversed. On the other hand, if all firms are certain that industry demand will continue to decline, it will facilitate the process of withdrawing capacity from the market in an orderly fashion. In acetylene, for example, it became quickly clear that the skyrocketing cost of natural gas would make ethylene a lower-cost substitute for many of the chemical processes using acetylene. Here the least efficient firms began early to develop strategies for withdrawal.

Firms may well *differ* in their perceptions of future demand; some firms may foresee a higher probability of revitalization, and these firms will be prone to hang on. Furthermore, there is some evidence in case histories of declining industries that a firm's perception of the likelihood of future decline is influenced by its position in the industry and its exit barriers. The stronger the firm's position or the higher the exit barriers it faces in leaving, the more optimism seems to exist in its projections of the future.

RATE AND PATTERN OF DECLINE

The more slowly decline is proceeding, the more it may be masked by short-run factors in firms' analyses of their positions, and the more uncertainty there usually is about future decline. Uncertainty greatly increases the volatility of this phase. If demand is declining precipitously, on the other hand, firms have a hard time in justifying optimistic future projections. In addition, large declines in sales make abandonments of whole plants or divestiture of whole divisions more likely, which can rapidly adjust industry capacity downward. The smoothness of decline also plays a part in uncertainty. If the industry's sales are inherently erratic such as in rayon and acetate, it may be difficult to separate the downward trend in sales from the confusion caused by period-to-period fluctuations.

The rate of decline is partly a function of the pattern in which firms actually decide to withdraw capacity from the business. In industrial businesses whose product is an important input to customers, demand can decline precipitously if one or two major producers decide to withdraw. Customers fear for the continued availability of a key input, and they are prone to shift to a substitute more quickly than otherwise. So firms that announce exit early can strongly influence the rate of decline. The rate also has a tendency to accelerate as decline proceeds because shrinking volume raises costs and perhaps prices.

Structure of Remaining Demand Pockets

As demand declines, the nature of the pockets of demand that remain plays a major role in determining the profitability of the remaining competitors. These may offer more or less favorable prospects for profitability, based on a complete structural analysis like that outlined in Chapter 1. For example, one of the major remaining pockets of demand in the cigar industry is the premium segment. This segment is quite immune to substitution, has price-insensitive buyers, and is amenable to the creation of high levels of product differentiation. The firms that can maintain a position in this segment are well placed to earn above-average returns, even as the industry declines, because they can defend their positions from competitive forces. In the leather industry, upholstery leathers have been a surviving pocket in which technology and differentiation have the same effect. In acetylene, on the other hand, the market segments where acetylene has not been displaced by ethylene are threatened by still other substitutes, and in those markets acetylene is a commodity product subject to price warfare because of its high fixed manufacturing costs. Thus profit potential in the remaining pockets is pretty dismal.

In general, an end game can be profitable for the survivors if the remaining pockets of demand involve price-insensitive buyers or those who have little bargaining power, because they have high switching costs or other traits like those discussed in Chapter 6. Commonly, remaining demand is price-insensitive when it is replacement demand and when demand from the manufacturers of the original equipment has disappeared. The profitability of the end game will also depend on the vulnerability of remaining pockets of demand to substitutes and to powerful suppliers, as well as the presence of mobility barriers, which protect firms serving the remaining segments from attack by firms seeking to replace sales lost in disappearing segments.

CAUSES OF DECLINE

Industry demand declines for a number of different reasons, which have implications for competition during the decline phase:

Technological Substitution. One source of decline is substitute products created through technological innovation (electronic calculators for sliderules) or made prominent by shifts in relative costs and quality (synthetics for leather). This source can be threatening to industry profits because increasing substitution usually depresses profits at the same time it cuts into sales. This negative effect on profits is mitigated if there are pockets of demand in the industry that are immune or resistant to the substitute and have favorable characteristics in the sense previously described. Substitution may or may not be accompanied by uncertainty over future demand, depending on the industry.

Demographics. Another source of decline is shrinkage in the size of the customer group that purchases the product. In industrial businesses, demographics cause decline by reducing demand in downstream industries. Demographics as a source of decline is not accompanied by the competitive pressure of a substitute product. Thus if capacity can leave the industry affected by demographics in an orderly way, surviving firms may have profit prospects comparable to those before decline. However, demographic shifts are often subject to great uncertainty, which is destabilizing for competition in decline as has been discussed.

Shifts in Needs.   Demand can fall because of sociological or other reasons which change buyers' needs or tastes. For example, cigar consumption has fallen in large part because of cigars' plummeting social acceptability. Like demographics, shifts in needs do not necessarily lead to increased pressure of substitutes for remaining sales. However, shifts in needs can also be subject to great uncertainties, like those in cigars, which have led many firms to continue to forecast a resurgence of demand. This situation is very threatening to profitability in decline.

The cause of decline, then, gives clues about the probable degree of uncertainty firms perceive about future demand as well as some indications about the profitability of serving the remaining segments.

EXIT BARRIERS

Crucial to competition in declining industries is the manner in which capacity leaves the market. Just as there are barriers to entry, however, there are *exit barriers* which keep firms competing in declining industries even though they are earning subnormal returns on investment. The higher the exit barriers, then, the less hospitable the industry will be to the firms that remain during decline.

Exit barriers stem from a number of fundamental sources:

DURABLE AND SPECIALIZED ASSETS

If the assets of a business, either fixed or working capital or both, are highly specialized to the particular business, company, or location in which they are being used, this creates exit barriers by diminishing the liquidation value of the firm's investment in the business. Specialized assets either must be sold to someone who intends to use them in the same business (and if they are specialized enough, to use them in the same location) or their value is greatly diminished and they must often be scrapped. The number of buyers wishing to use the assets in the same business is usually few, because the same reasons that make the firm want to sell its assets in a declining market will probably discourage potential buyers. For example, an acetylene manufacturing complex or a rayon plant has such specialized equipment that it must be sold to another owner for the same use or scrapped. An acetylene plant, futhermore, is so difficult to dismantle and transport that the costs of doing so may equal or exceed the scrap value. Once the acetylene and rayon industries began to decline, the potential buyers willing to continue to operate the plants up for sale were close to nonexistent; those plants that were sold were sold at enormous discounts to book value and often to speculators or desperate employee groups. Inventory in a declining industry may also be worth very little, particularly if it normally turns over very slowly.

If the liquidation value of the assets of a business is low, it is economically optimal for the firm to remain in the business even if the expected discounted future cash flows are low. If the assets are durable, the book value may greatly exceed the liquidation value. Thus it is possible for a firm to earn a book loss but it be economically appropriate to remain in the business because the discounted cash flows exceeded the opportunity cost of capital on the investment that could be released if the business were divested. Divesting the business in any situation in which the book value exceeds the liquidation value also leads to a write-off, which has some deterring effects on exit that will be discussed later.

In assessing the exit barriers caused by asset specialization in a particular business, the question is whether or not there are any markets for the assets as, or as part of, a going concern. Sometimes assets can be sold to overseas markets at a different stage of economic development, even though they have little value in the home country. This move raises the liquidation value and lowers exit barriers. Whether there are overseas markets or not, however, the value of specialized assets will usually diminish as it becomes increasingly clear that the industry is declining. For example, Raytheon, which sold its vacuum tube-making assets in the early 1960s when tube demand was strong for color TV sets, recovered a much higher liquidation value than the firms that tried to unload their vacuum tube facilities in the early 1970s, after the industry was clearly in its twilight years. Few, if any, U.S. producers were interested in purchasing by this later time, and foreign firms supplying vacuum tubes to less advanced economies either had already purchased tube-making equipment or were in a much stronger bargaining position once U.S. decline was obvious.

Fixed Costs of Exit

Often substantial fixed costs of exiting elevate exit barriers by reducing the effective liquidation value of a business. A firm often must face the substantial costs of labor settlements; in fact in some countries, like Italy, fixed costs of exit are effectively huge because government does not sanction a loss of jobs. The costly full-time efforts of a number of skilled managers, attorneys, and accountants will usually be consumed for a significant period when a company is divesting. Provision must sometimes be made for maintaining availability of spare parts to past customers after exit; this requirement involves incurring a loss which, discounted, becomes a fixed cost of exiting. Management or employees may need to be resettled and/or retrained. Breaking long-term contracts to purchase inputs or sell products may involve substantial cancellation penalties, if they can be abrogated at all. In many cases the firm must pay the cost of having another firm fulfill such contracts.

There are often also hidden costs of exit. Once the decision to divest becomes known, employee productivity may be prone to sag and financial results to deteriorate. Customers quickly pull out their business, and suppliers lose interest in meeting promises. These sorts of problems, also problems in executing a harvest strategy as will be discussed later, may accelerate losses in the waning months of ownership and may prove to be significant costs of exit.

On the other hand, sometimes exit can allow the firm to avoid fixed investments it would otherwise have had to make. For example, requirements to invest in order to comply with environmental regulations may be avoided, as may other requirements to reinvest capital just to stay in the industry. Requirements to make such investments *promote* exit, unless making them yields an equivalent or greater increase in the discounted liquidation value of the firm, because they raise investment in the business without raising profits.

Strategic Exit Barriers

Even if a diversified firm faces no exit barriers from economic considerations relating solely to the particular business, it may face barriers because the business is important to the company from an overall strategic point of view:

Interrelatedness: The business may be part of a total strategy involving a group of businesses, and leaving it would diminish the impact of the strategy. The business may be central to the corporation's identity or image. Exiting may hurt the company's relationships with key distribution channels or may lower overall clout in purchasing. Exit may idle shared facilities or other assets, depending on whether or not they have alternative uses by the firm or can be rented on the open market. A firm terminating a sole supply relationship to a customer may not only foreclose sales of other products to that customer but also hurt its chances in other businesses in which it is relied on to supply key raw materials or components. Vital to the height of interrelatedness barriers is the corporation's ability to transfer resources freed up from the declining business to new markets.

Access to Financial Markets: Exiting may reduce the confidence of the capital markets in the firm or worsen the firm's ability to attract acquisition candidates (or buyers). If the divested business is large relative to the total, its divestment may strongly reduce the financial credibility of the firm. Even though a write-off is justified economically from the point of view of the business itself, it may negatively affect earnings growth or otherwise act to raise the cost of capital.[3] Small losses over a period of years through operating the business may be preferable to a single large loss from this standpoint. The size of write-offs will obviously depend on how depreciated the assets in the business are relative to their liquidation value, as well as the ability of the firm to divest the business incrementally as opposed to having to make a once and for all decision.

Vertical Integration. If the business is vertically related to another in the company, the effect on barriers to exit depends on whether the cause of decline affects the entire vertical chain or just one link. In the case of acetylene, its obsolescence made downstream chemical synthesis businesses using acetylene as a feed stock obsolete. If the firm was in acetylene as well as in one or more of these downstream processes, closing the acetylene plant either closed the downstream facilities or forced the firm to find an outside supplier. Although it might negotiate a favorable price from an outside supplier because acetylene demand was falling, ultimately the firm would have to exit from the downstream operations as well. Here the exit decision would have to encompass the whole chain.

In contrast if an upstream unit sold to a downstream unit an input that had been made obsolete by a substitute, the downstream unit would be strongly motivated to find an outside supplier to sell it

[3]A diversified firm may be able to utilize the tax loss from such a write-off, which mitigates the negative cash flow impact of exit decisions. However, the write-off can still affect the financial markets.

the substitute input, to avoid worsening its competitive position. Thus the fact that the firm was integrated forward might hasten the decision to exit because the business' strategic value had been eliminated and it had become a strategic liability to the company as a whole.

INFORMATION BARRIERS

The more related a business is to others in the company, particularly in terms of sharing assets or having a buyer-seller relationship, the more difficult it can be to develop clear information about the true performance of the business. Businesses performing poorly can be hidden by the success of interrelated ones, and the firm might consequently fail even to consider economically justified exit decisions.

MANAGERIAL OR EMOTIONAL BARRIERS

Although the exit barriers described above are based on rational economic calculations (or the inability to make them because of failures in information), the difficulty of exiting from a business seems to go well beyond the purely economic.[4] A consideration that turns up in case study after case study is management's emotional attachments and commitment to a business, coupled with pride in their abilities and accomplishments and fears about their own future.

In a single business company, exit costs managers their jobs, and thus may be perceived as having some very unpleasant consequences from a personal standpoint:

- A blow to pride, and the stigma of "giving up"
- Severance of an identification with the business that may be longstanding
- An external sign of failure which reduces job mobility

The longer the history and tradition of the firm and the lower the likely mobility of senior management to other companies and careers, the more serious these considerations are likely to be in deterring exit.

Ample evidence suggests that personal and emotional barriers also extend to top managements of diversified companies. Managers

[4]This statement presupposes that managements have some degree of effective control in order to act in a manner not in the best interest of the shareholders. In the extreme case in which managers are the shareholders, the opportunity for and likelihood of emotional barriers to exit is probably the greatest.

of the sick division are in much the same position as those of a single business firm. It is difficult for them to propose divestment, so the burden of deciding when to exit usually falls on top management. Identifications with particular businesses can still be strong at the top management level, however, particularly if they are long-standing or early businesses for the firm, are part of the historical core of the firm, or were started or acquired with the incumbents' direct participation. The decision of General Mills to divest its original business (commodity flour) was surely an agonizing choice, for example, and one that actually took many years to make.

Just as identification can extend to top management of the diversified firm, so can pride and concern for external image. This is particularly true, once again, when top management of the diversified company played some personal role in the business that is a candidate for divestment. Moreover, diversified companies have the luxury, in comparison to single business firms, of funding poor performers with profitable businesses, and sometimes of being able to avoid disclosing poor results in a sick division. This ability perhaps allows emotional factors to creep into decisions to divest in diversified companies, even though ironically one of the benefits of diversification is supposed to be a more detached, dispassionate review of investments.

Managerial exit barriers can be so strong that, as illustrated in a number of studies of divestment case histories, divestments did not occur until a change in top management took place even though the unsatisfactory performance had been chronic.[5] Although this may be the extreme situation, nearly everyone seems to agree that divestments are probably the most unpalatable decision managements have to make.[6]

Managerial barriers can be reduced by experience with exit. For example, they appear to be less prevalent in firms in the broad area of chemicals, where technological failure and product substitution are common; in firms in sectors where product lives are historically short; or high-technology firms, who are more liable to perceive possibilities for new businesses to replace declining ones.

GOVERNMENT AND SOCIAL BARRIERS

In some situations, especially in foreign countries, closing down a business is next to impossible because of government concern for jobs and impact on the local community. The price of divestment

---

[5]See, for example, Gilmour (1973).
[6]For a discussion of ways to cope with managerial barriers see Porter (1976).

may be concessions from other businesses in the company or other terms that are prohibitive. Even where government does not become involved formally, community pressure and informal political pressure not to exit can be very high, depending on the situation in which the company finds itself.

Closely akin is the social concern that many managements feel for their employees and local communities, which may not translate into dollars and cents but is nonetheless real. Divestment often means putting people out of work, and it can mean crippling a local economy. Such concerns often interplay with emotional barriers to exit. In Quebec, for example, there has been tremendous social concern about closing down pulp mills in the depressed Canadian dissolving pulp industry, many of which are in one-company towns. Executives are torn with concern for communities, and formal and informal government pressure has been brought to bear as well.[7]

Because of any or all of these types of exit barriers, a firm may continue to compete in an industry even though its financial performance is subnormal. Capacity does not leave the industry as it shrinks, and competitors grimly battle it out to survive. In a declining industry with high exit barriers, it is difficult even for the strongest and healthiest firms to avoid being hurt in the process of decline.

Mechanism for Asset Disposition

The manner in which the assets of firms are disposed of can strongly influence the potential profitability of a declining industry. In the Canadian dissolving pulp industry, for example, a major plant was not retired but sold to a group of entrepreneurs at a significant discount to book value. With a lower investment base, managers of the new entity could make decisions on pricing and other aspects of strategy that were rational for them but which severely crippled the remaining firms. Selling the assets to the employees at a discount can have the same effect. Thus if assets in a declining industry are disposed of *within the industry* and not then retired, it is even worse for subsequent competition than if the original owners of the firms stayed in business.

The situation in which government subsidies keep ailing firms alive in declining industries is nearly as bad. Not only does capacity not leave the market, but also the subsidized firm can depress profit

[7]For an in-depth discussion of the role of government in this declining industry, see Mehta (1978).

potential even further because it is basing its decisions on different economics.

VOLATILITY OF RIVALRY

Because of falling sales, the decline phase of an industry will be particularly susceptible to fierce price warfare among competitors. Thus the conditions that determine the volatility of rivalry outlined in Chapter 1 become particularly acute in influencing industry profitability in decline. Warfare among the firms that remain will be most intense in the decline phase in the following situations:

- the product is perceived as a commodity;
- fixed costs are high;
- many firms are locked by exit barriers into the industry;
- a number of firms perceive a high strategic importance in maintaining their position in the industry;
- the relative strengths of remaining firms are relatively balanced so that one or a few firms cannot easily win the competitive battle;
- firms are uncertain about their relative competitive strengths and many attempt ill-fated efforts at changing position.

The volatility of rivalry in decline can be accentuated by suppliers and distribution channels. The industry becomes a less important customer to suppliers as it declines, which may affect prices and service.[8] Similarly, the power of channels will increase as the industry declines if distribution channels handle multiple firms, control shelf space and shelf positioning, or can influence the ultimate customer's purchase decision. In cigars, for example, shelf positioning is crucial to success since cigars are an impulse item. The power of distribution channels for cigars has increased markedly during the industry's decline, and sellers' margins have correspondingly fallen.

Perhaps the worst situation from the standpoint of industry rivalry during decline is the situation in which one or two firms are relatively weak in terms of their strategic position in the industry, but they possess significant overall corporate resources and a strong strategic commitment to stay in the business. Their weaknesses force them to attempt to improve position by desperate action, like price

[8]If the industry is a key customer of suppliers, however, they may attempt to help it fight off decline.

cuts, that threatens the entire industry. Their staying power forces other firms to respond.

Strategic Alternatives in Decline

Discussions of strategy during decline usually revolve around disinvestment or harvest, but there is a *range* of strategic alternatives—although not all are necessarily feasible in any particular industry. The range of strategies can be conveniently expressed in terms of four basic approaches (shown in Figure 12-1) to competing in decline, which the firm can pursue individually or in some cases sequentially. In practice the distinctions among these strategies are rarely neat, but there are advantages in discussing their objectives and implications separately. These strategies vary greatly, not only in the goals they seek to achieve, but also in their implications for investment. In the harvest and divest strategies, the business is managed to produce disinvestment, the classic goal of decline strategies. In leadership or niche strategies, however, the firm may actually want to invest in strengthening its position in the declining industry.

Putting aside until the next section the question of approaches to matching the strategy to the industry and the particular firm, we can explore the motivations for each strategic alternative and the common tactical steps in implementing it.

FIGURE 12-1 Alternative Strategies

Leadership	*Niche*	*Harvest*	*Divest Quickly*
Seek a leadership position in terms of market share	Create or defend a strong position in a particular segment	Manage a controlled disinvestment, taking advantage of strengths	Liquidate the investment as early in the decline phase as possible

LEADERSHIP

The leadership strategy is directed at taking advantage of a declining industry whose structure is such that the remaining firm or firms have the potential to reap above-average profitability and leadership is feasible vis-à-vis competitors. The firm aims at being either the only firm or one of few firms remaining in the industry. Once this position is attained the firm switches to a holding position or controlled harvest strategy, depending on the subsequent pattern of industry sales.[9] The premise underlying this strategy is that by achieving leadership the firm is in a superior position to hold position or harvest than it would be otherwise (taking into account the investment required).

Tactical steps that can contribute to executing the leadership strategy are the following:

- investing in aggressive competitive actions in pricing, marketing, or other areas designed to build market share and insure rapid retirement of capacity from the industry by other firms;
- purchasing market share by acquiring competitors or competitors' product lines at prices above their opportunities for sale elsewhere; this has the effect of reducing competitors' exit barriers;
- purchasing and retiring competitors' capacity, which again lowers exit barriers for competitors and insures that their capacity is not sold within the industry; a leading firm in the mechanical sensor industry repeatedly offers to buy the assets of its weakest competitors for this reason;
- reducing competitors' exit barriers in other ways, such as by willingly manufacturing spare parts for their products, taking over long-term contracts, producing private label goods for them so that they can terminate manufacturing operations;
- demonstrating a strong commitment to staying in the business through public statements and behavior;
- demonstrating clearly superior strengths through competitive moves, which are aimed at dispelling competitors' thoughts of attempting to battle it out;
- developing and disclosing credible information that reduces uncertainty about future decline—which lowers the likelihood that competitors will overestimate the true prospects for the industry and remain in it;
- raise the stakes for other competitors to stay in the business by precipitating the need for reinvestment in new products or process improvements.

[9]Investing in a slow or negatively growing market is generally risky because capital may be frozen and resistant to retrieval through profits or liquidation. The premise of the leadership strategy is that a firm's position and industry structure more than allow for recovery of reinvestment even though it is made late in the development of the industry.

NICHE

The objective of this strategy is to identify a segment (or demand pocket) of the declining industry that will not only maintain stable demand or decay slowly but also has structural characteristics allowing high returns. The firm then invests in building its position in this segment. It may find it desirable to take some of the actions listed under the leadership strategy in order to reduce competitors' exit barriers or reduce uncertainty concerning this segment. Ultimately the firm may either switch to a harvest or divest strategy.

HARVEST

In the harvest strategy, the firm seeks to optimize cash flow from the business. It does this by eliminating or severely curtailing new investment, cutting maintenance of facilities, and taking advantage of whatever residual strengths the business has in order to raise prices or reap benefits of past goodwill in continued sales, even though advertising and research have been curtailed. Other common harvest tactics include the following:

- reducing the number of models;
- shrinking the number of channels employed;
- eliminating small customers;
- eroding service in terms of delivery time (inventory), speed of repair, or sales assistance.

Ultimately the business is sold or liquidated.

All businesses are not readily harvestable. The harvest strategy presupposes some genuine past strengths on which the firm can live, as well as an industry environment in the decline phase that does not degenerate into bitter warfare. Without some strengths, the firm's price increases, reduction in quality, cessation of advertising, or other tactics will be met with severely reduced sales. If the industry structure leads to great volatility during the decline phase, competitors will seize on the firm's lack of investment to grab market share or bid down prices, thereby eliminating the advantages to the firm of lowering expenses through harvesting. Also, some businesses are hard to harvest because there are few options for incremental expense reduction; an extreme example is one in which the plant will quickly fail to operate if not maintained.

A basic distinction in harvesting tactics are actions that are *visible* to the customer (e.g., price increases, lower advertising) and those that are not (e.g., deferred maintenance, dropping marginal accounts). The firm without relative strengths will probably have to confine itself to invisible actions, which may or may not yield a significant increase in cash flow depending on the nature of the business.

Of all the strategic alternatives in decline, the harvest strategy creates perhaps the greatest demands from an administrative standpoint, although these have been little explored in the literature. In practice, a controlled liquidation is very difficult to manage because of problems with employee morale and retention, suppliers' and customers' confidence, and the motivations of executives. Classifying a business as a dog to be harvested, based on portfolio planning techniques like those described in Chapter 3, is not a great motivating device either. Although efforts have been made in companies like General Electric and Mead Corporation to adapt managerial incentives to the peculiar conditions of harvest, the results of these efforts are not yet clear, and the other administrative problems in harvesting remain, nevertheless.

QUICK DIVESTMENT

This strategy rests on the premise that the firm can maximize its net investment recovery from the business by selling it early in decline, rather than by harvesting and selling it later or by following one of the other strategies. Selling the business early usually maximizes the value the firm can realize from the sale of the business, because the earlier the business is sold, the greater is the uncertainty about whether demand will indeed subsequently decline and the more likely other markets for the assets, like foreign countries, are not glutted.

In some situations it may be desirable to divest the business *before* decline, or in the maturity phase. Once decline is clear, buyers for the assets inside and outside the industry will be in a stronger bargaining position. On the other hand, selling early also entails the risk that the firm's forecast of the future will prove incorrect.

Diverting quickly may force the firm to confront exit barriers like image and interrelationships, although being early usually mitigates these factors to some extent. The firm can use a private label strategy or sell product lines to competitors to help ease some of these problems.

Choosing a Strategy for Decline

The previous discussion provides a series of analytical steps to determine the position of the firm in a declining industry:

- Is the structure of the industry conducive to a hospitable (potentially profitable) decline phase based on the conditions in Section I?
- What are the exit barriers facing each and every significant competitor? Who will exit quickly and who will remain?
- Of the firms that stay, what are their relative strengths for competing in the pockets of demand that will remain in the industry? How seriously must their position be eroded before exit is likely, given their exit barriers?
- What are the exit barriers facing the firm?
- What are the firm's relative strengths vis-à-vis the pockets of demand that remain?

The process of selecting a strategy for decline is one of matching the desirability of remaining in the industry with the firm's relative position. The key strengths and weaknesses of the firm in determining its relative position are not necessarily those that have counted earlier in the industry's development; instead they relate to the segments or pockets of demand that will remain and the particular conditions of the decline phase in terms of the nature of rivalry. Also central to the leadership or niche strategies is credibility in prompting the exit of competitors. Differently situated firms will have different optimal strategies for decline.

A crude framework for viewing the firm's choice of strategies is shown in Figure 12-2.

When the industry structure is conducive to a hospitable decline phase because of low uncertainty, low exit barriers, and so on, the firm with strengths can either seek leadership or defend a niche, depending on the structural desirability of competing in most of the remaining segments versus selecting one or two particular segments. The firm with strengths has the clout to establish a leadership position—competitors that lose the battle will exit—and the industry's

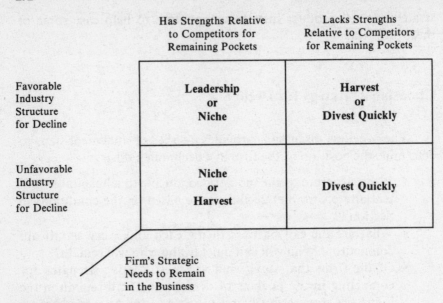

	Has Strengths Relative to Competitors for Remaining Pockets	Lacks Strengths Relative to Competitors for Remaining Pockets
Favorable Industry Structure for Decline	**Leadership** or **Niche**	**Harvest** or **Divest Quickly**
Unfavorable Industry Structure for Decline	**Niche** or **Harvest**	**Divest Quickly**

Firm's Strategic Needs to Remain in the Business

FIGURE 12-2.

structure yields rewards once such a position is achieved. When the firm has no particular strengths, it will be unlikely to capture leadership overall or in a niche, but it can take advantage of the favorable industry to harvest profitably. It may choose to divest early depending on the feasibility of harvest and the opportunities for sale of the business.

When the industry is unfavorable for decline, because of high uncertainty, high exit barriers for competitors, and/or conditions leading to volatile end-game rivalry, investing to achieve leadership is not likely to yield rewards, and a niche position may not either. If the firm has a strong relative position, it is usually better off taking advantage of it by shrinking to a protected niche and/or harvesting. If the firm has no particular strengths, it is well advised to get out as quickly as its exit barriers permit, because other firms stuck in the industry with high exit barriers will probably soon begin to attack its position successfully.

There is a third dimension to this simple framework, which is a firm's strategic needs to remain in the business. Strategic needs for cash flow, for example, may skew the decision toward harvest or early sale even though the other factors point to leadership. Operationally, the firm must assess the nature of its strategic needs and overlay them with the other conditions for decline to determine the right strategy.

There may be advantages to an *early commitment* to one decline strategy or another. An early commitment to leadership may provide the signals necessary to encourage competitors to exit and the timing advantage necessary to achieve leadership. An early commitment to divestment yields the benefits that have been discussed. Postponing a choice of decline strategy tends to eliminate the polar options and forces the firm toward either niche or harvest.

A key part of strategy in declining industries, particularly aggressive strategies, is to find ways to encourage particular competitors out of the industry. Some ways of doing so are discussed under the leadership option earlier. Sometimes the actual exit of a competitor with high market share may be necessary before an aggressive decline strategy makes sense. In such cases, the firm may want to bide its time by harvesting until the major competitor resolves the exit decision one way or another. If the leader decides to exit, the firm can be prepared to invest, and if the leader stays, the firm may continue to harvest or divest immediately.

Pitfalls in Decline

Finding the firm's position on Figure 12-2 requires a great deal of subtle analysis, and many firms violate the basic consistency between industry structure and strategic choice embodied in the figure. Study of declining industries also reveals a number of other potential pitfalls.

Failure to Recognize Decline. With the benefit of hindsight, it is all too easy to admonish firms for being overly optimistic about the prospects for revitalization of their declining industries. Yet discounting for legitimate uncertainty about the future, there seems to be a failure in some companies to look objectively at the prospects of decline, either because of long identification with the industry or overly narrow perception of substitute products. The presence of high exit barriers may also subtly affect how managers perceive their environment; they look for optimistic signs since pessimistic ones are so painful. From my examination of many declining industries, the firms that seem to be the most objective about managing the decline process are those that also participate in the substitute industry. They have a clearer perception concerning the prospects of the substitute product and the threat of decline.

A War of Attrition.   Warfare with competitors having high exit barriers usually leads to disaster. Such competitors are forced to respond vigorously to moves and will not yield position without a significant investment.

Harvesting without Clear Strengths.   Unless industry structure is very favorable for the decline phase, harvesting strategies by firms without clear strengths usually collapse. Customers quickly take their business elsewhere once marketing or service deteriorates or prices are raised. In the process of harvesting, the resale value of the business may also be dissipated. The competitive and administrative risks of harvesting make this strategy one that must be based on clear justification.

Preparing for Decline

If the firm can forecast industry conditions in the decline phase, it may be able to improve its position by taking steps during the maturity phase that greatly improve its position for decline; sometimes these moves cost little in terms of strategic position in maturity.

- Minimize investments or other actions that will raise exit barriers from any of the sources outlined above.
- Place strategic emphasis on market segments that will be favorable under decline conditions.
- Create switching costs in these segments.

13
Competition in Global Industries

A global industry is one in which the strategic positions of competitors in major geographic or national markets are fundamentally affected by their overall global positions.[1] IBM's strategic position in competing for computer sales in France and Germany, for example, is significantly improved by the technology and marketing skills developed elsewhere in the company combined with a coordinated worldwide manufacturing system. To analyze competition in a global industry, it is necessary to examine industry economics and competitors in the various geographic or national markets jointly rather than individually.

Global industries require a firm to compete on a worldwide, coordinated basis or face strategic disadvantages. Some industries that are international in the sense of being populated by multinational companies do not have the essential characteristics of a global industry. In many consumer packaged food products, for example, multinational firms like Nestlé, Pet, and CPC have operations in many countries. Except to a limited extent in product development, how-

[1]This chapter has benefited from assistance by Thomas Hout, Eileen Rudden, and Eric Vogt, of The Boston Consulting Group, as well as Neal Bhadkamkar, research assistant and MBA, 1979.

ever, subsidiaries are autonomous and the competitive balance is struck on a country-by-country basis. A firm need not compete internationally to be successful. Thus, industries with multinational competitors are not necessarily global industries. It must be recognized, though, that "globalness" is inevitably a matter of degree, since the extent of the strategic advantages that accrue to firms that compete internationally can vary a great deal from industry to industry.

An increasing number of industries have become or are becoming global industries in the 1970s, and this important structural setting is likely to become even more prevalent. By any measure, trade and foreign investment have risen significantly, and the shifts in strategic position that have accompanied industry evolution to global status are both dramatic and rapid. Television receivers, motorcycles, sewing machines, and automobiles are some particularly visible though not atypical examples. The movement to globalization can be compared to the shift in U.S. industries from regional to national competition between 1890 and 1930; as we will indicate, many of the fundamental causes are the same. Moreover, the movement toward global competition might be just as far-reaching. Managers in nearly every industry must consider global competition a possibility if not already a reality.

There are many differences in competing internationally versus nationally, and these are usually emphasized in developing international competitive strategy.

- factor cost differences among countries;
- differing circumstances in foreign markets;
- different roles of foreign governments;
- differences in goals, resources, and ability to monitor foreign competitors.

However, the *structural factors and market forces operating in global industries are the same* as those in more domestic industries. Structural analysis in global industries must encompass foreign competitors, a wider pool of potential entrants, a broader scope of possible substitutes, and increased possibilities that firms' goals and personalities will differ as well as their perceptions of what is strategically important. But the same five competitive forces described in Chapter 1 are at work, and the same underlying structural factors determine their strength. As we will see, most successful global strategies have been based on recognition of these market forces, in their somewhat different (and more complex) context.

This chapter will draw on the conceptual base established in Part I to examine some of the particular economic and competitive issues that arise in global industries. The central issue to be examined can be framed in both positive and negative terms. Does the firm gain a strategic advantage from competing on a global basis in its industry? How threatened will the firm be by international competition? In examining this issue, I will first develop the structural conditions that promote competition on a global basis, as well as the impediments to global competition. This analysis is an essential building block for understanding the evolution of industries to global status, including the environmental changes and strategic innovations of firms which can trigger global competition. Within this context I will consider some important strategic issues in competing in global industries, and alternative strategies for doing so. Finally, some trends that may affect global competition will be explored, including a look at the circumstances that promote or impede competition from firms of newly developed countries (NDC's) like Korea and Singapore, which have become increasingly important fixtures in global industries.

Sources and Impediments to Global Competition

Firms can participate in international activities through three basic mechanisms: licensing, export, and foreign direct investment. Usually a firm's first foray overseas involves export or licensing, and only after it has gained some international experience will it consider foreign direct investment. Export or foreign direct investment will be present in industries where competition is truly global. Major flows of exports among many countries are a reliable sign of global competition, but major direct foreign investment in an industry may not be. These investments can consist of essentially independent subsidiaries in foreign countries, with each subsidiary's competitive position depending essentially on its assets and particular circumstances in its country of location.

Fundamentally, an industry becomes a global industry because there are economic (or other) advantages to a firm competing in a coordinated way in many national markets. There are a number of distinct sources of such global strategic advantage, as well as impediments to achieving them.[2] The task for the analyst is to assess these items for the particular industry under study, understanding either why it is not global or, conversely, which sources of global advantage have outweighted the impediments.

SOURCES OF GLOBAL COMPETITIVE ADVANTAGE

The sources of global advantage stem broadly from four causes: conventional comparative advantage, economies of scale or learning curves extending beyond the scale or cumulative volume achievable in individual national markets, advantages from product differentiation, and the public–good character of market information and technology:[3]

Comparative Advantage. The existence of comparative advantage is a classic determinant of global competition. When a country or countries have significant advantages in factor cost or factor quality used in producing a product, these countries will be the sites of production and exports will flow to other parts of the world. In such industries, the strategic position of the global firm in those countries possessing a comparative advantage is crucial to its world position.

Production Economies of Scale. If there are economies of scale in production (or providing service) that extend beyond the size of major national markets, the firm can potentially achieve a cost advantage through centralized production and global competition. For example, modern high-speed steel mills have a minimum efficient scale that appears to be as much as 40 percent of worldwide demand. Sometimes advantages of vertical integration are the key to achieving global production economies, because the efficient scale of the vertically integrated system is greater than the size of national markets. Achieving production economies necessarily implies movement of exports among countries.

[2]These parallel, albeit on a different level, the causes of industry fragmentation and ways of overcoming them discussed in Chapter 9.

[3]A public good, such as a technological innovation, is something that can be used repeatedly at no cost once the initial investment has been made.

Global Experience.   In technologies subject to significant cost declines due to proprietary experience, the ability to sell similar product varieties in many national markets can bring benefits. Cumulative volume per model is greater if the model is sold in many national markets, leading to a cost advantage for the global competitor. This situation has probably occurred in the manufacture of light-duty lift trucks, in which Toyota has gained a commanding position. Global competition can allow *faster* learning, even if the learning curve flattens at cumulative volumes achievable eventually by competing in an individual geographic market. Since a company potentially can gain experience by sharing improvements among plants, a cost advantage from global competition potentially can be gained even if production is not centralized but takes place in each national market.

Logistical Economies of Scale.   If an international logistics system inherently involves fixed costs that can be spread by supplying many national markets, the global competitor has a potential cost advantage. Global competition may also allow the achievement of economies of scale in logistics that stem from the ability to use more specialized systems, such as specialized cargo ships. For example, Japanese firms have achieved significant cost savings in the use of specialized carriers to transport raw materials and finished products in steel and autos. Operating at world volume may allow a complete rethinking of logistical arrangements.

Marketing Economies of Scale.   Although many aspects of the marketing function must inherently be carried out in each national market, there may be potential marketing economies of scale that exceed the size of national markets in some industries. The most obvious are in industries in which a common sales force is deployed worldwide. In heavy construction and in the manufacture of aircraft or turbine generators, for example, the sales task is highly complex and is carried out infrequently with relatively few buyers. Thus the global firm can spread the fixed costs of a group of highly skilled and expensive salespersons over many national markets.

There may also be potential marketing economies through global use of proprietary marketing techniques. Since the knowledge gained from one market can be used at no cost in other markets,[4] the

---

[4]There may be costs of adapting the knowledge to the particular geographic market—see discussion later in this chapter.

global firm can have a cost advantage. The McDonald's "formula" or Timex's "torture test" marketing campaign have worked worldwide, for example. Some brand names have carryover among geographic markets, although usually the firm must invest to establish its brand name in each one. However, some brand names develop recognition internationally through trade press, technical literature, cultural prominence, or other reasons that do not require investments by the firm.

Economies of Scale in Purchasing. When there are opportunities to achieve economies of scale in purchasing as a result of bargaining power or lower suppliers' cost in producing long runs, which go beyond what is needed to compete in individual national markets, the global firm will have a potential cost advantage. For example, worldwide producers of television sets appear to be able to purchase transistors and diodes at lower costs. Such an advantage is most probable when the volumes purchased by the industry are moderate compared to the size of the industry producing the raw materials or components; if purchases are large, most bargaining leverage may well have been exhausted. If the firm is engaged directly in raw material extraction (minerals) or production (agricultural products), the potential advantage is similar. If the efficient scale of mine for a particular mineral is greater than the firm's need for that mineral to compete in a large national market, for example, the firm that mines at efficient scale and competes globally will have a cost advantage. However, the need to compete globally to achieve this advantage presupposes that the firm cannot mine at efficient scale and then sell excess minerals to other firms.

Product Differentiation. In some businesses, particularly technologically progressive ones, global competition can give the firm an edge in reputation and credibility. In the high-fashion cosmetics industry, for example, a firm significantly benefits from a presence in Paris, London, and New York in order to have the image to compete successfully in Japan.

Proprietary Product Technology. Global economies can result from the ability to apply proprietary technology in several national markets. This ability is particularly important when economies of scale in research are large relative to the sales of individual national markets. Computers, semiconductors, aircraft, and turbines are industries in which technological advantages of global-scale firms appear to be particularly great. Some advances in technology are so costly as to virtually require global sales to recoup them. Global competition can also give the firm a series of taps into technological developments worldwide which can improve its technological competitiveness.

Mobility of Production. An important special case of economies due to scale and sharing of proprietary technology arises where the production of a product or service is mobile. For example, in heavy construction the firm moves its crew from country to country to build projects; oil tankers can carry oil anywhere in the world; seismic crews, oil rigs, and consultants are also mobile. In such industries, fixed costs of creating and maintaining an organization and developing proprietary technology can be readily spread over operations in many national markets. In addition, the firm can invest in skilled people or mobile equipment whose employment would not be justified by the demand for the product in any one national market—hence another example of economies of scale exceeding single-market size.

Often the sources of global advantage occur in combination, and there can be interactions among them. For example, production economies can provide the basis for invasion of foreign markets, which then leads to logistical economies or those from purchasing.

The significance of each source of global advantage clearly depends on one of two things. First, how significant to total cost is the aspect of the business subject to global economies? Second, how significant to competition is the aspect of the business in which the global competitor has an edge? An advantage in an area that represents a fairly low percentage of total costs (e.g., sales force) can still be extremely important to competitive success or failure in some industries. In this case, even a small improvement in cost or effectiveness brought about by global competition can be significant.

It is also important to note that all the sources of advantage also *imply the presence of mobility barriers* for global firms. This factor will be important to our discussion of competitive issues in global industries.

IMPEDIMENTS TO GLOBAL COMPETITION

There are a variety of impediments to achieving these advantages of global competition, and they can block the industry from becoming a global industry altogether. Even when the advantages of global competition outweigh the impediments overall, the impediments can still yield viable strategic niches for national firms that do not compete globally. Some of these impediments are economic and raise the direct cost of competing globally. Others do not necessarily affect cost directly but raise the complexity of the managerial task.[5] A third category relates to purely institutional or governmental restraints that do not reflect economic circumstances. Finally, some impediments can relate solely to perceptual or resource limitations of industry incumbents.[6]

ECONOMIC IMPEDIMENTS

Transportation and Storage Costs.   Transport or storage costs offset economies of centralized production, as well as the efficiency of production in an integrated system involving specialized plants in a number of countries and transshipment. For products like prestressed concrete, hazardous chemicals, and fertilizer, high transport costs mean that plants must be built in each market, even though production costs alone might be reduced by plants whose scale exceeds individual national market needs. Competition is essentially on a market-by-market basis.

Differing Product Needs.   Global competition is impeded when national markets demand different product varieties. Because of differences in culture, state of economic development, income levels, climate, and so on, national markets might demand product varieties differing in trade-offs among cost, quality, and performance; in style; in size; and in other dimensions. For example, although computerized sewing machines are being sold in the United States and Western Europe, simpler pedal-powered varieties adequately meet the needs of the developing world. Different legal strictures, building codes, or technical standards might also compel different varieties to be demanded in different national markets even though intrinsic product needs were otherwise the same. The need to produce differing varieties impedes the achievement of global economies of scale or learning. It may also impede benefits from global

---

[5]The presence of these impediments in extreme form can mean that an industry is actually regional rather than national.

[6]This discussion focuses on the particular impediments to competition globally. The firm seeking entry into international markets must of course overcome the full range of entry barriers discussed elsewhere in this book.

sourcing if the differing varieties imply differing requirements for raw materials or components.

The barrier to global competition raised by differing product needs clearly depends on the *cost of altering products* to fit national markets. If required product differences are cosmetic or can otherwise be accommodated without significant cost in an otherwise standard production process, the global firm can still reap most of the global economies of scale.

Established Distribution Channels. The need to gain access to distribution channels in each national market can impede global competition. When customers are numerous and individual purchase amounts are small, the firm may well require access to already established independent stocking distributors to compete successfully. In electrical products, for example, any individual item, such as a load center or circuit breaker, is too small a sale to justify in-house distribution. In such situations it can be very difficult for a foreign firm to penetrate entrenched distribution channels. The channels have little incentive to substitute a foreign firm's line for a domestic one unless a significant (and perhaps prohibitive) concession is made. If distribution channels are less well established because the industry is new or in flux, this bottleneck may not be so great. Also, if much volume moves through a few channels, the foreign firm may have a better chance of gaining access than if it must convince many small channels to take on its line.

Sales Force. If the product requires a local manufacturer's direct sales force, the international competitor confronts a potential scale economy barrier, most severe if national competitors' sales forces sell a wide line of products. This factor may be impeding futher globalization in industries such as medical products in which costly detailing to doctors is required.

Local Repair. The need to offer local manufacturer's repair can impede the international competitor in much the same way as the need for a local sales force.

Sensitivity to Lead Times. Sensitivity to lead times because of short fashion cycles, rapidly moving technology, and the like tends to work against global competition. The distance between the national market and centralized production, product development, or marketing activities tends to create delays in responding to market needs that can be unacceptable in businesses like fashion clothing and distribution. This problem is accentuated if local product needs differ.

A related issue is the lead time required to physically transport goods globally. This lead time generally translates to cost, since in theory every good could be airshipped, although possibly at prohibitive expense. The point is that even though the cost of moving a product by a low-cost means might not preclude global shipment, the lead times involved are too great to allow the responsiveness demanded by the market.

Complex Segmentation Within Geographic Markets.   Complex price-performance trade-offs among competing brands by customers in national markets have the same basic effect as national product variety differences in impeding global competition. Complex segmentation increases even more the need for product lines with many varieties or the ability to produce custom products. Depending on the cost of producing additional varieties, it may effectively preclude cost advantages from centralization of production in an integrated manufacturing system. The local firm will be well suited to perceive and adapt to the various segments of the local market.

Lack of World Demand.   Global competition cannot occur if demand does not exist in a significant number of major countries. This situation could be present because the industry was new or because the product or service only fit the needs of an unusual customer group which was present in only a few national markets.

That industry newness might imply a lack of world demand follows from the so-called product life cycle of international trade.[7] This concept holds that products are initially introduced in markets where their attributes have the greatest value (e.g., labor-saving innovations in high-wage countries). Eventually product imitation and diffusion result in demand in other countries, leading in turn to export by the pioneering firms and eventually foreign investment by them. Overseas production by foreign firms may also begin once demand spreads abroad and technology diffuses. Upon maturity of the industry and subsequent product standardization and price competition, overseas firms may take prominent positions in the industry,

[7]For further discussion of this concept see Vernon (1966); Wells (1972).

based on cost advantages they achieve by starting late in the industry's development or from comparative advantages. All these arguments suggest that generally some degree of maturity is necessary for global competition to be present, although it seems clear that less maturity is necessary today than a decade ago because of the prevalence of multinational competitors with experience in global competition who can rapidly diffuse new products globally.[8]

MANAGERIAL IMPEDIMENTS

Differing Marketing Tasks.   Even if globally sold product varieties are similar, the marketing task can vary geographically. The nature of distribution channels, marketing media, and cost effective means of reaching the buyer can differ so much from country to country that the global competitors not only are unable to exploit marketing knowledge from other markets but also have a great deal of difficulty being as effective at local marketing as local competitors. Although there is no reason why a global competitor could not have centralized production and/or R&D combined with local marketing, in practice it may be difficult to manage. In some businesses, there may also be a customer bias toward dealing with local firms for a variety of reasons.

Intensive Local Services.   Where intensive localized marketing, service, or other customer interaction is required to compete in the industry, the firm can find it tough to operate on an integrated, global basis in competition with local rivals. Although a global firm could conceivably perform these functions through decentralized units, in practice the managerial task is so complex that the local firm can be more responsive. Where intensive local marketing and distribution (not subject to global economies) are crucial, the benefits achieved by other centralized activities of the global firm can be outweighed by the local firm. Even though a global metal fabricator might gain some production and technological benefits of multinational operations, for example, the need for intensive local marketing, responsive service, and quick turnaround means that the local firm can equal or outperform the global one.

Rapidly Changing Technology.   The global firm may have difficulties in operating where rapidly changing technology requires frequent product and process redesign attuned to the local markets.

---

[8]For evidence of this theory, see Vernon (1979).

The self-contained, national firm may well be better able to adapt to such conditions.

INSTITUTIONAL IMPEDIMENTS

Governmental Impediments.   There are a wide variety of government impediments to global competition, most under the guise of protecting local firms or local employment:

- tariffs and duties, which have the same effect as transport costs in limiting achievement of economies in production;
- quotas;
- preferential procurement from local firms by government and quasi-government entities (e.g., telephone companies, defense contractors);
- governmental insistence on local R&D or requiring locally produced components in the product;
- preferential tax treatment, labor policies, or other operating rules and regulations benefiting local firms;
- bribery laws, tax laws, or other policies by home governments that are disadvantageous to their firms in international operations.

Government impediments can either aid locally owned firms or else require production in the country, which nullifies potential scale economies from global production. Government regulations can also force the sale of product varieties peculiar to the particular country and affect marketing practices in ways that make them more country-specific.

Government impediments will be most likely to occur in industries that are "salient," or that affect some important government objectives such as employment, regional development, indigeneous sources of strategic raw materials, defense, and cultural significance. For example, government impediments are great in such industries as electric power generating and telecommunications equipment.

Perceptual or Resource Impediments.   A final category of impediments to global competition relates to perceptual or resource limitations of incumbent firms in the industry. Perceiving the opportunities to compete globally is *itself an innovation*, particularly since it may involve international issues well beyond the scope of heretofore domestic activities. Incumbents may lack the necessary vision.

Information and search costs are high in becoming established. Also substantial resources may be necessary for such things as the construction of world-scale facilities or start-up investments in penetrating new national markets. These investments may be beyond the abilities of incumbents, as may be the required managerial and technical skills for global competition.

The impediments to global competition are nearly always present to some degree in an industry. As a result, even in industries that are generally global in their competitive character, there may be aspects of "localness" that remain. In some markets, or in some segments, the national firm will be preeminent over global competitors because of the presence of particularly significant impediments to global competition.

Evolution to Global Industries

Few industries begin as global industries, but they tend to evolve into them over time. A number of triggers most common in creating global industries will be discussed. They involve either establishing or enhancing the sources of global competitive advantage or reducing or eliminating impediments to global competition. The latter will not lead to globalization, however, unless significant sources of strategic advantage are present. In all cases, it takes a strategic innovation by a firm or firms to make the industry global even though economic or institutional changes may have created the potential.

ENVIRONMENTAL TRIGGERS TO GLOBALIZATION

Increased Scale Economies. Technological advances that increase scale economies in production, logistics, purchasing, or R & D clearly provide a trigger for global competition.

Decreased Transportation or Storage Costs. Falling transport or storage costs are a clear stimulus to globalization. The long-run real decline in transportation that has occurred in the last twenty years is one of the key causes of the increased global competition we observe today.

Rationalized or Changed Distribution Channels.   If distribution channels are in flux, the burden of foreign firms gaining access to them may be eased. Rationalized channels may have the same effect. For example, if distribution for a product shifts from many fragmented retailers to a few national department stores and mass merchandiser chains, the problem of gaining distribution facing the foreign firm may shrink dramatically.

Changed Factor Costs.   Shifts in factor costs can strongly enhance the sources of globalization. Increases in the cost of labor, energy, and raw materials can shift the optimum production or distribution configuration in ways that make global competition more beneficial.

Narrowed National Economic and Social Circumstances.   The need for differing product varieties and marketing tasks and the problems of obtaining local distribution stem in part from differences in the state of economic circumstances of different geographic markets. They differ in their state of economic development, relative factor costs, income level, nature of distribution channels, available marketing media, and so on. As geographic markets become more similar in their economic and cultural circumstances as they relate to a particular industry, the potential for world competition increases, provided sources of global advantage are present in the industry. For example, energy cost increases in the United States, bringing it more in line with those abroad, coupled with a general reduction in per-capita income disparity between the United States and other countries, are causing U.S. automobile firms to move aggressively into small cars for sale worldwide; the automobile industry is becoming increasingly global. Rapid growth in the Far East and South America relative to the United States and Europe seems to be bringing the economic circumstances of these markets closer together for consumer goods, and increased global competition in consumer products may be a result.

Reduced Government Constraints.   Government policy changes that remove quotas, reduce tariffs, promote international cooperation on technical standards, and the like serve to increase the possibilities for global competition. For example, the formation of the European Economic Community promoted a major increase of U.S. direct investment in Europe.

STRATEGIC INNOVATIONS STIMULATING GLOBALIZATION

Even in the absence of environmental triggers, a firm's strategic innovations can begin the process of globalization.

Product Redefinition.   If required product differences among countries lessen, other potential advantages from global competition may be reaped. Sometimes national product differences erode naturally as the industry matures and products become standardized. However, firms can redesign products to make them acceptable in many markets, as General Motors and other firms are doing with the "world car." In other cases, a marketing innovation which redefines the image or concept of the product is sometimes instrumental in unlocking possibilities for global competition. For example, Honda redefined the image of a motorcycle in the United States to a practical, easy to ride, clean-cut mode of transportation and away from the image of a greasy, powerful, threatening device ridden by leather-jacketed hoods. With new U.S. volume to combine with Japanese volume, Honda was able to reap substantial global economies of scale in motorcycle production. Redefining product image may also ease difficulties in gaining access to distribution.

Indentification of Market Segments.   Even if there are required product differences among countries, there may be *segments* of the market that are common to many countries and that are being poorly served in many of them. For example, Japanese and European firms were able to take significant positions in the United States in the sale of small forklifts and small refrigerators because these market segments were badly served by U.S. manufacturers, who concentrated on the main part of their businesses. These segments required distinct technology, facilities, and/or marketing approaches which were subject to global economies and unmatchable by domestic firms. There may also be segments of the market less subject to impediments to global competition. In printing, for example, the long-run high-quality segment that is least sensitive to lead times is served on a global basis while other segments remain national.

Reduced Costs of Adaptations.   The impediment to global competition posed by national product differences is eased if firms can create ways of lowering the cost of altering basic products to meet these local needs. Matsushita, for example, is reportedly close to developing a television receiver capable of receiving signals of both the PAL and SECAM technologies that have differentiated France and other countries. Needs in telecommunications switching equipment vary dramatically by country, but Erickson has been developing a library of modular software packages which can be used to adapt a common piece of hardware to local needs. Any innovation that modularizes a product for easy adaptation or increases its range of compatibility opens up possibilities for global competition. So do production technology changes that lower the cost of producing special varieties.

Design Changes. Design changes leading to more standardized components that are subject to global purchasing economies, or those requiring new components subject to such economies, can trigger shifts toward global competition.

Deintegration of Production. In some industries government constraints requiring local production can be circumvented by assembling locally while producing some or all components centrally. If scale economies stem largely from one or more key components, their central production can strongly stimulate globalization of competition.

Elimination of Constraints from Resources or Perception. The entry of new firms can eliminate resource constraints to global competition. New entrants may also be able to start fresh with new strategies unencumbered by having competed in the industry in its preglobal era. For example, Japanese firms and recently firms from other Asian countries, such as Hong Kong, Singapore, and South Korea, have been quite successful in transforming industries in this way.

Foreign firms have sometimes been better able to perceive possible product redefinitions or opportunities for serving segments globally than U.S. firms, often because they have had experience competing in this way in their home markets. For example, Japanese motorcycle firms have long faced a market in which the motorcycle was a regular form of transportation; European firms have long produced small refrigerators because of historically smaller European dwelling units compared to those in the United States, among other reasons.

ACCESS TO THE U.S. MARKET

In many industries, globalization has hinged critically on foreign firms having access to the U.S. market because of its uniquely large size. Recognizing the strategic nature of the U.S. market, foreign firms have pressed for innovations in order to gain access to it. On the other hand, U.S. firms, because they were based in this huge market, have sometimes felt less pressure to design truly global methods of competition.

It is striking how freely U.S. government policy has allowed access to this volume, compared to the policies of many other governments. Some of this freedom is a legacy of postwar efforts to help the Japanese and German economies.

Competition in Global Industries

Competition in global industries presents some unique strategic issues compared to domestic competition. Although their resolution depends on the industry and the home and host countries involved, the following issues must be confronted in some way by global competitors.

Industrial Policy and Competitive Behavior. Global industries are characterized by the presence of competitors operating worldwide from home bases in different countries. Particularly outside of the United States, firms and their home governments must be regarded together in competitor analysis. The two have complex relationships which can involve many forms of regulation, subsidy, and other assistance. Home governments often have objectives, such as employment and balance of payments, that are not strictly economic, certainly from the point of view of the firm. Government industrial policy can shape companies' goals, provide R&D funds, and in many ways influence their position in global competition. Home governments can help negotiate for the firm in world markets (heavy construction, aircraft), help finance sales through central banks (agricultural goods, defense products, ships), or apply political leverage to advance its interests in other ways. In some cases the home government is directly involved in the firm through partial or complete ownership. A consequence of all this support is that *barriers to exit* may well increase.

Competitor analysis is impossible in world industries without a thorough examination of the relationships between firms and home countries. The home country's industrial policy must be well understood, as well as the political and economic relations of the home government vis-à-vis governments in major world markets for the industry's product.

It is often true that competition in world industries is distorted by political considerations which may or may not be related to the economics involved. Purchases of aircraft, defense products, or computers may depend as much on the political relations between home countries and buying countries as they do on the relative merits of one firm's product against another's. This factor implies not only that the competitor in a global industry needs a high degree of information about political matters but also that the firm's particular relationships with its home government and governments in buying countries become truly strategic in importance. Competitive strategy may have to include actions designed to build political capital, such as locating assembly operations in the major markets, even if they are not economically efficient.

Relationships with Host Governments in Major Markets. The firm's relationship with host governments in major markets becomes a key competitive consideration in global competition. Host governments have a variety of mechanisms that can impede the operation of global firms. In some industries they are major buyers, whereas in others their influence is more indirect but potentially as strong. Where host governments are prone to exercise their power, they can either block global competition altogether or create a number of different strategic groups in an industry. Studies by Doz have identified three groups.[9] The first consists of firms *competing globally* on a coordinated basis; the second, of multinational companies (often with smaller market shares) that follow a strategy of *local responsiveness* rather than integration. These firms escape many government impediments and may actually receive host government support. Final-

[9] Doz (1979).

ly, the third group is made up of local firms. For international companies, the *degree of responsiveness* to host government concerns becomes a key strategic variable. I will describe the broad alternatives to competing globally in some detail below.

The firm trying to compete globally may need to compete in certain major markets to gain necessary economies. For example, it may need the volume of certain major markets in order to fulfill a global manufacturing strategy. It must therefore concern itself strategically with protecting its position in those markets that affect its ability to implement the global strategy as a whole. This requirement gives the host governments in these countries bargaining power, and the firm may have to make concessions in order to preserve the whole strategy. For example, Japanese firms in the television and automobile industries may have to manufacture partly in the United States, to appease U.S. political concerns, in order to maintain the U.S. volume that is a key source of their global competitive advantage. Another example is IBM's policies of local full employment, balanced intra-company transfers of goods among countries, and some local R & D.[10]

Systemic Competition. A global industry, by definition, is one in which firms view competition as global and build strategies accordingly. Thus competition involves a coordinated worldwide pattern of market positions, facilities, and investments. The global strategies of competitors will usually involve only partial overlap in served markets, geographic location of plants, and so on. In maintaining a competitive balance from a systemic viewpoint, it may be necessary for firms to make defensive investments in particular markets and locations so as not to let competitors reap advantages that can be factored into their overall global posture. Knickerbocker's study of international competition found much evidence of this pattern of behavior.[11]

Difficulty in Competitor Analysis. Although the same sorts of factors as described in Chapter 3 are important in analyzing international competitors, this analysis is difficult in global industries because of the prevalence of foreign firms and the need to analyze systemic relationships. Data on foreign firms are generally less available than on U.S. firms, although the differences are narrowing.

[10]For a discussion of IBM see Doz (in press).
[11]Knickerbocker (1973).

Analysis of foreign firms also may involve institutional considerations that are hard for outsiders to understand, such as labor practices and managerial structures.

Strategic Alternatives in Global Industries

There are a number of basic strategic alternatives in a global industry. The most fundamental choice a firm must make is whether it must *compete* globally or whether it can find niches where it can build a defensible strategy for competing in one or a few national markets.

The alternatives are the following.

Broad Line Global Competition.   This strategy is directed at competing worldwide in the full product line of the industry, taking advantage of the sources of global competitive advantage to achieve differentiation or an overall low cost position. Implementing this strategy requires substantial resources and a long time horizon. To maximize competitive advantage the emphasis in the firm's relationships with governments is to reduce impediments to competing globally.

Global Focus.   This strategy targets a particular segment of the industry in which the firm competes on a worldwide basis. A segment is chosen where the impediments to global competition are low and the firm's position in the segment can be defended from incursion by broad line global competitors. The strategy yields either low cost or differentiation in its segment.

National Focus.   This strategy takes advantage of national market differences to create a focused approach to a particular national market that allows the firm to outcompete global firms. This variation of the focus strategy aims at either differentiation or low cost in serving the particular needs of a national market, or the segments of it most subject to economic impediments to global competition.

Protected Niche.   This strategy seeks out countries where governmental restraints exclude global competitors by requiring a high proportion of local content in the product, high tariffs, and so on. The firm builds its strategy to deal effectively with the particular national markets with such restrictions, and places extreme attention on the host government in order to insure that protection remains in force.

In some global industries, strategies of national focus or seeking a protected niche are unavailable because there are no impediments to global competition, while in other industries these strategies are defendable against global competitors. An increasingly prevalent approach to implementing the more ambitious strategies in global industries is transnational *coalitions*, or cooperative agreements between firms in the industry of different home countries. Coalitions allow competitors to team up to surmount the difficulties of implementing a global strategy in areas like technology, market access, and the like. Aircraft (GE-Snecma), automobiles (Chrysler-Mitsubishi; Volvo-Renault) and electrical products (Siemens-Allis-Chalmers; Gould-Brown-Boveri) are just a few global or near-global industries in which coalitions have become prevalent.

Trends Affecting Global Competition

In the context of our discussion, there appear to be a number of trends that hold great importance for competition in existing global industries and for the creation of new ones.

Reduction in Differences Among Countries. A number of observers have pointed out that the economic differences among developed and newly developed countries may be narrowing in areas like income, factor costs, energy costs, marketing practices, and distribution channels.[12] Part of this reduction may be due to the aggressiveness of multinational companies in spreading techniques around the world. Whatever the causes, it works toward reducing impediments to world competition.

More Aggressive Industrial Policy. Industrial policies of many countries are in flux. From passive or protective postures, governments like Japan, South Korea, Singapore, and West Germany

[12]For example, Vernon (1979).

are taking aggressive postures to stimulate industry in carefully selected sectors. They are also facilitating the abandonment of sectors
deemed less desirable. This new industrial policy is giving firms in
such countries the support to make bold moves that will transform
industries to global status, like the construction of massive plants
and large up-front investments in breaking into new markets. Thus,
although firms in sectors not favored by their governments may
drop out, those firms that remain in global industries may well
behave differently. As the latter are increasingly backed by governments taking an aggressive stance, the resources available for competition and the stakes involved are increased. Noneconomic objectives made central by government involvement come increasingly
into play. There is the possibility that international rivalry will
escalate as a result of these factors and that barriers to exit will also
increase, which further increases rivalry.

National Recognition and Protection of Distinctive Assets.
Governments seem to be increasingly cognizant of which of their
resources are distinctive from the point of view of economic competition, and they are increasingly prone to capture the economic benefits from possession of these assets. Natural resources (e.g., oil,
copper, tin, rubber) are obvious examples of assets that have been
controlled either directly by government ownership or indirectly
through joint ventures of governments and producers. The presence
of abundant low-waged semiskilled and unskilled labor (South
Korea, Taiwan, Hong Kong) is another asset explicitly recognized in
some countries. The proactive exploitation of such distinctive assets
by governments is a reflection of changing philosophy toward industrial policy, as previously discussed.

This posture has potentially fundamental implications for
world competition in industries where such protected assets are important strategically. Foreign firms may be cut out of effective control of key resources. In oil, for example, such a reorientation of
government has caused a reorientation of oil companies' strategies
away from saturation retailing and other activities designed to reap
profits at the production stage and toward making profits in each
vertical stage. In other industries it may give certain firms of the
home country fundamental advantages in global competition.

Freer Flow of Technology.   A freer flow of technology appears
to be giving a wide variety of firms, including NDC competitors, the

ability to invest in modern, world-scale facilities. Some firms, notably the Japanese, have become quite aggressive in selling their technology abroad. Also some firms that have purchased technology are willing to resell it to others at bargain prices. All this activity tends to promote more global competition.

Gradual Emergence of New Large-Scale Markets.   Whereas the United States has long been the strategic market for global competition because of its unique size, China, Russia, and possibly India may ultimately emerge as huge markets in the future. This possibility has a number of implications. First, if China and Russia control access to their markets, their firms may become major global powers. Second, gaining access to one or both of these markets may well become a crucial strategic variable in the future because of the scale it will provide to the successful firm.

NDC Competition.   A phenomenon of the last ten to fifteen years is competition from NDC's in world industries, particularly the emergence of Taiwan, South Korea, Singapore, and Brazil. Traditionally NDC's competed on the basis of cheap labor and/or natural resources, which still occurs (textiles, light manufacturing such as toys and plastic products). However, NDC competition has increasingly made a major impact in such capital-intensive industries as shipbuilding and the manufacture of television sets, steel, fibers, and soon possibly even automobiles.

Newly developed countries are increasingly well prepared, because of some of the arguments presented above, to make major capital investments in large-scale facilities, aggressively to seek to buy or license the latest technology, and to take enormous risk. Those industries most vulnerable to NDC competition are those who *lack* the following entry barriers:

- rapidly changing technology that can be kept proprietary;
- highly skilled labor;
- sensitivity to lead times;
- complex distribution and service;
- high consumer marketing content;
- complex, technical selling task.

Some of these factors will be recognized as impediments to global competition, as described earlier. Although they may not deter competitors from developed nations, they are particularly difficult problems for NDC firms to solve because of the unavailability of resources or skills, inexperience, lack of credibility and established relationships, or inability to understand the requirements (e.g., distribution, consumer marketing and selling) in the traditional developed markets because of wide differences from local conditions.

III
Strategic Decisions

Part III draws on the analytical structure in Part I to examine each major type of strategic decision that occurs in an industry:

- vertical integration (Chapter 14);
- major capacity expansion (Chapter 15);
- entry (Chapter 16).

Divestment, the other major type of strategic decision, is considered in detail in Chapter 12, which analyzes the problems of competing in declining industries.

Each chapter in Part III draws on the concepts in Part I that relate to the particular strategic decision under examination. Part III also introduces additional economic theory and administrative considerations of managing and motivating an organization that relate to each type of strategic decision.

Part III is designed not only to help the firm make these strategic decisions itself but also to give it insight into how its competitors, customers, suppliers, and potential entrants might resolve them. Thus it reinforces and deepens concepts presented in Parts I and II.

14
The Strategic Analysis of Vertical Integration

Vertical integration is the combination of technologically distinct production, distribution, selling, and/or other economic processes within the confines of a single firm. As such, it represents a decision by the firm to utilize internal or administrative transactions rather than market transactions to accomplish its economic purposes. For example, a firm with its own sales force instead could have contracted, through the market, an independent selling organization to supply the selling services it requires. Similarly, the firm mining the raw materials it fabricates into end products could have contracted an independent mining organization to supply its needs.

In theory, all the functions we now expect a corporation to perform could be performed by a consortium of independent economic entities, each contracting with a central coordinator, which itself need be little more than a desk and a single manager. In fact, segments of the book publishing and recording industries take approximately this form. Many publishers contract for editorial services, layout, graphics, printing, distribution, and selling, retaining for the firm little more than decisions about which books to publish, marketing, and finance. Some recording companies similarly contract with independent artists, producers, recording studios, disc-pressing facilities, and distribution and marketing organizations to create, manufacture, and sell each record.

In most situations, however, firms find it advantageous to perform a significant proportion of the administrative, productive, distributive, or marketing processes required to produce their products or services in-house rather than through contracts with a series of independent entities. They believe that it is cheaper, less risky, or easier to coordinate when these functions are performed internally.

Many vertical integration decisions are framed in terms of the "make or buy" decision, focusing on the financial calculations such a decision entails.[1] That is, they are preoccupied with estimating the cost savings of integration and balancing them with the investment required. However, the vertical integration decision is much broader than this. The essence of the vertical integration decision is not the financial calculation itself but rather the numbers that serve as the raw material for the calculation. The decision must go beyond an analysis of costs and investment requirements to consider the broader strategic issues of integration versus use of market transactions, as well as some perplexing administrative problems in managing a vertically integrated entity that can affect the success of the integrated firm. These are very hard to quantify. It is the magnitude and strategic significance of the benefits and costs of vertical integration, both in direct economic terms and indirectly through its affect on the organization, that are the essence of the decision.

This chapter examines the economic and administrative consequences of vertical integration, in order to help the manager determine the appropriate degree of vertical integration in a strategic context and to guide decisions to vertically integrate or disintegrate. To find the strategically appropriate extent of vertical integration for the firm requires balancing the economic and administrative benefits of vertical integration with the economic and administrative costs. This balance, as well as the particular costs and benefits themselves, will differ greatly depending on the particular industry and on the particular strategic situation of the firm. The benefits and costs are also affected by whether the firm adopts a policy of *tapered* integration (producing some of its own requirements internally and contracting for the rest) or full integration. Also, many of the benefits of integration can sometimes be gained without incurring all of the costs through the use of *quasi-integration*—the use of debt or equity

[1]No attempt will be made here to review the techniques for making make or buy calculations per se. For treatments of them see Buffa (1973); Moore (1973).

investments and other means to create alliances between vertically related firms without full ownership.

The framework presented here is not a formula but rather a guide to insure that the important benefits and costs of vertical integration have been considered, to sensitize the manager to some chronic pitfalls, and to raise some possible alternatives to obtain the benefits of full vertical integration. The framework will need to be combined with a careful industry and competitive analysis of the particular situation under study and a careful strategic assessment by the firm making the decision.

Strategic Benefits and Costs of Vertical Integration

Vertical integration has important generic benefits and costs which need to be considered in any decision but whose significance will depend on the particular industry. They apply to both forward and backward integration, with the necessary changes in perspective. I will discuss these generalized benefits and costs here, saving for later sections an examination of some issues peculiar to a company integrating forward or one integrating backward. For purposes of this discussion, the *upstream* firm is the selling firm and the *downstream* firm is the buying firm in the vertical chain.

VOLUME OF THROUGHPUT VERSUS EFFICIENT SCALE

The benefits of vertical integration depend, first of all, on the volume of products or services the firm purchases from or sells to the adjacent stage relative to the size of the efficient production facility in that stage. For ease in exposition let us take the case of a firm integrating backward. The volume of purchases of the firm contemplating backward integration must be large enough to support an in-house supplying unit large enough to reap all economies of scale in producing the input, or the firm faces a dilemma. Either it must accept a cost disadvantage in producing the input internally, or it must sell some of the production of the upstream unit in the open market. As will be discussed extensively later, selling extra output on the open market may be difficult because the firm might have to sell to its competitors. If the firm's needs *do not* exceed the scale of an efficient unit, the firm faces one of two costs of integrating, which must then be figured against the benefits. Either it builds an inefficiently small facility that meets only its needs, or it builds an efficient facility and must bear the possible risk of sales or purchases on the open market.

STRATEGIC BENEFITS OF INTEGRATION

ECONOMIES OF INTEGRATION

If the volume of throughput is sufficient to reap available economies of scale,[2] the most commonly cited benefit of vertical integration is the achievement of *economies*, or cost savings, in joint production, sales, purchasing, control, and other areas.

Economies of Combined Operations. By putting technologically distinct operations together, the firm can sometimes gain efficiencies. In manufacturing, for example, this move can reduce the number of steps in the production process, reduce handling costs, reduce transportation costs, and utilize slack capacity which arises from indivisibilities in one stage (machine time, physical space, maintenance facilities, etc.). In the classic case of the hot rolling of steel, the steel billet need not be reheated if the steelmaking and rolling operations are integrated. Metal may not have to be treated with a finish to prevent oxidation before the next operation; slack inputs such as the capacity of particular machines can be used on both processes. Facilities can be located in close proximity to each other, as is the case with the many large sulfuric acid users (fertilizer companies, oil companies) who have established backward integration into sulfuric acid production. This step eliminates transportation costs, which are substantial for a hazardous and difficult to handle product like sulfuric acid.

Economies of Internal Control and Coordination. The costs of scheduling, coordinating operations, and responding to emergencies may be lower if the firm is integrated. Adjacent location of the integrated units facilitates coordination and control. There is also likely to be more trust placed on an insider to keep the needs of its

[2]Or the cost penalty is small enough to be offset by other benefits of integration to be discussed.

sister unit in mind, and therefore, less slack built into the business to cope with unforeseen events. Steadier supply of raw materials or the ability to smooth deliveries may result in better control of production schedules, delivery schedules, and maintenance operations. This is because the revenue foregone by suppliers who fail to deliver may be much less than the cost of disruption, and hence their motivation to deliver punctually is hard to assure. Styling changes, product redesign, or introduction of new products may also be easier to coordinate internally, or coordination may occur more rapidly. Such economies of control can reduce idle time, the need for inventory, and the need for personnel in the control function.

Economies of Information. Integrated operations may reduce the need for collecting some types of information about the market, or more likely, may reduce the overall cost of gaining information. The fixed costs of monitoring the market and predicting supply, demand, and prices can be spread over all parts of the integrated firm, whereas they would have to be borne by each entity in an unintegrated firm.[3] For example, the integrated food processor can use sales projections for the final product in all segments of the vertical chain. Similarly, market information may well flow more freely through an organization than through a series of independent parties. Integration may thus allow the firm to obtain faster and more accurate information about the marketplace.

Economies of Avoiding the Market. By integrating, the firm can potentially save on some of the selling, price shopping, negotiating, and transactions costs of market transactions. Although there will usually be some negotiating in internal transactions, its cost should not be nearly as great as that of selling to or purchasing from outside parties. No sales force and no marketing or purchasing departments are needed. Moreover, advertising is unnecessary, as are other marketing costs.

Economies of Stable Relationships. Both upstream and downstream stages, knowing that their purchasing and selling relationship is stable, may be able to develop more efficient, specialized proce-

[3]Some of the benefits of vertical integration, such as information economies, can be achieved even if the products do not actually move between units related vertically in the firm, but each deals with outside parties.

dures for dealing with each other that would not be feasible with an independent supplier or customer—where both the buyer and the seller in the transaction face the competitive risk of being dropped or squeezed by the other party. Specialized procedures for dealing with customers or suppliers can include dedicated, specialized logistical systems, special packaging, unique arrangements for record keeping and control, and other potentially cost-saving ways of interacting.

It is also possible that stability of the relationship will allow the upstream unit to tune its product (in quality, specifications, etc.) to the exact requirements of the downstream unit, or for the downstream unit to adapt itself more fully to the characteristics of the upstream unit. To the extent that such adaptation would lock independent parties into each other, its occurrence without vertical integration may require payment of a risk premium, which raises costs.

Characteristics of Vertical Integration Economies. Economies of integration are at the core of the analysis of vertical integration, not only because they matter in and of themselves, but also because they contribute to the significance of some other issues in integration to be discussed below. Clearly their importance *varies from firm to firm* in an industry, depending on each firm's strategy and its strengths and weaknesses. A firm with a strategy of low-cost production may place a greater value on achieving economies of all types, for example. Similarly, a firm with a weakness in marketing may save more by avoiding market transactions.

TAP INTO TECHNOLOGY

A second potential benefit of vertical integration is a tap into technology. In some circumstances it can provide close familiarity with technology in upstream or downstream businesses that is crucial to the success of the base business, a form of economy of information so important as to deserve separate treatment. For example, many mainframe computer and minicomputer firms have instituted backward integration into semiconductor design and manufacturing to gain a better understanding of this essential technology. Manufacturers of components in many areas integrate forward into systems to develop a sophisticated understanding of how the components are used. Often, if not usually, integration to tap into technology is tapered, or partial, integration because full integration carries with it some technological risks.

Assure Supply and/or Demand

Vertical integration assures the firm that it will receive available supplies in tight periods or that it will have an outlet for its products in periods of low overall demand. Integration only assures demand to the extent that the downstream unit can absorb the output of the upstream unit. The ability of the downstream unit to do so clearly depends on the effect of competitive conditions on the demand of the downstream unit. If demand is down in the downstream industry, the sales of the internal unit may also be low, and its needs for the output of its internal supplier corresponding low. Thus integration may only reduce the uncertainty that the firm will be arbitrarily cut off by its customers rather than assure demand in the literal sense.

Although vertical integration can reduce the uncertainty of supply and demand, and hedge the firm against fluctuations in prices, this does not mean that internal transfer prices should not reflect market disturbances. Products should pass from unit to unit within the integrated company at transfer prices reflecting market prices to insure that each unit will manage its business properly. If transfer prices diverge from market prices, one unit will be subsidizing the other compared to what it could achieve on the open market (one unit will be better off and the other worse off). Then the managements of the upstream and downstream units may make decisions based on these artificial prices which reduce the efficiency and harm the competitive position of their units. For example, if an upstream unit supplies a downstream unit at prices significantly lower than those it could receive on the open market, the corporation as a whole will probably suffer. The downstream manager, acting on the basis of the artificially low prices, may well seek to expand the market position of the downstream unit—which will then require the upstream unit to supply more subsidized products.

Assurance of supply and demand should thus *not* be viewed as complete protection from ups and downs in the market but rather as reducing uncertainty about their effects on the firm. Both the upstream and downstream unit should be able to plan better with lower risks of interruptions, elimination of changes in suppliers or customers, and lower risks of being caught in a situation in which prices in excess of average market prices must be paid to meet an emergency. This reduction of uncertainty is especially important when one or both stages is capital intensive. The assurance of supply and demand has been mentioned prominently as a motivation for integration in such industries as petroleum, steel, and aluminum.

OFFSET BARGAINING POWER AND INPUT COST DISTORTIONS

If a firm is dealing with suppliers or customers who wield significant bargaining power and reap returns on investment in excess of the opportunity cost of capital, it pays for the firm to integrate even if there are no other savings from integration. Offsetting bargaining power through integration may not only lower costs of supply (by backward integration) or raise price realization (by forward integration) but also allow the firm to operate more efficiently by eliminating otherwise valueless practices used to cope with the powerful suppliers or customers. The bargaining power of suppliers or customers will be determined by the structure of their respective industries relative to the firm's industry.

Backward integration to offset bargaining power has other potential benefits. Internalizing the profits earned by suppliers of an input can reveal the true costs of that input. The firm then has the choice of adjusting the price of its final product to maximize overall profits of the two entities before integration. The fact that the firm knows the true cost of inputs also means that it might improve efficiency by changing the mix of the various inputs used in the downstream business' production process.[4] This move can also increase total profitability.

Although the benefits of adjusting to the true opportunity costs of inputs are clear from the perspective of the corporation, it is important to note that conventional transfer pricing policies work against reaping these benefits. If external suppliers of an input have bargaining power, internal transfers at the market price will occur above the true opportunity cost of the input. However, transfers at market price can have administrative benefits in terms of managerial incentives.

ENHANCED ABILITY TO DIFFERENTIATE

Vertical integration can improve the ability of the firm to differentiate itself from others by offering a wider slice of value added under the control of management. This aspect can, for example, allow better control of channels of distribution in order to offer superior service or provide opportunities for differentation through in-house

---

[4]This decision of course depends on the ability of the downstream unit to vary the mix of its inputs.

manufacture of proprietary components. The effect of vertical integration on differentiation will be discussed further below.

ELEVATE ENTRY AND MOBILITY BARRIERS

If vertical integration achieves any of these benefits, it can raise mobility barriers. The benefits give the integrated firm some competitive advantage over the unintegrated firm, in the form of higher prices, lower costs, or lower risk. Thus the unintegrated firm must integrate or face a disadvantage, and the new entrant into the business is forced to enter as an integrated firm or bear the same consequences. The more significant the net benefits of integration, the greater the pressure on other firms to also integrate. If there are significant economies of scale or capital requirements barriers to integration, the compulsion to integrate will raise mobility barriers in the industry. If scale economies and capital requirements are not significant, on the other hand, then the compulsion to be integrated will have little competitive significance.

ENTER A HIGHER-RETURN BUSINESS

A firm may sometimes increase its overall return on investment by vertically integrating. If the stage of production into which integration is being contemplated has a structure that offers a return on investment greater than the opportunity cost of capital for the firm, then it is profitable to integrate even if there are no economies of integration per se. Of course the integrating firm must include the cost of overcoming entry barriers into the adjacent stage in its calculation about the return on investment to be earned in the adjacent industry, and not just consider the returns being earned by incumbents. Thus, as will be discussed in Chapter 16, it must have some potential advantages over other potential entrants.

DEFEND AGAINST FORECLOSURE

Even if there are no positive benefits of integration, it may be necessary to defend against foreclosure of access to suppliers or customers if competitors are integrated. Widespread integration by competitors can tie up many of the sources of supply or the desirable customers or retail outlets. In this case the unintegrated firm faces the grim prospect of having to scramble for the remaining suppliers or customers and bears the risk that they may be inferior to those captured by integrated firms. Foreclosure thus raises the mobility barrier of access to distribution channels or the absolute cost barrier of access to favorable suppliers of raw materials.

For defensive purposes, a firm may have to integrate or face a disadvantage from foreclosure, the disadvantage being more serious the greater the percentage of customers or suppliers who are foreclosed. These same considerations mean that the new entrant must enter the business on an integrated basis. Need for integration will raise mobility barriers in the same way previously described if there are significant economies of scale or capital requirements involved. The foreclosure problem has triggered much defensive integration in such U.S. industries as cement and shoes.

STRATEGIC COSTS OF INTEGRATION

The strategic costs of vertical integration basically involve entry cost, flexibility, balance, ability to manage the integrated firm, and the use of internal organizational incentives versus market incentives.

Cost of Overcoming Mobility Barriers

Vertical integration obviously requires the firm to overcome the mobility barriers to compete in the upstream or downstream business. Integration is, after all, a special case (though a common one) of the general strategic option of entry into a new business.[5] Because of the internal buying and selling relationship implied by vertical integration, the integrating firm can often readily surmount some mobility barriers into the adjacent business, such as access to distribution channels and product differentiation. However, overcoming barriers caused by cost advantages from proprietary technology or favorable sources of raw materials can be a cost of vertical integration, as can overcoming other sources of mobility barriers, such as economies of scale and capital requirements. As a result, vertical integration occurs most frequently in industries like metal containers, aerosol packaging, and sulfuric acid, in which the technology is well known and the minimum efficient scale of a plant is not great.

Increased Operating Leverage

Vertical integration increases the proportion of a firm's costs that are fixed. If the firm was purchasing an input on the spot market, for example, all the costs of that input would be variable. If the input is produced internally, the firm must bear any fixed costs in-

[5]See Chapter 16 for an examination of the economic and strategic issues in entry decisions generally.

volved in its production even if a downturn or some other cause reduces the demand for it. Since the sales of the upstream business are derived from the sales of the downstream business, factors that cause fluctuations in either business cause fluctuations in the whole chain. Fluctuations can be caused by the business cycle, by competitive or market developments, and so on. Thus integration increases the operating leverage of the firm, exposing it to greater cyclical swings in earnings. Vertical integration thereby *increases business risk* from this source, though the net effect of integration on risk depends on whether it decreases business risk in other dimensions, as has been discussed. The degree to which integration will increase operating leverage in a particular business clearly depends on the amount of fixed costs present in the business in which integration occurs. If the business has low fixed costs, for example, the effective increase in operating leverage can be minor.

A good example of the risk of operating leverage created by extensive vertical integration is the Curtis Publishing Company. Curtis built an immense vertical enterprise to supply its relatively few magazines, primarily the *Saturday Evening Post*. When the magazine ran into difficulty in the late 1960s, the impact on the financial performance of Curtis was disastrous.

REDUCED FLEXIBILITY TO CHANGE PARTNERS

Vertical integration implies that the fortunes of a business unit are at least partly tied to the ability of its in-house supplier or customer (who might be its distribution channel) to compete successfully. Technological changes, changes in product design involving components, strategic failures, or managerial problems can create a situation in which the in-house supplier is providing a high-cost, inferior, or inappropriate product or service or the in-house customer or distribution channel is losing position in its market and thus its suitability as a customer. Vertical integration raises the costs of changeover to another supplier or customer relative to contracting with independent entities. For example, Imasco, a leading Canadian cigarette producer, backward integrated into the packaging material used in its manufacturing process. However, technological change made this form of packaging inferior to other varieties, which the captive supplier could not produce. The supplier was eventually divested after many difficulties. Robert Hall's difficulties in the men's clothing business may have been caused in part by its total reliance on internally produced merchandise.

The extent of this risk depends on a realistic assessment of the likelihood that the in-house supplier or customer will get into trouble, and the likelihood of external or internal changes that will require adaptation by the sister unit.

HIGHER OVERALL EXIT BARRIERS

Integration that further increases the specialization of assets, strategic interrelationships, or emotional ties to a business may raise overall exit barriers. Any of the exit barriers (described in Chapter 12) can be affected.

CAPITAL INVESTMENT REQUIREMENTS

Vertical integration consumes capital resources, which have an opportunity cost within the firm, whereas dealing with an independent entity uses investment capital of outsiders. Vertical integration must yield a return greater than or equal to the firm's opportunity cost of capital, adjusting for the strategic considerations discussed in this chapter, in order for integration to be a good choice. Even if there are substantial benefits to integration, they may not be enough to raise the return from integrating above the corporate hurdle rate when the firm is contemplating integration into potentially low-return businesses like retailing or distribution.

This issue can manifest itself in the *appetite for capital* of the upstream or downstream business into which integration is contemplated. If its capital needs are likely to be great relative to the ability of the firm to raise funds, the need to reinvest funds in the integrated unit can expose the firm to strategic risks elsewhere. That is, integration can drain capital needed elsewhere in the company.

Integration can reduce the flexibility with which the firm allocates its investment funds. Since the performance of the entire vertical chain is dependent on each of its pieces, the firm may be forced to invest in marginal pieces to preserve the overall entity rather than allocate capital elsewhere. For example, it appears that some of the large, integrated firms that supply raw materials have been stuck in low-return businesses because they lacked the capital to diversify. Their capital-intensive, integrated operations have consumed most of the funds available for investment just to preserve the value of the assets in these operations.

FORECLOSURE OF ACCESS TO SUPPLIER OR
CONSUMER RESEARCH AND/OR KNOW-HOW

By integrating, the firm may cut itself off from the flow of technology from its suppliers or customers. Integration usually means that a company must accept responsibility for developing its own technological capability rather than piggybacking on others. However, if it chooses not to integrate (whereas other firms do), suppliers are often willing to support the firm aggressively with research, engineering assistance, and the like.

Foreclosure of technology can be a significant risk when there are numerous independent suppliers or customers doing research or where suppliers or customers have large-scale research efforts or have particular know-how difficult to replicate. This risk is inherent in integrating to provide a direct tap into technology in adjacent businesses, though it may be counterbalanced by the risk of not integrating for this reason. Even if the firm only integrates partially, still buying or selling some product in the open market, it may risk foreclosing technology because it puts itself in competition with its suppliers or customers (see below).

MAINTAINING BALANCE

The productive capacities of the upstream and downstream units in the firm must be held in balance or potential problems arise. The stage of the vertical chain with excess capacity (or excess demand) must sell some of its output (or purchase some of its inputs) on the open market or sacrifice market position. This step in such a circumstance may be difficult because the vertical relationship often compels the firm to sell or buy from its competitors. They may be reluctant to deal with the firm for fear of getting second priority or to avoid strengthening their competitor's position. If excess output can be readily sold on the open market or excess demand for inputs readily satisfied, on the other hand, the risks of imbalance are not great.

Vertical stages go out of balance for a variety of reasons. First, efficient increments to capacity are usually unequal for the two stages, creating temporary periods of imbalance even in a growing market. Technological change in one stage may require changes in methods that effectively increase its capacity relative to the other stage; or changes in product mix and quality may affect effective capacity in the vertical stages unequally. The risk of imbalance will depend on predictions about the likelihood of these factors.

DULLED INCENTIVES

Vertical integration means that buying and selling will occur through a captive relationship. The incentives for the upstream business to perform may be dulled because it sells in-house instead of competing for the business. Conversely, the business buying internally from another unit in the company may not bargain as hard as it would with outside vendors. Thus, dealing in-house can reduce incentives. A related point is that internal projects to expand capacity, or internal contracts to buy or sell, may get less stringent review than external contracts with customers or suppliers.

Whether or not these dulled incentives actually reduce performance in the vertically integrated firm is a function of the managerial structure and procedures that govern the relationship between the administrative units in the vertical chain. One often reads policy statements concerning internal transactions that give managers the freedom to use outside sources or to sell outside if the inside unit is not competitive. The mere presence of such procedures is not enough, however. The use of an outside instead of an inside source often places the burden of proof on the unit manager and requires an explanation to top management; most managers may well try to avoid interacting with top management on such a basis. Also there is a sense of fairness and comradeship within an organization that may make strictly arms-length agreements difficult, especially if one unit or the other is earning very low returns or otherwise is in serious trouble. Yet this is where arms-length relationships are the most necessary.

The difficulty just discussed, leads to the "bad apple" problem. If the upstream or downstream unit is sick (strategically or otherwise), its problems may spill over to its healthy partner. One unit can be pressured or even voluntarily attempt to rescue the troubled unit by accepting higher-cost products, products of inferior quality, or lower prices on internal sales. This situation can damage the healthy unit strategically. If the corporate parent seeks to help the troubled unit, it will do better to subsidize or support the unit directly rather than indirectly through its sister unit. Even if top management recognizes this point, however, human nature will make it difficult for the healthy unit to take a ruthless attitude toward the sick unit (although this does happen in some companies). Thus the presence of the sick unit can insidiously poison the healthy one.

DIFFERING MANAGERIAL REQUIREMENTS

Businesses can be different in structure, technology and management despite having a vertical relationship. Primary metal production and fabrication are quite different, for example; one is extremely capital intensive and the other, which is not, demands close supervision of production and a decentralized emphasis on service and marketing. Manufacturing and retailing are fundamentally different. Understanding how to manage such a different business can be a major cost of integration and can introduce a major element of risk in the decision.[6] A management capable of operating one part of the vertical chain very well may be incapable of effectively managing the other, to put the point in its most extreme form. Thus a common managerial approach and a common set of assumptions can be quite counterproductive for vertically related businesses.

Since vertically linked businesses transact business with each other, however, there is a subtle tendency to view them as similar from a managerial point of view. Organizational structure, controls, incentives, capital budgeting guidelines, and a variety of other managerial techniques from the base business may be indiscriminately applied to the upstream or downstream business. Similarly, judgments and rules that have grown from experience in the base business may be applied in the business into which integration occurs. This tendency to apply the same managerial style to both elements of the chain is another risk of integration.

When assessing the strategic benefits and costs of vertical integration, one must examine them in terms not only of the current environment but also of probable changes in industry structure in the future. Economies of integration that seem small today, for example, may be large in a more mature industry; or industry growth and resulting company growth may mean that the firm will soon be able to support an internal unit of efficient scale. Or slowing down of

[6]These potential differences in managerial requirements are attenuated if the vertically related business must necessarily operate in a foreign country, which is the case with many suppliers of raw materials. Foreign location adds additional differences in the managerial approach required in the vertically related business to the sort of differences that have been discussed. In addition, in certain circumstances a foreign owner may be at a disadvantage compared to local owners as a result of policies of the host government.

technological change can reduce the risk of being locked into the internal supplier.

Particular Strategic Issues in Forward Integration

In addition to the benefits and costs of integration previously discussed, there are some particular issues raised by forward integration.

Improved Ability to Differentiate the Product. Forward integration can often allow the firm to differentiate its product more successfully because the firm can control more elements of the production process or the way the product is sold. For example, Texas Instruments' forward integration into consumer products such as watches and calculators allowed it to develop a brand name, whereas its electronic components were essentially commodities. Monfort, a cattle feedlot operator, has forward integrated into meat-packing and distribution in part to develop a brand name at least with retailers.

Providing service for a product as well as selling the product itself may allow a company to differentiate itself even though its product is not superior to that of competitors. Forward integration into retailing sometimes allows the firm to control the salesperson's presentation, the physical facilities and image of the store's location, the incentives of the salesperson, and other elements of the retail selling function that help differentiate its product. The basic idea of integration in all these cases is to increase value added to provide a basis for differentiation that was unavailable or difficult in the unintegrated unit. In increasing product differentiation, the firm may at the same time increase mobility barriers as well.

Access to Distribution Channels. Forward integration solves the problem of access to distribution channels and removes any bargaining power the channels have.

Better Access to Market Information. In a vertical chain the underlying demand for the product (and the decision maker who actually makes the choices among competing brands) often are located in a forward stage. This stage determines both the size and the composition of demand of the upstream stages of production. For example, the demand for alternative construction materials is determined by the contractor or developer who balances customers' desires with the quality and cost of the materials available. The stage in which these key market decisions are made will be referred to here as the *demand leading stage*.

Forward integration toward or into the demand leading stage can provide the firm with critical market information, that allows the entire vertical chain to function more effectively. On the simplest level, it may allow the firm to determine the quantity of demand for its products sooner than if it had to infer it indirectly from orders by its customers. The interpretation of customers' orders is complicated by the presence of inventories held by each intervening stage. Earlier market information allows better adjustment of production levels and reductions in the costs of overages and underages.

Informational benefits may also be more subtle than simply the receipt of timely information on the size of the demand. By competing in the demand leading stage, the firm can gain, firsthand, timely information about the optimal product mix, trends in buyer tastes, and competitive developments that will ultimately affect its product. This information can facilitate rapid adjustments in product characteristics and mix in the upstream stages and lower the costs of adjustment.

A number of companies have followed implicit or explicit strategies of integration to the demand leading stage in all their businesses. Genstar Ltd., a leading Canadian firm, integrated forward into housing construction and heavy construction from its cement and building materials businesses. Indal Ltd., another Canadian firm, has a policy of going forward into final fabrication from its metal rolling, extruding, and coating businesses. Both companies place heavy weight on market information as a justification for forward integration.

The benefits of forward integration for this purpose depend on the degree to which market conditions are unstable or changing in the demand leading stage, whether production is to inventory or to order, and also on the ability of the firm to gain forward market information without resorting to integration. In both construction and metal fabricating, final demand is highly cyclical and its composition often rapidly changes. Cyclical, erratic, and changing demand increases the benefits of timely market information. If final demand is highly stable, market information gained from customers may be more than sufficient.

The degree to which accurate information can be gained from customers depends on the industry. Although it is hard to generalize, if there are many small customers, informal sampling probably gives an accurate indication of the situation in forward markets. The presence of a few large customers (particularly if they are powerful), on the other hand, means that accurate forward information may be hard to obtain. The consequences of changes in a particular customer's specifications or mix are much greater in this situation as well.

Higher Price Realization. In some cases forward integration can allow the firm to realize higher overall prices by making it possible to set different prices for different customers for essentially the same product. The problem with this practice is that arbitrage may occur, and the practice can be illegal in some cases under the Robinson-Patman Act. If the firm integrates into the businesses that should be charged with the lower price because its demand is more elastic, it may realize higher prices on sales to other customers. However, other firms selling the product must also be integrated, or the firm's product must be differentiated so that customers will not accept competitors' products as perfect substitutes.

Another practice is to integrate in order to allow the prices to be better matched to the elasticities of demand of the firm's ultimate customers. Some consumers may be willing to pay more for a product because they use it more intensively than others, for example. A firm may have difficulty in matching prices to different usage rates, however, because it cannot measure usage. But if it also provides service for a fee or sells supplies that must be used with the product, it can set the basic product price low and recoup the benefits of differing elasticities of demand through the sale of these associated products. This sort of approach has been employed in copiers and computers. As long as the buyer is not compelled to purchase the associated products from the firm as a condition of purchasing the basic product, this practice is legal under the antitrust statutes.

Particular Strategic Issues in Backward Integration

As with forward integration, there are some particular issues that must be examined in considering backward integration.

Proprietary Knowledge. By producing its needs internally, the firm can avoid sharing proprietary data with its suppliers, who need it to manufacture component parts or raw materials. Often the exact specifications for component parts reveal the key characteristics of the final product's design or manufacture to the supplier, or the component parts themselves are what is proprietary about the final product. If the firm cannot produce the component internally in such a situation, its suppliers will have considerable bargaining power and will pose a threat of entry. For a long time Polaroid has produced internally many of the proprietary components of its products, contracting out the rest, for just this reason.

Differentiation. Backward integration can allow the firm to enhance differentiation, though the circumstances are somewhat different than those of forward integration. By gaining control over the production of key inputs, the firm actually may be able to differentiate its product better or say credibly that it can. For example, if integration allows the firm to receive inputs with particular specifications, it may improve its final product or at least distinguish it from competitors. Even if Perdue chickens are indistinguishable from others, the fact that Frank Perdue raises them allows him to claim that they are treated specially. If he bought average chickens on the open market and merely processed them, the claim that Perdue chickens are different would be harder to make.

Long-Term Contracts and the Economies of Integration

It is essential to recognize the possibility that *some economies of integration could be gained by the right type of long-term or even short-term contract between independent firms*. For example, process savings could conceivably be gained by locating the plants of two independent entities right next to each other. Metal container plants are sometimes located next door to major food processors and connected by conveyor belts to avoid transportation costs. Or selling and coordination costs could be avoided with sole-source long-term contracts specifying a fixed delivery schedule.

However, contracts do not usually allow the achievement of all the economies of integration because they expose one or both parties to substantial risks of being locked in and because independent parties have interests that are probably dissimilar. These risks and divergent interests often make it impossible for independent firms to agree on a contract, either because of negotiating costs or the risk of post-contract haggling. Hence integration becomes necessary to achieve the benefits.

Nevertheless, a firm should always consider the option of contracting with an independent entity to achieve the same benefits as integration, especially when the risks and costs of integration, previously discussed, are great. One of the pitfalls in vertical integration is to be beset by its costs or risks when many of the benefits could have been achieved through more clever dealing with outside parties.

TAPERED INTEGRATION

Tapered integration is partial integration backward or forward, the firm purchasing the rest of its needs on the open market. It requires that the firm be able to *more than support* an efficiently sized in-house operation and still have additional requirements which are met through the marketplace. If the firm is not large enough for its in-house operations to be efficient, the disadvantage of small scale must be subtracted from the net benefits caused by tapered integration.

Tapered integration can yield many of the benefits of integration previously described while reducing some of the costs. It is undesirable if the foregone benefits due to incomplete integration exceed the reduction in the costs of integration brought about by taper. The choice between tapered integration and full integration will vary from industry to industry and from firm to firm in the same industry.

TAPERED INTEGRATION AND THE COSTS OF INTEGRATION

Tapered integration results in less elevation in fixed costs than full integration. Furthermore, the degree of taper (or the proportion of product or service purchased outside) can be adjusted to reflect the degree of risk in the market. Independent suppliers can be utilized to bear the risk of fluctuations, while in-house suppliers maintain steady production rates.[7] This is the case in the automobile industry, and it is a prevalent practice in many Japanese manufacturing industries. Taper can also be used to guard against imbalance between stages because of the problems described earlier. The optimal degree of taper varies with the size of the expected market fluctuations and the extent of probable imbalances between stages created by expected technological change and other events. It should be noted, however, that tapered integration by necessity requires the firm to buy or sell to competitors. If this is a serious risk, tapered integration is unwise.

Tapered integration reduces the risk of locked-in relationships to the extent of the degree of taper. It also gives the firm some access to outside R&D activities and can provide a partial solution to the problem of internal incentives. The juxtaposition of the in-house supplier or customer with independent suppliers or customers creates a form of competition among them that may improve their work.

TAPERED INTEGRATION AND THE BENEFITS OF INTEGRATION

Tapered integration allows the firm to prove that a threat of full integration is credible, which provides a strong discipline on suppliers or customers and may avoid the necessity of full integration to offset bargaining power. Furthermore, tapered integration gives the firm a detailed knowledge of the cost of operating in the adjacent industry and a source of emergency supply. These factors yield additional bargaining advantages. Such a strong bargaining position is characteristic of the major automobile companies and the international oil companies (who purchase tanker shipping services to complement their own fleets). Maintaining a pilot plant, short of full fledged in-house production, can in some cases provide many of the same effects as tapered integration with even less required investment.[8]

Tapered integration also gives the firm many of the informational benefits of integration. However, some other benefits of vertical integration discussed earlier are reduced, in some cases more than proportionately to the amount of taper. Taper may actually increase coordination costs in situations in which products produced by outside suppliers and the internal unit must match exactly.

---

[7]This practice presumes that suppliers willing to take this role and bear such fluctuations without charging a corresponding risk premium are available. They are most likely to be available where the supplier industry is fragmented and/or highly competitive.

[8]See Cannon (1968), p. 447.

QUASI-INTEGRATION

Quasi-integration is the establishment of a relationship between vertically related businesses that is somewhere in between long-term contracts and full ownership. Common forms of quasi-integration are as follows:

- minority equity investment;
- loans or loan guarantees;
- prepurchase credits;
- exclusive dealing agreements;
- specialized logistical facilities;
- cooperative R&D.

In some circumstances, quasi-integration achieves some or many of the benefits of vertical integration without incurring all the costs. It can create a greater community of interest between buyer and seller, which facilitates specialized arrangements (like logistical facilities) that lower unit costs, reduce the risk of supply and demand interruptions, mitigate against bargaining power, and so on. This community of interest stems from goodwill, sharing of information, more frequent and informal contacts between managements, and the direct financial stake each side has in the other. Quasi-integration can also reduce costs that may be present with full integration, and it eliminates the necessity to commit to the full supply and demand of the adjacent business. It also avoids the need to make the full capital investment required for integration and eliminates the necessity of managing the adjacent business, among other factors.[9]

Quasi-integration should be considered as an alternative to full integration. The key is whether the community of interest established through quasi-integration is sufficient to achieve enough of the benefits of integration to justify the reduction in the costs (and risks) over full integration. Some benefits of integration, such as increasing return on investment, raising product differentiation, or enhancing mobility barriers, may be quite difficult to achieve with quasi-integration. An analysis of each benefit and cost of vertical integration in the particular business with the alternative of quasi-integration in mind will be necessary to evaluate its desirability as a strategy.

[9]For further discussion of quasi-integration in the context of a particular raw material business, see D'Cruz (1979).

Illusions in Vertical Integration Decisions

There are some common misperceptions about the benefits of vertical integration that must be guarded against:

1. **A strong market position in one stage can automatically be extended to the other.**

It is often said that the firm with a strong position in its base business can integrate into a more competitive adjacent business and extend its position to that market. Suppose a strong manufacturer of consumer goods integrates forward into retailing, a very competitive business. Although the integrated retailer might pick up all the manufacturer's business, thereby increasing share, the manufacturer might well be better served if many retailers were competing actively to sell its products.[10] The manufacturer could indeed raise its prices to its captive retailer—though it would just be a bookkeeping transfer of profits from one unit to another—but if the captive retailer then adjusted its prices, its competitive position would be worsened. Thus the integration does not automatically allow the extension of a strong market position at all. Only if the *integration per se* produced some tangible benefits would integration allow the extension of market power, because under these circumstances it would improve the competitiveness of the combined entity.

2. **It is always cheaper to do things internally.**

As has been discussed, there are many potential hidden costs and risks in vertical integration that may be avoided by dealing with outside firms. There is also the possibility that clever contracting can reap the benefits of integration without the costs or risks. The economies of integration are often looked at much too narrowly, and integration decisions thereby ignore many of these issues.

3. **It often makes sense to integrate into a competitive business.**

The deck is stacked against the advisability of integration into a highly competitive industry. Firms in such an industry are earning low returns and are competing vigorously to improve quality and serve customers. There are many firms to choose from in buying or selling. Vertical integration can dull incentives and blunt initiative.

[10] If the adjacent industry into which integration is contemplated is very competitive, the firm may often be worse off if all its output is directed to a single captive customer or supplier than if it deals through the market. In the competitive industry the risks of being locked into one partner are usually the greatest.

4. Vertical integration can save a strategically sick business.

Although a strategy of vertical integration can bolster the strategic position of a business under certain conditions already discussed, it is rarely a sufficient cure for a strategically sick business. A strong market position cannot be automatically extended vertically except under particular circumstances. *Each stage* of a vertical chain must be strategically sound to insure the health of the enterprise as a whole. If one link is sick, the sickness is more likely to spread to the other healthy units, as the analysis presented earlier has shown, rather than vice versa.

5. Experience in one part of the vertical chain automatically qualifies management to direct upstream or downstream units.

As has been discussed, the managerial characteristics of vertically related businesses are often extremely different. A false sense of security growing out of the proximity of the business can lead to the destruction of the new upstream or downstream business, simply by the process of applying historical managerial approaches.

15
Capacity Expansion

Capacity expansion is one of the most significant strategic decisions faced by firms, measured both in terms of the amount of capital involved and the complexity of the decision-making problem. It is probably the central aspect of strategy in commodity-type businesses. Because capacity additions can involve lead times measured in years and capacity is often long lasting, capacity decisions require the firm to commit resources based on expectations about conditions far into the future. Two types of expectations are crucial: those about future demand and those about competitors' behavior. The importance of the former in capacity decisions is obvious. Accurate expectations about competitors' behavior is essential as well, because if too many competitors add capacity, no firm is likely to escape the adverse consequences. Thus, capacity expansion involves all the classic problems of oligopoly, in which firms are mutually dependent.

The strategic issue in capacity expansion is how to add capacity to further the objectives of the firm, in the hope of improving its competitive position or market share, while avoiding industry overcapacity. Undercapacity in an industry is rarely a problem, except temporarily, since it will usually attract new investment. However, because investments in capacity are largely irreversible, capacity overshooting demand may well persist for long periods of time.

Overbuilding is indeed a problem that has repeatedly and severely plagued many industries—paper, shipping, iron ore, aluminum, and many chemical businesses, just to name a few.

This chapter will explore the capacity expansion decision in a strategic context. First, the elements of the decision will be outlined. Since industry overbuilding is a chronic problem, the next section will examine the causes of overbuilding and some approaches to preventing it. Finally, the preemptive strategy for capacity expansion will be discussed, a strategy that has become more common in the 1960s and 1970s.

Elements of the Capacity Expansion Decision

The mechanics of making a capacity expansion decision in the traditional capital budgeting sense are quite straightforward—any finance textbook will supply the details. Future cash flows resulting from the new capacity are forecasted and discounted to weigh them against the cash outflows required for the investment. The resulting net present value ranks the capacity addition against the other investment projects available to the firm.

However, this simplicity masks an extremely subtle decision-making problem. The firm usually has a number of options for adding capacity which must be compared. In addition, to determine future cash inflow from the new capacity the firm must predict future profits. These will depend crucially on the size and timing of capacity decisions by each and every one of its competitors, as well as on any number of other factors. There is also usually uncertainty about future trends in technology, as well as about what future demand will be.

The essence of the capacity decision, then, is not the discounted cash flow calculation but the numbers that go into it, including probability assessments about the future. Estimating these is in turn a subtle problem in industry and competitor analysis (*not* financial analysis).

The simple calculation presented in finance textbooks does not allow for uncertainty and alternate assumptions about competitors' behavior. In view of the complexity of the discounted cash flow calculation that properly includes these elements, it is useful to model the capacity decision with as high a precision as possible. The steps in Figure 15-1 describe the elements of the modeling process.

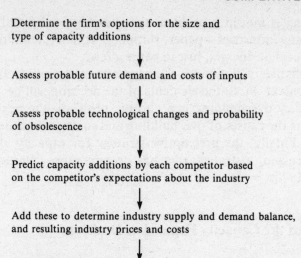

Determine the firm's options for the size and
type of capacity additions

Assess probable future demand and costs of inputs

Assess probable technological changes and probability
of obsolescence

Predict capacity additions by each competitor based
on the competitor's expectations about the industry

Add these to determine industry supply and demand balance,
and resulting industry prices and costs

Determine expected cash flows from capacity addition

Test the analysis for consistency

FIGURE 15-1.   Elements of the Capacity Expansion Decision

The steps in Figure 15-1 must be analyzed in an interactive fashion. The first step is to determine the realistic options available to the firm in adding capacity. Usually the size of the additions can vary, and the degree of vertical integration of the new capacity may be a variable as well. The addition of unintegrated capacity can be a hedge against risk. Since the firm's own decision about how much capacity to add can influence what its competitors do, each of its options must be analyzed separately in conjunction with competitor behavior.

Having developed the options, the firm then must make predictions about future demand, input costs, and technology. Future technology is important because it is necessary to forecast the likelihood that present additions to capacity will be made obsolete or that design changes will allow effective increases in capacity from in-place facilities. Forecasting input prices must account for the possibility that increased demand due to new capacity may increase input prices. These predictions about demand, technology, and input costs will be subject to uncertainty, and scenarios (Chapter 10) may be used as a device for coping with this uncertainty for analytical purposes.

The firm must next forecast how and when each and every one of its competitors will add capacity. This is a subtle problem in competitor analysis, which must draw on the full range of techniques presented in Chapters 3, 4, and 5. Competitors' capacity moves will, of course, be determined by *their* expectations about future demand, costs and technology. Thus, predicting their behavior involves uncovering (or guessing) what these expectations are likely to be.

Predicting competitors' behavior is also an iterative process, because what one competitor does will influence the others, particularly if that competitor is an industry leader. Therefore, competitors' capacity additions must be played against each other to predict a probable sequence of actions and resulting responses. There is a bandwagon process in capacity expansion, to be discussed later, which is important to try to forecast.

The next step in the analysis is adding competitors' and the firm's behavior to yield aggregate industry capacity and individual market shares, which can be balanced against expected demand. This step will allow the firm to estimate industry prices, and in turn, expected cash flows from the investment.

The whole process must be scrutinized for inconsistencies. If the result of the predictions is that one competitor fares poorly by not adding capacity, for example, the analysis may have to be adjusted to allow that competitor to see the error of its ways and add capacity late. Or if the entire process of predicted expansion leads to conditions that violate most firms' predicted expectations, it may have to be adjusted. The modeling of the capacity expansion process is complex and will involve a great deal of estimation. However, the process gives a firm a great deal of insight into what will drive expansion in the industry, as well as possible ways to influence it in its favor.[1]

A model of the capacity expansion process reveals that the *degree of uncertainty about the future* is one of the central determinants of the way the process proceeds. Where there is great uncertainty about future demand any differences in risk aversion and financial capabilities of firms will usually lead to an orderly expansion process. Risk taking firms, those loaded with cash or with high strategic stakes in the industry, will jump in, whereas most firms will wait and see what the future actually brings. However, if future demand is perceived to be fairly certain, the capacity expansion process becomes a *game of preemption*. With known future demand, firms will race to get the capacity on stream to supply that demand, and once they do so it will not be rational for others to add still more ca-

---

[1] A detailed computer model of capacity expansion in a complex industry is described in Porter and Spence (1978).

pacity. This game of preemption will generally be accompanied by heavy market signaling to try to deter other firms from investing. The problem occurs when too many firms try to preempt, and capacity is overbuilt because firms mistake each others' intentions, misread signals, or misjudge their relative strengths and staying power. Such a situation is one major cause of the overbuilding of industry capacity, which I will explore further.

Causes of Overbuilding Capacity

There seems to be a strong tendency toward overbuilding of capacity, particularly in commodity businesses, that goes far beyond that due to mistaken attempts at preemption. Since overbuilding is a key problem in capacity expansion, we must explore its causes in some detail.

The risk of overbuilding is most severe in commodity businesses for two reasons.

1. Demand is generally cyclical. Cyclical demand not only guarantees overcapacity in downturns but also seems to lead to excessively optimistic expectations in upturns.
2. Products are not differentiated. This factor makes *costs* crucial to competition, since the buyers' choice is heavily based on price. Also, the absence of brand loyalty means that firms' sales are closely tied to the *amount of capacity* they have. Thus, firms are under great pressure to have large, modern plants to be competitive and adequate capacity to achieve their target market share.[2]

A number of conditions lead to overbuilding in industries, both in commodity businesses and other businesses, which can be divided into the following categories. If one or more factors are present in an industry the risks of overbuilding can be severe.

TECHNOLOGICAL

Adding Capacity in Large Lumps.   The necessity to add capacity in large units increases the risk that bunching of capacity deci-

[2]Demand is also often quite inelastic in commodity businesses. Inelastic demand may lengthen periods of excess capacity because price cutting by firms is unsuccessful in filling capacity by stimulating demand.

sions will lead to serious overcapacity. This was a major factor in the overcapacity of color picture tubes that developed in the late 1960s. Many firms producing television sets perceived the need to assure a supply of tubes, but the size of an efficient tube plant was very large relative to that of a television set assembly plant. Demand did not grow rapidly enough to absorb the massive color tube capacity put on stream all at once.

Economies of Scale or a Significant Learning Curve. This factor makes it more likely that attempts at preemptive behavior like that previously described will occur. The firm with the largest capacity or which adds capacity early will have a cost advantage, putting pressure on all firms to move quickly and aggressively.

Long Lead Times in Adding Capacity. Long lead times require firms to base their decisions on projections of demand and competitive behavior far into the future or pay a penalty in not capitalizing on opportunity if demand materializes.[3] Long lead times increase the penalty to the firm who is left behind without capacity, and hence may cause risk-averse firms to be more prone to invest even though the capacity decision itself is risky.

Increased Minimum Efficient Scale (MES). Where MES is increasing and the new larger plants being built are significantly more efficient, unless demand is growing rapidly the number of plants in the industry must shrink or there will be overcapacity. Unless every firm has several plants and can consolidate them, some firms will necessarily have to reduce market share, something they may loathe to do. More likely every firm will build the larger new facilities, creating overcapacity.

A variation of this situation has been occurring in the oil tanker shipping industry, where the new Supertankers are many times the size of the older vessels. The capacity of Supertankers ordered in the early 1970s far exceeded the market demand.

Changes in Production Technology. Changes in production technology have the effect of attracting investment in the new technology, though plants using the old technology are left operating. The higher the exit barriers for the old facilities, the less likely will they be withdrawn from the market in an orderly way. This situation

---

[3]If a plant can be built in stages or if cancellation costs are not great, this problem is reduced.

is occurring in the production of chemicals, in which there is a changeover from natural gas to oil as a feedstock. When the oil-fed plants come on stream, serious excess capacity is expected to occur, which will slowly be eliminated as gas prices rise and gas-fed plants are shut down.

STRUCTURAL

Significant Exit Barriers.   Where exit barriers are significant, inefficient excess capacity does not leave the market smoothly. This factor accentuates and elongates periods of overcapacity.

Forcing by Suppliers.   Equipment suppliers, through subsidies, easy financing, price cuts, and the like, can increase overbuilding of capacity in their customers' industries. In a scramble for orders, suppliers can also make it possible for marginal competitors to build capacity who would be unable to under normal circumstances. Shipbuilders have forced capacity increases in the shipping industry, aided by heavy government subsidies, to maintain employment. Lenders for new capacity can also accentuate the overbuilding problem by providing capital to all comers. Aggressive real estate investment trusts (REITs) are partially to blame for overbuilding in the U.S. hotel industry in the late 1960s and early 1970s, for example.[4]

Building Credibility.   Some period of significant overcapacity is often virtually required in industries trying to sell new products to large buyers, particularly if a new product is an important input. Its buyers will not switch to the new product until sufficient capacity is on stream to meet their needs without making them vulnerable to a few suppliers. This has been the case with the high-fructose corn syrup industry.

A related, and very common, case is one in which buyers strongly encourage firms to invest in capacity with implied promises of future business. They may do so directly or indirectly through statements designed to indicate their feelings about the need for new capacity. Of course buyers are not required to actually place orders once the capacity is built; it is in their interest to insure that adequate capacity exists to serve their greatest possible needs even if putting

[4]See *Business Week,* July 17, 1978.

that much capacity in place is not the most prudent decision for suppliers—since this level of demand is quite unlikely.

The pressure of buyers is strongest where the industry faces close substitutes. Here lack of capacity can help substitutes penetrate the industry, and firms are motivated to prevent it.

Integrated Competitors. If competitors in the industry are also integrated downstream, pressures for overbuilding may be increased because each firm wants to protect its ability to supply its downstream operations. Under these circumstances, if the firm has insufficient capacity to supply demand, it will lose not only market share in the industry but also possibly share (or greater risks of obtaining input supplies) in its downstream unit. Therefore, it is more apt to insure it has enough capacity even if there is uncertainty about future demand. A similar argument holds if competitors are integrated upstream.

Capacity Share Affects Demand. In industries such as airlines the firm with the greatest capacity may get a disproportionate share of demand because buyers are prone to approach it first. This characteristic creates strong pressures for overbuilding capacity as several firms strive for capacity leadership.[5]

Age and Type of Capacity Affects Demand. In some industries, such as many service businesses, capacity is marketed directly to buyers. Having the most modern, well-decorated fast-food outlet, for example, may yield competitive benefits. In industries where buyers choose among firms based solely or in part on the type of capacity they have available, these pressures for overcapacity exist.

COMPETITIVE

Large Number of Firms. The tendency toward overbuilding is most severe when many firms have the strengths and resources to add significant capacity to the market, and they are all trying to gain market position and possibly to preempt the market. Paper, fertilizer, corn milling, and shipping are industries in which large numbers of firms have contributed to making overbuilding a severe problem.

[5]See Fruhan (1972).

Lack of Credible Market Leader(s).   If a number of firms are vying for market leadership and no firm or firms have the credibility to enforce an orderly expansion process, the instability of the process is increased. A strong market leader, conversely, can credibly add sufficient capacity to meet a major portion of industry demand, if necessary, and can credibly retaliate against overaggressive building by others. Thus a strong leader or small group of leaders can often orchestrate an orderly expansion through their announcements and actions. The conditions for credibility and the mechanisms used are discussed in Chapter 5.

New entry.   New entrants often create or aggravate the problem of overbuilding. They seek positions in the industry, often significant ones, and incumbent firms refuse to yield. Entry has been a major cause of overcapacity in such industries as fertilizer, gypsum, and nickel. Businesses with easy entry are also subject to overbuilding because entrants rush in in response to periods of favorable industry conditions.

First Mover Advantages.   Ordering and building capacity early may offer advantages that tempt many firms to commit early to capacity when future prospects look favorable. Possible advantages from committing early include short lead times in ordering equipment, lower equipment costs, and the first opportunity to take advantage of supply/demand imbalances.

INFORMATION FLOW

Inflation of Future Expectations.   There seems to be a process by which expectations about future demand can become overinflated as competitors listen to each other's public statements and to security analysts. This situation appears to have occurred, for example, in the ethylene and ethylene glycol industries. A related point is that managers may be optimists who prefer positive action to inaction or a negative posture.

Divergent Assumptions or Perceptions.   If firms have differing perceptions of each other's relative strengths, resources, and staying power, they tend to destabilize the capacity expansion process. Firms may misestimate (under or over) the likelihood that their rivals will invest, leading them either to invest unwisely or not to invest initially at all. The former case leads directly to overbuilding, whereas in the latter case, the firm left behind may make a desperate attempt to catch up, triggering a sequence of excessive investments.

Breakdown of Market Signaling. Where firms no longer trust market signals because of new entrants, changed conditions, recent outbreaks of warfare, or other causes, the instability of the capacity expansion process increases. Signaling that is credible, on the other hand, promotes an orderly expansion by allowing firms to warn others of planned moves, to plan for the expected starting and completion of capacity expansions, and so forth.

Structural Change. Related to the preceding point, industry structural change can often promote overbuilding of capacity, either because it requires firms to invest in new types of capacity or because the turmoil of structural change makes firms prone to misestimate their relative strengths.

Financial Community Pressure. Although the financial community can sometimes be a stabilizing force, often security analysts seem to accentuate pressures toward overbuilding of capacity by questioning managements who have not invested once their competitors have. Also, managements' need to make positive statements to the financial community to improve stock prices may lead to statements that can be misinterpreted by competitors as aggressive, prompting retaliation.

MANAGERIAL

Production Orientation of Management. Capacity overbuilding seems to be particularly liable to occur when production has been the traditional concern of management, as contrasted to marketing or finance. In such businesses, pride in having the shiniest new plants is high, and the perceived risk of being left behind in adding the newest and most efficient capacity is great. Thus pressures for overbuilding are compelling.

Asymmetric Aversion to Risk. A strong case can be made that managers lose more by being the only firm caught with insufficient capacity in a strong market than they do by having built too much capacity, along with all their competitors, if demand fails to materialize. In the latter case they can take safety in numbers and have not lost relative position. In the former case, their jobs as well as the company's strategic position may well be in jeopardy. Such an asymmetry between the consequences of building and not building insures that there will be strong pressures for all companies to build capacity once a few have taken the plunge.

GOVERNMENTAL

Perverse Tax Incentives.   Tax structures and/or investment tax credits can sometimes encourage overinvestment. This is an acute problem in shipping, where Scandinavian tax laws shelter profits reinvested in capacity but tax uninvested profits. This motivates all shippers to reinvest in capacity when industry conditions are good. Overbuilding is also promoted by tax-free retention of earnings by U.S. subsidiaries abroad.

Desire for Indigenous Industry.   Industries of such stature as to be subject to a nationalistic fervor to have an indigenous industry are prone to world overcapacity. Many countries will seek to establish a home-based industry, hoping to sell excess supply on world markets. If minimum efficient scale is large relative to the world market, it is likely to lead to overcapacity.

Pressures to Increase or Maintain Employment.   Governments sometimes exert great pressures on firms to invest (or not disinvest) to increase or maintain employment, a social goal. This factor accentuates problems of overcapacity.

LIMITS TO CAPACITY EXPANSION

There are some checks against the tendency for overbuilding, even when some of the conditions discussed are present. Some of the most common are the following:

- Financing constraints
- Company diversification, which raises the opportunity cost of capital and/or widens the horizons of management who

may have been production-oriented or prone to overbuild to protect their position in their traditional industry
- Infusion of top management with finance background to replace management with marketing or production backgrounds
- Pollution control costs and other increased costs of new capacity
- Great uncertainty about the future that is widely shared
- Severe problems because of previous periods of overcapacity

Several of these conditions were present in the aluminum industry in 1979, and as a result the industry may break from its pattern of boom or bust in capacity utilization. Poor earnings resulting from overcapacity in the late 1960s and restricted profits in high demand years because of wage-price controls have left this industry financially unable to make major investments until several good years swell the coffers. In addition the cost of constructing facilities has quadrupled since 1968.[6]

A firm can sometimes influence the capacity expansion process in a number of ways, by using its own behavior to signal to competitors about its expectations or plans or by otherwise trying to influence competitors' expectations. For example, the following actions will tend to discourage capacity additions by competitors:

- a large announced capacity addition by the firm (see the next section of this chapter on preemptive strategies);
- announcements, other signals, or information that carries a discouraging message about future demand;
- announcements, other signals, or information that elevates the perceived likelihood of technological obsolescence of the current generation of capacity.

Preemptive Strategies

One approach to capacity expansion in a growing market is the preemptive strategy, in which the firm seeks to lock up a major portion of the market to discourage its competitors from expanding and to deter entry. If future demand is known with certainty, for example, and a firm can build enough capacity to supply all the demand, other firms may be discouraged from building capacity. Usually a

[6]*New York Times*, February 11, 1979, p. D1.

preemptive strategy requires not only investments in facilities but also in withstanding marginal or even negative short-term financial results; capacity is added in anticipation of demand, and prices are often set in anticipation of future cost declines.

The preemptive strategy is an inherently risky one because it involves the early commitment of major resources to a market before the market outcome is known. In addition, if it is unsuccessful in deterring competition it can lead to disastrous warfare since major overcapacity results and the other firms attempting preemption have made a major strategic commitment to the market from which it may be hard to back down.

As a result of the cost and risk of a preemptive strategy, it is important to set forth the conditions that must be present for success. The preemptive strategy is risky partly because *all* these conditions must be satisfied.

Large Capacity Expansion Relative to Expected Market Size. If a move is not large in relation to the expected size of the market, it cannot be preemptive. Thus there are straightforward conditions for the size of the capacity expansion that must be made to preempt a market whose future demand conditions are known. However, a crucial issue is the expectations *each competitor and potential competitor* holds about future demand. If any competitor or potential competitor believes that future demand will be large enough to absorb the preemptive capacity move and then some, it may choose to invest as well. Thus a firm attempting preemption either must be confident it knows the expectations of its competitors or must try to influence those expectations in such a way as to insure that its move will be viewed as preemptive.[7] If competitors' view of potential demand is unrealistically high, the preempting firm must communicate a credible commitment to quickly add further capacity if future demand proves higher than initially anticipated.

Large Economies of Scale Relative to Total Market Demand, or Significant Experience Curve. If economies of scale are large relative to total market demand, an early preemptive capacity move may deny competitors enough residual demand to be efficient (see Figure 15-2). In this case, competitors who invest must invest heavily and risk a bloody battle to fill capacity, or they will have inherently

---

[7]Such as signaling certainty about future demand and technology.

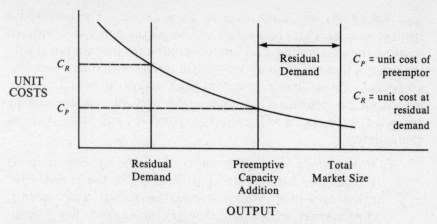

FIGURE 15-2. Preemptive Capacity Given Economies of Scale

higher costs if they invest on a small scale. Either they will be deterred from investing at all, or if they invest on a small scale they will have a permanent cost disadvantage.

If there is a significant experience curve operating whose benefits can be made proprietary, the early, large-scale investor in capacity will have a lasting cost advantage as well.

Credibility of the Preempting Firm.   The preemptive firm must carry credibility in its announcements and moves that it is committed to and able to execute the preemptive strategy. Credibility involves the presence of resources, needed technological capacity, historical delivery on planned investments, and so on.[8] Without credibility, competitors either will not perceive the move as preemptive or will be willing to take on the preemptor anyway.

Ability to Signal Preemptive Motive Before Competitors Act. A firm must be able to signal that it is preempting the market *in advance* of competitors' commitments to invest. Thus it must put a preemptive amount of capacity in place before competitors even consider capacity decisions, or more likely, it must be able to announce or otherwise credibly communicate its intentions. A firm must have credibility in executing the preemptive strategy as discussed, and it must also have a credible way of indicating that preemption is its motive.

[8]See Chapter 5 for a discussion of the factors that lead to a credible commitment.

Willingness of Competitors to Back Down.   The preemptive strategy assumes that competitors will weigh the potential returns of fighting the preempting firm and conclude that they do not justify the risks. A number of conditions may interfere with such a decision, a common thread being perceived high stakes in establishing or maintaining a significant position in the particular business being contested. Preemption will be risky against the following types of competitors:

1. Competitors with goals other than purely economic: If competitors highly value participation in the industry because of a long history or other emotional commitments, they may try to maintain their position against the preemptor despite the presence of other favorable conditions for preemption as described above.
2. Competitors for whom this business is a major strategic thrust or is related to others in their portfolio: In this situation, even though it might be rational not to fight the preemptor firm were a competitor to view the contested business in isolation, it perceives its presence in the business as broadly significant. Thus it may be nearly impossible to successfully preempt.
3. Competitors who have equal or better staying power, a longer time horizon, or a greater willingness to trade profits for market position: There may be competitors who will take a very long view of success in the business and be willing to battle it out for a long period of time. A preemptive strategy becomes questionable in such a situation.

16
Entry into New Businesses

This chapter examines the strategic decision to enter a new business. It takes the point of view of the entering firm, for whom acquisition is a strategy for entry as is entry through internal development.[1] Analytical techniques for looking at both forms of entry will be presented here, with an eye toward helping companies select the appropriate industry to enter and the best entry strategy.

Although there are many complexities in finding, negotiating, integrating, organizing, motivating and managing acquisitions and internal development of new businesses, my purpose in this chapter is somewhat narrower. The emphasis will be on how the tools of industry and competitor analysis described elsewhere in this book can help managers make entry decisions. As we will see, some crucial economic principles identify businesses that are attractive targets for entry and help determine what company assets and skills will make an entry profitable. These principles are essential to the success or failure of entry, though they are quite often lost in the legitimate concern for all the human, organizational, financial, legal, and ad-

---

[1] My frame of reference is improvement in the performance of the entering firm. I do not consider explicitly the question of how the stockholder fares from entry. Salter and Weinhold's (1979) interesting book explores that question in great detail.

ministrative factors that can also be important to the success or failure of a particular entry move.

The economics of entry rests on some fundamental market forces that are operating whenever entry occurs. If these market forces work perfectly, in the economist's sense, then *no entry decision can ever yield an above-average return on investment*. This startling statement is the key to analyzing the economics of entry—finding industry situations in which the market forces are not working perfectly. The overriding conclusion from our analysis is that even putting aside all the problems of integrating and managing new businesses, the acquisition or internal development of sound, well-managed businesses in favorable industry environments is far from sufficient to assure successful entry, despite the widespread belief to the contrary. However, there are many possibilities for successful entry, as I will discuss.

Entry through Internal Development

Entry through internal development involves the creation of a new business entity in an industry, including new production capacity, distribution relationships, sales force, and so on. Joint ventures raise essentially the same economic issues because they are also newly started entities, although they create complicated questions about the division of efforts among the partners and who has effective control.[2]

The first important point in analyzing internal development is that it requires the firm *to confront directly the two sources of entry barriers into an industry*—structural entry barriers and the expected reaction of incumbent firms. The entrant through internal development (hereafter termed *internal entrant*) must pay the price of overcoming structural entry barriers and face the risk that existing firms will retaliate. The cost of the former usually involves up-front investments and start-up losses, which become part of the investment base in the new business. The risk of retaliation by existing firms can be viewed as an additional cost of entry, equal to the magnitude of

[2]Joint ventures should be analyzed in the same fashion as an internal entry. If a joint venture passes this hurdle, the *partner* must then be scrutinized for any clues about whether its goals, expectations, or managerial proclivities concerning the venture diverge from that of the firm. Such differences may make even a sound business proposition unworkable as a joint venture.

the adverse affects of retaliation (e.g., lower prices and escalated marketing costs) multiplied by the likelihood that retaliation will occur.

In Chapter 1, I described in some detail the sources of structural entry barriers and the factors that determine the likelihood of retaliation. The appropriate analysis of a decision to enter will balance the following costs and benefits:

1. the investment costs required to be in the new business, such as investment in manufacturing facilities and inventory (some of which may be elevated by structural entry barriers);
2. the additional investment required to overcome other structural entry barriers, such as brand identification and proprietary technology[3];
3. the expected cost from incumbents' retaliation against the entry, *balanced against*
4. the expected cash flows from being in the industry.

Many capital budgeting treatments of the entry decision neglect one or more of these factors. For example, too often the financial analysis assumes the industry prices and costs prevailing before entry and measures only the clearly visible investments necessary to the business, like constructing manufacturing facilities and assembling a sales force. Ignored are the more subtle costs of overcoming structural entry barriers, such as established brand franchises, distribution channels tied up by competitors, competitors' access to the most favorable sources of raw materials, or the need to develop proprietary technology. Also, new entry can raise the prices of scarce supplies, equipment, or labor, which means that the entering firm must bear higher costs.

Another factor often neglected is the *effect the entrant's new capacity* will have on the supply-demand balance in the industry. If the internal entrant's addition to industry capacity is significant, its efforts to fill its plant will mean that at least some other firms will have excess capacity. High fixed costs are likely to trigger price cutting or other efforts to fill capacity which will persist until someone exits from the business or until the excess capacity is eliminated by industry growth or retirement of facilities.

[3]The investments required to enter an industry through internal development may seem high relative to the cost of acquisition depending on the state of the acquisition market, to be discussed later. Currently, the perceived high costs of internal entry are driving many companies to the acquisition market.

Even more often neglected in the entry decision is the impact of the *probable reactions of existing firms*. Under conditions described below, existing firms will react to an entry in a variety of ways. One common reaction is to shave prices, which may mean that the industry prices assumed in *pro forma* calculations of the desirability of entry must be *lower* than those prevailing before entry. Prices are often depressed for years after an entry occurs, as they were in corn wet milling following the entries of Cargill and Archer-Daniels-Midland. Entry by Georgia-Pacific also has been disruptive to prices in the gypsum industry.[4]

Other reactions of existing firms may be escalation in marketing activities, special promotions, extension of warranty terms, easier credit, and product quality improvements.

Another possibility is that an entry will trigger a round of excessive capacity expansion in the industry, particularly if the new entrant comes in with more up-to-date facilities than some incumbents have. Industries differ in their instability with regard to capacity expansion, and some of the factors that will make an industry volatile have been described in Chapter 15.

The extent of these reactions and their probable duration must be forecast, and the prices or costs built into the *pro forma* entry calculation adjusted accordingly.

WILL RETALIATION OCCUR?

Incumbents will retaliate to entry if it pays to do so based on economic and noneconomic considerations. Internal entry is most likely to be disruptive and to provoke retaliation, which will harm future prospects, in the following kinds of industries (they are therefore risky entry targets):

Slow Growth. Internal entry will always take some market share from existing firms. However, in a slow-growing market this will be especially unwelcome because it may involve a drop in absolute sales, and vigorous retaliation is likely. If the market is growing rapidly, incumbents can continue strong financial performance even though an entrant takes some market share, and capacity added by the entrant is more quickly utilized without destroying prices.

[4]See *Forbes*, September 18, 1978.

Commodity or Commodity-Like Products.   In such businesses there are no brand loyalties or segmented markets to insulate incumbents from the effects of a new entrant, and vice versa. Entry in such a situation affects the entire industry, and price cutting is especially likely to occur.

High Fixed Costs.   When fixed costs are high, the addition of the new entrant's capacity to the market is prone to trigger retaliatory action by competitors if their capacity utilization falls significantly.

High Industry Concentration.   In such industries an entrant is particularly noticeable and may make a significant dent in one or more incumbent's market position. In a highly fragmented industry, the entrant may affect many firms but have only marginal impact. None of them will be hurt badly enough to retaliate vigorously, and none is likely to have the capability to inflict a penalty on the new entrant. In assessing probable retaliation it is obviously important to identify how seriously each of the incumbents will be affected. The more the effects are felt unequally by incumbents, the more likely are the most seriously affected firms to retaliate. If the shock of the entrant is spread over all the incumbents, it may be less threatening.

Incumbents Who Attach High Strategic Importance to Their Position in the Business.   When there are incumbents affected by the new entrant who place a high premium strategically on maintaining their share in the business, entry can evoke sharp retaliation. Strategic importance may be the result of heavy dependence on the business for cash flow or future growth, its position as a flagship business for the company, interrelationship between the business and others in the company, and so on. The factors that make a business strategically important to a company are described in Chapter 3 and in the discussion of exit barriers in Chapter 12.

Attitudes of Incumbent Management.   The presence of long-established incumbents, particularly if they are single business companies, can result in a volatile reaction to an entry move. In such industries entry is often taken as an affront or an injustice, and retaliation can be very bitter. More generally, the attitudes and backgrounds of the managements of incumbents can play a major role in retaliation. Some managements may have histories or orientations that make them feel more threatened by entry or more likely to react vindictively.[5]

The past behavior of incumbents concerning entry threats will often provide some indication of how they will react to a new entrant. Behavior toward past entrants and toward incumbents trying to shift strategic groups are especially useful clues.

IDENTIFYING TARGET INDUSTRIES FOR INTERNAL ENTRY

Assuming the potential entrant will properly analyze the elements of the decision described above, where is internal entry most likely to be attractive? The answer to this question flows from the basic framework of structural analysis. The expected profitability of firms in an industry depends on the strength of the five competitive forces: rivalry, substitution, bargaining power of suppliers and buyers, and entry. Entry acts as a balance in determining industry profits. If an industry is stable, or in equilibrium, the expected profits of entrants should *just reflect* the height of structural barriers to entry and the legitimate expectations of entrants about retaliation. The potential entrant, calculating its expected profits, should find that they are normal, or average profits, even though the profits of incumbents may be high. Because the entrant must overcome structural entry barriers and bear the risk of reaction from going firms, it faces higher costs than the successful firms in the industry, and these costs eliminate its above-average profits. If the costs of entry did not offset the above-average returns, other firms would already have entered and driven profits down to the level where the costs of entry and the benefits of entry cancel. *Thus it will rarely pay to enter an industry in equilibrium unless the firm has special advantages*—market forces are at work that eliminate the returns.

How, then, does a company expect to achieve above-average returns from entry? The answer lies in identifying those industry situations in which the market mechanism I have described is not working perfectly. Prime targets for internal entry by a firm fall into one of the following categories:

1. The industry is in disequilibrium.
2. Slow or ineffectual retaliation from incumbents may be expected.

[5]For some discussion about this point, see Chapter 3.

3. The firm has lower entry costs than other firms.
4. The firm has distinctive ability to influence the industry structure.
5. There will be positive effects on a firm's existing businesses.

INDUSTRIES IN DISEQUILIBRIUM

Not all industries are in equilibrium.

New Industries.   In new, rapidly growing industries, the competitive structure is usually not well established and the costs of entry may be much less than they will be for later entrants. Probably no firm will have locked up supplies of raw materials, created significant brand identification, or have much proclivity to retaliate to an entry. Going firms may face limits on the rate at which they can expand. However, a firm should not enter a new industry just because it is a new industry. Entry will not be justified unless a full structural analysis (Chapter 1) leads to the prediction of above-average profits for a period long enough to justify the investment. It is also important to note that in some industries the cost of entry for pioneers is *greater* than that for firms entering later, just because of the costs of pioneering. Some analytical techniques for identifying whether early or later entry is appropriate are discussed in Chapter 10 on emerging industries. Finally, other entrants may well be forthcoming into a new industry, and in order for it to expect profits to remain high the firm must have some economic basis for believing that later entrants will face entry costs higher than its own.

Rising Entry Barriers.   Increasing entry barriers mean that future profits will more than offest the *current* costs of entry.[6] Being first or one of the early entrants can minimize entry costs and also sometimes yield an advantage in product differentiation. However, if many other firms also enter early, this door may be closed. Thus the premium in such industries is on moving early and then facilitating the rise in entry barriers to block later entrants.

Poor Information.   A long-run imbalance between the cost of entry and expected profits may be present in some industries because of lack of recognition of this fact by potential entrants. This situa-

[6]Entry barriers often are rising in new industries.

tion may occur in "backwater," or obscure, industries which do not come to the attention of many established firms.

It is essential to realize that market forces will be working against the success of the entering firm to some extent. Where the prospects for entry are good because of disequilibrium, the market will be sending the same signals to others, who will be prone to enter as well. Thus a decision to enter must carry with it some clear notion of why the entrant and not other firms will reap the benefits of disequilibrium. Often the ability to forecast this rests on the advantages of getting in early by spotting the disequilibrium first. But unless the entrant can create some barriers to imitation, the advantages of being early may be eroded (though not eliminated) over time. An entry strategy must include consideration of such issues and a plan for dealing with them.

Slow or Ineffectual Retaliation

There may also be a favorable imbalance between expected profits and the cost of entry in industries whose incumbents are profitable but are sleepy, poorly informed, or otherwise impeded from timely or effective retaliation. If a firm can be among the first to discover such an industry, it can reap above-average profits.

Industries that may be ripe targets for entry do *not* have the characteristics leading to vigorous retaliation (given earlier) and possess some other unique factors.

Incumbents' cost of effective retaliation outweighs the benefits. The firm considering entry must examine the calculation each significant incumbent will make in deciding how vigorously to retaliate. It must forecast how large a profit erosion the incumbent must bear if it tries to inflict losses on the entrant. Are incumbents likely to think they can outlast the entrant? The larger the costs of retaliation versus the benefits incumbents want to achieve, the less likely they will retaliate.

The entrant not only can choose industries in which incumbents are less likely to retaliate but also can *influence* the probability of retaliation. For example, if the entrant can convince incumbents that it will never give up in its quest for a viable position in the industry, they may not waste money attempting to dislodge it completely.[7]

[7]See Chapter 5 for a discussion of ways in which a firm, including an entrant, might communicate such a commitment.

There is a paternal dominant firm or tight group of longstanding leaders. A dominant firm with a paternal view toward the industry may have never had to compete and may be slow to learn. The leader (or leaders) may see itself as the protector of the industry and its spokesperson. It may behave in ways that are best for the industry (e.g., hold up prices, preserve product quality, maintain high levels of customer service or technical help) but not necessarily best for it. An entrant can take a significant position as long as the leader is not provoked to (or is unable to) respond. This sort of situation may well have existed in nickel and corn milling, in which INCO and CPC have lost major positions to new players. Of course the risk in this strategy is that the sleeping giant will be awakened, and thus a judgment about the nature of its management is crucial.

Incumbents' costs of responding are great given the need to protect their existing businesses. This situation offers possibilities for the mixed-motive strategy discussed in Chapter 3. For example, responding to an entrant who is using a new distribution channel may alienate existing distributors' loyalties. Opportunity is also present if an incumbent's response to a new competitor will cut into sales of its bread and butter products, will help legitimize the strategy of the entrant, or will be inconsistent with the incumbent's image in the marketplace.

The entrant can exploit conventional wisdom. When incumbents believe in conventional wisdoms or certain key assumptions about how to compete in the industry, a firm with no preconceived notions can often see situations in which the conventional wisdom is inappropriate or outmoded. Conventional wisdom can creep into product line, service, plant location, and nearly any other aspect of a competitive strategy. Incumbents may cling tenaciously to such conventional wisdom because it has worked well in the past.

LOWER ENTRY COSTS

A more common and less risky situation where market forces do not negate the attractiveness of internal entry is an industry in which not all firms face the same entry costs. If a firm can *overcome structural entry barriers into an industry more cheaply* than most other potential entrants, or if it can *expect less retaliation*, a firm can reap above-average profits from entry. The firm also may have special advantages in competing in the industry that outweigh entry barriers.

The ability to overcome structural entry barriers more cheaply than other potential entrants usually rests on the presence of assets or skills drawn from the entrant's existing businesses or on innovations that provide a strategic concept for entry. The firm can look for industries in which it has capability to overcome entry barriers because of proprietary technology, established distribution channels, a recognized and transferable brand name, and so on. If many other potential entrants have the same advantages, then these advantages will probably already be reflected in the balance between the cost of entry and the benefits of entry. However, if the firm's ability to overcome structural entry barriers is unique or distinctive, the entry is likely to be profitable. Examples are General Motors' entry into recreational vehicles, utilizing chassis, engines, and a dealer network drawn from its automobile operations; and John Deere's entry into construction equipment, utilizing manufacturing technology and experience in product design and service drawn from its agricultural equipment business.

A firm might also receive less vigorous retaliation by incumbents than other potential entrants, either because the firm commanded great respect as a competitor or because its entry was somehow deemed not threatening. The entrant could command respect because of its size and resources or because of its reputation as a fair competitor (or conversely a ruthless one). The entrant might be seen as nonthreatening because of its history of confining its operations to small niches in the market, of not cutting prices, and so on. If the firm has a distinctive advantage in expecting less retaliation for any of these reasons, its expected cost of retaliation will be lower than other potential entrants, and entry can thereby offer potentially above-average profits.

DISTINCTIVE ABILITY TO INFLUENCE INDUSTRY STRUCTURE

Internal entry will be profitable despite the market forces if the firm has some distinctive ability to change the structural equilibrium in the target industry. If the firm can increase mobility barriers in the industry for subsequent entrants, for example, the structural equilibrium in the industry will change. The initiator will then be in a position to reap above-average profits from entry. Also, entry into a fragmented market can sometimes start in motion a process that greatly increases mobility barriers and leads to consolidation, as was discussed in Chapter 9.

Positive Effect on Existing Businessess

Internal entry will be profitable, even in the absence of the conditions described above, if it has a beneficial impact on the entrant's existing businesses. This impact could occur through the improvement of distributor relations, company image, defense against threats, and so on. Thus even if the new business earns an average return, the company as a whole will be better off.

Xerox's proposed entry into national digital data transmission networks may be an example of entry on this basis.[8] Xerox seems to be trying to build a broad base in the "office of the future." Since data transmission among computers, electronic mail, and elaborate linkage of company locations is likely to be part of this future—as well as conventional copying—Xerox may be trying to protect its existing strong base even though it has no special advantages in the data network business. Another example is Eaton Corporation's recent move into auto repair outlets. As a leading manufacturer of repair parts, Eaton has a stake in opening up markets and in keeping business away from the automobile manufacturers' captive dealer service departments, who use manufacturers' parts exclusively. Even though Eaton may have no reason to suspect above-average returns in auto repair per se, such an entry can boost its overall returns.

GENERIC CONCEPTS FOR ENTRY

Some common approaches to entry, which rest on various concepts for overcoming entry barriers more cheaply than other firms, are as follows:

Reduce Product Costs. Finding a way to produce the product at lower cost than incumbents. Possibilities are (1) an entirely new process technology; (2) a larger plant, reaping greater economies of scale; (3) more modern facilities, incorporating technological im-

---

[8]For a brief discussion of this planned move, see *Business Week*, November 27, 1978.

provements; (4) shared activities with existing businesses that yield a cost advantage.

Buy in with Low Price.   Buy into the market by sacrificing returns in the short run to force competitors to yield share. The success of this approach depends on competitors' unwillingness or inability to retaliate in the face of the particular strengths of the entrant.

Offer a Superior Product, Broadly Defined.   Offer an innovation in product or service that allows the entrant to overcome product differentiation barriers.

Discover a New Niche.   Find an unrecognized market segment or niche which has distinctive requirements the firm can cater to. This move allows the entrant to overcome existing barriers in product differentiation (and perhaps distribution channels).

Introduce a Marketing Innovation.   Find a new way to market the product which overcomes product differentiation barriers or circumvents distributors' power.

Use Piggybacked Distribution.   Build an entry strategy on established distribution relationships drawn from other businesses.

Entry Through Acquisition

Entry through acquisition is subject to a completely different analytical framework than entry through internal development because acquisition does not add a new firm to the industry in the direct sense. As we will see, however, some of the same factors that determine the attractiveness of an internal entry will affect a candidate for acquisition.

The critical point is the recognition that *the price of an acquisition is set in the market for companies.* The market for companies is the marketplace in which owners of companies (or business units) are sellers and acquiring companies are buyers. In most industrialized nations, particularly the United States, the market for companies is a very active market in which many companies are bought and sold every year. The market is well organized, involving finders, brokers, and investment bankers all seeking to match buyers and sellers and often reaping large commissions for doing so. The market has become more organized in recent years as both intermediaries and participants have become more sophisticated.[9] Intermediaries now work actively to generate multiple bidders for selling firms, and multiple bids are common. The market for companies is also a market about which much is written in the press and many statistics are now collected. All these things suggest that the market will function relatively efficiently.

An efficient market for companies works to *eliminate any above-average* profits from making an acquisition. If a company has sound management and attractive future prospects, its price will be bid up in the market. Conversely, if its future is dim or if it requires massive infusions of capital, its sale price will be low relative to book value. To the extent that the market for companies is working efficiently, then, the price of an acquisition will eliminate most of the returns for the buyer.

Contributing to the market's efficiency is the fact that the seller usually has the option of keeping and operating the business. In some situations the seller has compelling reasons to sell and is thereby vulnerable to accepting whatever price the market for companies sets. However, to the extent that the seller has the alternative of operating the business it will not rationally sell if the sale price does not exceed the expected present value of continuing to operate the business. This expected present value puts a *floor* under the price for the business. The price that results from the bidding process in the market for companies must exceed this floor, or the transaction will not take place. In practice, the price for the acquisition must significantly exceed the floor to give the owners a premium for selling. In today's market for companies, large premiums over market value are the rule rather than the exception.

This analysis suggests that it is quite difficult to win at the acquisition game. The market for companies and the seller's alternative of continuing to operate the business work against reaping above-average profits from acquisitions. Perhaps this is why acquisitions so often seem not to meet managers' expectations, as is sug-

[9] Historically the market for companies has functioned much less formally, and predominantly through personal contacts.

gested by much survey evidence. This analysis is also consistent with the conclusions of a number of studies by economists which suggest that the seller, and not the buyer, usually captures most of the spoils from an acquisition.

However, the real power of this analysis lies in directing attention toward the conditions that determine whether or not a particular acquisition will have a good chance of yielding an above-average return. Acquisitions will most likely be profitable if

1. the floor price created by the seller's alternative of keeping the business is low;
2. the market for companies is *imperfect* and does not eliminate above-average returns through the bidding process;
3. the buyer has a *unique* ability to operate the acquired business.

It is crucial to note that the bidding process can eliminate the profitability of an acquisition even if the floor price is low. Thus favorable conditions in at least two of the areas are necessary for success.

THE HEIGHT OF THE FLOOR PRICE

The floor price for an acquisition is set by the seller's alternative of keeping the business. It clearly depends on the perceptions of the *seller*, and not the perceptions of buyers or of the market for companies. Obviously the floor will be lowest when the seller feels the greatest compulsion to sell, for example, because of the following:

- the seller has estate problems;
- the seller needs capital quickly;
- the seller has lost key management or sees no successors for existing management.

The floor price will also be low if the seller is not optimistic about its prospects if it were to continue to operate the business. The seller may believe its ability to operate the business is inferior to that of buyers if

- the seller perceives capital constraints to growth;
- the seller recognizes its managerial weaknesses.

IMPERFECTIONS IN THE MARKET FOR COMPANIES

Despite its high level of organization, the market for companies is subject to a variety of imperfections, that is, situations in which the bidding process will not completely eliminate the profits from an acquisition. These imperfections stem from the fact that the market for companies is trading products each of which is unique, that information is highly incomplete, and that buyers and sellers often have complex motives. Imperfections in the market leading to successful acquisitions will occur in the following situations, among others:

1. *The buyer has superior information.* A buyer may be in a better position to forecast favorable future performance from an acquisition than other buyers. It may know the industry or the trends in technology or have insights that other potential bidders do not. In this case the bidding will stop short of eliminating all above-average returns.

2. *The number of bidders is low.* The probability that the bidding process will not eliminate all the returns from the acquisition is increased if the number of bidders is small. The number may be low if the candidate is an unusual business that would not fit with or be understood by many potential acquirors or if the candidate is very large (and not many buyers can afford it). The way in which the buyer conducts negotiations can discourage the seller from seeking other bidders ("we will not participate in a bidding war").

3. *The condition of the economy is bad.* It appears that the state of the economy affects not only the number of buyers but also what they are willing to pay. Thus a company may reap potentially above-average returns by being willing to deal during economic downturns if it is suffering less than other bidders.

4. *The selling company is sick.* There is some evidence that sick companies are more heavily discounted than a true expected-value analysis would suggest, perhaps because acquirors all seem to be looking for sound companies with good management. Thus the number of bidders for sick companies may be lower, as well as the prices they are willing to pay. White Consolidated appears to have successfully taken advantage of this situation by purchasing ailing companies or divisions at below book value and apparently making them profitable.

5. *The seller has objectives besides maximizing the price received for the businesses.* Luckily for acquirors, not all sellers try to maximize the price they receive for their business. Since the selling prices of companies are often well in excess of what their owners believe they need for financial well-being, sellers often value other things. Common examples are the name and reputation of the buyer, the way in which the seller's employees will be treated, whether the seller's management will be retained, and how much the buyer will interfere in running the business if the owner plans to stay on. Companies selling divisions are somewhat less likely to have such noneconomic objectives than are owners or owner-managers selling an entire company, although they still can be present.

This analysis suggests that acquirors should look for companies who will have noneconomic objectives and should cultivate these objectives. It also suggests that certain acquirors may have advantages because of the story they can tell sellers. If they can demonstrate good treatment of employees and management of acquisitions in the past, for example, their case with potential sellers will be made more credible. Large prestigious acquirors may also have an edge for similar reasons, since owners want to associate their life's work (their company) with a blue chip organization.

UNIQUE ABILITY TO OPERATE THE SELLER

The buyer can bid more than other buyers and still achieve above-average returns under the following conditions:

1. *The buyer has a distinctive ability to improve the operations of the seller.* A buyer with distinctive assets or skills that can improve the strategic position of the acquisition candidate can achieve above-average returns from the acquisition. The other bidders, assuming less improvement of the acquisition in their calculations, will stop bidding before the returns are eliminated. Well-known examples of such acquisitions are Campbell's of Vlasic and Gould's of ITE.

Possessing the ability to improve the acquisition candidate is not enough in and of itself. This ability must to some degree be distinctive, because if it is not, there are likely to be other firms around who will see the same potential. These firms may keep the bidding going until the returns from making the improvements are eliminated by the price.

Entry through acquisition and through internal development are the most similar in this approach. In both cases, the buyer must have some distinctive ability to compete in the new business. In the case of acquisition, the firm is able to outbid others for the candidate and still earn above-average profits. In the case of internal development, the firm is able to overcome barriers to entry more cheaply than other firms.

2. *The firm buys into an industry that meets the criteria for internal development.* Many of the same points about favorable industries made in the context of internal entry can apply here. If the acquiror can use the acquisition as a base from which to change industry structure or to exploit conventional wisdom, or can take advantage of slow or ineffective response by incumbents to strategy changes, for example, possibilities for above-average returns in the industry are good.

3. *The acquisition will uniquely help a buyer's position in its existing businesses.* If the acquisition can add something to bolster the buyer's position in its existing businesses, the profitability of the acquisition may not be eliminated in the bidding process. A good example of this logic as a motivation for acquisition is R.J. Reynolds' recent acquisition of Del Monte. Reynolds has a number of food brands (Hawaiian Punch, Chun King, Vermont Maid, and others) but has failed to achieve significant market penetration for most of them. The acquisition of Del Monte will provide a distribution system, more clout with food brokers, and entrance into international markets where Reynolds' existing brands are weak. Even if Del Monte yields only average returns, its positive affect on the rest of Reynolds' food strategy may mean an above-average return from the transaction.

IRRATIONAL BIDDERS

When bidding for acquisition candidates, it is extremely important to examine the motives and situation of other bidders. Although bidding will usually stop once above-average returns are eliminated, it is important to recognize that some competing bidders may continue long after, from one firm's point of view, the returns are eliminated. This might happen for a number of reasons:

• the bidder sees a unique way to improve the acquisition target;

- the acquisition will help the bidder's existing business;
- the bidder has goals or motives other than the maximization of profit—perhaps growth is the primary objective, the bidder sees the possibility for a one-shot financial gain, or the bidder desires a firm of the type of the acquisition target because of the idiosyncracies of its management.

In such a case, it is important *not* to take the willingness of the bidder to raise the price as an indication of the acquisition's value. A careful analysis of the factors entering into the bidder's reservation price is indicated.

Sequenced Entry

Any decision to enter an industry must include a target strategic group. However, the discussion in Chapter 7 combined with the analysis earlier in this chapter suggests that a firm can adopt a sequential strategy of entry involving initial entry into one group and subsequent mobility from group to group. For example, Procter and Gamble acquired the Charmin Paper Company, which had high-quality toilet tissue and some production facilities, but little or no brand identification and only regional distribution. Starting from a base in this strategic group, Procter and Gamble invested substantial resources in creating brand identification, achieving national distribution, and improving the product and production facilities. Thus, Charmin was shifted into a new strategic group.

Such a strategy of sequential entry may lower the total cost of overcoming mobility barriers into the strategic group that is the ultimate target, and may lower the risks. Costs can be lowered by accumulating knowledge and brand indentification in the industry through entry into the initial group, which is then used at no cost for mobility into the ultimate target group. Managerial talent can be developed in a more measured way in this fashion. Also the reaction of existing firms to entry might be tempered by such a sequenced strategy.

A sequenced strategy often lowers the risks of entry because the firm can segment the risk. If it fails in its initial entry, the firm is spared the cost of going further; it would have to put all its chips on the table if it tried to enter the ultimate target group right away. Sequenced entry also allows the firm to accumulate capital for subsequent shifts in position, for which it might have to pay a stiff price if all were needed at once. In addition, a firm can choose to take its first step into a strategic group in which overcoming mobility barriers requires relatively reversible investments (plant capacity that is salable). For example, a firm's initial entry might be into production for a private label. Only if it is successful at this step will the firm then attempt entry into a strategic group where heavy investments in advertising, R & D, or other unsalvageable areas are required to overcome mobility barriers.

The analysis of sequenced entry can be turned around to derive implications for existing firms in the industry. If there are particularly safe sequenced entry strategies, then it clearly pays to direct investments in mobility barriers to close them off.

Appendixes

APPENDIX A
Portfolio Techniques In Competitor Analysis

Since the late 1960s a number of techniques have been developed for displaying a diversified firm's operations as a "portfolio" of businesses. These techniques provide simple frameworks for charting or categorizing the different businesses in a firm's portfolio and determining the implications for resource allocation. Techniques for portfolio analysis have their greatest applicability in developing strategy at the corporate level and in aiding in corporate review of business units, rather than in developing competitive strategy in individual industries. Nevertheless, if their limitations are understood, these techniques can play a part in answering some of the questions in competitor analysis raised in Chapter 3, particularly if a firm is competing with a diversified rival who uses them in its strategic planning.

There have been many written accounts of the most-used techniques for portfolio analysis, and an extensive discussion of their mechanics will not be presented here.[1] Rather the focus will be on outlining the key elements of the two most commonly used techniques—the growth/share matrix identified with the Boston Consulting Group (BCG) and the company position/industry attractiveness

[1] For extensive discussion of these techniques see Abell and Hammond (1979), chaps. 4, 5; Day (1977); Salter and Weinhold (1979), chap. 4.

screen identified with GE and McKinsey—and discussing their use in competitor analysis.

The Growth/Share Matrix

The growth/share matrix is based on the use of industry growth and relative market share[2] as proxies for (1) the competitive position of a firm's business unit in its industry and (2) the resulting net cash flow required to operate the business unit. This formula reflects the underlying assumption that the experience curve (discussed in Chapter 1) is operating and that the firm with the largest relative share will thereby be the lowest cost producer.

These premises lead to a portfolio chart like that shown in Figure A-1, on which each of a firm's business units can be plotted. Although the cut-offs in terms of growth and relative market share are arbitrary, the growth/share portfolio chart is usually divided into

FIGURE A-1. Growth/Share Matrix

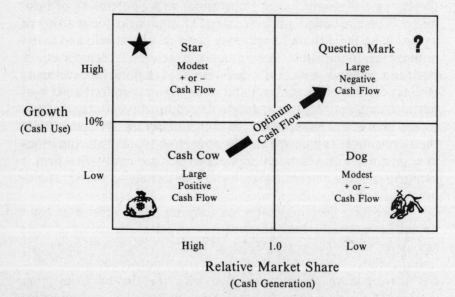

[2]Relative market share is the market share of the firm relative to that of the largest competitor in the industry.

four quadrants. The key idea is that business units located in each of these four quadrants will be in fundamentally different cash flow positions and should be managed differently, which leads to some implications for how the firm should try to build its overall portfolio.

- Cash Cows: Businesses with high relative share in low-growth markets will produce healthy cash flow, which can be used to fund other, developing businesses.
- Dogs: Businesses with low relative share in low-growth markets will often be modest cash users. They will be cash traps because of their weak competitive position.
- Stars: Businesses with high relative share in high-growth markets usually will require large amounts of cash to sustain growth but have a strong market position that will yield high reported profits. They may be nearly in cash balance.
- Question Marks (sometimes called wildcats): Businesses with low relative share in rapidly growing markets require large cash inflows to finance growth and are weak cash generators because of their poor competitive position.

Following the logic of the growth/share portfolio, cash cows become the financiers of other developing businesses in the firm. Ideally, cash cows are used to make question marks into stars. Since doing so requires a great deal of capital to keep up with rapid growth as well as to build market share, the decision about which question marks to build into stars becomes a key strategic one. Once a star, a business eventually becomes a cash cow as its market growth slows. Question marks that are not chosen for investment should be harvested (managed to generate cash) until they become dogs. Dogs should either be harvested or divested from the portfolio. A firm should manage its portfolio, according to BCG, so that this desirable sequence occurs and so that the portfolio is in cash balance.

LIMITATIONS

The applicability of the portfolio model depends on a number of conditions, some of the most important of which are summarized below:

- The market has been defined properly to account for important shared experience and other interdependencies with other markets. This is often a subtle problem requiring a great deal of analysis.

- The structure of the industry (Chapter 1) and within the industry (Chapter 7) are such that relative market share is a good proxy for competitive position and relative costs. This is often not true.
- Market growth is a good proxy for required cash investment. Yet profits (and cash flow) depend on a lot of other things.

USE IN COMPETITOR ANALYSIS

In view of these conditions, the growth/share matrix by itself is not very useful in determining strategy for a particular business. A great deal of analysis of the sort described in this book is necessary in order to determine the competitive position of a business unit, and to translate this competitive position into a concrete strategy.[3] Once this front-end analysis has been done, the value added of the portfolio plot itself is low.

However, the growth/share matrix can be one component of a competitor analysis when combined with the other kinds of analysis described in Chapter 3. A firm can plot, as best it can, the corporate portfolio for each of its significant competitors, ideally at several points in time. The portfolio position of the business unit against which the firm competes will give some indications about the questions raised in Chapter 3 and about the goals the competitor's parent may be expecting it to meet and its vulnerability to various types of strategic moves. For example, a business being harvested may be vulnerable to attacks on its market share. The comparison of competitors' portfolios over time can identify even more clearly shifts in the position of a competitor's business unit relative to others in its company, and it can provide further clues about the strategic mandate being given to the competitor. If the competitor is known to use the growth/share portfolio approach in planning, the predictive power of portfolio analysis is all the greater. However, even if a competitor does not formally use the technique, the logic of the need for broad allocation of resources may mean that the portfolio provides useful clues.

[3]The advice to "harvest" or "grow into a star" is far from sufficient to guide managerial action.

The Company Position/Industry Attractiveness Screen

Another technique is the three-by-three matrix variously attributed to General Electric, McKinsey and Company, and Shell. One representative variation of this technique is shown in Figure A-2. The two axes in this approach are the attractiveness of the industry and the strength, or competitive position, of the business unit. Where a particular business unit falls along these axes is determined by an analysis of that particular unit and its industry, using criteria like those listed in Figure A-2. Depending on where a unit falls on the matrix, its broad strategic mandate is either to invest capital to *build* position, to *hold* by balancing cash generation and selective cash use, or to *harvest* or divest. Expected shifts in industry attractiveness or company position lead to the need to reassess strategy. A firm can plot its portfolio of businesses on such a matrix to insure that the appropriate allocation of resources is made. The firm can also try to balance the portfolio in terms of its mix of developing and

FIGURE A-2. Company Position/Industry Attractiveness Screen

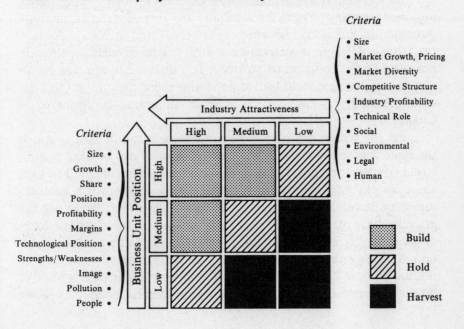

developed businesses and the internal consistency of cash generation and cash use.

The company position/industry attractiveness screen is less precisely quantifiable than the growth/share approach, requiring inherently subjective judgments about where a particular business unit should be plotted. It is often criticized for being more vulnerable to manipulation. As a result, sometimes quantitative weighting schemes, using criteria determined to lead to industry attractiveness or company position in the particular industry, are employed to make the analysis more "objective." The screening technique reflects the assumption that every business unit is different and requires its own analysis of competitive position and industry attractiveness. As noted above, actually constructing the growth/share portfolio in practice involves the same type of particularistic analysis of each business unit. Hence its actual "objectivity" may really not be far from that of the company position/industry attractiveness screen.

Like the growth/share portfolio matrix, the company position/industry attractiveness screen offers little but a basic consistency check in formulating competitive strategy for a particular industry. The real issues involve deciding where to plot the business on the grid, deciding if position on the grid implies the indicated strategy and working out a detailed strategic concept for building, holding, or harvesting. These steps require the sort of detailed analysis described in this book, because the criteria listed in Figure A-2 are far from sufficient to determine industry attractiveness, company position, or the appropriate strategy. It is difficult to see, for example, how the screen could lead to a recommendation to invest in a declining industry, sound advice in some situations as discussed in Chapter 12.

Yet the screen can play a part in competitor analysis, in much the same way as the growth/share matrix can. It can be used to construct competitors' portfolios at different points in time and to gain some insight into what strategic mandate a competitor's business unit may be receiving from its corporate office. Whether to use the growth/share or company position/industry attractiveness technique is largely a matter of taste (basically the same analysis is required to use either of the techniques properly), unless a competitor is known to use one or the other. In the latter case the best predictive power is gained from the technique the competitor itself uses. Note that the growth/share technique is inextricably tied with the experience curve concept. Hence if a competitor is known to be strongly influenced by the experience curve concept, the growth/share portfolio approach will probably be a better predictor of its goals and behavior.

APPENDIX B
How to Conduct an Industry Analysis

How should one go about analyzing an industry and competitors? What types of data does one look for and how can they be organized? Where does one look for these data? This appendix deals with these questions and some of the other practical problems involved in conducting an industry analysis. There are basically two types of data about industries: published data and those gathered from interviews with industry participants and observers (field data). The bulk of discussion in this appendix will center on identifying the important sources of published and field data, their strengths and weaknesses, and strategies for approaching them most effectively and in the right sequence.

A full-blown industry analysis is a massive task, and one that can consume months if one is starting from scratch. In beginning an industry analysis there is a tendency to dive in and collect a mass of detailed information, with little in the way of a general framework or approach in which to fit this information. This lack of method leads to frustration at best, and confusion and wasted effort at worst. Thus before considering specific sources, it is important to consider an overall strategy for conducting the industry study and the critical first steps in initiating it.

Industry Analysis Strategy

There are two important aspects in developing a strategy for analyzing an industry. The first is to determine just what it is one is looking for. "Anything about the industry" is much too broad to serve as an effective guide for research. Although the full list of specific issues that need to be addressed in an industry analysis depends on the particular industry under study, it is possible to generalize about what important information and raw data the researcher should look for. The chapters in this book have identified the key structural features of industries, the important forces causing them to change, and the strategic information necessary about competitors. These are the factors that are the target of an industry analysis, and the core of the framework that identifies these factors has been presented in Chapters 1, 3, 7, and 8 and extended in the rest of the book. However, since these characteristics of structure and competitors are generally not raw data but rather the result of *analysis* of raw data, researchers may also find it useful to have a framework for systematically collecting raw data. A simple but exhaustive set of areas under which to collect raw data is given in Figure B-1. The researcher who can fully describe each of these areas should be in a position to develop a comprehensive picture of industry structure and competitors' profiles.

With a framework for assembling data, the second major strategy question is how sequentially to develop data in each area. There are a number of alternatives, ranging from taking one item at a time to proceeding randomly. As hinted earlier, however, there are important benefits in getting a general *overview* of the industry first, and only then focusing on the specifics. Experience has shown that a broad understanding can help the researcher more effectively spot important items of data when studying sources and organize data more effectively as they are collected.

A number of steps can be useful in obtaining this overview:

1. *Who is in the industry*. It is wise to develop a rough list of industry participants right away, especially the leading firms. A list of key competitors is helpful for quickly finding other articles and company documents (some of the sources discussed later will aid in this process). An entering wedge for many of these sources is the indus-

FIGURE B-1.   Raw Data Categories for Industry Analysis

Data Categories	*Compilation*
Product lines	By company
Buyers and their behavior	By year
Complementary products	By functional area
Substitute products	

Growth
    Rate
    Pattern (seasonal, cyclical)
    Determinants

Technology of production and distribution
    Cost structure
    Economies of scale
    Value added
    Logistics
    Labor

Marketing and Selling
    Market segmentation
    Marketing practices

Suppliers

Distribution channels (if indirect)

Innovation
    Types
    Sources
    Rate
    Economies of scale

Competitors—strategy, goals, strengths and
weaknesses, assumptions

Social, political, legal environment

Macroeconomic environment

try's *Standard Industrial Classification* (SIC) code, which can be determined from the Census Bureau's *Standard Industrial Classification Manual*. The SIC system classifies industries on a variety of levels of breadth, with two-digit industries overly broad for most purposes, five-digit industries often too narrow, and four-digit industries usually about right.

2. *Industry studies.* If one is lucky, there may be a relatively comprehensive industry study available or a number of broadly-based articles. Reading these can be a quick way of developing an overview. (Sources of industry studies are discussed later.)

3. *Annual reports*. If there are any publicly held firms in the industry, annual reports should be consulted early. A single annual report may contain only modest amounts of disclosure. However, a quick review of the annual reports for a number of major companies over a ten- or fifteen-year period is an excellent way to begin to understand the industry. Most aspects of the business will be discussed at one time or another. The most enlightening part of an annual report for an overview is often the president's letter. The researcher should look for the rationales given for both good and bad financial results; these should expose some of the critical success factors in the industry. It also is important to note what the company seems to be proud of in its annual report, what it seems to be worried about, and what key changes have been made. It is also possible to gain some insights into how companies are organized, the flow of production, and numerous other factors from reading between the lines in a series of annual reports from the same company.

The researcher will generally want to come back to annual reports and other company documents later in the study. The initial early reading will fail to uncover many nuances that become apparent once the knowledge of the industry and the competitor is more complete.

GET INTO THE FIELD EARLY

If there is any common problem in getting industry analyses underway, it is that researchers tend to spend too much time looking for published sources and using the library before they begin to tap field sources. As will be discussed later, published sources have a variety of limitations: timeliness, level of aggregation, depth, and so on. Although it is important to gain some basic understanding of the industry to maximize the value of field interviews, the researcher should not exhaust all published sources *before* getting into the field. On the contrary, clinical and library research should proceed simultaneously. They tend to feed on each other, especially if the researcher is aggressive in asking every field source to suggest published material about the industry. Field sources tend to be more efficient because they get to the issues, without the wasted time of reading useless documents. Interviews also sometimes help the researcher identify the issues. This help may come, to some extent, at the expense of objectivity.

GET OVER THE HUMP

Experience shows that the morale of researchers in an industry study often goes through a U-shaped cycle as the study proceeds. An initial period of euphoria gives way to confusion and even panic as the complexity of the industry becomes apparent and mounds of information accumulate. Sometime later in the study, it all begins to come together. This pattern appears to be so common as to serve as a useful thing for researchers to remember.

Published Sources for Analysis of Industry and Competitors

The amount of published information available varies widely by industry. The larger the industry, the older it is, and the slower the rate of technological change, the better the available published information tends to be. Unfortunately for the researcher, many interesting industries do not meet these criteria, and there may be little published information available. However, it is *always* possible to gain some important information about an industry from published sources, and these sources should be aggressively pursued. Generally, the problem the researcher will face in using published data for analyzing an economically meaningful industry is that they are *too broad*, or too aggregated, to fit the industry. If a researcher starts searching for data with this reality in mind, the usefulness of broad data will be better recognized and the tendency to give up too easily will be avoided.

Two important principles can greatly facilitate the development of references to published materials. First, every published source should be combed tenaciously for references to other sources, both other published sources and sources for field interviews. Often articles will cite individuals (industry executives, security analysts, and so on) who usually do not appear by accident; they tend to be either well-informed or particularly vocal industry observers, and they make excellent leads.

The second principle is to keep a thorough bibliography of everything that is uncovered. Although it is painful at the time, taking down the full citation of the source not only saves time in compiling the bibliography at the end of the study but also guards against wasteful duplication of efforts by members of research teams and the agony of not being able to remember where some critical piece of information came from. Summary notes on sources or Xerox copies of useful ones are also useful. They minimize the need for rereading and can facilitate communication within a research team.

Although the types of published sources are potentially numerous, they can be divided into a number of general categories, which are discussed briefly below.[1]

INDUSTRY STUDIES

Studies that provide a general overview of some industries come in two general varieties. First are book-length studies of the industry, often (but not exclusively) written by economists. These can usually best be found in library card catalogs and by cross-checking references given in other sources. Participants in or observers of an industry will almost always know of such industry studies when they exist, and they should be questioned about them as the study proceeds.

The second broad category is the typically shorter, more focused studies conducted by securities or consulting firms, such as Frost and Sullivan, Arthur D. Little, Stanford Research Institute, and all the Wall Street research houses. Sometimes specialized consulting firms collect data on particular industries, such as SMART, Inc., in the ski industry and IDC in the computer industry. Often access to these studies involves a fee. Unfortunately, although there are a number of published directories of market research studies, there is no one place where they are all compiled, and the best way to learn about them is through industry observers or participants.

TRADE ASSOCIATIONS

Many industries have trade associations, which serve as clearing houses for industry data and sometimes publish detailed industry statistics.[2] Trade associations differ greatly in their willingness to

---

[1]L. Daniels (1976) is an excellent general source of business information. There are also a number of computerized abstract services for references and articles available at major business libraries, which can speed the task of finding articles and sorting the useful ones from those that are not so useful.

[2]There are a number of published directories of trade associations.

give data to researchers. Usually, however, an introduction from a member of the association is helpful in gaining the cooperation of staff in sending data.

Whether or not the association is a source of data, members of the staff are extremely useful in alerting the researcher to any published information about the industry that exists, identifying the key participants and discussing their general impressions of how the industry functions, its key factors for company success, and important industry trends. Once contact with a trade association staff member has been made, this person can in turn be a useful source of referrals to industry participants and can identify participants who represent a range of viewpoints.

TRADE MAGAZINES

Most industries have one or more trade magazines which cover industry events on a regular (sometimes even daily) basis. A small industry may be covered as part of a broader-based trade publication. Trade journals in customer, distributor, or supplier industries are often useful sources as well.

Reading through trade magazines over a long period of time is an extremely useful way to understand the competitive dynamics and important changes in an industry, as well as to diagnose its norms and attitudes.

BUSINESS PRESS

A wide variety of business publications cover companies and industries on an intermittent basis. To obtain references, there are a number of standard bibliographies, including the *Business Periodicals Index*, *The Wall Street Journal Index*, and the *F&S Index*, United States (and companions for Europe and International).

COMPANY DIRECTORIES AND STATISTICAL DATA

There are a variety of directories of both public and private U.S. firms, some of which give a limited amount of data. Many directories list firms by SIC code, and thus they provide a way to build a complete list of industry participants. Comprehensive directories include *Thomas Register of American Manufacturers*, the Dun and Bradstreet *Million Dollar Directory* and *Middle Market Directory*, *Standard and Poor's Register of Corporations*, *Directors and Executives*, and the various *Moody's* publications. Another broad list of companies classified by industry is the Newsfront *30,000 Leading U.S. Corporations*, which gives some limited financial information as well. In addition to these general directories, other potential sources of broad company lists are financial magazines (*Fortune, Forbes*) and buyers guides.

Dun and Bradstreet compiles credit reports on all companies of significant size, whether they be public or private. These reports are not available to any library and provided only to subscribing companies who pay a high fixed cost for the service plus a small fee for individual reports. Dun and Bradstreet reports are valuable as sources about private companies, but since data provided by the companies are not audited, it must be used with caution; many users have reported errors in the information.

There are also many statistical sources of such data as advertising spending and stock market performance.

COMPANY DOCUMENTS

Most companies publish a variety of documents about themselves, particularly if they are publicly traded. In addition to annual reports, SEC form 10-K's, proxy statements, prospectuses, and other government filings can be useful. Also useful are speeches or testimony by firm executives, press releases, product literature, manuals, published company histories, transcripts of annual meetings, want ads, patents, and even advertising.

MAJOR GOVERNMENT SOURCES

The Internal Revenue Service provides in the *IRS Corporation Source Book of Statistics of Income* extensive annual financial information on industries (by size of organizations within the industry) based on corporate tax returns. A less detailed, printed version of the data is in the IRS's *Statistics of Income*. The main drawback of this source is that the financial data for an entire company are allocated to that company's principle industry, thereby introducing biases in industries in which many participants are highly diversified. However, the IRS data are available annually back to the 1940s, and it is the only source that gives financial data covering all firms in the industry.

Another source of government statistics is the Bureau of the Census. The most frequently used volumes are *Census of Manufacturers, Census of Retail Trade*, and *Census of the Mineral Industries*, which are available quite far back in time. As with the IRS data, the census does not refer to specific companies but rather breaks down statistics by SIC code. Census material also has considerable regional data for industries. Unlike IRS data, census data are based on aggregates of data from establishments within corporations, such as plant sites and warehouses, rather than corporations as a whole. Therefore, the data are not biased by company diversification. One feature of the *Census of Manufacturers* that can be particularly useful is the special report, *Concentration Ratios in Manufacturing Industry*. This section gives the percentages of industry sales of the largest four, eight, twenty, and fifty firms in the industry for each SIC four-digit manufacturing industry in the economy. Another useful government source for price level changes in industries is the Bureau of Labor Statistics, *Wholesale Price Index*.

Leads on further government information can be obtained through the various indexes of government publications, as well as by contacting the U.S. Department of Commerce and the libraries of other government agencies. Other government sources include regulatory agency filings, congressional hearings, and patent office statistics.

OTHER SOURCES

Some other potentially fruitful published sources include the following:

- antitrust records;
- local newspapers in which a competitor's facilities or headquarters are located;
- local tax records.

Gathering Field Data for Industry Analysis

In gathering field data it is important to have a framework for identifying possible sources, determining what their attitude toward cooperation with the research is likely to be, and developing an approach to them. Figure B-2 gives a schematic diagram of the most important sources of field data, which are participants in the industry itself, firms and individuals in adjacent businesses to the industry (suppliers, distributors, customers), service organizations that have contact with the industry (including trade associations), and industry observers (including the financial community, regulators, etc.). Each of these sources has somewhat differing characteristics, which are useful to identify explicitly.

CHARACTERISTICS OF FIELD SOURCES

Industry competitors will perhaps be the most uncertain about cooperating with researchers, because the data they release have a real potential of causing them economic harm. Approaching sources in the industry requires the greatest degree of care (some guidelines will be discussed later). Sometimes they will not cooperate at all.

The next most sensitive sources are service organizations, such as consultants, auditors, bankers, and trade association personnel, who operate under a tradition of confidentiality about individual clients, though usually not about general industry background information. Most of the other sources are not threatened directly by industry research, and in fact they often perceive it as a help. The most perceptive outside observers of the industry are often suppliers' or customers' executives who have taken an active interest in the whole range of industry participants over a long period of time. Retailers and wholesalers are often excellent sources as well.

The researcher should attempt to speak with individuals in all of the major groups since each of them can supply important data and provide useful cross-checks. Because of their differing perspectives, the researcher should *not* be surprised if they make conflicting and even directly contradictory statements. One of the arts of interviewing is cross-checking and verifying data from different sources.

FIGURE B-2.   Sources of Field Data for Industry Analysis

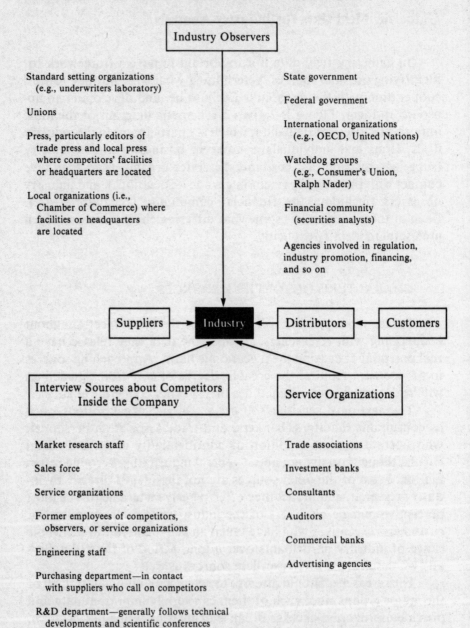

Industry Observers

Standard setting organizations
  (e.g., underwriters laboratory)

Unions

Press, particularly editors of
  trade press and local press
  where competitors' facilities
  or headquarters are located

Local organizations (i.e.,
  Chamber of Commerce) where
  facilities or headquarters
  are located

State government

Federal government

International organizations
  (e.g., OECD, United Nations)

Watchdog groups
  (e.g., Consumer's Union,
  Ralph Nader)

Financial community
  (securities analysts)

Agencies involved in regulation,
industry promotion, financing,
and so on

Suppliers → Industry ← Distributors ← Customers

Interview Sources about Competitors
Inside the Company

Service Organizations

Market research staff

Sales force

Service organizations

Former employees of competitors,
  observers, or service organizations

Engineering staff

Purchasing department—in contact
  with suppliers who call on competitors

R&D department—generally follows technical
  developments and scientific conferences
  and publications

Trade associations

Investment banks

Consultants

Auditors

Commercial banks

Advertising agencies

The researcher can make the initial field contact at any point shown in Figure B-2. Initially, to gather background, it is best to make contact with someone who is knowledgeable about the industry *but who does not have a competitive or direct economic stake in it*. Such interested third parties are usually more open and provide the best way of gaining an unbiased overview of the industry and of the key actors involved, which is important early in the research. When the researcher is in a position to ask more perceptive and discriminating questions, direct industry participants can be tackled. However, to maximize the chances of success in any interview, it is important to have a personal introduction, no matter how indirect. This consideration may dictate the choice of where to begin. Field research always involves an element of opportunism, and following a method of analysis should not deter the researcher from pursuing good leads.

It is important to remember that many participants in an industry or observers of it know each other personally. Industries are not faceless; they are composed of people. Thus one source will lead to another if the researcher is adept at his task. Particularly receptive subjects for field interviews are often individuals who have been quoted in articles. Another good method to develop interviews is to attend industry conventions to meet people informally and generate contacts.

FIELD INTERVIEWS

Effective field interviewing is a time-consuming and subtle process, but one that will amass the bulk of critical information for many industry studies. Although each interviewer will have his or her own style, a few simple points may be useful.

Contacts. It is generally most productive to make contacts with potential sources by telephone, rather than by letter, or by a telephone call following up a letter. People are apt to put a letter aside and avoid a decision about whether to cooperate. A telephone call forces the issue, and people are more likely to cooperate with an articulate and well-informed verbal request than they are with a letter.

Lead Time. Researchers should begin to arrange interviews as early as possible, since lead times may be long and travel schedules difficult to coordinate; it may take months to arrange and complete them. Although at least a week is necessary lead time for most interviews, often the researcher can get an interview on very short notice as peoples' schedules change. It is desirable to have identified a number of alternative sources for any interview trip; if time becomes available they just might be willing to meet on short notice.

Quid Pro Quo.   When arranging an interview, one should have something to offer the interviewee in return for his or her time. This can range from an offer to discuss (selectively of course) some of the researcher's observations based on the study, to thoughtful feedback on the interviewees' comments, to summaries of results or extracts of the study itself when feasible.

Affiliation.   An interviewer must be prepared to give his or her affiliation and make some statement about the identity or (at least) the nature of his or her client if the study is being conducted for another organization. There is a moral obligation to alert an interviewee if information may be used to his or her detriment. If the identity of the interviewer's firm or client cannot be disclosed, some general statement must be made regarding the economic stake of the firm or client in the business being studied. Otherwise interviewees generally will not (and should not) grant an interview. Failure to disclose the identity of the firm or client will often limit (though not necessarily destroy) the usefulness of the interview.

Perseverance.   No matter how skillful the interviewer, scheduling interviews is invariably a frustrating process; many times an interview is declined or the interviewee is openly unenthusiastic about it. This is in the nature of the problem and must not deter the interviewer. Often an interviewee is much more enthusiastic once a meeting has commenced and the relationship between interviewer and interviewee has become more personal.

Credibility.   Interviewers greatly build credibility in arranging interviews and conducting them by having some knowledge of the business. This knowledge should be displayed early both in initial contacts and in interviews themselves. It makes the interview more interesting and potentially useful for the subject.

Teamwork.   Interviewing is a tiring job and should ideally be done in teams of two if resources permit. While one member asks a question, the other can be taking notes and thinking up the next round of questions. It also allows one interviewer to maintain eye contact while the other takes notes. Teamwork also allows for a debriefing session immediately after the interview or at the end of the day, which is extremely useful in reviewing and clarifying notes, checking for consistent impressions, analyzing the interview, and synthesizing findings. Often much creative work in industry research is done in such sessions. A solo interviewer should leave time for such activity as well.

Questions.   Gathering accurate data depends on asking unbiased questions, which do not prejudge or limit the answer nor expose the interviewer's own leanings. The interviewer must also be sensitive not to signal with his or her behavior, tone of voice, or expression what the "desired" answer is. Most people like to be cooperative and agreeable, and such signaling may bias the answer.

Notes.   In addition to taking notes, the researcher can benefit from writing down observations about the interview itself. What publications does the individual use? What books are on the shelves? How are the offices decorated? Are they plush or sparse? Does the interviewee have any sample products in the office? This type of information often provides useful clues in interpreting the verbal data that result from the interview and also provides leads for additional sources.

Relationships.   It is important to recognize that the subject is human, has never met the researcher before, has his or her own set of personal characteristics, and may be quite uncertain about what to say or not say. The style and vocabulary of the subject, his or her posture and attitude, body language, and so on give important clues and should be diagnosed quickly. A good interviewer is usually adept at quickly building a relationship with the subject. Making an effort to adapt to the style of the interviewee, to lower the level of uncertainty, and to make the interaction personal rather than keeping it on an abstract business level will pay off in the quality and candor of the information received.

Formal Versus Informal.   Much interesting information often comes after the formal interview is over. For example, if the researcher can get a plant tour, the interviewee may become much more open as the setting becomes removed from the more formal setting of the office. The researcher should attempt to engineer interviews so that the inherent formality of the situation is overcome. This may be done by meeting on neutral ground, getting a tour, having lunch, or discovering and discussing other topics of common interest besides the industry in question.

Sensitive Data. It will generally be most productive to start an interview with nonthreatening general questions rather than asking for specific numbers or other potentially sensitive data. In situations in which concern over sensitive data may be likely, it is usually best to state explicitly at the beginning of an interview that the researcher is not asking for proprietary data but rather impressions about the industry. Often individuals will be willing to provide data in the form of ranges, "ball park" figures, or "round numbers" that can be extremely useful to the the interviewer. Questions should be structured as follows: "Is the number of salespersons you have closer to 100 or 500?"

Pursuing Leads. A researcher should always devote some time in interviews to asking questions such as the following: Whom else should we speak to? What publications should we be familiar with? Are there any conventions going on that might be useful to attend? (A large number of industries have conventions taking place in January and February.) Are there any books that might be enlightening? The way to maximize the use of interviews is to gain further leads from each one. If an interviewee is willing to provide a personal reference to another individual, the offer should always be taken. It will greatly facilitate the arrangement of further interviews.

Phone Interviews. Phone interviews can be quite productive relatively late in a study when questions can be highly focused. Phone interviews work best with suppliers, customers, distributors, and other third-party sources.

Bibliography

ABELL, D. F., AND HAMMOND, J. S. *Strategic Market Planning: Problems and Analytical Approaches.* Englewood Cliffs, N.J.: Prentice-Hall, 1979.

ABERNATHY, W. J., AND WAYNE, K. "The Limits of the Learning Curve," *Harvard Business Review*, September/October 1974.

ABERNATHY, W. J. *The Productivity Dilemma: Roadblock to Innovation in the Automobile Industry.* Baltimore, Md.: Johns Hopkins Press, 1978.

ANDREWS, K. R. *The Concept of Corporate Strategy.* New York: Dow Jones-Irwin, 1971.

ANSOFF, H. I. "Checklist for Competitive and Competence Profiles." *Corporate Strategy*, pp. 98-99. New York: McGraw-Hill, 1965.

BROCK, G. *The U.S. Computer Industry.* Cambridge, Mass.: Ballinger Press, 1975.

BUCHELE, R. "How to Evaluate a Firm." *California Management Review*, Fall 1962, pp. 5-16.

BUFFA, E. S. *Modern Production Management.* 4th ed. New York: Wiley, 1973.

BUZZELL, R. D. "Competitive Behavior and Product Life Cycles." In *New Ideas for Successful Marketing*, edited by John Wright and J. L. Goldstucker, pp. 46-68. Chicago: American Marketing Association, 1966.

BUZZELL, R. D., GALE, B. T., AND SULTAN, R. G. M. "Market Share—A Key to Profitability." *Harvard Business Review*, January-February 1975, pp. 97-106.

BUZZELL, R. D., NOURSE, R. M., MATTHEWS, J. B., JR., AND LEVITT, T. *Marketing: A Contemporary Analysis*. New York: McGraw-Hill, 1972.

CANNON, J. T. *Business Strategy and Policy*. New York: Harcourt, Brace and World, 1968.

CATRY, B., AND CHEVALIER, M. "Market Share Strategy and the Product Life Cycle." *Journal of Marketing*, Vol. 38, October 1974, pp. 29-34.

CHRISTENSEN, C. R., ANDREWS, K. R., AND BOWER, J. L. *Business Policy: Text and Cases*. Homewood, Ill.: Richard D. Irwin, 1973.

CLIFFORD, D. K., JR. "Leverage in the Product Life Cycle." *Dun's Review*, May 1965.

COREY, R. *Industrial Marketing*. 2nd ed. Englewood Cliffs, N.J.: Prentice-Hall, 1976.

COX, W. E., JR. "Product Life Cycles as Marketing Models." *Journal of Business*, October 1967, pp. 375-384.

DANIELS, L. *Business Information Sources*. Berkeley: University of California Press, 1976.

DAY, G. S. "Diagnosing the Product Portfolio." *Journal of Marketing*, April 1977, pp. 29-38.

D'CRUZ, J. "Quasi-Integration in Raw Material Markets." DBA Dissertation, Harvard Graduate School of Business Administration, 1979.

DEAN, J. "Pricing Policies for New Products." *Harvard Business Review*, Vol. 28, No. 6, November 1950.

DEUTSCH, M. "The Effect of Motivational Orientation Upon Threat and Suspicion." *Human Relations*, 1960, pp. 123-139.

DOZ, Y. L. *Government Control and Multinational Strategic Management*. New York: Praeger, 1979.

————. "Strategic Management in Multinational Companies." *Sloan Management Review*, in press, 1980.

FORBUS, J. L., AND MEHTA, N.T. "Economic Value to the Customer." Staff paper, McKinsey and Company, February 1979.

FORRESTER, J. W. "Advertising: A Problem in Industrial Dynamics." *Harvard Business Review*, Vol. 37, No. 2, March/April 1959, pp. 100-110.

FOURAKER, L. F., AND SIEGEL, S. *Bargaining and Group Decision Making: Experiments in Bilateral Monopoly*. New York: McGraw-Hill, 1960.

FRUHAN, W. E., JR. *The Fight for Competitive Advantage*. Cambridge, Mass.: Division of Research, Harvard Graduate School of Business Administration, 1972.

————. *Financial Strategy*. Homewood, Ill.: Richard D. Irwin, 1979.

GILMOUR, S. C. "The Divestment Decision Process." DBA Dissertation, Harvard Graduate School of Business Administration, 1973.

HARRIGAN, K. R. "Strategies for Declining Industries." DBA Dissertation, Harvard Graduate School of Business Administration, 1979.

HUNT, M. S. "Competition in the Major Home Appliance Industry." Ph.D. Dissertation, Harvard University, 1972.

KNICKERBOCKER, F. T. *Oligopolistic Reaction and Multinational Enterprise.* Cambridge, Mass.: Division of Research, Harvard Graduate School of Business Administration, 1973.

KOTLER, P. *Marketing Management.* 2nd ed. Englewood Cliffs, N.J.: Prentice-Hall, 1972.

LEVITT, T. "Exploit the Product Life Cycle." *Harvard Business Review,* November/December 1965, pp. 81-94.

_____. "The Augmented Product Concept." In *The Marketing Mode: Pathways to Corporate Growth.* New York: McGraw-Hill, 1969.

MEHTA, N. T. "Policy Formulation in a Declining Industry: The Case of the Canadian Dissolving Pulp Industry." DBA Dissertation, Harvard Graduate School of Business Administration, 1978.

MOORE, F. G., *Production Management.* 6th ed. Homewood, Ill.: Richard D. Irwin, 1973.

NEWMAN, H. H. "Strategic Groups and the Structure-Performance Relationship." *Review of Economics and Statistics,* Vol. LX, August 1978, pp. 417-427.

NEWMAN, W. H., AND LOGAN, J. P., *Strategy, Policy and Central Management.* Chapter 2. Cincinnati, Ohio: South Western Publishing, 1971.

PATTON, ARCH. "Stretch Your Product's Earning Years." *Management Review,* Vol. XLVII, No. 6, June 1959.

POLLI, R., AND COOK, V. "Validity of the Product Life Cycle." *Journal of Business,* October 1969, pp. 385-400.

PORTER, M. E. *Interbrand Choice, Strategy and Bilateral Market Power.* Cambridge, Mass.: Harvard University Press, 1976a.

_____. "Strategy Under Conditions of Adversity." Discussion paper, Harvard Graduate School of Business Administration, 1976b.

_____. "Please Note Location of Nearest Exit: Exit Barriers and Planning." *California Management Review,* Vol. XIX, Winter 1976c, pp. 21-33.

_____. "The Structure Within Industries and Companies' Performance." *Review of Economics and Statistics,* LXI, May 1979, pp. 214-227.

PORTER, M. E., AND SPENCE, M. "Capacity Expansion in a Growing Oligopoly: The Case of Corn Wet Milling," Discussion paper, Harvard Graduate School of Business Administration, 1978.

QUAIN, MITCHELL. *Lift-Truck Industry: Near Term Outlook.* New York: Wertheim & Company, June 22, 1977.

ROTHSCHILD, W. E. *Putting It All Together.* New York: AMACOM, 1979.

SALTER, M., AND WEINHOLD, W. *Diversification Through Acquisition.* New York: Free Press, 1979.

SCHELLING, T. *The Strategy of Conflict.* Cambridge, Mass.: Harvard University Press, 1960.

SCHOEFFLER, S., BUZZELL, R. D., HEANY, D. F. "Impact of Strategic Planning on Profit Performance." *Harvard Business Review*, March/April 1974, pp. 137-145.

SKINNER, W. "The Focused Factory." *Harvard Business Review*, May/June 1974, pp. 113-121.

SMALLWOOD, J. E. "The Product Life Cycle: A Key to Strategic Market Planning." *MSU Business Topics*, Vol. 21, No. 1, Winter 1973, pp. 29-36.

SPENCE, A. M. "Entry, Capacity, Investment and Oligopolistic Pricing." *Bell Journal of Economics*, Vol. 8, Autumn 1977, pp. 534-544.

STAUDT, T. A., TAYLOR, D., AND BOWERSOX, D. *A Managerial Introduction to Marketing*, 3rd ed. Englewood Cliffs, N.J.: Prentice-Hall, 1976.

SULTAN, R. *Pricing in the Electrical Oligopoly. Vols. I and II.* Cambridge, Mass.: Division of Research, Harvard Graduate School of Business Administration, 1974.

VERNON, R. "International Investment and International Trade in the Product Cycle." *Quarterly Journal of Economics*, Vol. LXXX, May 1966, pp. 190-207.

————. "The Waning Power of the Product Cycle Hypothesis." Discussion paper, Harvard Graduate School of Business Administration, May 1979.

WELLS, L. T., JR. "International Trade: The Product Life Cycle Approach." In *The Product Life Cycle in International Trade*, edited by L. T. Wells, Jr. Cambridge, Mass.: Division of Research, Harvard Graduate School of Business Administration, 1972.

Case Studies

Note on the Watch Industries in Switzerland, Japan and the United States. Intercollegiate Case Clearinghouse, 9-373-090.

Prelude Corporation. Intercollegiate Case Clearinghouse, 4-373-052, 1968.

Timex (A). Intercollegiate Case Clearinghouse, 6-373-080.

Periodicals

Business Week, August 13, 1979; June 11, 1979; November 27, 1978; October 9, 1978; July 17, 1978; August 15, 1977; February 28, 1977; December 13, 1976, November 18, 1976.

Dun's, February 1977.

Forbes, December 25, 1978; September 18, 1978; July 15, 1977; November 15, 1977.

New York Times, February 11, 1979.

Index

Abell, D., 361n.
Abernathy, W.J., 16n., 217n., 243n.
Accounting procedures, 52
Acetylene industry, 23, 29, 156, 256, 259, 260–262
Acquisitions, 30, 350–356; see also Entry
  effect on rivalry, 21
  forecasting, 50
  fragmented industries, 204
Advertising, 9–10
  and the product life cycle, 159–161
  and substitutes, 23–24
Aerosol packaging industry, 21, 31, 170, 172–173, 232, 309
Agricultural cooperatives, 140
Agricultural products industry, 191
Air cargo, 8
Aircraft industry, 12, 280, 292, 295
Air filter industry, 206
Airline industry, 331
Allis-Chalmers, 44, 295
Aluminum extrusion industry, 207
Aluminum fabricating industry, 198
Aluminum industry, 335
American Hospital Supply Corporation, 104–105
American Motors Corporation, 98, 127, 150
Ammonium fertilizer industry, 19, 130, 140
Ancell, N., 209n.
Announcements, 76–81
Ansoff, H.I., 63n.
Antitrust policy, 53, 56, 85–86
Appliance industry, 129–130, 244
Aquaculture industry, 220
Archer-Daniels-Midland, 342
Arthur D. Little, Inc., 373
Asset disposition, 265–266
Automatic drip coffee maker industry, 221
Automobile industry, 15, 16n., 25, 37, 43, 45, 98, 127, 143, 150, 162, 163, 168,

176, 218, 276, 288, 289, 293, 295, 297, 320
Automotive parts industry, 349
Automotive repair shops, 349
Automotive tune-up centers, 223

Baby food industry, 58–59
Baby products industry, 9, 165, 244
Backpack industry, 166
Baldor, Inc., 43
Bank cash dispenser industry, 162
Baxter Travenol Laboratories, 104–105
Beauty care industry, 198
Beef cattle industry, 201
Berkey Photo, Inc., 77
Bhadkamkar, N., 275n.
Bic-Pen Corporation, 52, 54, 98
Bicycle industry, 158, 166, 224
Biological separation industry, 215
Black and Decker, 13, 36
Blue jean industry, 166
Board of directors, 53
Bosch, R., 20
Boston Consulting Group, 275n., 361
Bottled water industry, 215, 224
Bowersox, 161n.
Bowmar, Inc., 78
Brewing industry, 7, 9, 21, 60, 146, 156, 244
Briggs and Stratton, 36
British Leyland, 43
Brock, G., 77
Brown-Boveri, 295
Buchele, R., 63n.
Buffa, E.S., 301
Building supply industry, 198
Bulova Watch Company, 174n.
Burger King, 252
Burroughs Corporation, 126
Business cycle, 168

389

Business forms industry, 198

Buyers
  bargaining power, 24–27, 113–114
  behavior in declining industries, 257–258,
    261–262
  effect on industry fragmentation, 197
  in emerging industries, 219
  growth potential, 110–113
  learning, 170–171
  in mature industries, 238–239
  price sensitivity, 114–118
  repeat buyers, 167–168
  strategy toward, 108–122
Buyer segments, 169–170
Buyer selection 26–27, 108–122, 244–245
Buzzell, R.D., 145*n*., 161*n*.

Calculator industry, 17, 315
Campbell Soup Company, 354
Campground industry, 203
Candy industry, 165, 166
Cannon, J.T., 320*n*.
Canteen Corporation, 243
Capacity expansion
  determinants, 78, 239, 324–338
  effect on rivalry, 19
Capital budgeting, 325–326, 341
Capital markets, 10, 23, 78, 223, 262, 333,
    350–356
Cargill, Inc., 342
Carpet industry, 146, 148
J.I. Case, Inc., 62
Cash cow, 363
Cash trap, 247
Castle & Cooke, 134
Caterpillar Tractor, 37, 38, 84, 202
Catry, B., 161*n*.
Cattle feedlots, 315
CBS, Inc., 203
Cement industry, 197
Century 21, Inc., 203
Cessna, 175–176
Chain saw industry, 153, 224
Charles River Breeding Laboratories, 201
Charmin Paper Company, 21, 356
Chemical industry, 24, 140, 197, 282
Chevalier, M., 161*n*.
Chloride industry, 19
Chrysler Corporation, 25, 43, 127, 295
Cigarette industry, 310
Cigar industry, 257, 259, 266
Clark Equipment, 42
Clifford, D., 161*n*.
Clinical laboratory industry, 181
Clothing industry, 148, 168
Coal gassification industry, 219, 222, 228
Coalitions, 295
Coca-Cola Company, 51, 85, 145
Coffee industry, 70, 84, 85
Coleman Company, 37
Commitment, 89, 99, 100–105
Competitive forces, 3–33, 126–153, 157
Competitive moves, 88–107

Competitive reaction, 50–51, 67–71, 88–107,
    130, 154–155, 341–344, 346–347
Competitor analysis
  blind spots, 59, 60
  competitor assumptions, 48–49, 58–63,
    92–93, 96, 238, 247
  competitor capabilities, 48–49, 63–67,
    91–92, 111, 149–150
  competitor goals, 48–49, 50–58, 92,
    95–100
  in emerging industries, 233–234
  in global industries, 293–294
  market signals, 75–87
  in mature industries, 238
  mixed motives, 70–71
  organizational structure, 52
  picking the battleground, 70
  theory, 47–74
  use of portfolio models, 361–367
Competitor intelligence, 48, 71–74
Competitor intelligence systems, 71–74
Complementary products, 167
Computer Automation, Inc., 218
Computer industry, 7, 77, 126, 134, 275,
    280, 305, 317
Computer memories, 78–79
Computer service bureau industry, 179, 204
Computer software, 192
Conducting industry analyses, 368–382
Construction equipment industry, 37, 38,
    84, 118, 143, 316, 348
Consulting industry, 116, 198
Consumer electronics industry, 45–46
Consumer finance industry, 244
Consumer needs, 165–166
Consumer packaged food industry, 62, 275
Control Data Corporation, 126*n*., 134
Control systems, 40–41, 52, 250–251
Convenience store industry, 244
Conventional wisdom, 60, 219, 347
Cook, P., 158*n*.
Copier industry, 10, 317
Corey, R., 117*n*.
Corning Glass Works, 231
Corn milling industry, 23, 24, 330, 331,
    342, 347
Corporate culture, 41, 42
Cosmetics industry, 4, 9, 127
Cost curves, 245
Cost leadership, 35–37, 40, 45, 148
Cost of servicing buyers, 110–111, 118
Cox, W.E., Jr., 161*n*.
CPC International, 275, 347
Creative industries, 191, 198
Cross-parry, 84–85
Cross subsidization, 242
Crown Cork and Seal, Inc., 37, 127, 246,
    252
Curtis Publishing Company, 310
Cutlery industry, 148

Daniels, L., 373*n*.
Data collection, xv

Data General Inc., 218
Data sources, 368–382
Data transmission industry, 223, 349
Day, G.S., 361*n*.
D'Cruz, J., 321*n*.
Dean Foods, 246
DeCastro, E., 218
Declining industries, 159–161, 254–274
John Deere, 84, 143, 348
Defense industry, 292
Defensive strategy, 98–105
Del Monte Company, 355
Demographics, 164–165, 258
De Novo entrants, 220–221
Department stores, 137
Design and Manufacturing Corporation, 130
Deutsch, M., 102*n*.
Developing countries, 277, 297–298
Diffusion of knowledge, 172–174
Digital Equipment Corporation, 109, 218
Dillon Companies, 207
Discount retailing, 61
Diseconomies of scale, 197–199, 202–203
Dishwasher industry, 238
Disposable lighters, 15
Distribution industries, 191
Diversification; *see also* Entry
  acquisition, 7
  impact of industry structure on, 5, 15–16, 31–32, 55, 135, 263, 264
  shared operations or functions, 8, 13
Divestment: *see* Exit barriers
Dog business, 363
Doz, Y., 292, 293*n*.
Dr. Pepper Company, 85
Drug industry, 9, 148
Dry cleaning industry, 200
Du Pont Corporation, 36, 66
Durable goods, 168

Early markets, 225–229
Eaton Corporation, 44
Economic value to the customer, 121*n*.
Economies of scale
  and capacity expansion, 329
  in emerging industries, 218
  in fragmented industries, 196, 201–202, 203, 204
  in global industries, 278–281
  joint costs, 8–9
  and preemption, 336–337
  and strategic groups, 132–134, 143, 146
  theory, 7–9, 12
  vertical integration, 9, 302
Economies of vertical integration, 302–305
Educational testing industry, 166
Electrical controls industry, 115
Electrical products industry, 295
Electric coffee percolator industry, 221
Electric motor industry, 8
Electric ranges, 37
Electric utilities, 224

Electronic alarm systems, 24
Electronic calculator industry, 136–137, 169, 178, 222, 232, 237
Electronic component distribution industry, 109, 162, 192, 196, 208
Embryonic industries: *see* Emerging industries
Emerging industries, 158–161, 215–236
Emerson Electric, 13, 36, 43
Entry
  and capacity expansion, 332
  choice of industries to enter, 235–236
  into emerging industries, 220–221, 232–233
  encouraging entry, 233–234
  of foreign firms, 182*n*.
  into fragmented industries, 205–206
  and industry evolution, 163, 175–176, 182–183
  sequential entry, 356–357
  signaling and, 82
  theory, 6–7, 99, 132–136, 171, 339–357
  timing, 142, 144
Entry barriers; *see also* Mobility barriers
  access to distribution channels, 10–11
  capital requirements, 9–10
  cost disadvantages, 11–13
  economies of scale, 7–9, 15–16
  in emerging industries, 220–221
  and entry, 340–350
  excess capacity, 8*n*.
  experience curve, 11–13, 15–17
  in fragmented industries, 196
  and global competition, 297
  government policy, 13
  and industry maturity, 241
  product differentiation, 9
  switching costs, 10
  theory, 7–17, 30–31, 142–144
  vertical integration, 9, 308–310
Entry deterring price, 14
Erickson, L.M., 290
Estee Lauder, 127
Ethan Allen, Inc., 208–209
Ethylene glycol industry, 332
Ethylene industry, 257
Evolutionary processes, 162–184
Excess capacity, 249
Exchange rates, 176–177
Exclusive dealers, 11
Exit, 182–183
Exit barriers
  approaches to reducing, 268
  and capacity expansion, 330
  and entry barriers, 22–23
  in global industries, 292
  and industry concentration, 186
  and industry fragmentation, 199
  and rivalry, 20–21
  theory, 66, 183, 225, 259–265, 311
Expectations, 324–327, 332
Experience curve
  and capacity expansion, 329

in emerging industries, 217–218
in fragmented industries, 196, 201–202
in global industries, 279
and industry evolution, 174–175
and preemption, 336–337
theory, 11–13, 15–17
Extended rivalry, 6
Externalities, 230

Fabricated aluminum products industry, 192
Factor costs, 288
Farm equipment industry, 62, 84, 143, 156, 176, 246
Fashion clothing industry, 284
Fastener industry, 39, 116
Fast food industry, 203, 252
Federated Department Stores, 61
Fertilizer industry, 282, 331
Fiat, 43
Fiberglass insulation industry, 23
Fiber optics industry, 200, 215, 217, 231
Fibers industry, 297
Fieldcrest Mills, 37
Field interviewing, 379–382
Fighting brand, 85, 99
Fire engine industry, 199
Firm capabilities: *see* Competitor analysis
Firm profitability, 126–151
Firm size, 175–176
Fishing industry, 199
Fixed costs, 18, 24, 211, 260–261, 343
Fleetwood, Inc., 207
Flour industry, 264
Fluid milk industry, 197, 246
Focal points, 95, 105–106
Focus strategies, 38–40; *see also* Generic strategies
Folgers Coffee, 70, 84
Food and Drug Administration, 105
Food wholesaling industry, 40
Footwear industry, 148
Forbus, J.L., 121*n*., 224*n*.
Ford Motor Company, 25, 45, 127, 143, 168
Forecasting, 157–188, 234–235, 273
Foreclosure, 308–309
Foreign competitors, 18, 19; *see also* Global industries
Foreign direct investment, 277
Forest products industry, 28
Forest Service, U.S., 28
Forrester, J.W., 161*n*.
Fort Howard Paper, 39
Fouraker, L.F., 75*n*.
Fractional horsepower electric motor industry, 43
Fragmented industries, 191–214
Franklin Electric Co., 43
Free-market return, 5–6
Freight forwarding industry, 13
Frost and Sullivan, 373
Fruhan, W.E., Jr., 223*n*., 331*n*.
Functional strategy, xiii, xvi–xvii
Furniture industry, 208–209

Gallo Wine Company, 183*n*.
Gambling equipment industry, 166
Game theory, 88–107
Garbage collection industry, 192
General Electric Company, 7, 43, 105, 121, 129, 238, 270, 295, 362, 365
General Instrument Corporation, 221
General management and strategy, 42, 55–56, 61–63, 252–253
General Mills, Inc., 264
General Motors Corporation, 25, 43, 45, 126–127, 143, 168, 211, 289, 348
Generic strategies
definition, 34–46, 54, 120, 206, 208, 245
in mature industries, 241
and strategic groups, 152
Genstar Ltd., 316
Georgia-Pacific, 342
Gerber Products Company, 58, 244
Gillette, 15, 98, 100
Gilmour, S.C., 264*n*.
Global industries, 275–298
Gould, Inc., 43, 295, 354
Government policy
and capacity expansion, 334
in competitor analysis, 53
and demand, 166
and divestment, 264–265
in emerging industries, 223–224
as an entry barrier, 11
as an exit barrier, 21
and global industries, 286, 288
impact on competition, 28–29
and industry evolution, 181–182
affect on industry fragmentation, 200
affect on new product adoption, 229
subsidy, 219–220
and substitutes, 167*n*.
Grain mill products industry, 148
Growth/share matrix, 362–364
Gulf Oil Corporation, 62
Gypsum industry, 332, 342

Hammond, J., 361*n*.
Hanes Corporation, 54, 151
Harley-Davidson, 46
Harnischfeger Company, 36–37
Harrigan, K.R., 254*n*.
Harvard Business School, 225*n*.
Harvest strategy, 56, 254, 255, 267–274, 363, 366
Heavy construction industry, 281, 292
Heilman Brewing Company, 244
Hertz Corporation, 242, 248
Heublein, Inc., 183
Hewlett-Packard, 17, 136–137
High speed steel industry, 278
H.K. Porter Paint, 39
Hobart Corporation, 238
Honda, 289
Honeywell, Inc., 126*n*., 134, 218
Hosiery industry, 151
Hospital management industry, 181, 230
Hospital supply industry, 104–105

Host governments, 292–293
Hot buttons, 68
Hotel industry, 330
Household Finance Corporation, 62, 244
Household paper products industry, 21
Hout, T., 275*n.*
Hudson Motor Car Company, 218
Hunt, M., 138*n.*
Hyster, 37, 42, 44

IBM, 70, 77, 98, 126, 134, 275, 293
IDC, Inc., 373
Illinois Tool Works, 39, 116
Imasco, Ltd., 31
Imitation, 171–172
Incentive systems, 40–41, 52, 55, 250–251
Inco, 347
Income elasticity, 165
Indal, Inc., 207, 316
Industrial policy, 291–292, 295–296
Industry concentration, 18, 24, 27, 123,
    185–186
Industry consolidation, 185–186, 200–206
Industry cooperation, 231
Industry data, 71–74
Industry definition, 5, 32–33, 44, 136, 146,
    186–187
Industry elasticity of demand, 23*n.*
Industry evolution
    and buyers, 122
    capacity expansion, 324–338
    in declining industries, 254–274
    in emerging industries, 215–236
    and entry, 345, 348–349
    and the experience curve, 174–175
    and overcoming fragmentation, 200–206
    and strategic group mapping, 153–155
    and strategic groups, 135–136, 151–152
    and strategy formulation, 30–31
    theory of, 156–188
    and transition to maturity, 237–253
Industry forecasting, 71, 153–155
Industry growth
    determinants of, 164–169
    and complementary products, 167
    and consumer needs, 165–166
    and demographics, 164–165
    and penetration, 167–168
    and rivalry, 18
    and substitute products, 166–167
Industry profitability, 3–4, 5–6, 19, 22–23,
    142–148, 186, 240
Industry salience, 286
Industry structure, 3–33, 90–91, 126–153,
    156–188, 196
Information in markets, 26, 91, 106–107,
    263, 287, 304, 315, 345–346
Initial structure, 162
Instability of sales, 197
Internal development, 340–350
International competition, 5, 181, 240, 246;
    see also Global industries
Interviewing: *see* Field interviewing
Intravenous solutions industry, 10

Inventory costs, 197
Investment banking industry, 9, 116
ITE, Inc., 354

Jenn-Air, 37
J.I. Case, Inc., 62
Joint ventures, 340*n.*

Kawasaki, 46
Knickerbocker, F.T., 293
KOA, Inc., 203
Kodak, 15, 77
Komatsu, 42
Kotler, P., 158*n.*

Label industry, 206
Labor, 28
Laboratory animal industry, 201–202
Land, E., 62
Lawrence, M.O., 225*n.*
Lead times, 329
Leather industry, 257
Letraset, Inc., 118
Letter transfer industry, 118
Levitt, T., 120*n.*, 161*n.*, 162*n.*
Lift truck industry, 42, 43, 279, 289
Light aircraft industry, 169
Lincoln Electric Company, 36
Liquidation value, 260
Liquor industry, 148
Liquor retailing, 13, 192
Lobster fishing industry, 196, 211
Logan, J.P., 63*n.*
Logging equipment industry, 10*n.*
Long-term contracts, 318–319

Machine tool industry, 244
MacIntosh, 37
Make or buy decisions, 301
Management skills, 252–253
Mark Controls, 242–243
Market for companies, 350–356
Market leadership, 191, 201–211, 234,
    246–247, 267–269, 332
Market share
    and cost position, 36
    in maturing industries, 248
    and profitability, 42–44, 145–148
Market signals, 75–87, 89, 94, 102–105,
    268, 328, 333, 337
Martin-Brower, 40
Massey Fergusen, 246
Matsushita, 290
Mature industries, 237–253
Maxwell House, 70, 84, 85
Maytag, 130, 238
McDonald's Corporation, 203, 252, 280
McKinsey and Company, 121*n.*, 224*n.*, 362,
    365
Mead Corporation, 270
Meat packing industry, 148, 201
Mechanical calculator industry, 178
Medical products, 283
Mehta, N.T., 121*n.*, 265*n.*

Men's clothing industry, 310–311
Mercedes-Benz, 37, 43
Metal container industry, 37, 127, 180, 246, 252, 309, 318
Metal distribution industry, 208
Metal enclosure industry, 26
Metal fabrication industry, 191
Microcomputer industry, 204
Miller Brewing Company, 7, 60
Minicomputer industry, 17, 70, 109, 137, 173, 179, 204, 218, 223, 227, 305
Mining industry, 137–138
Mitsubishi, 295
Mixed motives, 70–71, 97
Mobile home industry, 176, 207
Mobility barriers; *see also* Entry barriers
  in emerging industries, 220–221, 231–232
  in global industries, 281
  and industry concentration, 185–186
  and marketing innovation, 178
  and process innovation, 178–180
  and product innovation, 177–178
  and R&D, 173–174
  theory, 132–136, 154
  and vertical integration, 308–310
Modular housing industry, 223, 224
Monfort, 315
Moore, F.G., 301
Motorcycle industry, 46, 158, 276, 289, 290
Motorola, 78–79
Movie industry, 60, 177, 178
Mr. Coffee, Inc., 221
Mr. Pibb, 85
Mushroom farming industry, 134, 197, 201–202, 206

Nash, 218
National Can Corporation, 127
Nature of entrants, 232
Nestlé, 275
New industries: *see* Emerging industries
Newman, H.H., 63n., 138n.
Newspaper industry, 207
Nickel industry, 332, 347
Nightclub industry, 198
Norton-Villers-Triumph, 46

Obsolescence, 228
Oil field equipment industry, 4, 26
Oil industry, 140, 296
Oil tanker shipping industry, 6, 10n., 192, 281, 320, 329, 331
Oligopoly, 88
Operating leverage, 309–310
Optical, medical and opthalmic goods industry, 148
Optical character reader industry, 169
Organizational structure
  in competitor analysis, 40–41, 52, 55
  decentralized organization, 207
  implications of industry maturity, 249–253
  overcentralization, 211–212
Owner-managed firms, 19, 198, 212

Packaged food industry, 355
Packard, 218
Paint industry, 39, 81n.
Panasonic (Matsushita), 46
Panty hose industry, 54
Paper industry, 4, 39, 331
Paramount Pictures, 60
Patton, A., 161n.
Pepsi Cola, 145
Perdue, F., 318
Perdue Chicken, 134, 318
Perfectly competitive industry, 6
Perfume industry, 148
Periodicals industry, 148
Perrier, 215
Personal computer industry, 215, 218
Pet, Inc., 275
Philip Morris, 6, 60
Philips, 20, 217
Photofinishing industry, 21
Photographic equipment industry, 15, 77, 148
Pioneering, 232–234
Pizza Hut, 203
Plastics industry, 297
Pleasure boat industry, 179–180
Polaroid Corporation, 15, 62, 318
Polli, R., 158n.
Pollution control industry, 13
H.K. Porter Paint, 39
Portfolio models, 53–54, 56–57, 255, 270, 361–367 (Appendix A)
Potential competitors, 49–50
Potential industry structure, 163
Pottery industry, 148
Poultry industry, 134, 318
Preemptive strategy, 76–77, 79, 327–328, 335–338
Prelude Corporation, 211
Prestressed concrete, 282
Price competition, 17, 248
Pricing, 242–243
Prisoner's dilemma, 88–89
Privately held firms: *see* Owner-managed firms
Process innovation, 243
Procter and Gamble, 21, 84, 143–144, 356
Product differentiation
  and economies of scale, 16
  effect of buyer learning on, 170–171
  effect on industry fragmentation, 199
  effect on rivalry, 19
  in global industries, 280
  and the product life cycle, 159–161
  and suppliers, 28
  theory, 21–22, 31, 37–38, 46, 116, 119, 192, 208
  and vertical integration, 307–308, 315, 318
Product innovation, 168–169, 177–178, 240
Product life cycle, 30, 157–162
Product life cycle of international trade, 284–285
Product line rationalization, 241–242

Product quality, 223
Product standards, 222
Product testing, 13
Public accounting industry, 9
Public goods, 278
Publishing industry, 300, 310
Pulp and paper industry, 265
Purchasing strategy, 122–125, 280

Quasi-integration, 301, 321
Question mark business, 363

Radio broadcasting industry, 166, 168, 180
Railroad industry, 13
Ralston Purina, 134
Rate of industry decline, 256–257
Rate of market penetration, 225–229
Raw materials industry, 11, 13, 220, 221–222
Rayon industry, 23, 256, 259, 260
Raytheon Company, 260
Razor blade industry, 15, 96
RCA Corporation, 178, 217, 242, 248
Ready-to-wear clothing industry, 26
Real estate brokerage industry, 203
Real estate investment trusts industry, 330
Recognition Equipment Company, 169
Recording industry, 165, 180–181, 199, 203, 300–301
Recreational vehicle industry, 15, 21, 168, 171, 176, 222, 232, 348
Refrigerator industry, 289, 290–291
Regional industries: *see* Fragmented industries
Regulation: *see* Government policy
Renault, 295
Repeat buyers, 167–168
Replacement demand, 168
Research and development, 7, 10, 27, 173–174
Retailers, 26
Retailing industry, 180, 191, 192, 200, 240
Retaliation: *see* Competitive reaction
Retaliation lags, 95–98
Rivalry, 17–23, 138–142, 266–267
R.J. Reynolds, 62, 355
Robert Hall, Inc., 310–311
Robinson-Patman Act, 317
Roijtman, M., 62
Roper Corporation, 130
Rothschild, W.E., 63*n*.
Rough terrain cranes, 36–37
Rudden, E., 275*n*.

Salter, M., 339*n*., 361*n*.
Saturday Evening Post, 310
Scale economies: *see* Economies of scale
Scenarios, 234, 326
Schelling, T., 106
Schlumberger, 116
Sears Roebuck, 137, 187
Secrecy, 106–107
Securities brokers, 23
Securities and Exchange Commission, 80

Securities industry, 181
Security equipment industry, 166
Security guard industry, 24, 166, 181–182, 186
Seismographic services industry, 116, 281
Semiconductor industry, 129, 173, 280
Service industries, 6, 191, 197, 198
Sewing machine industry, 276, 282
Shared costs, 8, 9, 13; *see also* Portfolio models
Sharp, 45–46
Shell, 365
Sherwin-Williams, 81*n*.
Shipbuilding industry, 12, 292, 297, 330
Siegel, S., 75*n*.
Siemens, 295
Size of company, and profitability, 145–148
Skiing equipment industry, 186
Skinner, W., 245–246
Small appliance industry, 180
Small gasoline engine industry, 36
Smallwood, J.E., 161*n*.
Smart, Inc., 373
Smoke alarm industry, 215, 217, 222, 224, 231
Snecma, 295
Snowmobile industry, 21, 168, 227, 237
Soap industry, 148
Soft drink industry, 85, 145, 148, 152, 166
Solar heating industry, 29, 31, 171, 182, 192, 200, 215, 217, 218, 219, 222–223, 224
Sony Corporation, 20, 46
Southland Corporation, 244
Spence, A.M., 102*n*., 327*n*.
Spin-off firms, 172, 218–219
Sporting goods industry, 21, 148
Standard Industrial Classification Code, 370
Stanford Research Institute, 373
Star business, 363
Staudt, T.A., 161*n*.
Storage costs, 18, 28
Steel industry, 4, 6, 297
Strategic dimensions, 127–129
Strategic distance, 139–140
Strategic group mapping, 131–132, 140–141, 152–155
Strategic groups, 129–155
Strategic planning processes, xix–xx, 183–184
Strengths and weaknesses: *see* Competitor analysis
Substitute products, 6, 23–24, 137–138, 166–167, 258
Sugar industry, 23
Sulfuric acid industry, 114, 303, 309
Sulphur industry, 11
Sultan, R.G.M., 105*n*.
Sundstrand Corporation, 244
Supermarket industry, 207, 210
Suppliers
　bargaining power, 27–28
　role in emerging industries, 231
　strategy toward, 122–125

Sustainable growth, 66
Switching costs, 19, 21, 25, 26, 28, 114, 120, 122, 124, 227–228, 274
Switzerland, 94

Talent agencies, 199
Tapered integration, 25, 125, 301, 319–320
Tariffs, 286
Tax losses, 262*n*.
Tax policy, 334
Taylor, D., 161*n*.
Technological change, 216–217, 222, 329–330
Technological innovation, 12, 16, 21, 229
Telecommunications equipment industry, 290
Television broadcasting industry, 166
Television set industry, 9, 146, 148, 178, 217, 221, 276, 290, 293, 297, 329
Tennis industry, 237
Tests for consistency of strategy, xix
Texas Gulf Sulphur, 11
Texas Instruments, 13, 36, 51, 78–79, 100, 129, 315
Texfi, 252
Textile industry, 262, 297
Timber industry, 186
Timex Corporation, 11, 94, 96, 97–98, 150–151, 280
Timing of entry, 142, 144
Tire industry, 4, 6
Toiletries industry, 4, 146, 180
Toilet tissue industry, 144
Towels and linen industry, 37
Toy industry, 148, 202, 297
Toyota, 42, 279
Transactions costs, 113–114
Transfer pricing, 306
Transportation costs, 197, 282
Trucking industry, 13
Turbine generator industry, 105, 121, 280

Uncertainty
  and capacity expansion, 327–328
  role in declining industries, 256–257
United Brands, 183
U.S. Census, 376

Vacuum tube industry, 221, 260
Value added, 18, 207–208
Valve industry, 242–243
Varian Associates, 218
Vernon, R., 294*n*., 295*n*.
Vertical integration
  and buyer power, 25
  and capacity expansion, 331
  in declining industries, 262–263
  in emerging industries, 232
  as an entry barrier, 9
  in fragmented industries, 207–208, 210
  and global industries, 290
  implications for purchasing strategy, 122–125
  and industry evolution, 176
  and innovation, 178, 179
  theory, 15, 30–31, 114, 300–323
Video disc industry, 217
Video game industry, 171, 215, 221, 223
Vinyl chloride industry, 19
Vlasic Pickles, 354
Vogt, E., 275*n*.
Volkswagen, 98
Volvo, 295

Wall Street, 223, 233
Warner Brothers, 203
Watch industry, 11, 94, 97–98, 100, 151, 178, 180, 222, 223, 315
Wayne, K., 16*n*.
Weinhold, W., 339*n*., 361*n*.
Welding equipment and supplies industry, 36
Wells, L.T., Jr., 161*n*., 284*n*.
Wertheim and Company, 42*n*.
Westinghouse, 244
White Consolidated, 244, 253
Wholesalers, 26
Windfall profits, 6, 22
Wind industry, 15, 178, 182–183, 185, 205
Women's clothing industry, 146, 198
Word processing industry, 215
World industries: *see* Global industries
Writing instrument industry, 52

Xerox Corporation, 7, 10, 174*n*., 349

About the Author

Michael E. Porter is the Bishop William Lawrence University Professor at the Institute for Strategy and Competitiveness, based at the Harvard Business School. He is a leading authority on competitive strategy and the competitiveness and economic development of nations, states, and regions. The author of sixteen books and more than a hundred articles, Professor Porter has developed ideas that have guided economic policy throughout the world. *Competitive Strategy: Techniques for Analyzing Industries and Competitors* introduced his first area of research: competitive strategy for companies. His 1990 book, *The Competitive Advantage of Nations,* motivated by his appointment by President Ronald Reagan in 1983 to the President's Commission on Industrial Competitiveness, launched his second major body of work on competitiveness and economic development. Professor Porter's research on economic development gave rise to his third major body of work: the relationship between competition and society. The holder of nine honorary doctorates, Professor Porter has won numerous awards for his books, articles, public service, and influence on several fields.